Dutch Reformed Protestants in the Holy Roman Empire, c. 1550–1620

Changing Perspectives on Early Modern Europe

Additional Titles of Interest

The Consistory and Social Discipline in Calvin's Geneva
Jeffrey R. Watt

Consuls and Captives:
Dutch-North African Diplomacy in the Early Modern Mediterranean
Erica Heinsen-Roach

The Politics of Piety:
Franciscan Preachers During the Wars of Religion, 1560–1600
Megan C. Armstrong

Reformation and the German Territorial State:
Upper Franconia, 1300–1630
William Bradford Smith

Pragmatic Toleration:
The Politics of Religious Heterodoxy in Early Reformation Antwerp, 1515–1555
Victoria Christman

The Scourge of Demons:
Possession, Lust, and Witchcraft in a Seventeenth-Century Italian Convent
Jeffrey R. Watt

Jenatsch's Axe:
Social Boundaries, Identity, and Myth in the Era of the Thirty Years' War
Randolph C. Head

A complete list of titles in the Changing Perspectives on Early Modern Europe series may be found on our website, www.urpress.com.

Dutch Reformed Protestants in the Holy Roman Empire, c. 1550–1620

A Reformation of Refugees

Jesse Spohnholz and Mirjam van Veen

University of Rochester Press

A digital edition of this book is openly available thanks to generous funding from the Dutch Research Council.

First published 2024

University of Rochester Press
668 Mt. Hope Avenue, Rochester, NY 14620, USA
www.urpress.com
and Boydell & Brewer Limited
PO Box 9, Woodbridge, Suffolk IP12 3DF, UK
www.boydellandbrewer.com

ISBN-13: 978-1-64825-076-7
ISSN: 1542-3905

Library of Congress Cataloging-in-Publication Data

Names: Spohnholz, Jesse, 1974– author. | Veen, Mirjam van, author.
Title: Dutch Reformed Protestants in the Holy Roman Empire, c.1550–1620 : a Reformation of refugees / Jesse Spohnholz and Mirjam van Veen.
Description: Rochester, NY : University of Rochester Press, 2024. | Series: Changing perspectives on early modern Europe, 1542-3905 ; 23 | Includes bibliographical references and index. | Identifiers: LCCN 2023034976 (print) | LCCN 2023034977 (ebook) | ISBN 9781648250767 (paperback) | ISBN 9781805431619 (pdf) | ISBN 9781805431626 (epub)
Subjects: LCSH: Religious refugees—Holy Roman Empire. | Religious refugees—Netherlands. | Dutch—Holy Roman Empire—Religious life and customs. | Intergroup relations—Holy Roman Empire. | Reformed (Reformed Church)—Holy Roman Empire. | Holy Roman Empire—Church history—16th century.
Classification: LCC BX9476.E8515 S66 2024 (print) | LCC BX9476.E8515 (ebook) | DDC 284/.2492094309031—dc23/eng/20231122
LC record available at https://lccn.loc.gov/2023034976
LC ebook record available at https://lccn.loc.gov/2023034977

A catalogue record for this title is available from the British Library.

This book is dedicated to Marieke Ridder and Sheri Six

Contents

Illustrations

Figures

Tables

Acknowledgments

Our collaboration began when we accidentally bumped into each other, intellectually speaking. In March 2011, we had been assigned to the same panel by another colleague at a scholarly conference in Montreal, Quebec. At the time, we knew one another only casually. First, Jesse Spohnholz presented about a series of pastors and other Reformed churchmen who were refugees in Wesel (the topic of his first book). Next, Mirjam van Veen presented on a series of opponents of orthodox Calvinists who rejected dogmatic forms of religion (the topic of her first book). As it turned out, our papers were on the exact same people! Many of the Dutch Republic's most notorious so-called libertines had spent time in refugee communities in the Holy Roman Empire in the 1560s and 70s. Did these examples demand that we rethink the commonplace treatment of exile as a contributor to doctrinaire and steadfast forms of orthodox Calvinism? Why had scholars—including ourselves—failed to see these counterexamples before? Through conversations that followed, we began asking all sorts of new questions and wondering what would happen if we started looking at a fuller spectrum of refugees' experiences and impacts.

Over time, we developed a collaborative research project. Our goal was to understand the diversity of exiles' experiences and to see if we could make sense of the resulting impacts of those experiences. We did not set out to prove that exiles were either more or less tolerant than anyone else, or that exile had any particular effect on migrants, their hosts, or their future homes. Instead, we were driven by an open curiosity. In 2014, the Dutch Research Council (*Nederlandse Organisatie voor Wetenschappelijk Onderzoek*) awarded us a grant to investigate our questions and develop answers to them.

We wish to thank a number of colleagues who provided particular help as this project developed. They include (alphabetically) Ana Barnes, Kora Baumbach, David de Boer, Daniel Herbert Fogt, Paul van Geest, Martin van Gelderen, Jaap Geraerts, Peter Gorter, Aza Goudriaan, Craig Harline, August den Hollander, Geert Janssen, Carina Johnson, Benjamin Kaplan, Susanne Lachenicht, Andreas Mühling, Johannes Müller, Silke Muylaert, Inge Schipper, Herman Selderhuis, Violet Soen, and Nicholas Terpstra. We would like to give a special thanks to the librarians and archivists who made this book possible, including Gerhard Nessler and Martin Roelen. This project has been collaborative from start to finish, and we value the contributions made by those who helped in that spirit.

Abbreviations

BF	Bonali-Fiquet, F. ed. *Jean Calvin: Lettres à Monsieur et Madame de Falais*. Geneva: Librairie Droz, 1991.
BLGNP	Biografisch Lexicon voor de geschiedenis van het Nederlands Protestantisme, resources.huygens.knaw.nl/retroboeken/blnp.
DNRM	Database of Netherlandish Reformed Migrants, 1550–1600. Held at the Department of History, Washington State University.
CO	Calvin, John. *Ioannis Calvinis Opera Quae Supersunt Omnia*. Edited by G. Baum, E. Cunitz, and E. Reuss. 59 vols. Brunswick: C. A. Schwetschke, 1863–1900.
COR	Calvin, John. *Ioannis Calvini Opera Omnia. Denuo Recognita et adnotatione critica instructa notisque illustrate*. Geneva: Librairie Droz, 1992–.
CPG	Codex Palatinus Germanicus, Universitätsbibliothek Heidelberg
DvdM	Erfgoed Leiden en Omstreken. 0096 Daniël van der Meulen en Hester de la Faille, zijn vrouw, 1550–1648.
EKAW	Evangelisches Kirchenarchiv Wesel.
FRH	*Franckfurtischer Religions-Handlungen* ... 2 vols. Frankfurt am Main: Franz Varrentrapp, 1735.
RGP 196	Jongbloet-Van Houtte, Gisela, ed. *Brieven en andere bescheiden betreffende Daniel van der Meulen, 1584–1600*, vol 1: augustus 1584–september 1585. Rijks Geschiedkundige Publicatiën, 196. The Hague: Martinus Nijhoff, 1986.
SAW	Stadtarchiv Wesel.
StAF	Stadtarchiv Frankenthal.
WMV 1/3	Janssen, H. Q., ed. *Handelingen van den kerkerraad der Nederlandsche gemeente te Keulen*. Werken der Marnix-Vereeniging, serie I, deel III. Utrecht: Kemink & zoon, 1881.

WMV 2/2 — Janssen, H. Q. and J. J. van Toorenenbergen, ed. *Acten van Classicale en Synodale Vergadering der verstrooide gemeente in het land van Cleef, Sticht van Keulen en Aken, 1571–1589.* Werken der Marnix-Vereeniging, serie II, deel II. Utrecht: Kemink en zoon, 1882.

WMV 3/2 — Janssen, H. Q. and J. J. van Toorenenbergen, eds. *Brieven uit onderscheidene kerkelijke archieven.* Werken der Marnix-Vereeniging, serie III, deel II. Utrecht: Kemink en zoon, 1878.

WMV 3/4 — Janssen, H. Q, and J. J. van Toorenenbergen, eds. *Brieven uit onderscheidene kerkelijke archieven.* Werken der Marnix-Vereeniging, serie III, deel IV. Utrecht: Kemink en zoon, 1880.

WMV 3/5 — Toorenenbergen, J. J., ed. *Brieven uit onderscheidene kerkelijke archieven.* Werken der Marnix-Vereeniging, serie III, deel V. 2 vols. Utrecht: Kemink en zoon, 1882–84.

WW — Coornhert, Dirck Volkersz. *Dieryck Volckertsz. Coornherts wercken, waer van eenige noyt voor desen gedruct zyn.* 3 vols. Amsterdam: Jacob Aertsz Colom, 1630.

Introduction

In recent years, the world has sometimes seemed to be overwhelmed by the plight of refugees, as well as with passionate debates about which migrants deserve support as refugees and which pose dangers to their hosts. The causes of these widespread forced migrations today are diverse and complex. War, poverty, fear of persecution, and the wish to build a more prosperous future elsewhere have all convinced people to migrate. Responses in host societies vary. Sometimes, locals struggle with the changes to their neighborhoods that this migration entails, including the introduction of different values and cultures that migrants bring with them. On other occasions, hosts are perfectly content to welcome migrants because of their economic or cultural contributions or because they pity the newcomers for the hardships they have endured. In these debates, the use of the word "refugee" matters. The very word conveys a sense of tragedy that someone has had to abandon their home due to fear of persecution, violence, or even death. It asks readers or listeners to pity migrants for their plight or to celebrate them for their perseverance. Some so-called migrants resent the term, because it downplays their self-dignity and autonomy. Others grow frustrated when people will not recognize them as refugees. There is no escaping the difficult moral and ethical questions surrounding refugees.

Taking a long-term historical perspective helpfully allows us to step away from these urgent debates to offer critical analysis that sees beyond the rhetoric. It helps us distinguish between short-term anxieties and long-term outcomes. It permits us to explore multiple perspectives that contemporaries could not see at the time. And it provides us with an emotional distance that permits us to sympathize with people whose values and culture we do not share as well as to critique those whose heritage we might cherish. As historians, we did not set about a research project in the hopes that we might offer policy suggestions for today. But we do hope that our readers might find in the history of sixteenth-century refugees some wisdom or insight that helps them better navigate their world.

As the historian Nicholas Terpstra has demonstrated, religious refugees first became a mass phenomenon in Europe during the sixteenth century, as a quest for religious purity fueled widespread projects to purge ideas and people that threatened that vision.[1] Terpstra's synthetic approach was made possible by the work of other scholars whose interest has centered on Reformation-era refugees, even as he has inspired still more research on related topics.[2] Previously, historians primarily stressed the exile experiences faced by members of the Jewish diaspora or the movement often known as International Calvinism.[3] But all this recent scholarship has made it clear that the early modern era saw increased refugee movements among Muslims, Catholics, Lutherans, Anabaptists, and others.[4] There can be no doubt of the massive demographic, cultural, economic, and intellectual impact of refugees in early modern Europe. Major host cities became centers of activism for energized religious reformers. Reformed migrants brought new skills, trade contacts, and manufacturing techniques to host communities, bolstering lagging economies. Refugee centers also became major disseminators of publications, which could then be smuggled back home. Famous religious exiles penned powerful writings that changed minds and shifted religious worldviews across the continent. Refugees from Europe also spilled into North Africa and the emerging Atlantic world, shaping the religious cultures of the Ottoman Empire and colonies in the Americas.

Besides the benefit of providing critical reflection on issues of our own day, this attention to the history of Reformation-era refugees has also offered contributions to scholarship on the early modern era. First, it helps historians see beyond processes of state building, decentering political elites and instead centering those marginalized by their efforts to consolidate authority. Because refugees moved across jurisdictions, it also provides a framework to follow historians' subjects across archival collections, which are not neutral repositories of evidence, but themselves ideological constructions.[5] Those advantages, of course, also bring enormous challenges for historians. In our case, conducting research capable of crossing the same boundaries that Reformation-era refugees crossed required considerable teamwork and cooperation among a group of scholars.

One of the largest and most dramatic cases of forced migrations of refugees during the Reformation era was sparked by religious persecution in the Low Countries, that assortment of territories under the rule of Charles V

1 Terpstra, *Religious Refugees.*

2 For a few English-language examples, see Janssen, *Dutch Revolt and Catholic Exile*; Muylaert, *Shaping the Stranger Churches*; Lachenicht, "Refugees"; Müller, *Exile Memories*; Corens, *Confessional Mobility*; Ó hAnnracháin, *Confessionalism and Mobility.*

3 Schilling, "Christliche und jüdische Minderheitengemeinden."

4 For an overview, see Jesse Spohnholz, "Refugees," in Holder, *John Calvin in Context*, 147–54.

5 See Corens, Peters, and Walsham, *Social History of the Archive.*

and, beginning in 1555, his son Philip II. In the 1540s, Charles stepped up his campaign against religious dissenters. Authorities reacted with measures to check the influence of all dissenting movements and with persecutions. As pressure on dissenters mounted, by the mid-1550s, Reformed Protestantism was also becoming a prominent dissenting Christian movement in the territories. Many members of these new Reformed churches fled the Habsburg Netherlands altogether. Persecution and the violence of the civil war that broke out in 1566–68 dramatically increased these outmigrations of refugees.[6] Tens of thousands of Protestants escaped to England and the Holy Roman Empire. When Protestant-allied rebels secured victories in the provinces of Holland and Zeeland, in the summer of 1572, they began establishing a new independent government, with the grand nobleman William of Orange as its leading figure. But war continued. Crackdowns on heretics, sedition, and the misery of the war in the Habsburg-controlled south led to continued flows of migrations. In the late 1570s, the rebels made gains in the southern provinces of Brabant and Flanders, conquering large cities. In 1581, the allied rebel-led lands abjured the authority of King Philip II and established the United Provinces of the Netherlands, a political and military alliance that formed the basis of what would become the Dutch Republic. But a string of military victories by the general Alexander Farnese starting in the early 1580s led to Habsburg consolidation in the southern Netherlands. Habsburg forces began re-Catholicizing Brabant and Flanders, including the great trade city of Antwerp after its fall in 1585. New flows of Reformed refugees escaped, some for the independent United Provinces in the north, where the Dutch Reformed Church becomes the public church, but many also fled to England and the Holy Roman Empire.

In the historiography of Reformed Protestantism, an influential argument presented by Heiko Oberman, and later repeated by Heinz Schilling, has suggested that Calvinism offered a theological system (*Eine Exulantentheologie*) that bolstered the faith of beleaguered Reformed exiles.[7] Historians following Oberman's argument have suggested that, bound together by the Word of God and free to work unhindered by state authority, Reformed Protestants established institutions and patterns of religious life that allowed them to live out their ideology in its most perfected form.[8] Calvinism's doctrines of providence and predestination comforted refugees in the face of

6 Kooi, *Reformation*, 110–21.

7 Oberman, "'Europa Afflica'"; Heinz Schilling, "Peregrini und Schiffchen Gottes: Flüchtlingserfahrung und Exulantentheologie des frühneuzeitlichen Calvinismus," in Reiss and Witt, *Calvinismus*, 160–68.

8 H. J. Selderhuis and P. Nissen, "De zestiende eeuw," in Selderhuis ed., *Handboek Nederlandse Kerkgeschiedenis*, 287.

displacement.[9] Calvinists' stress on strict church discipline also provided a well-regulated model capable of operating without state sponsorship.[10] In short, Calvinism's intellectual, social, and institutional characteristics allowed it not only to survive but even thrive in the conditions of exile.[11]

Many historians of the Dutch Reformation have used this argument to suggest that Dutch Reformed refugees' experiences fleeing Habsburg persecution and war galvanized their movement into a doctrinally steadfast and well-disciplined force.[12] Cast off from their homes, according to this view, refugees formed isolated communities of like-minded believers who developed an even deeper commitment to their cause. The trauma of persecution and exile, historians have suggested, explain why Dutch Reformed Protestants embraced volunteeristic and confessionalized Calvinism, and rejected any governmental oversight in the Dutch Republic. While seventeenth- and eighteenth-century historical reflections offered by sympathetic coreligionists sometimes bemoaned the sufferings of sixteenth-century Dutch Reformed refugees, they did not see them as possessing any distinct ideas, behaviors, or influence, compared to other Protestants.[13] In the nineteenth century, though, an early version of what would become Oberman's exile narrative became instrumentalized by advocates of Neo-Calvinism, who saw the origins of liberty and freedom in the sixteenth-century Reformed refugees, which they understood as expressed through the refugees' commitment to the Reformed confession and their supposed independence from governmental interference.[14] Their opponents used the same narrative to explain Calvinism as a foreign intrusion trying to impose dogmatic extremism on an otherwise moderate and peace-loving Dutch population.[15] More recent historians have similarly applied elements of this exile narrative to explain why the Dutch Reformed Church emerged as orthodox Calvinist and staunchly opposed to any governmental oversight.[16]

---

9 Grell, *Brethren in Christ*.

10 Robert Kingdom, "International Calvinism," in Brady, Oberman, and Tracy, *Handbook of European History*, 2:229–45; Klueting, "Obrigkeitsfreie reformierte Flüchtlingsgemeinden."

11 Pettegree, *Emden*.

12 This paragraph paraphrases from Spohnholz and Van Veen, "Disputed Origins."

13 Cleyn, *Dank-offer*, 48.

14 For example, Abraham Kuyper, "De eeredienst der Hervormde kerk in de zamenstelling van haar kerkboek," in Ter Haar and Moll, *Geschiedenis der christelijke kerk*, 80.

15 For example, Reitsma, *Geschiedenis*, 99–133, 159–60, 195–98, 432–33.

16 Geyl, *Revolt*, 110; Bremmer, *Reformatie en rebellie*, 173; Van Gelder, *Revolutionnaire Reformatie*; Pettegree, "Politics of Toleration," 187–88;

This narrative has been reinforced by more politically centered stories about the civil war raging in the Netherlands. A combination of Habsburg-sponsored warnings against the influence of foreigners combined with William of Orange's calls for refugee communities to support his revolt have led many historians to portray the Reformed refugee communities as a key backbone of anti-Habsburg resistance. In this version, refugees took a central place in the fragile alliance developing between Orange (whose commitment to the Reformed cause was tepid at best) and zealous Reformed preachers that was central for politics in the new United Provinces. Scholars have stressed, for instance, that members of these refugee communities collected money to support Orange's campaigns and even joined the rebel troops as soldiers. In this vision, refugees look like radicals on two fronts, seeking to topple both the political and religious status quo in the Catholic, Habsburg-ruled Low Countries, with violence if necessary. According to this version of events, the return of former exiles posed a serious threat to Habsburg order.[17] Exiles thus have often been treated as being filled orthodox zeal, as uncompromising, militant and ready to fight for what they believed.[18] Sometimes, historians even instrumentalized exile as a self-evident catalyst for radicalization.

This version of events *is* rooted in facts. From 1568, Orange *did* make numerous attempts to convince the refugee communities to support his revolt. There *were* examples of returning refugees who supported rebel troops. Some former refugees *did* become political leaders in the United Provinces and zealous promoters of Reformed orthodoxy. But these facts do not prove that there existed a specific mindset or any shared political and religious commitment among the refugees. It could well be that Orange's appeals were only so frequent because they were proving so unsuccessful. Many refugees had strong reasons to distance themselves from the rebels. It turns out, many refugee communities were more interested in their own survival than in supporting an anti-Habsburg revolt or building a Reformed church in the "fatherland."[19] Many refugees also proved reluctant to support armed insurrection and refused to support the use of violence.[20] Experiences

---

Kooi, *Calvinists and Catholics*, 181–96; Judith Pollmann, "Freiwillige Religion in einer 'öffentlichen' Kirche: Die Anziehungskraft des Calvinimus in der Niederländischen Republik," in Reiss and Witt, *Calvinismus*, 178–79.

17 Van Nierop, *Het foute Amsterdam*, 14. For refugees' influence on Amsterdam, see Deen, *Publiek debat en propaganda*, 105–36.

18 Van Stipriaan, *De Zwijger*, 350–53; Fagel and Pollmann, *1572*, 48–53, 88; De Boer, "De verliezers van de opstand," 20–21.

19 Gorter, *Gereformeerde Migranten*, 173–76.

20 Mout, "Armed Resistance and Calvinism"; Muylaert, *Shaping the Stranger Churches*, 154–94.

abroad might have encouraged some to embrace orthodox Calvinism, but many refugees also had strong reasons to compromise on matters of belief and worship. After all, in order to survive abroad, they often learned to live alongside Lutherans and Catholics, to moderate their religious positions, and even to worship alongside people of different faiths.

The picture of Calvinists radicalized in exile stands in remarkable contrast to historical characterizations of the origins and nature of religious toleration in the Dutch Republic. A long scholarly tradition, going back to the seventeenth century, but crystalizing in the nineteenth century into a powerful Romantic nationalist version, emphasized that religious toleration reflected the Dutch national character.[21] These arguments relied on circular logic that explained little. By contrast, recent research has suggested that a mixture of religious, political, economic, and social factors explains religious pluralism in the Republic.[22] However, these newer histories of confessional coexistence have little to say about the massive migrations of Dutch Protestants fleeing to the Holy Roman Empire and England.[23] When refugees do appear, often histories only briefly instrumentalize the exile narrative presented above, as a way of explaining the confessionalized character of the Dutch Reformed Church.[24] Other historians of the early Dutch Republic are unconcerned with these migrations, often because they limit their research to municipal or state government archives and thus focus their attention on tracing people's activities within—not across—political boundaries.[25] We believe that there is much to be gained by moving across political boundaries, both to compare

21 Benjamin J. Kaplan, "'Dutch' Religious Tolerance: Celebration and Revision," in Hsia and Van Nierop, *Calvinism and Religious Toleration*, 8–26.

22 Spohnholz, "Confessional Coexistence"; Frijhoff, *Embodied Belief*; Christine Kooi, *Calvinists and Catholics*; Maarten Prak, "The Politics of Intolerance: Citizenship and Religion in the Dutch Republic (Seventeenth to Eighteenth Centuries)," in Hsia and Van Nierop, *Calvinism and Religious Toleration*, 159–75.

23 More attention has been given to the migration of Southern Netherlanders northward after 1585. Briels, *Zuidnederlanders in de Republiek*. As Judith Pollmann has pointed out, non-Dutch historians made important contributions recognizing the international characteristics of the Dutch Revolt. Pollmann, "Internationalisering en de Nederlandse Opstand."

24 Kooi, *Liberty and Religion*, 10.

25 For one excellent example, see Hibben, *Gouda in Revolt*. This book includes a discussion of Herman Herberts's role in Gouda starting in 1582 but does not mention Herbert's role in serving simultaneum and multiconfessional churches in the Holy Roman Empire in the 1560s and 1570s.

situations in each but also to understand how people interacted between and moved among different locations.[26]

This book explores the broad range of experiences in Dutch-speaking Reformed refugee communities in the Holy Roman Empire during the second half of the sixteenth century, and assesses their impact on the religious culture of the Dutch Republic. It focuses especially on eleven refugee communities that fall into three basic categories: (1) free imperial cities (*Reichstädte*) with Lutheran or Catholic majorities, (2) small towns in the confessionally mixed borderlands duchy of Cleves, and (3) one Dutch Reformed colony in the Electoral Palatinate. The first group—Cologne, Aachen, and Frankfurt—is distinguished by shared economic and constitutional features. As imperial cities, their magistrates were largely free to shape local policies (including the terms of the Netherlanders' stay) within the confines of imperial law. They were also large trade cities with significant long-distance economic connections, including with the Low Countries. Finally, the Reformed were a confessional minority in each of these cities, and they (largely) organized separate congregations from those of their German hosts.

The second group—towns in Cleves—includes the medium-sized territorial city of Wesel as well as smaller towns within its orbit, including Emmerich, Goch, Gennep, Kalkar, Rees, and Xanten. The politics of the duchy of Cleves were marked by the confessional ambiguity—even some spiritualist leanings—of Duke Wilhelm of the United Territories of Jülich-Cleves-Mark-Berg (r.1539–1592) before 1567 as well as by the inability of the duke's court to enforce obedience to the Roman Church, even despite his advisors' earnest attempts after 1567.[27] In Wesel, all Dutch immigrants were required to join the officially Lutheran (but in practice multiconfessional) city parishes. While this arrangement caused some conflict, this "comprehension church" generally functioned without significant violence through the high period of refugees.[28] While some of the smaller towns had similar confessional accommodations, for the most part the Netherlanders were members of unstable and underground Reformed congregations. They shared pastors, were often faced with insecurity, and relied to a greater or lesser degree on their ties to Wesel's Dutch consistory and its city pastors' willingness to perform sacraments and other rites for their members. While

26 Corpis, *Crossing the Boundaries of Belief*; Scholz, *Borders*; Schmale, "Grenze"; Soen et al., *Transregional Reformations*; De Ridder et al., *Transregional Territories*; Corens, *Confessional Mobility*.

27 To avoid confusion, in this book we use the English convention of spelling the duchy "Cleves," while using the German language "Kleve" to refer to the town of the same name.

28 On the concept of comprehension, Kaplan, *Divided by Faith*, 127–43.

Netherlanders fled to other towns in Cleves as well—we discuss some who fled to Duisburg in chapter 6, for example—we focus our attention on those with more substantive surviving evidence.

The last Dutch Reformed refugee community in our study is Frankenthal, a newly formed Dutch-speaking colony established in 1562 in the Electoral Palatinate, the most powerful officially Reformed territory in the Empire. The community was founded by a group of Netherlandish migrants who had left Frankfurt out of frustration with the terms of their settlement there. The Elector Palatine, Friedrich III (r.1559–1576) granted them an empty tract of land around a recently closed cloister (after the Augustinian friars had been resettled), and set the terms for their new colony. This is the only example in our study in which the Dutch Reformed refugees did not have to adapt to a local population. However, they did have to build their own city, essentially from scratch, street by street and building by building. Frankenthal became a kind of sixteenth-century experiment in Reformed purity.

Depending on our frame of reference, other communities move in and out of our focus. Periodically, we reference Heidelberg, the capital of the Palatinate. Few Netherlanders ever moved to Heidelberg, so we did not focus on the refugee population there; yet the city proved relevant to our research for two reasons. First, many Dutch ministers studied theology at the University of Heidelberg, which became one of the leading centers for Reformed thinking in Europe. Such students were not refugees, though, since their move was more about their traveling for training than fleeing danger. Second, Heidelberg was the Palatinate's capital, and some Netherlanders there gained access to the elector's ear. Heidelberg thus became the most important link between the Dutch Reformed and German Reformed traditions, connecting them both theologically and politically. Chapter 1 also discusses individuals who also lived elsewhere in the diaspora or who maintained relations with people abroad, including Duisburg, Bremen, Hamburg, Lemgo, Nuremberg, and Danzig (present-day Gdańsk). We have not otherwise focused on such communities because of a dearth of sources, because the Dutch Reformed population there was small, or because they were not central to the religious networks in our study. However, we cannot pretend that the eleven communities around which this book revolves formed some kind of isolated network. Rather, they simply constituted key nodes of activity of Dutch Reformed migrants in the Empire within the larger Dutch Reformed diaspora. In addition, Dutch congregations in our study maintained significant interactions with German- and French-speaking congregations within the same host communities or in the surrounding region. That is, the Dutch Reformed diaspora was neither ethnically nor linguistically isolated but operated within multilingual regional, transregional, and transnational networks.[29] Thus, although the eleven communities mentioned above form the center of our analytical framework, they need to be understood as embedded within a larger and more varied set of networks as well.

It's also important to recognize that the Netherlands from which these refugees fled was not unified linguistically or politically.[30] While the Burgundian heartlands fell under Habsburg patrimony in the late fifteenth century, institutionally they remained divided into multiple duchies, counties, and lordships. Charles of Luxembourg (later Charles V, Holy Roman Emperor and king of Spain), who ruled these lands starting in 1506, also expanded his possessions north and east to include territories outside the Burgundian lands from the 1520s to 1540s. Linguistically, Dutch was the most common language, but there were extensive French-speaking areas in the Walloon provinces in the southwest, as well as Frisian and Low German dialects in the east. French was also the language of the central government, so many Dutch political elites were multilingual.

Chronologically, our book begins in the 1540s, when Charles V's government started to take repressive measures against religious dissenters, inducing some to take refuge elsewhere, forming the first migrant congregations of Reformed Netherlanders among cities and towns along the Rhine.[31] Our attention really increases after 1553, when small but politically significant migrations of Reformed refugees arrived in a few of the host communities in our study from England, following the ascension of the Catholic queen, Mary I. Larger waves of refugees came following the Habsburg crackdowns on the widespread preaching and iconoclasm in the Low Countries, known as the Wonderyear (1566–67). Other smaller migrations often depended on local developments in cities or towns of the Low Countries or even on personal experiences. The last major emigration came in the mid-1580s, following the Habsburg conquest of a series of rebel-held cities in Flanders and Brabant. Some of this last group of migrants, however, went to the rebel-controlled United Provinces in the north, which later became known as the Dutch Republic. It's important to recognize that through this entire period of migration, movement was never one way. People moved back and forth between the Low Countries and the Empire depending on the exigencies of war, personal

29 See Monge and Muchnik, *Early Modern Diasporas,* 6–22.

30 Kooi, *Reformation*, 15–26; Hugo de Schepper, "The Burgundian-Habsburg Netherlands," in Brady, Oberman, and Tracy, *Handbook of European History*, 1:499–527.

31 See Denis, *Les églises d'étrangers.*

circumstances, and economic opportunities. They also moved between host communities in the Empire for a similarly diverse set of reasons.

We end our study at the end of the sixteenth century because around that time most religious dissenters fleeing Habsburg rule were heading to the Dutch Republic, not the Empire or England. By this time, too, most migrants in the Empire who preferred to move to the Dutch Republic had already done so. Meanwhile, those who stayed were now building permanent lives for themselves abroad.[32] In our final chapter, we trace the influence of these migrations of Reformed refugees and then examine the memory culture of these migrations for the subsequent decades and centuries. If exile played a role in later generations, it was insofar as the memory of exile served as a particular rhetorical tool, rather than via personal experience.

In general, Reformed refugees escaping the Habsburg Netherlands fled in three directions. Some crossed the English Channel to England.[33] Others fled to the northeast, to the imperial county of East Friesland, especially to its largest city, Emden.[34] The rest fled south and east, utilizing both land and river routes long used for trade and migration. These are the people we chose to follow, largely because we recognized early in our research that their experiences were more diverse than the historiographical paradigm suggested. While leaders in these congregations maintained correspondence and relationships with people in England and East Friesland, their ties to one another were both more sustained and more substantial.[35] The smaller congregations in Cleves maintained regular interactions with Dutch Reformed migrants in Wesel. Trade contacts also connected Dutch traders in Wesel, Cologne, and Frankfurt. Regional ecclesiastical bodies called classes linked the congregations in Aachen and Cologne to one another, just as other classes linked congregations in Frankfurt and Frankenthal, Wesel and Kalkar. Additionally, pastors and other church leaders moved frequently between these congregations, as between Goch and Gennep and between Frankfurt and Frankenthal. Thus, although each congregation in our study faced distinct opportunities and challenges, based on these personal bonds of positive associations, we treat them as a loose network of congregations that can be studied separately from those of East Friesland and England.

---

32 Though that did not necessarily involve abandoning an identity as part of the Dutch diaspora. Müller, *Exile Memories.*

33 Muylaert, *Shaping the Stranger Churches*; Esser, *Niederländische Exulanten*; Pettegree, *Foreign Protestant Communities*; Spicer, *French-speaking Reformed Community.*

34 Pettegree, *Emden*; Fehler, *Poor Relief and Protestantism*; Schilling, "Reformation und Bürgerfreiheit."

35 Some also moved between these regions, and thus some people who had been in London and Emden are included in our study.

This book's parameters are further defined by answers to three questions. Who counts as Reformed? Who counts as Dutch? And who counts as a refugee? What determines whether someone was Reformed is a thorny question. Casually associating "Reformed refugees" of the sixteenth century with "Calvinism"—as used to be common—is problematic. In the sixteenth century, the term "Calvinism" was a derogatory epithet used by enemies of the Reformed to suggest that they followed beliefs and practices put forward by an ordinary man rather than Christ.[36] It was only in the nineteenth century that Dutch Reformed Protestants began to treat Calvin as the central figure in their religious tradition.[37] Other reformers proved as influential—or more so—for the movement overall, including Jan Łaski, Heinrich Bullinger, and Philip Melanchthon.[38] Calvin played a role in advising Reformed refugees but as part of a larger pool of resources from which the leaders of those churches drew. Thus, we risk misunderstanding both the refugees and the International Reformed movement if we privilege Calvin's role over the diversity of other thinkers who made significant contributions.

But our unwillingness to define the Dutch Reformed tradition by its "Calvinism" alone does not solve the problem of whom to include (or who to exclude). For the most part, we chose to include only people who had some positive affiliation to the Dutch Reformed churches in our study. However, we have tried to operate under a broad definition of "affiliation." Of course, we include all the church officers and full members we were able to identify. These people receive the bulk of our attention in this book. But since these communities did not keep complete membership lists, determinations can sometimes be tricky. To be included in our study, individuals need to have made some positive effort—submitting to Reformed discipline, attending Reformed services, or defending Reformed beliefs. But those included some people who also sometimes worshipped with or took rites in Lutheran, Anabaptist, or Catholic congregations. That is, for the most part, we include all people who were involved in personal networks of relationships that included some markers of a positive association with the Dutch Reformed ecclesiastical networks in the host cities and towns in our study. But not everyone who did so was as steadfast and inflexible in their faith as the older exile narrative imagined.

---

36 Plath, "Zur Entstehungsgeschichte des Wortes 'Calvinist.'"

37 Schutte, *Het Calvinistisch Nederland*; Paul, "Johannes Calvijn."

38 Muller, "Demoting Calvin"; Becker, *Gemeindeordnung und Kirchenzucht*; Springer, *Restoring Christ's Church*; Neuser, "Die Aufnahme der Flüchtlinge," 28–49; Mühling, *Heinrich Bullingers europäische Kirchenpolitik*. For arguments that Zwinglian ideas are reflected in Dutch refugee churches, see Pettegree, *Foreign Protestant Communities*, 70–71.

Defining the linguistic and ethnic boundaries of our project poses similar challenges. The term *Netherlands* described the entirety of the multilingual Low Countries. But we focus on Dutch-speaking congregations rather than French-speaking ones. Reformed Walloons facing the same dangers as Dutch Reformed fled abroad too. For the most part, they joined French-speaking Reformed communities, which developed in Aachen, Cologne, Frankfurt, Wesel, and Frankenthal. However, making too absolute of a distinction between Walloons and Dutch is problematic. Many Netherlanders spoke Dutch and French. Some also already knew German, some learned it while in the Empire, and since the linguistic border was fluid, understanding German proved little problem for others. Thus, some migrants from the Low Countries were capable of moving between French-, Dutch-, and German-speaking churches. Thus, while we focus on Dutch-speaking congregations, these communities also included individuals from Hainaut, Walloon Flanders, Artois, Cambrai, and Namur, as well as the semiautonomous prince-bishopric of Liège. In terms of our research methods, thus, sharply distinguishing Walloon from Dutch can prove tricky.

Despite this, we have limited ourselves to focusing on the Dutch-speaking refugee communities—rather than all Reformed Protestants from the Low Countries. We made this decision for practical reasons and historiographical ones. Practically speaking, distinguishing Walloon migrants from migrants from France would prove far more challenging, since they were mostly part of the same congregations. Including the Walloons would also have doubled the already vast research requirements for this book. Historiographically, it would also raise entirely separate questions about the history of the French Reformation and Wars of Religion.[39] But the historiographical problem that we began with—the influence of exiles on the religious culture of the early Dutch Republic—centered on Dutch-speaking migrants, so that's where we focused. Thus, while we recognize that separating Netherlandish Dutch and French speakers does not fully reflect their shared experiences as subjects of the Habsburg Netherlands, it does correspond to the ways that Reformed refugees from the Netherlands organized their lives and their churches abroad.

We also need to define what we mean by *refugee*. There are two important considerations: the definition that we used to select our subjects, and the language that our subjects used to describe themselves. For the first, we define refugees as people who fled from their place (or places) of residence out of fear of ongoing or anticipated hardships that posed a serious threat to life, safety, or livelihood.[40] The word thus emphasizes the "push

39 Diefendorf, "Reformation and Wars."

40 Spohnholz, *Ruptured Lives*, 2–4.

factors" that caused people to flee, rather than "pull factors" that draw them to a specific location. Yet sometimes examining pull factors also proves critical to understanding the nature of a specific community. They help us see, for instance, why the Dutch Reformed communities in Frankfurt and Cologne resemble Dutch expatriate communities in Venice and Hamburg. Yet because the push factors were persecution and war, all the migrants in our study can generally be regarded as refugees in the sense that these push factors explain why they moved. Still, economic incentives, political calculations, family relationships, and other considerations played roles in these migrations too. Thus, while it's appropriate to use the word "refugees" for these migrants as whole, when we get to specifics, sometimes the more neutral "migrant" or the more legally defined "exile" seem more appropriate.

However, we don't use these different terms to subdivide the refugees. Yes, some refugees may have been exiles: that is, people who were explicitly barred from their hometown or from the Habsburg lands for crimes against the government, including heresy and sedition. But in practice, it can be difficult to distinguish between the two. A head of household may have been exiled but traveled with his whole family. Do we call *them* exiles too, or do we split family members into separate categories of migrants? Exiles also lived together, intermarried, and built social relationships with other kinds of refugees and migrants. We do not parse these differences too carefully. After all, emphasizing the difference between exiles and refugees privileges the legal perspectives of the Habsburg authorities which comes at the expense of undervaluing the perspectives of the migrants themselves. In other cases, the legal status of a refugee was unclear or unknown, or was known at the time but cannot be determined today. Thus, while there are good reasons at times to distinguish between exiles, refugees, and other forced migrants, in general, we avoid rigid distinctions.

We also do not divide the refugees we study according to the reasons for their migration. Did they flee religious persecution, political threats, or economic adversity? Often multiple reasons factored into decisions to flee. Trying to deduce an individuals' decision-making process often proves fruitless, even impossible.[41] In many cases people probably tried to balance different and even contradictory interests: their religious beliefs, their political views, their economic prospects, and their social interests. Some emphasized the religious reasons for their escape and the extreme suffering they endured to elicit sympathy from their hosts, even if that meant omitting less convenient parts of their stories.[42] That is, the rhetorical strategies that people

41 See Schunka, "Konfession und Migrationsregime"; Van der Linden, *Experiencing Exile*; Lougee, *Facing the Revocation*.

42 Such was the case for Utenhove, *Simplex et fidelis narratio*.

used in times of hardship do not always provide particularly useful windows into understanding why they left. Accordingly, although we are primarily interested in Reformed migrants who fled as religious refugees, we do not pretend that such clear lines can be drawn. When considering whether to use terms like "migrant," "refugee," "exile," or otherwise, we try to use the most appropriate word for the circumstances we are describing, but we recognize the inexact nature of these categories.

At the same time, we are careful to consider the nuances of meaning in individuals' self-descriptions. In an early modern context, calling oneself an "exile" (in Latin *exul* or in Dutch *balling*) necessarily invoked a comparison with the tribulations of the ancient Israelites as described in the Old Testament. It also emphasized that the suffering was involuntary. Some people also described themselves as living in Babylon, which carried similar connotations. Others described themselves as pilgrims (Latin *peregrinus*, Dutch *pelgrim*), drawing on a medieval tradition of leaving one's home as an expression of one's devotion to God.[43] In the course of our research we found that some people invoked these connotations self-consciously. Others used a broad repertoire of language to describe righteous Christian suffering. Sometimes it was living in a foreign land, away from one's home, that constituted the suffering, while at other times living abroad marked a release from the suffering of living in fear back home. Other times that suffering merely constituted the more general struggles that humans face on earth before being released to heaven. Especially in chapters 1 and 6, we pay attention to these nuances to understand these migrants' experiences of, whether because they provide insights into the migrants' worldviews or their rhetorical strategies.

A persistent challenge during this project was confronting the influence of anachronistic national and religious classifications, not only on the prevailing scholarship but also on our own understandings. Despite so much useful revisionism in recent years, modern political boundaries and confessional categories still deeply influence how scholars describe early modern migrants, their relationships to their hosts, and the long-term significance of migrations. Such categories have sometimes encouraged historians to essentialize the experience of migration or to overlook diversities within migrant populations.[44] But early modern political and cultural boundaries were flexible and permeable. For instance, it is impossible to make neat political, social, or cultural distinctions between the Low Countries and the Holy Roman Empire. Politically, following the imperial constitutional reforms of the late fifteenth and early sixteenth century, the Netherlands remained an official part of

43 Van Veen, "'Reformierte Flüchtlinge"; Janssen, "Legacy of Exile."

44 Monge and Muchnik, *Early Modern Diasporas,* 11–12.

the Burgundian Circle, an institutional subset of the Empire. In practice, the Burgundian Circle largely operated independently from the rest of the Empire and, from 1555, had a separate sovereign. Yet, some Netherlandish entities still sent delegates to meetings of imperial diets or appealed to imperial legal institutions. Additionally, from a linguistic and cultural perspective, the border was more fluid and the differences gradual, so some migrations were less dramatic than others.

Methodologically, we have combined social, cultural, and intellectual history. To do so, we have drawn on records produced by refugee churches, such as consistory records, classis and synodal minutes, as well as attestations and letters between pastors and elders. Where possible, we also examined the correspondence of laypeople in these communities. Additionally, we used records from several of the host governments, such as parish church records (including baptismal, marriage, and funeral registries), city council minutes, and legal records. Together, these sources enabled us to understand religious life and social interactions from the perspective of both refugees and locals, including the legal frameworks for their welcome, modes of boundary-drawing around communities of faith, and ritual behaviors at both a prescriptive and descriptive level. Finally, we examined published and unpublished writings of both refugees and former refugees. Our goal has been to understand how refugees' experiences affected the ways that the authors articulated their worldviews but also how authors rhetorically emphasized or elided components of their exile, both during and after, to serve strategic purposes.

We found it helpful to compare refugees' experiences in different kinds of environments rather than treating this migration into the Empire as a monolith. In this effort, we followed the example of Heinz Schilling, who compared Dutch refugee communities, looking for correlations between the extent to which Dutch migrants challenged local economic structures and local religious norms.[45] His 1972 study suggested that newcomers' challenges to local economic structures often underpinned conflicts over confessional norms and help us understand why Netherlanders successfully integrated into some places but found hostile receptions elsewhere. Schilling's work was pioneering, but it was mostly based on secondary sources and tended toward larger structuralist and functionalist generalities. While Schilling's study usefully examined how economic structures shaped exiles' experiences, it often reduced humans to sociological categories, downplaying contingency and personal experience. To a large degree, these limitations are understandable: one person could not possibly undertake the kind of research that such a broad comparison would require. When we began this project, we were aware of the challenges such a study would entail

45 Schilling, *Niederländische Exulanten.*

and that its successful completion would require a team of five researchers working together over many years.[46]

The prosopographical database we produced allowed members of our team to collect evidence in a relatively consistent manner in order to compare these migrants across the communities under consideration, even if no team member had read all the sources for the entire project. The five researchers who cooperated on this project produced a database with evidence about more than nineteen thousand individuals who lived in these communities, mostly Netherlanders who associated with one of these congregations.[47] In chapter 3, we used this database to look for demographic patterns across these communities. More often, we used the database to provide a repository—arranged in a format that was consistent regardless of our individual research methods and habits—for tracing individuals when they appeared in different types of primary or secondary sources as well as for when they moved from one community to another. The process of following migrants in demographically unstable communities has not been easy. German-speaking scribes sometimes Germanized Dutch names and Dutch-speaking scribes sometimes Dutchified German names. Additionally, sixteenth-century naming and spelling conventions were inconsistent. Finally, some kinds of migrants left far more traces in our sources than others. Thus, although 70 percent of the individuals in our database are men, we cannot use this number to make an accurate estimate about the gender balance in these communities because women's presence frequently went unreported in the sixteenth century. Further, records have not survived consistently in all the communities we studied. The Dutch Reformed consistory of Wesel left meticulous records starting in 1573, for instance, while similar sources for Aachen only begin in 1592. Although our results differ according to community, we have been able to learn about intermarriage patterns, correspondence networks, demographic patterns, residency patterns, and formal legal and political interactions but also more informal social interactions as well as trace movements between communities.

The book consists of six chapters. Chapter 1 explores the religious, political, and economic developments and personal experiences that forced Netherlanders to flee their homelands for the Empire. It demonstrates the extent to which modern religious and political categories—anachronistically

46 Other members of our team included two doctoral researchers, Peter Gorter and Inge Schipper, and one postdoctoral researcher, Silke Muylaert. We draw on their research for this book. Gorter, *Gereformeerde migranten*. Schipper, "Across the Borders of Belief." Muylaert is currently writing her book.

47 Because our parameters for data collection in each community were not fixed, but flexible, there are some people in this number who were not refugees or exiles or even migrants.

projected back into the sixteenth century—have shaped understandings of this migration. It also shows how fruitless it is to distinguish between economic migrants, political exiles, and religious refugees. And it demonstrates that for some migrants the distinction between the Low Countries and the Holy Roman Empire—or as the distinction is often made today, between Dutch and German—was not straightforward. And finally, it looks for factors that explain the multifaceted and ambiguous reasons that people fled and the factors that influenced where they decided to go.

Chapters 2 and 3 examine the kinds of relationships migrants developed with their hosts. Chapter 2 focuses on the institutional political and ecclesiastical compromises that migrants had to make, depending on the religious and political situations in which they found themselves. Changing structures of the imperial constitution and the dynamic ways that local magistrates interpreted that constitution dramatically impacted migrants' experiences. Most importantly, chapter 2 makes it clear that, from the autumn of 1555 onward, the way in which authorities applied the Peace of Augsburg—formally and informally—played the most critical role in determining the legal and institutional frameworks for Dutch Reformed living in the Empire. Here we see how the malleability of confessional categories and the variability in the enforcement of the imperial constitution resulted in a variety of arrangements.

Chapter 3 examines how refugees interacted with host communities more broadly. Scholarship on the relationships between refugees and hosts has often fallen under the purview of scholars interested in German or English history who have largely focused on the contributions of migrants to local economies (and to a lesser extent cultures), the extent to which the migrants converted locals to "Calvinism," or the pace at which the migrants assimilated.[48] Most of that work, though, has accepted the distinction between "Dutch" and "German" as straightforward national, ethnic, or linguistic categories. In this chapter, we examine the specific linguistic and socioeconomic profiles for each migrant community relative to its host community to better understand the social relations between migrants and hosts. As we learned, the further migrants traveled from their homes, the less like their hosts they were—not just linguistically but socially as well. Thus, the strategies for coexistence in some areas relied on a blurring of social distinctions, while elsewhere those strategies depended on clearly demarcated social boundaries.

48 For example, Goose, "'Dutch' in Colchester"; Pettegree, "Progress towards Integration"; Sarmenhaus, *Die Festsetzung*; Rotscheidt, "Übergang der Gemeinde Wesel"; Hantsche, "Niederländische Glaubensflüchtlinge."

Chapters 4 and 5 examine the religious lives of these refugee communities. Chapter 4 looks at how Dutch migrants worshipped while living in the Empire. Certainly, the distinctiveness of each as described in the previous chapters played a key role in shaping the opportunities for religious practice. But belief systems and the variable significance of ritual practices also mattered. As we explain, migrants proved more willing to compromise with local restrictions on their faith when it came to rites of passage—baptisms, weddings, and funerals—than they were from the central rite of community of their faith—the celebration of the Lord's Supper. In Catholic cities, the fact that the migrants shared a commitment to infant baptism—and Catholics' fear that migrants might be harboring Anabaptists—proved critically important in shaping the compromises that developed. Meanwhile, in Protestant cities that followed the Augsburg Confession (in scholarship, commonly referred to as Lutheran cities), Dutch Reformed baptized their infants, married spouses, and buried their loved ones in local churches. By contrast, in order to preserve the purity of the Lord's Supper, migrants sometimes put their communities in grave danger by celebrating it separately.

Chapter 5 examines the religious life of these refugee communities in the context of the international ecclesiastical structures and the networks for communal assistance that refugees developed abroad. While scholarship has stressed that the structures and networks of "international Calvinism" helped refugees to survive (and even thrive) in diaspora, our research yielded a different conclusion. We found that the institutions and networks binding this diaspora of Reformed Protestants were quite dynamic, diverse, and provisional. Communication networks were patchy. Transnational ecclesiastical institutions bound migrants together but were not primarily oriented toward the Netherlands or the Dutch Reformed Church. This chapter examines the construction of ecclesiastical institutions, the supplying of pastors for congregations, charity efforts to aid communities across the diaspora, and letters of attestation to monitor mobile church members. Our research suggests that Reformed migrants adapted to serve their own local, regional, and transregional needs, including closely collaborating with French- and German-speaking coreligionists living nearby, while they were less oriented to supporting the Dutch Reformed Church, the Dutch Revolt, or the Netherlands per se.

The final chapter examines how migrants remembered their experiences and asks to what extent those experiences contributed to the religious landscape of the Dutch Republic. Surprisingly, we found that few refugees played any direct role in shaping Dutch religious life. Many of the refugees remained abroad, with little fanfare. While the number of Netherlanders who did move to the Dutch Republic was never large, some became outspoken champions of Reformed confessionalism. However, there is little indication that they developed their zeal in exile, nor is there any indication that they were ever imprinted with an exile identity. Meanwhile, other refugees who moved back to the Netherlands explicitly rejected confessional forms of religion altogether. As we have shown in this book, life as an exile was not exceptionally traumatic for those who experienced it—at least no more so than any of the other dramatic political and religious upheavals of the late sixteenth century in this region of Europe. The memories of these migrants centered on the general suffering of the faithful for the true church. Many Dutch Reformed Protestants remembered the fight against the authority of Rome and against Habsburg rule in terms of the utmost suffering, which they interpreted as a kind of "bearing of the cross." For many, though, living abroad brought an escape from that suffering. Over time, this memory culture began changing as the children of exiles started to record their families' histories. In their writings, exile gradually emerged as an important theme to explain the suffering experienced by Reformed Protestants living abroad during previous generations. In the nineteenth century, this story of the transformative power of exile to crystallize Dutch Calvinism really took shape, inspired by the Romantic nationalism of the era.[49] By the mid- to late twentieth century, when these kind of confessional and nationalist studies of the Reformation were being replaced with a more secular and less confessionally invested brand of history, this exile narrative had become so entrenched that even some of the most talented and creative historians of the day repeated it without a second thought.

In each of these earlier iterations, historical reflections on the history of refugees provided meaning for people struggling with questions of their own day. In many cases, however, that meaning carried with it the implicit moral and ethical connotations that the word "refugee" connotes, dividing the world into heroes and villains. We do hope that readers will find meaning in these stories, though we do not offer any clear morality tales. Instead, readers will find the nuances, complexities, and contradictions that are found in real life and that our discourses about migration today often cannot quite capture.

49 Spohnholz and Van Veen, "Disputed Origins."

Chapter One

Leaving Home

According to standard historical convention, sixteenth-century Dutch Reformed migrants fled because of their shared commitment to the Reformed truth. These Reformed believers were prepared to leave their homes, family, and friends to give up their financial and social security and to face a period of suffering abroad for their faith. Challenges to this rather simple narrative are not new. Already in 1937, L. J. Rogier questioned the religious commitment of migrants, many of whom, he pointed out, never even became members of the foreign churches. Later, social historians like Raingard Esser also emphasized how migrants balanced religious commitment with economic interests. More recently, we have tried to show that while some migrants developed orthodox Reformed ideas, others developed more libertine visions.[1] This chapter analyzes seven migrants' decisions to go into exile, describes the circumstances under which they decided to flee, and elaborates on early modern travel and the challenges that migrants faced before arriving at their destination. We will first introduce our seven migrants: Jacques de Falais, Yolande van Brederode, Dirck Volckertsz Coornhert, Neeltje Simonsdr, a maid known to us only as Sybilla, Hendrik van den Corput, and Daniel van der Meulen.

Jacques de Falais (d.1556) and his wife Yolande van Brederode (1525–c.1555) were among the earliest Dutch Reformed migrants. They belonged to the noble elites of the Low Countries and had the means and opportunity to prepare their migration carefully. Jacques was an illegitimate son of Philips le Bon, and a cousin of Emperor Charles V. For her part, Yolande van Brederode was a descendant of the counts of Holland. At the urging of John Calvin, they decided to leave "Babylon" for a place where they could serve Christ in Reformed purity.[2] They left their home in Fallais, near the city of Liège, and went to Cologne, where they became one of the driving forces

1 Rogier, "Over karakter en omvang"; Esser, *Niederländische Exulanten*; Van Veen and Spohnholz, "Calvinists vs. Libertines."

2 This correspondence has been edited. BF.

behind the first attempt to establish a Reformed church.[3] In a sense these early migrants paved the way for the other exiles. They established foreign churches that were able to support future migrants. The networks this first generation created provided subsequent migrants with useful information.

Dirck Volckertsz Coornhert (1522–1590) and his wife Neeltje Simonsdr (1510 [?]–1584) belonged to the wave of exiles who left the Low Countries after the riotous iconoclasm in 1566.[4] Following waves of image breaking by Reformed zealots and angry mobs that year, the Habsburg government took severe measures against these rebels and heretics. Religious and political persecution forced large groups to look for safe harbor elsewhere. Coornhert's decision to flee was primarily motivated by his political actions. Coornhert was born in Amsterdam to a well-to-do merchant and lived in Haarlem as a member of the urban elites. He had family connections to Hendrik van Brederode, the Reformed noble and early leader of resistance to Habsburg rule. We know little about Neeltje's origins, but we do know that her sister was a mistress of Reinout van Brederode, the father of Hendrik van Brederode. Anna Simonsdr was the mother of six of Reinout's extramarital children, including Artus van Brederode, who helped Coornhert to flee.[5] Although Coornhert had written a ferocious attack on John Calvin's calls to commit to the Reformed faith and distance oneself from Catholic idolatry, he still took part in Reformed and rebel networks in 1566. Habsburg authorities, indeed, had many reasons to suspect him of fostering heretical and antigovernment ideas. During the turbulent 1560s, he had been present at a religious disputation, and he was in touch with Hendrik van Brederode. In 1567 Coornhert was apprehended and imprisoned but managed to escape to Xanten. Coornhert is a clear example of the permeability of religious boundaries. He seems to have participated in compromise church services (church services that combined elements of different liturgies), and he exchanged letters with more libertine-minded Reformed believers. Leading libertines fulfilled important roles in the young Dutch Reformed Church and opposed the attempts of orthodox Reformed to rigidly define the Reformed confession. The church they envisioned did not define ecclesiastical boundaries but welcomed all believers.[6] However,

3 Denis, "Jacques de Bourgogne, Seigneur de Falais."

4 On Coornhert see, Bonger, *Leven en werk.* Some 40 years after Coornhert's death, Jacob Aertsz Colom published his collected works Coorhnert, *Dieryck Volckertsz. Coornherts wercken*, here abbreviated as WW. Bruno Becker published archival sources on Coornhert: Becker, *Bronnen.*

5 Van Nierop, "Coornherts huwelijk."

6 In an early modern context, "libertine" was a slur. Its modern use suggests a clarity that was probably alien to the sixteenth-century context. Margolin, "Réflexions sur l'emploi du terme Libertin." With their pleas for a

during Coornhert's stay abroad, his revulsion for the Reformed orthodoxy increased, and he started a polemic against the Reformed doctrine of predestination.[7] In 1572, he returned to Holland, but soon after he decided to migrate again. This second migration need not concern us since it was only during his first migration that Coornhert participated in Reformed networks and supported William of Orange's revolt.

About Sybilla we know virtually nothing. She lived in Frankfurt am Main as a maid of Mathijs Schats, a Reformed migrant from Brussels. She first appears in the consistory records in April 1577, when it was recorded that Schats was harassing her. We have identified six women who shared this first name in this community. It is possible she is one (or more) of these women. The earliest record of Schats's presence in Frankfurt was only the year before, so it is possible that Sybilla arrived with him in 1576. As the consistory records inform us, Mathijs Schats, an elder, beat her when she struggled with her loom.[8] As a result of her injuries she was unable to use her arm for a couple of days. The consistory chose (more or less) to side with Sybilla, admonishing Sybilla and Mathijs to behave more peacefully while suspending Mathijs from the upcoming celebration of the Lord's Supper. Sybilla belonged to a large group of maids in Frankfurt.[9] Unfortunately, Sybilla and her fellow maids left few traces in the archives and hence we know nothing more of where she came from or how she came to live in Frankfurt.[10]

The Van den Corput family were members of the local elites in Breda who, because of the Reformed faith, fled for Duisburg in 1567.[11] Hendrik

---

nonconfessional church, their optimism about human perfectibility, and their critique of Reformed doctrines such as predestination, libertines were a stumbling block to orthodox Reformed ministers. Such libertines were active within and outside the Reformed Church. See Kaplan, *Calvinists and Libertines*; Augustijn, "Die Reformierte Kirche."

7 Bonger, *Leven en werk*.

8 Meinert, and Dahmer, *Das Protokollbuch*, 159–60.

9 On the occupational profile of Dutch Reformed migrants in Frankfurt, see chapter 3.

10 Gorter, *Gereformeerde migranten*, 101.

11 Crucial for our study of the Van den Corput family are A. J. M. Beenakker's articles that are only published online. "Pendelen tussen Heidelberg en Breda in de zestiende eeuw," "Brieven van de familie van de Corput," and "Brieven 1597–1612," (https://docplayer.nl/7757511-Pendelen-tussen-heidelberg-en-breda-in-de-zestiende-eeuw-dr-a-j-m-beenakker-samengebracht-zijn-hier.htmlhttps://www.yumpu.com/nl/document/view/20133579/pdf-brieven-1562-1584-brieven-van-den-corputnl). The family's correspondence has also been digitized: Codex Palatinus Germanicus, Universitätsbibliothek

van den Corput (1536–1601) was to become one of Holland's leading ministers. After becoming a minister in Holland's oldest town, Dordrecht, in 1578, he helped define the course of the Dutch Reformed congregation in that city. Together with the other leading reformer, Arent Cornelisz, he insisted on the introduction of a church order and embraced the Heidelberg Catechism as a means of instructing believers but to also to provide doctrinal clarity and foster the bonds between Reformed Protestants across Europe. No wonder he clashed with Coornhert, who saw the introduction of a church order and a confession as a new kind of tyranny. Coornhert equated the Reformed insistence on a church order as the reintroduction of a canon law (*jus canonicum*) and warned his readers that the Reformed commitment to a written confession undermined their only recently acquired freedom.[12] Van den Corput, who fled his hometown of Breda with other family relatives in 1567 (about the same time as Coornhert), had been an elder and *voorlezer* (a reader of Bible passages during church services) of Breda's clandestine Reformed church. As we will see, he continued to feel closely connected with his hometown of Breda, and yet his stay abroad offered him the opportunity to study theology in Heidelberg and thus to start a career as a pastor. His time in this leading center of Reformed scholarship may well have first instilled him with an international outlook. We don't know exactly where he started his ministry, but he soon became pastor in Frankenthal. As we will see, Frankenthal offered the Reformed the possibility to establish a Reformed town and to pursue their efforts to promote Reformed purity with few compromises.

Finally, Daniel van der Meulen (1554–1600) was an extremely successful merchant. He co-owned a large, international firm—founded by his parents—with his brother Andries. Van der Meulen, who had spent parts of his youth in Cologne, returned to Antwerp in 1579 during the heyday of Reformed Protestantism there. In 1584 when Antwerp was under siege, the city government sent him as a deputy to try to convince the States of Holland to help them. In 1585, after Alexander Farnese's conquest of Antwerp, he moved to Bremen. In each move, his decisions were motivated by a mix of his Reformed conviction, his political involvement, and his commercial interests. As we will see, the decision to move from Holland to Bremen was also motivated by the wish to avoid the confiscation of his belongings in Antwerp. We also found evidence of other members of Daniel's family

---

Heidelberg, abbreviated CPG. On the flight of this family see Schipper, "Across the Borders of Belief," 159–88.

12 Coornhert, *Remonstrance of vertooch*, b1r–b3r. Coornhert, *Proeve vande Heydelberghsche catechismo, omme te verstaen, of die voort-gekomen is uyt de Godtlijcke Schrift, dan uyt het menschelijcke vernuft*, WW 3, 466v.

fleeing to Frankfurt and Cologne creating points of support for their international firm, and thus linking him to the network of congregations under examination in this book.[13]

These individuals represent some of the diversity of the migrants in our study. Extensive correspondence regarding the decisions of De Falais, and members of the Van der Meulen and Van den Corput families to go into exile have been preserved. Coornhert's treatises and his correspondence with leaders of the revolt against Habsburg authority in the Low Countries allow us to analyze his reasons for going into exile as well. Records drawn from our database help us understand the patterns in movement from a more quantitative perspective. As we will see, these migrants had religious, political, social, and economic reasons for leaving their homes. Some were able to make their own decisions: they had the financial and social resources to collect information about potential refuges and they had reliable means of transportation. Others lacked these resources and, as a result, their agency in the decision-making process was limited. The way people fled had a tremendous impact on their lives abroad. Some migrants were able to prepare carefully: they secured their belongings in the Netherlands and sometimes even managed to arrange for proper and convenient housing at their destination. Many others had to flee in the night, sacrificing their belongings in the process. With little means of securing their futures, they depended on the benevolence of others.

The migrants described above also belonged to different waves of migration. The number of people leaving the Netherlands was closely linked to the course of religious persecutions and the course of the ongoing civil war in the Netherlands. Below, we will describe the political and religious circumstances that caused these waves of migration.[14]

The Reformation gained sympathizers in the Low Countries shortly after Martin Luther's attacks on what he saw as abuses in the old church.[15] The harsh measures the Habsburg regime took toward religious dissenters incited some to migrate. By the early 1560s, Reformed Protestantism had become an important aspect of the religious landscape, and many nobles and town leaders had begun to rail against Philip's anti-Protestant policies. The year 1566 marked a watershed in the religious and political history of the

13 On the Van der Meulen family, see Sadler, "Family in Revolt." On the archival resources on this family, see Kernkamp, "Het Van der Meulen-archief ca." For the correspondence between members of the family preceding their flight, see RGP 196.

14 De Graaf, *Oorlog, mijn arme schapen*; Van der Lem, *De Opstand in de Nederlanden.*

15 For a recent overview of the Reformation in the Low Countries, see Kooi, *Reformation.*

Low Countries. Angry mobs and zealous Protestant believers "cleansed" the churches of idolatry, breaking religious images and desecrating holy objects. The Habsburg regime momentarily gave in and allowed Protestants to convene, but Margaret of Parma, Philip's regent in Brussels, soon succeeded in restoring the old order. King Philip II responded by dispatching the duke of Alba to the Low Countries to repress dissent. Outmigration of Reformed Protestants became a mass phenomenon after these tumults of 1566. The noble leader William of Orange was among the thousands who decided to leave the Low Countries at this moment; he fled to his ancestral home in Dillenburg. Like Orange, other Netherlandish nobles sympathetic to the revolt also fled to the Empire, where they already owned property. Hence, from a certain perspective such migration was not quite an exile to foreign lands as much as an expedient move to their second homes.[16]

From his safe haven in Dillenburg, Orange organized a revolt against the Habsburg regime. He encouraged people back home to resist Habsburg rule, attempted to gain support among German nobles, and tried to use the networks of Netherlandish communities abroad to raise money and amass troops. Coornhert served as one of his agents charged with the task of collecting money. In 1568, Orange launched a military campaign against Philip's rule. This campaign failed, but it marked the start of a civil war that lasted decades. Only four years later, in 1572, the rebels gained a foothold in the province of Holland when they took Den Briel.[17] The seizure of this port had been the initiative of rebel sailors known as "Sea Beggars." Orange tried to use these rather unorganized troops in his military campaigns but failed to bring them under his authority. No wonder: to make their living the beggars were largely dependent on piracy (and Orange allowed them to continue this behavior).[18]

During the following years, in the rebel-held lands William of Orange tried to promote a compromise based on a policy of religious coexistence. However, efforts were undermined from multiple sides. Rebel troops, known as "Beggars," continued to loot on land, rob monasteries, and harass people, especially clerics.[19] When they conquered a city, Reformed Protestants were hardly willing to share church buildings with Catholics. Meanwhile, Catholics were inclined to regard Protestant believers as heretics who

16 Asaert, *1585*, 169. This pattern was not new: Rutger van Randwijck and his wife Jacoba van den Bongart, for example, were able to make use of family property across the border. After having been imprisoned for a year, they left Gelderland and around 1534 they went to Gennep, where Jacoba owned House Berkenbosch. Schipper, "Across the Borders of Belief," 43.

17 See now Fagel and Pollmann, *1572*.

18 Doedens and Houter, *De Watergeuzen*.

19 On the term "beggar," see Van Nierop, "Beggars' Banquet."

threatened humanity itself. From the outset, the so-called middle party risked being crushed by more outspoken people on both sides.[20] Coornhert's fate may serve as an example. After the successes of Orangist troops, he decided to return to Holland and was commissioned by the States of Holland to investigate atrocities committed by the beggars. But Coornhert gradually became a suspicious figure in the eyes of the rebels, and two Reformed ministers understood his second flight in 1572 as a betrayal of the "fatherland."[21] The ongoing war—which brought economic decline, miseries, and mutual hatred—was, perhaps, hardly compatible with moderation. In these years, the military action of rebel troops and royal troops continued to push people to look for a better life elsewhere.

In 1579, the Union of Utrecht—the treaty that aligned the rebel provinces in the north—and the Union of Arras—aligning southern provinces with the Spanish Habsburgs, further entrenched the religious lines. While defense of the Habsburgs had become a Catholic enterprise, Orange's rebellion increasingly became understood as a Protestant endeavor. After Alexander Farnese's successful military campaigns in the south, starting with his victory at Gembloux in January 1578, this confessional and political divide became a geographical divide as well. This military campaign produced a new flood of migrants. The conquest of Antwerp in 1585, especially, caused a mass migration to the northern parts of the Low Countries as well as to the Holy Roman Empire. The Van der Meulen family was part of this second wave of migrants.

Our database allows us to see patterns in the arrival of Dutch Reformed migrants in the Holy Roman Empire in these years. We have traced the first appearance of migrants in the extant sources for each of these communities. We cannot be sure how soon the individual showed up in the sources after their arrival, so we cannot actually measure this. However, the fact that these first appearances generally match the periods of increased crackdowns by Habsburg officials on Protestants and periods of more intensive warfare suggests that they provide a generally accurate picture of the inflows of migrants to these communities. That is, large spikes of migration occurred in the later 1560s and the early 1580s, as King Philip's armies made major gains in quashing political and religious dissent in the Low Countries.

Although the reasons to flee—the "push factors"— were clear, the decision to migrate was far from evident. In the following, we will describe how

20 Woltjer, *Friesland in hervormingstijd*, 292–311; Woltjer, *Tussen vrijheidsstrijd en burgeroorlog*, 64–88. Woltjer elaborated extensively on this middle party, as he called people who tried to avoid a choice between staunch Catholics and staunch Protestants.

21 R. Donteclock and A. Cornelisz to Coornhert, September 11, 1579, in WW 2, 264r. Coornhert included this letter in his *Sendt-brief*, WW 2, 257v–267r.

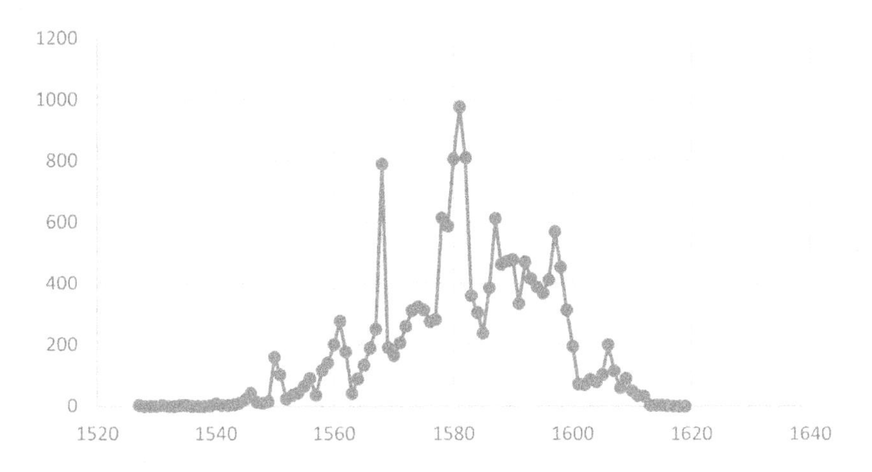

Figure 1.1. Dutch Reformed migrants' first appearance in the eleven communities of this study.

early modern people regarded migration. As we will see, this is not a straightforward story. Early modern Europeans fostered mixed feelings about migration. Urban residents of the Low Countries had long been mobile, and many towns and villages saw the advantages of welcoming foreigners. Because mortality rates in cities were high, towns needed newcomers simply to maintain population levels.[22] Academics, merchants, and journeymen were accustomed to traveling, and towns and villages were accustomed to welcoming them. Magistrates were often aware of the contribution that newcomers' skills and trade networks could make to local economies. At the same time, people in the early modern era expected one another to maintain legal and social ties to their hometowns. People were expected to seek permission from political authorities to leave their territory of residence. Some associated migration with criminality. The problem of discerning between migrants, exiles, vagabonds, vagrants, beggars, and foreigners illustrates how close mobility could come to disorder.[23] Contemporaries rarely understood migrants' decisions to leave in terms of heroic steadfastness. Instead, they often saw it in terms of betrayal. The warnings of Habsburg authorities in Brussels against leaving the Netherlands, especially as the duke of Alba was arriving from Spain to repress political and religious dissent, and the

22 See the discussion in chapter 2.

23 Coy, *Strangers and Misfits*; Kamp, *Crime, Gender, and Social Control*, 211–74.

confiscation of these migrants' property reflected attempts to enforce social norms.[24] The request in 1567 of some Reformed believers in Amsterdam for permission to leave was probably motivated by financial and social concerns. To be sure: Reformed refugees tried to avoid the loss of their property, but their motivation to avoid being seen as vagabonds may have also motivated them to maintain their status as respectable members of society.[25]

Just as there were reasons to remain where one was born and raised, there were risks in moving to a foreign land. Foreigners were vulnerable in many respects. Although, as indicated above, local magistrates were often aware of the need to attract new inhabitants to survive, early modern people still often had strong prejudices against foreigners. Foreigners were seen as an infringement of the normal order, people who endangered the normal set of beliefs or the normal rules of local societies. It was not by coincidence that, when requesting permission to stay, newcomers tried to assure local authorities that they respected the local order and were obedient citizens.[26] Thus leaving one's homeland implied a loss of security. After all, early modern Europeans were dependent on their family and social networks for help. They maintained ties with friends, family members, or neighbors and turned to these networks in case of illness, conflicts with others, poverty, or other problems. Such networks were usually bound to a specific region.[27] Literate people were able to maintain bonds of friendship by writing letters (the conversation between friends at a distance),[28] but this was not a possibility for most early modern Europeans. Thus, the decision to migrate could easily lead to a dramatic decline in social stability. Migrants were less able to draw on their preexisting networks for help. Meanwhile, churches, towns, and villages were careful to direct their poor relief to help their own poor, excluding foreigners. Social welfare rules, whether ecclesiastical or secular, explicitly excluded foreigners.[29] Delegates at the synod of Emden in October 1571 noted that people who moved too easily placed a heavy burden on social

24 See, for example, Van der Lem, *De Opstand in de Nederlanden*, 70.

25 Pontanus, *Historische beschrijvinghe,* 78.

26 This topic is the subject of a study currently being completed by Mirjam van Veen as it relates to the sixteenth-century churchman, Jan Utenhove.

27 Kooijmans, "Andries & Daniel."

28 Augustijn and Van Stam, *Ioannis Calvini Epistolae*, 11.

29 Kamp, *Crime, Gender and Social Control*, 213–17; Jütte, *Obrigkeitlichte Armenfürsorge*. See also Lieuwes, "Dorpsreglementen," 659–60; Van Zalinge-Spooren, *Gemeint en gemeenschap*, 200–202. Geneva was an exception since it allowed foreigners to draw on the local charity. This caused tension between foreigners and the "children of Geneva" as the local charity was often overtaxed by the number of foreigners. Naphy, *Calvin*, 122–26; Olson, *Calvin and Social Welfare.*

welfare systems and tried to set limits on the degree to which foreign travelers leaned on Reformed deacons.[30]

Because of the loss of social stability, migration was easier for strong, young men who were able to make a living elsewhere. The risk that elderly people might fall prey to poverty was often simply too big to justify their migration. Friends of the Van den Corput family were especially concerned about the well-being of parents.[31] Children also added to the vulnerability of migrants: in one of his letters written during his stay abroad, Coornhert mentioned his neighbor who struggled to get around and make a living not only for himself but also for his children.[32]

Migration was riskier for women. In our study, we have traced far more Dutch men than Dutch women who traveled to the Holy Roman Empire (70 percent men). To some extent, this overrepresentation of men is due to the sources we have used to make our database: men were more likely to be mentioned in many of the political and ecclesiastical sources on which we based much of our research. Still, for those communities with complete marriage records (listing both the wife's and husband's names) and baptismal records (listing the mother's and father's names), like Frankenthal, we find greater gender parity, even if we still learn little qualitatively about the women listed. However, still fully 65 percent of Netherlanders recorded as living in Frankenthal in our database were men. Certainly, there were female migrants whose identities were never recorded in Frankenthal's records, including married women who arrived with their husbands (and thus their identities may have been subsumed under their husbands'), who never bore children in Frankenthal (and thus were never listed as mothers on baptismal certificates), who never served as godmothers for other families, or who predeceased their husbands (and thus were never widows). Still, while men could travel alone without attracting suspicion in early modern Europe, such was not the case with women, whose social stability often depended on their ties to patriarchal authority. Thus, as elsewhere, it is likely that the majority of migrants were indeed male.[33] By planning their migration carefully, how-

30 Rutgers, *Acta*, 81. For further discussion of this point, see chapter 5.

31 Maria Adriaensdr to Anna van den Corput, Breda, first half of January 1568, in CPG 841, 45v. Anna received the letter on January 17. It had made a detour: Maria Adriaensdr had sent the letter to Duisburg, but it was forwarded to Wesel.

32 Coornhert to Dirck Jacobsz van Montfoort, undated, in Coornhert, *Brievenboeck*, ep. 30, 71. Coornhert wrote that he really wanted to speak with his friend in Holland in a personal meeting, instead of writing letters. This shows that he wrote his letter during one of his stays abroad.

33 Hippel, *Armut*; Kamp, "Female Crime"; Dürr, "Die Migration von Mädgen"; Fehler, "Refugee Wives, Widows, and Mothers."

ever, migrants could limit the dangers associated with migration. In the following we will describe the means migrants might have to plan their journey.

Gathering information was key for migrants deciding where to go. They needed to know whether a potential place of refuge could offer job opportunities, whether they could obtain housing, and whether such a place was within traveling distance. The possibility of staying in touch with people back home, either because a place was close by or because it had a working postal system, counted as a strong asset. Accordingly, one's place of origin determined, to some extent, where one was likely to migrate. People fleeing Amsterdam, for instance, often went to Emden because there were preexisting travel routes but also the regular exchange of news back and forth. Early modern migrants tried to maintain their networks. For the same reason they migrated as a group.[34] Traveling a relatively short distance was less expensive, offered more information about circumstances back home, and made it easier to return.[35] Migrants from Nijmegen, thus, often went to Gennep and Goch, which were both within a day's walk.

Distance was also a factor in measuring the impact of migration. To people from the northeastern parts of the Netherlands, migrating to small towns along the Lower Rhine did not necessarily imply a major change in their lives. Guelders had only become part of the Netherlands in 1543. People living in Guelders and in neighboring Overijssel maintained long-standing ties with the Empire.[36] Indeed, there was a strong tradition of people in these regions identifying as members of the Holy Roman Empire rather than as members of the Burgundian Netherlands. In 1566, for example, magistrates in Deventer argued that the Peace of Augsburg applied to their city because, as they understood it, people living there were members of the Empire. This argument was mingled with political strategy: in 1566 Deventer wanted to allow its Protestant inhabitants to assemble. Moreover, some people from the northeastern part of the Netherlands shared their Lower Saxon language with people living in the small towns across the border in the Empire.[37] Likewise, people from Limburg shared their language with people in Aachen. Meanwhile, the language in the duchy of Cleves was much closer to Brabantine Dutch than High German. In those cases, the decision to migrate was probably not terribly difficult. In chapter 3, we will discuss language in

34 Spicer, *French-Speaking Reformed Community,* 159. See also Raymond Fagel, "Immigrant Roots: The Geographical Origins of Newcomers from the Low Countries in Tudor England," in Goose and Luu, *Immigrants,* 41–56.

35 Lesger, "Variaties in de herkomstpatronen," 122.

36 Aart Noordzij, "Against Burgundy. The appeal of Germany in the Duchy of Guelders," in Stein and Pollmann, *Networks, Regions and Nations,* 111–29; Reitsma, *Centrifugal and Centripetal Forces,* 88.

37 Van der Sijs, *15 eeuwen Nederlandse taal.*

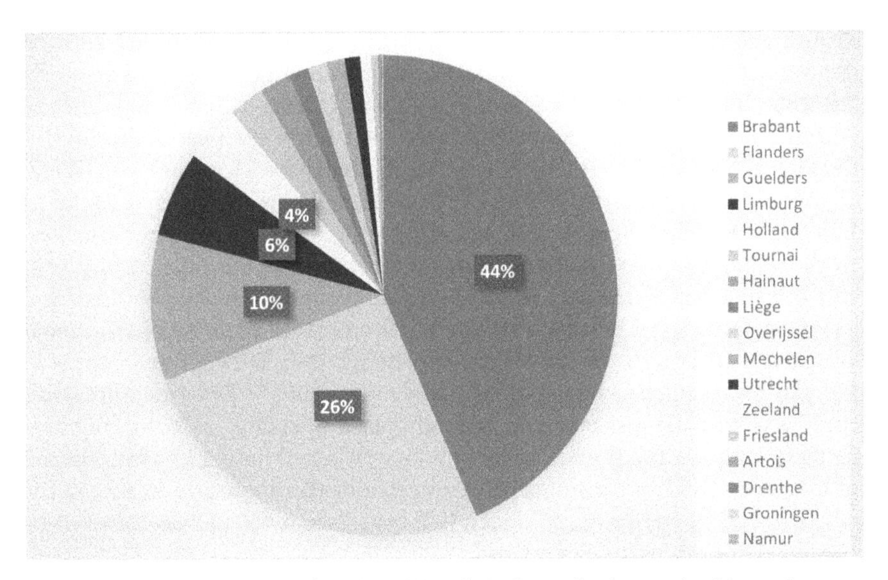

Figure 1.2. Territory of origin of Dutch Reformed migrants in this study.

more depth, but for our purposes here, it is enough to recognize that not all migration involved the sudden and disorientating experience of confronting a wholly unfamiliar culture.

Figure 1.2 gives an impression of the territory of origin of migrants coming from the Low Countries. It should be kept in mind that some people participating in these Reformed communities originally came from the Holy Roman Empire (and are not included in this chart). It should also be stressed that we do not know the origins of most of the migrants in these communities. It is nevertheless clear that most Dutch Reformed migrants from the Netherlands came from Brabant and Flanders.

Migrants used several methods to obtain information about possible places of refuge. In the case of Hendrik van den Corput, his younger brother Johan was a source of information about Duisburg. Johan van den Corput had studied at Duisburg's gymnasium. Although Johan's father regretted his son's preference of Duisburg over Leuven, and although his family repeatedly urged him to come home, Johan would have been an important source of information and assistance when the other family members decided to go into exile. It seems that the family benefited from the networks Johan had established during his stay in Duisburg as a gymnasium student.[38] Another reason to head for Duisburg was probably that a number of other Reformed

38 Postema, *Johan van den Corput*, 24.

Protestants from Breda had also gone there: migration to Duisburg allowed the Van den Corputs to stay (in part) within the same network. Personally knowing someone who lived in a city in the Empire could help someone decide to move there.[39] Some migrants even knew political authorities in their place of refuge: De Falais was acquainted with Hermann von Wied, Cologne's reform-minded bishop;[40] Coornhert knew Wilhelm V, Duke of Jülich-Cleves-Mark-Berg.[41] The Van der Meulen family used their large network to find a possible place of refuge and even took the time to find suitable housing before leaving. In 1585, Andries van der Meulen, for instance, wrote to Daniel van der Meulen about a house that their cousin Gommar Govaerts had bought in Frankfurt, explaining that, if necessary, others in the Van der Meulen family could probably stay there.[42] Reformed networks could also provide assistance in finding a place of refuge, offering migrants financial support and providing them with new social networks. After the fall of Ghent in 1584, for instance, Reformed ministers took care to spread the news that the government of Baden had expressed a willingness to welcome expelled believers as coreligionists.[43]

The presence of a preexisting Dutch community was a strong asset in identifying a potential place of refuge. Not only could such a community help migrants in cases of need, but also the presence of other migrants often helped them to feel more at home. Johan van den Corput (the elder) and his wife Anthonina Montens, along with their daughter Anna, were happy to meet other migrants in Duisburg. They made new friends, rejoiced about the preaching of the Word, and felt they were not lacking in anything. Other refugees in their surroundings were worse off.[44] During his stay in Wesel, Coornhert was in close contact with his friend Cornelis Fabius to discuss pious matters, and Coornhert definitively missed the relationship

39 See also Peeter van den Meere to Anna van den Corput, August 24, 1567, in CPG 841, 49r–v.

40 Denis, *Les églises d'étrangers*, 150. For a map with routes see De Graaf, *Oorlog*, 42.

41 Bonger, *Leven en werk*, 47–64.

42 "Gommar Govarts, ons cousijn, heeft ons gheschreven een huys tot Francfort ghecost te hebben, dat soude in noot moghen voor iemanden van onsen huysse te passe comen. Ick zal hem schrijven oft van grooter commoditeyt is." Andries van der Meulen to Daniel van der Meulen, Antwerp, January 30, 1585, in RGP 196, 145.

43 Van den Corput aan Arent Cornelisz, February 15, 1585, in WMV 3/2, ep 53, 252. Van den Corput probably referred to the margravate of Baden-Durlach, in the Upper Rhine region.

44 Anna van den Corput to Johanna and Anthonina, Duisburg, March 6,1568, in CPG 841, 60v.

after settling in Xanten.[45] Anna van de Meulen felt isolated in Stade where she missed her family and friends and bemoaned the absence of a Dutch-speaking community.[46]

Once people had decided to leave their homelands, they had to plan their journey. Traveling was challenging in the sixteenth century. People could travel by foot, horseback, carriage, or ship. Most roads were poorly maintained and travelers risked falling prey to robbers or meeting bad weather.[47] Moreover, in times of war soldiers were often about looting the lands, including those in the areas of the Rhine watershed.[48] No wonder the Van der Meulen brothers worried about the journey their pregnant wives would have to undertake.[49] More than once, families sent a male member ahead to prepare lodgings for others who would arrive.[50] And indeed, travel was only for the physically able. After De Falais arrived in Strasbourg, he seems to have been exhausted.[51] His feeble health kept him from traveling.[52] Coornhert's story is another clear example of the dangers involved in early modern travel. His initial plan was to head for Emden, as his brothers had done. He embarked on a ship to cross the Zuiderzee, but once asea, Coornhert's ship faced bad weather. Facing a dangerous storm required Coornhert to make a change of plans and disembark in Harderwijk. From there, he instead traveled inland to Deventer where Hendrick van Marckel, a burgomaster, provided lodging for him in his house.[53]

Before leaving, migrants tried to secure their belongings in their homeland. Coornhert's friend Cornelis Meynertsz Boon, for instance, sold his

---

45 Coornhert to Cornelis Fabius, 1571, Coornhert, *Brievenboeck*, ep. 58, 158.

46 Sadler, "Family in Revolt," 564–65.

47 Scholz, *Borders*, 42.

48 For example, Consistory of Cologne to the Classis, Cologne, October 31, 1572, in WMV 3/5, ep. 25, 66.

49 Jacques della Faille to Daniel van der Meulen and Hester della Faille, Haarlem, September 10, 1585, in RGP 196, ep. 177, 340. For the same reason, Anna van der Meulen worried about her old mother traveling. Anna van der Meulen to Sara van der Meulen, Cologne, September 18, 1585, in RGP 196, ep. LXVII, 506.

50 Jacques della Faille to Daniel van der Meulen, Haarlem, September 6, 1585, in RGP 196, ep. 172, 335. Della Faille advised Van der Meulen to look for a suitable place to stay while the others stayed where they were. Likewise, Peter Marimont first went to London before he wanted his wife and children to come over. See Katharina van Court to Anthonina van den Corput, July 19, 1567, in CPG 841, 30r.

51 Jean Crespin to Calvin, undated, CO 12, ep. 637, 73.

52 On the many challenges of traveling see Herborn, "Die Reisen und Fahrten."

53 Bonger, *Leven en werk*, 46.

house and furniture before going to Wesel.[54] Other migrants gave a debt note to an intermediary for them to reclaim the money if the migrants' property was confiscated, later returning the money to the migrant.[55] Andries van de Meulen took care to sublet two houses the family owned in Antwerp on his second escape from that city.[56] Networks were once again key to organizing his migration properly. These networks could even help if authorities confiscated the property of a refugee. Jan Utenhove was able to regain his possessions thanks to his influential family; his noble birth helped to nullify the legal measures taken against him.[57]

Time proved another important factor in the success or failure of early modern migration. People fleeing from Antwerp had considerable time to consider their options and balance their interests. The capture of Antwerp in 1585 took months, and, even after his victory, Farnese allowed Protestants four years to make up their minds about whether to leave Antwerp or return to the Catholic Church. Thus, those considering flight had plenty of time to organize their migration. Eighteen years earlier, in September 1567, Katharina Court told Anna van den Corput that Protestants in Breda packed their belongings in order to send them ahead of their journeys. They too had the time to organize their departure.[58] More than a decade later, Protestants in Breda lacked the time to properly prepare themselves. In a rather dramatic letter from July 1581, Hendrik van den Corput informed Arent Cornelisz about the miseries faced by Reformed Protestants in Breda after Habsburg troops took the town by surprise in the previous month. Van den Corput bemoaned the fates of highly esteemed people who had once been rich but were now impoverished.[59] A lack of time robbed migrants of options and could easily prelude a dramatic departure.

The seven migrants we mentioned at the start of this chapter had different reasons to flee: Jacques de Falais, Yolande van Brederode, and Hendrik van den Corput and his family fled for religious reasons; Dirck Volckersz Coornhert and his wife Neeltje fled for political reasons; we don't know why Sybilla left, but she may have simply been following her employer; and Daniel van der Meulen and his family had political, religious, and economic

---

54 Ten Boom, *De reformatie in Rotterdam*, 256, n. 123.

55 Decavele, *De dageraad van de reformatie*, 523.

56 Andries van der Meulen to Daniel van der Meulen, Antwerp, August 16, 1585, in RGP 196, ep. 163, 324.

57 Pijper, *Jan Utenhove*, 17–18.

58 Katharina Court to Anna van den Corput, September 16, 1567, in CPG 841, 32r.

59 Hendrik van den Corput to Arent Cornelisz, July 8, 1581, in WMV 3/2, ep. 19, 149.

reasons to flee. These seven migrants also had very different options in terms of planning their migrations. In fact, the social status one had in one's homeland determined to a high degree the possibilities a migrant had to steer their life in a specific direction. As the examples of Jacques de Falais and Yolande van Brederode show, social status shaped migrants' experiences too. Jacques de Falais and Yolande van Brederode were warmly welcomed when they arrived in Strasbourg, both by Martin Bucer, whom they already knew, and Strasbourg's magistrates, who welcomed them with wine.[60] Strasbourg's magistrates were also ready to help its new inhabitants to find suitable housing.[61] Additionally, they had the means to plan their migration carefully. They had networks to provide them with relevant information on possible places of refuge and to support them in case of need, and their financial resources helped make travel less strenuous. The same applied to the Van der Meulen family. Their networks helped them to balance religious, political, and economic interests, and their financial resources allowed them to search for proper housing. Sybilla, however, lacked the means to make her own choices and was not even supposed to determine her own future. As a woman, she was supposed to be the member of a patriarchal household, and she was expected to not travel alone.[62] As a maid, she could not choose her own profession and was excluded from more profitable occupations.[63]

The challenges Sybilla had to overcome once she arrived in her place of refuge were probably more significant than the challenges people like De Falais and Van der Meulen faced. We know that Frankfurt's ruling elites were aware of the economic contribution wealthy migrants could make to the local economy, but as the number of foreigners grew, Frankfurt became more reluctant to offer commoners (*gemeine Leut*) opportunities to become part of the urban community.[64] Sybilla probably suffered more from feelings of unease with foreigners than the rich and wealthy. Similarly, there were stronger prejudices against her than, as the city council records called them, "wealthy, stately people" (*narhafftige statlich personen*). Moreover, she had few resources to bypass such prejudices. In 1572, Frankfurt's city leaders were inclined to keep the city gates closed to people who were of little use to the local economy.[65]

60 Denis, *Les Églises d'Étrangers*, 154–56.
61 Van Veen, "In exelso honoris gradu," 11.
62 Dürr, "Die Migration von Mägden."
63 Ogilvie, *Bitter Living*, 79–139, esp. 130–31.
64 Frankfurter Ratsprotokollen, August 27, 1585, in Meinert, *Die Eingliederung*, 310–11.
65 Frankfurter Ratsprotokollen, March 14, 1572, in Meinert, *Eingliederung*, 197.

Social status also mattered within the Dutch Reformed churches in the Holy Roman Empire. Although Reformed Protestants confessed to have no master in their church but Christ, they still respected people of high social status. Calvin took care to meet the needs of De Falais: he asked after De Falais's health,[66] wrote an apology on his behalf[67] and sent him a minister to attend to his spiritual care when requested.[68] In an era of inherited status, church authorities' willingness to give exceptions to social elites was perfectly normal.[69] Besides, the often overwhelmed and undersupplied Reformed churches relied upon wealthy members, able to contribute financially, to lobby on behalf of and organize for the Reformed movement. Nevertheless, the political and financial support the nobility could offer was only one side of the coin: using noble families to spread the Gospel was not without risks. These noble believers occasionally had their own ideas about what it meant to be Reformed. For instance, it was not always clear to them that, regardless of their noble ancestry, they had to obey the rules of a Reformed synodal-presbyterial church system. The Flemish noblewoman living in the duchy of Cleves, Clara van der Dilft, for example, organized Reformed worship at her property in Goch, separate from the Reformed services that already took place in that town. Godfried Loeffs acted as a minister for this alternative church. The Reformed elders in Goch tried to convince "the Lady of Arnhem," as Van der Dilft was known to them, to integrate her own church into the ecclesiastical structure of the Reformed church in the region, but for years she refused to do so.[70]

Although the Reformed church was deeply patriarchal, and although social status mattered within the church, it provided some security to women like Sybilla. Deacons tried to address the needs of poor church members and felt called to care for the sick. Consistories offered some protection against violence against women: they urged their male church members to abstain from using violence against women or harassing their spouses.[71] They also knew about the vulnerability of women during travel. Accordingly, when, in 1571, Reformed Protestants in Cologne were worried that they might have to leave the town, Dutch-speaking elders in Cologne wrote to

66 Calvin to De Falais [September 1545], BF, ep. 11, 73.

67 Calvin, *L'Excuse du Noble Seigneur.*

68 Hollweg, "Calvins Beziehungen zu den Rheinlanden,"136.

69 Gorter, *Gereformeerde migranten*, 139.

70 Schipper, "Across the Borders of Belief," 97–98. On Reformed church structures among migrant congregations in the duchy of Cleves, see chapters 2 and 3.

71 Though they also reprimanded victims of spousal abuse for disobedience to their husbands. Spohnholz, *Tactics of Toleration*, 90. For the situation in the early Dutch Republic, see Roodenburg, *Onder censuur*, 362–69.

members of the Reformed consistory in Wesel about the widow of Willem de Mulenslaegher.[72] Given the dangers of travel for women especially, Cologne's Dutch consistory asked Wesel's elders and deacons to care for the widow in case the Reformed community in Cologne had to be dissolved.[73]

Jacques de Falais was among the early refugees. By birth and by dint of his marriage to Yolande van Brederode, he belonged to the highest nobility of the Low Countries. Yolande van Brederode probably played a crucial role in the decision to leave the ancestral lands in Fallais[74] to go to Cologne: she likely preceded her husband in embracing the new religious ideas. John Calvin played a major role in the migration history of Yolande van Brederode and Jacques de Falais: he wrote several letters urging them to take the example of Abraham and Sarah to heart and leave the land from which Christ had been banned.[75] These letters were all written in French, although De Falais knew Latin as well. Calvin's decision to write in French may have been an attempt to include Yolande van Brederode in his correspondence with her husband. In the summer of 1544, Jacques de Falais reported to Calvin that he had decided to honor God. Calvin seems to have been delighted, and he was very ready to support De Falais's efforts to establish a church in Cologne.[76]

De Falais's decision was exceptional because in the 1540s few people felt the need to migrate. When De Falais exchanged letters with Calvin, the Reformed were still relatively inconspicuous in the religious landscape of the Low Countries. The response of the secular authorities was just as unclear as the official Catholic response to the calls for reform in the Netherlands. Charles V was determined to defend Catholicism, though his anti-Protestant policies were harsher in the Netherlands than in the Holy Roman Empire, the decentralized nature of politics the Low Countries left sufficient room for dissenters to maneuver.[77] De Falais's decision to migrate was definitely

---

72 See Gorter, *Gereformeerde migranten*, 75–79.

73 Consistory of Cologne to the consistory of Wesel, December 6, 1571, in WMV 3/5, esp. 7, 26–27. See also chapter 5.

74 Roughly 25 km west of the city of Liège. The prince-bishopric Liège has a complicated history; at the time, it was a semi-independent state with close ties to the court in Brussels.

75 John Calvin to Jacques de Falais, [Geneva, October 14, 1543], BF, ep. 1, 35–40. Calvin to Madame de Falais, [Geneva], October 4, [1543], BF, ep. 2 41–43. Calvin to Jacques de Falais, [Geneva, March 1544], BF, ep. 3, 44–47.

76 Van Veen, "In exelso honoris gradu."

77 Seibt, *Karl V*. For an overview of how the inquisition operated see: Goosens, *Les inquisitions modernes*. See also Augustijn, "Die Ketzerverfolgungen." On the use of the term "inquisition" for the Netherlands, see Gielis and Soen, "The Inquisitorial Office."

inspired by his heterodoxy, but it is difficult to accurately gauge his beliefs. In this way, his religious views reflected the rather inchoate religious situation in the Low Countries. Although John Calvin rejoiced that he had won De Falais over to the Reformation, De Falais assured the emperor that he wished to live and to die "in the true ancient and Catholic religion" ("*en la vraye aucyenne et catholique religion*") and that he abhorred sects.[78] In his later years, by contrast, De Falais sided with the Anabaptist visionary David Joris, and he might have already fostered these ideas when he decided to migrate.[79]

Calvin might well have seen De Falais's decision to go to Cologne as a unique opportunity. First, his stay in Cologne coincided with the attempts of Archbishop Hermann von Wied to steer his territory toward Protestantism. For Protestants, winning the archbishopric of Cologne over for the Reformation cause would have been a strategic coup. For this reason, Martin Bucer did everything he could to assist Wied. De Falais's wish to have a minister at his disposal and to establish a small church conveniently coincided with these larger developments. Second, De Falais's story was an excellent propaganda tool, and Calvin took full advantage of it. He dedicated one of his commentaries to De Falais, hallowing his choice for the Reformation.[80] With the full support of the pope and the emperor, the defenders of the Catholic Church managed to restore the old power balance, and Hermann von Wied was forced to retreat.[81] Small reform-minded and clandestine Reformed communities continued to exist nevertheless, including in the city of Cologne. The small communities established in the 1540s, like the one established by De Falais in Cologne, became important havens for refugees during these years. The same happened in Wesel and Aachen.[82] The existence of a foreign community was an important reason for migrants to head for that very place. These preexisting small migrant communities could provide later migrants with information on, for example, the job market, allowing them to make a better-informed decision about where to move. Moreover, as soon as these small foreign Protestant communities managed to stabilize (to become what in French was known as *une église dressée*, or an

78 Jacques de Falais to Emperor Charles V, Cologne, April 16, 1545. Denis, *Les Églises d'étrangers*, annexe 11, 656, 657.

79 Van Veen, "In exelso honoris gradu."

80 Calvin to De Falais, *Dedicatio prioris epistolae Pauli ad Corinthios*, CO, ep. 753, 258–60.

81 Badea, *Kurfürstliche Präeminenz.*

82 On the first years of these small communities see, especially, Denis, *Les églises d'étrangers.*

"established church"), they also had a deaconry that could, in case of need, provide poor relief.[83]

De Falais could not stay in Cologne. His proximity to the court at Brussels probably worsened matters for him since Charles V, being aware of the propagandistic use of De Falais's decision as well, was not inclined to ignore the conversion of his cousin. Charles V wrote to his cousin that he planned to visit him in Cologne. De Falais didn't need another warning and decided to move to Strasbourg. But Strasbourg was not the end of his journey: once again, his old ties with the emperor were not exactly beneficial. When, during the Schmalkaldic War, Strasbourg came under threat from the emperor, De Falais felt compelled to leave again. In 1547, he went to Basel and later to Veigy, a small town northeast of Geneva.[84]

Unlike De Falais, Dirck Volckertsz Coornhert and his wife Neeltje Simonsdr were part of the large wave of refugees of the 1560s. Authorities had many reasons to be suspicious about Coornhert. For one thing, he had ties with the Brederode family. As we saw his sister-in-law, Anna Simonsdr, had been Reinoud van Brederode's *maitresse*. Coornhert himself worked for a short time at Batestein Castle, the residence of Brederode in Vianen. Reinoud's son Hendrik was to become a rebel leader, and Vianen was to become a nest of heretical thinking and political resistance against Charles V. After his move to Haarlem, probably in 1540, where he became a member of the urban elite, Coornhert stayed in touch with the Brederode family.[85] These ties with the Brederode family were probably an important reason why Coornhert became a suspicious figure in the eyes of Habsburg authorities.

Coornhert's connections with Brederode were not his only problem. Heresy ran in his family, with his two brothers, Frans and Clement, choosing sides with the Reformed. Although Reformed ministers described Coornhert as a man contaminated with the worst ideas imaginable, he certainly fostered dissenting ideas and participated in some Reformed networks.[86] His early writings show the influence of spiritualist thinkers like Sebastian Franck, who emphasized that humans had to choose to reject sin in order to become perfect.[87] Coornhert's attendance of a religious debate in 1566 testifies to his interest in religious renewal as well. During this debate between Catholic clerics and representatives of the Reformed, Coornhert acted as

83 On this term, see Wilcox, "'Églises plantées' and 'églises dressées.'"

84 Van Veen, "In exelso honoris gradu," 13–14.

85 Bonger, *Leven en werk*, 22–24.

86 For a report on Coornhert, see Beza's brothers in Holland to Beza, Amsterdam, September 1, 1565, De Vries van Heekelingen, *Genève Pépinière*, ep. 2:107, 283.

87 Van Veen, *Verschooninghe van de roomsche afgoderye*, 158–59, 172–79.

scribe.[88] Coornhert was also in touch with leading Reformed Protestants in Amsterdam. In a letter written in July 1566, he wrote that he would really like to speak with three people who led Amsterdam's religious agitation, Maarten Jansz Coster, Andries Boelensz Loon, and Reynier Simonsz van Neck, "about matters that can't be written on paper."[89] He was probably also in touch with Cornelis Meynaartszoon Boon who was active in organizing the Reformed church in Rotterdam.[90] In 1574, the Reformed consistory in Rotterdam blamed Boon for spreading Coornhert's ideas. By that time, he was one of the men who unsuccessfully tried to convince the magistrates in Rotterdam to hire Pieter de Zuttere as pastor, who was, as the consistory scribe remarked, close to "anabaptists, erroneous spirits and libertines."[91] It seems clear that at that time Coornhert sympathized with those striving for religious renewal. He used the ideas of Sebastian Franck and was in touch with Reformed believers who would later try to steer their church in a more libertine direction.[92]

During the years preceding the iconoclastic outbreaks in the summer of 1566, Coornhert became involved in the policy of William of Orange. We know that the two met in September 1565, when Orange together with Wilhelm V, duke of Jülich-Cleves-Mark-Berg visited Haarlem. They met again in February 1566 and discussed the persecution of heretics. Orange informed Coornhert of the lists he had in his possession with the names of thirty-six thousand people sought by the inquisition.[93] Meanwhile, in his role as the town's secretary, Coornhert contributed to the preservation of

---

88 *Tsamenspraeck*, in Dodt van Flensburg, *Archief*, 1:297–99.

89 Coornhert to Willem Dircksz Bardes, Haarlem, July 30, 1566, Becker, *Bronnen*, 143–44.

90 N. van der Blom, "Geen stilzitter," in Van der Blom, *Grepen uit de geschiedenis*, 43–62. During his exile, Coornhert exchanged letters with Boon or Fabius, and these letters testify to their meetings in Wesel. They likely already knew each other before going to the duchy of Cleves. Coornhert and Boon were both involved in Brederode's efforts to convince Orange not to escape to the Empire but to protect Holland against the inquisition in October 1566. In September, Brederode received deputies from towns from Holland in Vianen, likely including Boon and Coornhert. See also Becker, *Bronnen*, nr. 63, 40–42; nr. 66, 44.

91 Consistory of Rotterdam to Emden, undated, in WMV 3/2, ep. 8, 15. See also Van der Blom, "Geen stilzitter," in Van der Blom, *Grepen uit de geschiedenis*, 50. On De Zuttere in Rotterdam, see Ten Boom, *De reformatie in Rotterdam*, 162–66.

92 See n. 6 above.

93 Bonger, *Leven en werk*, 37–39.

peace and concord in Haarlem.[94] When a wave of iconoclasm swept through the Low Countries, together with others, Coornhert succeeded in safeguarding Haarlem's churches. But although Coornhert was certainly among those who abhorred the iconoclastic violence, he decided not to distance himself from those protesting against the royal policy of cracking down on the image breakers. His translation of the Three Million Guilder Request into Dutch, made by a group of leading Netherlanders offering a large sum of money to King Philip II if he agreed to stop persecuting Protestants, testifies to his ongoing involvement in the political upheavals.[95]

No wonder Coornhert became extremely concerned when Orange's efforts failed. Apparently, he made preparations to flee; he tried to sell his house and asked to be relieved from his duties as town secretary. From a sixteenth-century perspective, Coornhert's initial plan to go to Emden made sense. Emden already harbored a community of religious dissidents who had fled the neighboring Low Countries to escape persecution. There were existing travel routes between Holland and Emden, and Coornhert's brothers, Frans and Clement, who ran a printing press in Amsterdam, were heading for Emden.[96] However, when bad weather caught him on the Zuiderzee, Coornhert changed plans and went instead to Deventer, where he stayed with Van Marckel.

Meanwhile, Coornhert attempted to get to Cologne, but this plan failed as well. When he found out that his books were actually in Emmerich, he decided to go there. In Emmerich, he received a letter from William of Orange urging him to travel as fast as he could to Dillenburg to discuss some issues.[97] Unfortunately, we don't know anything about Coornhert's meeting with Orange, but it seems plausible that Coornhert became part of Orange's plans for a military campaign during the spring of 1568.[98]

After a prolonged stay at Van Marckel's in Deventer, Coornhert decided to go home to Haarlem in July. It is not clear what convinced him to make this decision, but possibly this trip had to do with Coornhert's meeting with

94 Bonger, *Leven en werk*, 41.

95 Bonger, *Leven en werk*, 43. See also Van Stipriaan, *De Zwijger*, 269.

96 Together with others, Dirck Volckertsz Coornhert had started a printing office in Haarlem. This office was moved to Sedan and later to Emden. Paul Valkema Blouw showed that Frans and Clement probably took over Dirck's role in managing this office. During their time in Emden, this printing office bore a decisively Protestant stamp. Valkema Blouw, "A Haarlem Press in Sedan and Emden, 1561–1669," in his *Dutch Typography*, 275–348.

97 Bonger, *Leven en werk*, 46. William of Orange in Siegen to Dirck Volckertsz Coornhert in Emmerich, December 8, 1567, *De briefwisseling van Willem van Oranje*, briefnummer 7901.

98 On his campaign see De Graaf, *Oorlog*, 150.

Orange. After all, at the time Orange was trying to gain support in Holland for a revolt, as becomes clear from his letter of commission for Johannes Basius, Coornhert's former Latin teacher, in March 1567.[99] According to a witness during his later trial, Coornhert had tried to raise support for the revolt after his return to Haarlem.[100] The idea that Coornhert returned to Haarlem for this purpose is not too far-fetched; after all, he would do the same during his later exile. But since sources remain silent on Coornhert's reasons for returning, we can't be sure. In any case, it turned out to be an unfortunate decision. Just a few months later, in September, he was apprehended and sent to jail in The Hague. However, supported by Artus van Brederode, the son of Anna Simonsdr, he managed to escape and fled to the duchy of Cleves together with his wife Neeltje. Someone tried to convince Neeltje to stay in Holland and claim her portion of Coornhert's property—it was not uncommon for one spouse to stay at home while the other fled. The Reformed consistory of Cologne even asked Emden's synod for guidelines, wondering whether the refusal of a spouse to go into exile nullified the bond of marriage.[101] Neeltje, however, stayed with her husband, although it would result in her also being banned from Holland. Duke Wilhelm V of Jülich-Cleves-Mark-Berg (whom he had met in Haarlem) granted Coornhert permission to stay in his territories, and for short periods he stayed in Goch, Wesel, and Emden. In 1570, he moved to Xanten where he stayed until his return to Holland.[102]

Coornhert's decision to go to the duchy of Cleves instead of Emden seems to reflect his ties to Orange. During Coornhert's stay in Cleves, the duchy was an important center of fundraising activity to finance the revolt. Jacob van Wesembeke was Orange's most important envoy in the area. He

99 William of Orange, Dillenburg, March 25, 1567, in Groen van Prinsterer, *Archives*, première série, t. 3, ep. 104a, 196–200.

100 Becker, *Bronnen*, 146–47.

101 "Punten ter overweging gegeven op de algemeene Synode te Emden," in WMV 3/5, ep. 4, 14.

102 Bonger, *Leven en werk*, 47–64. On Neeltje's decision, see D.V. Coornhert, *Lied-boeck*, song 30, WW 1, 504r. According to Bonger, Coornhert stayed several weeks with Van Montfoort in Leiden, but as far as we have been able to ascertain, Coornhert only stayed with Van Montfoort during his second flight, not during his first flight. Boomgaert, who described Coornhert biography, mentioned Artus van Brederode's help to escape from prison but remains silent on possible help from Van Montfoort's side. WW 1, 1v. In addition, in a grateful letter to Van Montfoort, Coornhert mentioned the occasions on which Van Montfoort offered him support. He also described his financial help during Coornhert's stay in prison, and his hospitality in 1572 (and not in 1568). Coornhert to [Van Montfoort], undated, Becker, *Bronnen*, ep. 6, 209.

tried to raise funds, gain information relevant to the revolt, and convince people to side with Orange.[103] Another important envoy of Orange was Johannes Basius, a jurist who had taught Coornhert Latin and who traveled around Holland to gain support for Orange's planned military campaign but also stayed occasionally in Cleves. During one of these tours, Coornhert and Basius met up. The two men were still close: Basius counseled Coornhert not to bemoan his exile but to seize the God-given opportunity to bear his cross.[104] Among the Reformed in Wesel we find a number of Orange's commissioners, trying to raise funds, gather troops, and raise support: Pieter de Rycke, Jean Desmaistres, Jacques Tayart, Cornelis Taymon, Cornelis le Brun, Tylman Bruyn, Jacques Liebart, Jean Salengre, Reinier Cant, Gerard van Weshem, and Philippe du Gardin. In these letters of commission, Orange explicitly tried to involve the consistories and ministers as well.[105] According to his plan, consistories should collect money to support the revolt; others should do so only if the consistories did not.[106] According to Orange, exiles were obliged take up arms or at least pay for someone to take up arms.[107] Wesel played an important role in William's strategy: it harbored a group of agents and served as a meeting point. In 1570, for example, Albert Verbeke and Orange's deputies met in Wesel to negotiate the weapons Verbeke would sell to the prince.[108] Coornhert (and Neeltje) played a role in this princely network as well. Together with his brother, Frans Dirck testified to the authenticity of at least one commission letter between Orange and

103 See also *Nationaal Biografisch Woordenboek*, sv. The correspondence between Orange and Jacob van Wesenbeke has been edited: Van Someren, "Oranjes Briefwisseling met Jacob van Wesenbeke."

104 Coornhert, *Eene lieffelijcke samensprekinge van de droefheydt*, WW 3, 379r–384v.

105 On the meager financial contributions of Reformed congregations abroad to Orange's military efforts, see chapter 5.

106 William of Orange, Dillenburg, June 10, 1568, *De briefwisseling van Willem van Oranje*, briefnummer 8862. See also William of Orange, Siegen, June 15, 1570, Van Someren, "Oranjes Briefwisseling," ep. 5, 94–96. See also William of Orange to Jacob van Wesenbeke, August 19, 1570, in Van Someren, "Oranjes Briefwisseling," ep. 19, 208.

107 William of Orange, June 15, 1570, Van Someren, "Oranjes Briefwisseling," ep. 6, 147–50. According to this letter, Orange saw these contributions as a loan and promised to repay the loan as soon as the land had been reconquered.

108 Trade agreement between Jonker A. van Huchtenbrouck, Diederik Sonoy and Jacob van Wesenbeke with Aert Verbeke, October 20, 1570, Van Someren, "Oranjes Briefwisseling," ep. 30, 23–24.

Dirck (and in his absence Neeltje) preserved money that had been collected.[109] He was also involved in collecting news from Holland that would be useful to Orange, taking great care that such news reached the prince.[110] Coornhert's request to Orange for permission to stay longer in the duchy of Cleves instead of returning to Haarlem in 1572 confirms our thesis that Coornhert's decision regarding where to go and where to stay depended, at least in part, on Orange's strategy.[111] Coornhert's migration is thus a complicated mix of political and religious motives in addition to political strategy. His proximity to Brederode, his involvement in networks of Reformed believers, and his support for Orange explain his flight. Notably, among other acts of service, he used his migration to support Orange's attempts to organize a military campaign.

Like Dirck Volckertsz Coornhert, Hendrik van den Corput was a member of the local elite. But unlike Coornhert, Hendrik's migration was embedded in the decisions of his family. His father, Johan van den Corput was the secretary of the city of Breda. Hendrik, who had studied law in Leuven, became an attorney at the city's Aldermen's Court. Together with his wife, Anthonina Montens, Johan had eighteen children, but only ten, Bartholomeus, Hendrik, Anthonie, Severijn, Johan, Johanna, Anthonina, Adriana, Anna, and Elisabeth, seem to have survived childhood. Hendrik van den Corput was a committed member of the clandestine Reformed church in Breda. He was married to Adriana van Bregt.[112] The other members of the family, with the exception of his brother Anthonie, became Reformed as well. Hendrik served the church as an elder and as a *voorlezer* (a reader of biblical texts during worship services). Brothers and sisters of Hendrik van den Corput married Reformed elites: Severijn married Anna van der Meulen (sister of Daniel van der Meulen); Johanna married Hendrik de Smet, a doctor; and Elisabeth married Franciscus Junius, a well-known theologian.[113]

The early Reformed clandestine church in Breda probably came close to Calvin's ideal vision of an organized Reformed congregation, called an "*église dressée*" in French. The Reformed consistory there had been founded by 1565. A series of itinerant Reformed preachers preached in Breda, among them were Franciscus Junius and Herman Moded.[114] Johan van den Corput

109 Cornelis Boon to Neeltje Simonsdr, Wesel, November 28, [1570], Van der Blom, "Geen stilzitter," 49–50.

110 Diary of Van Wesenbeke's journey through the Netherlands, July 1570, Van Someren, "Oranjes Briefwisseling," ep. 11, 157–58.

111 *Het leven van D.V. Coornhart*, WW 1, 2r.

112 BLGNP, s.v.

113 Postema, *Johan van den Corput*, 17–21.

114 Beenakker, *Breda*, 41–43.

sometimes hosted visiting ministers himself. The Reformed community received strong support from two noblewomen: Philipotte van Belle (Philip van Marnix van St Aldegonde's wife) and Henrica des Barres. When iconoclasts began attacking religious objects in Breda, in August 1566, members of the Van den Corput family made preparations to flee. In 1567, Hendrik van den Corput, his parents, Anthonina, Anna and Elisabeth, Johanna and Hendrik de Smet (aka Henricus Smetius), left Breda. Hendrik's brothers Anthonie and Nicolaas remained at home; Bartholomeus left later, while Severijn fled to Frankfurt, where he earned a living as a merchant.[115] The family moved to Duisburg, where they rented a house. But the Van den Corputs remained highly mobile. They even occasionally lost track of one another. For that reason, the whereabouts of family members are not always certain.[116] Within a short time, Johanna and Hendrik de Smet, together with the ever-ill Anthonina, moved on to Lemgo. The parents, along with their daughter Elisabeth, followed, while Hendrik and Anna remained in Duisburg. Soon after this, however, Anna moved to Lemgo as well. After six years in Lemgo, Hendrik de Smet became the physician of the Elector Palatine. Consequently, Johanna and Hendrik de Smet also moved to the Palatinate, first to Neustadt and later to Heidelberg, where Hendrik de Smet became a professor. Johanna and Elisabeth were reunited again. Elisabeth married Junius in 1578, then a professor in Neustadt. They too moved to Heidelberg in 1584, where Elisabeth died in 1587. In 1592, Junius became a professor in Leiden where he lived for the rest of his life. Meanwhile, Hendrik used his flight to effect a major change in his own life: he embarked on an ecclesiastical career, taking up his studies in Heidelberg. He eventually became a minister, first in a place not known to us, later in Frankenthal, and finally in Dordrecht where he helped to build the Dutch Reformed Church.

We don't know precisely why Johan van den Corput, his wife Anthonia Montens and their daughters Elisabeth and (later) Anna moved to Lemgo, where Anthonina lived together with Hendrik de Smet and Johanna van den Corput. This decision to move to Lemgo might have had to do with Anthonina's ill health. In any case, Anthonina described Lemgo as a small paradise. According to her, the local bread tasted far better than in the duchy of Cleves and the women were friendly and beautiful.[117] Their arrival in Lemgo came too late: by the time other members of her family

---

115 Schipper, "Across the Borders of Belief," 172–73.

116 See also Postema, *Johan van den Corput*, 22–24. Schipper, "Across the Borders of Belief," 172–80.

117 "*Die vrouwen syn hier int gemeyn veel vreyndelycker dan int lant van Cleve. Het syn al lange vrouwen, veel schoon.*" Anthonina van den Corput to Anna van den Corput, Lemgo, November 12, 1567, in CPG 841, 65r.

entered Lemgo, Anthonina had passed away. Other family members decided where to go based on career opportunities. As we saw, Hendrik succeeded in his ecclesiastical career, and Junius and De Smet worked in Neustadt and Heidelberg, respectively. Why Hendrik moved to the Dutch Reformed settlement Frankenthal remains a matter of conjecture. It might be that Hendrik was attracted to the vision of Reformed purity that the town represented.

All in all, the Van den Corput family offers a clear example of confessional migration. Their commitment to the Reformed movement was an important and probably decisive factor in their migration. But this religious motive merged with other motives. Hendrik used his time in the Empire to start a new career; Hendrik de Smet became a physician of the elector and a professor at the university; Junius embarked on a theological career and also became a professor in the Palatinate. Although life in the Empire was not bad for the Van den Corputs, some members of the family continued to feel deeply connected to the "fatherland."[118] They took care to stay in touch with people back home, shared news about what happened in Brabant, and regarded their stay in exile as temporary.[119]

While sources reveal many details about the decision of other migrants to go into exile, we know virtually nothing about Sybilla's journey to Frankfurt. Like most migrants, she left few traces in written records. We can only speculate about the details of her own migration and her decision-making process. Only a small minority of early modern people had the writing skills and leisure time to record their own experiences. As a result, information on how commoners understood their displacement is scanty at best. We do not know where Sybilla came from, nor do we know why she decided to go to Frankfurt; although she may have traveled from Brussels with her master. Frankfurt's Reformed community included many maids and servants who worked for the rich merchants in that city.[120] People like Sybilla probably had little choice but to follow the religious decisions of the heads of their households, like the wealthy Dutch Reformed merchants who were so important to this migrant community.[121] Nevertheless, early modern women were often mobile and although women were less likely to travel

118 It is unclear whether this term referred to the entire Netherlands, the duchy of Brabant, or the city of Breda. In most cases in our research for this project, however, this term referred to the Netherlands generally. For a discussion of this concept, see Poelhekke, "Het naamloze vaderland" (an English version appeared in *Acta Historiae Neederlandicae* 7 [1974]: 54–87). Tilmans, "De ontwikkeling van een vaderland-begrip."

119 Anthonina van den Corput to Anna van den Corput, Lemgo, November 12, 1567, in CPG 841, 64r.

120 See chapter 3.

121 Gorter, *Gereformeerde migranten*, 44, 86.

unaccompanied than men, some did. Of course, such outliers paid a price: their contemporaries regarded these women with suspicion and associated their decision with immorality.[122]

In any case, Sybilla's agency was limited and people of means were probably more likely to move than the poor. In a letter written in 1584, Andries van der Meulen suggested that displacement was a condition primarily for people with financial means. Writing during the siege of Antwerp, he warned his brother that the poor were likely to stay in Antwerp, while those with means planned to flee.[123] Indeed, travel often required significant funds, including for transport, food, and lodging. Thus, someone like Sybilla probably had few options in deciding where to go and what to do. Her gender further limited her agency in life as well as within the Reformed church. Although Reformed congregations elsewhere counted deaconesses among their members, the new church remained deeply patriarchal.[124] Women continued to be excluded from congregations' decision-making processes: they were not allowed to become ministers or elders, nor were they allowed to vote for church officers. In addition to her gender, Sybilla remained in the margins of Frankfurt's Reformed church because of her lower social status as a servant.

Meanwhile, the impact of displacement on Sybilla's life was probably greater than it was for migrants from more privileged backgrounds. Whereas Jacques de Falais and Dirck Volckertsz Coornhert were able to use their networks as resources for information and support, Sybilla was unlikely to have had any such network. This put people like her in a more vulnerable position. Sybilla also probably had little means of staying in touch with friends and family back home or of returning periodically for a visit, as more wealthy migrants occasionally did. It is also unlikely that she was able to read or write, let alone send letters back home. Sybilla's break from her old home was likely more complete than, for example, Coornhert's, and her ability to build a new life for herself more constrained.

The difference between Sybilla's migration and Daniel van der Meulen's migration could hardly be bigger. Daniel had many opportunities to combine religious and political zeal with self-interest and managed to turn his displacement into a success story. As we will see, Daniel's decision to head for Bremen was part of a business strategy. Just like Hendrik van den Corput's migration, his own migration was very much linked to the dispersal of his

122 Kamp, *Crime, Gender and Social Control*, 225–30. Dürr, "Die Migration von Mädgen."

123 Andries van der Meulen to Daniel van der Meulen, Antwerp, November 12, 1584, RGP 196, ep. 39, 81.

124 Van Booma, *Onderzoek*, 67–68; Spohnholz, "Instability and Insecurity."

entire family. After Farnese's siege of Antwerp, the Van der Meulen family had to find new avenues to continue their thriving business. Part of this new business strategy was a plan regarding where family members should move. Many archival resources on this family have been preserved, allowing us to learn in detail about their decisions about where to go, where to live, and how to create a more prosperous future for themselves.

Daniel's parents, Jan van der Meulen and Elizabeth Zeghers, were the founders of the family-owned trade firm. After their marriage in 1543 they had six children, three sons Jan (born in 1547 or 1548), Andries (born in 1549) and Daniel (born in 1554), and three daughters, Anna, Sara, and Maria, whose birth years are unknown. It is not clear when the Van der Meulens converted to the Reformed faith, but the names of Sara and Daniel might give a clue. These Old Testament names were not used in their family's lineage. Indeed, given the widespread popularity of Old Testament names for members of the Reformed tradition specifically, the use of these names should probably be interpreted as a sign of sympathy for the Reformed church.[125] After Jan Sr. died in 1563, Elizabeth was forced to both care for her children and run the firm. When political and religious tensions mounted in the Low Countries, in the later 1560s she sent her three daughters and her youngest son to Cologne, a choice that likely reflected that city's long-standing trade connections to Brabant, which, in turn, attracted Protestant migrants from the Netherlands despite the city's fame as a center of Catholicism. As mentioned above, Anna van der Meulen married Severijn van den Corput during this stay in Cologne. In 1574, Elizabeth left Antwerp for Cologne as well. Elizabeth attempted to start a firm together with her son-in-law, but Severijn died in 1575, only a few months after they had decided to work together. Severijn left one son behind: Hanske van den Corput. During this time, Jan and Andries played a significant role in Elizabeth's business: they commuted between Antwerp, Frankfurt, and Strasbourg depending on when the cities' large trade fairs took place. But in 1576, Elizabeth Zeghers lost her oldest son, Jan. By then, Daniel had started to participate in Elizabeth's business as well. He continued to live in Cologne.

After Reformed Protestants had launched a successful overthrow of the government in Antwerp in 1577, and after rebels in that city had signed the Union of Utrecht in 1579—marking their political alliance with rebels elsewhere in the Netherlands against Habsburg rule—Daniel seized the opportunity to return to Antwerp. Meanwhile, Elizabeth found a new business partner in François Pierens, a merchant from Comines (in Flanders). At

125 On the use of Old Testament names among Reformed Protestants see Benedict, *Christ's Churches Purely Reformed*, 504–6. Naming practices in migrant communities varied, however. See chapter 3.

a certain point (we don't know the precise date) he became her son-in-law by marrying Elizabeth's daughter Anna. While Anna van der Meulen and François Pierens continued to live in Cologne, in 1582 Elizabeth joined her two sons in Antwerp. The Van der Meulens became involved in the political affairs of Antwerp. Andries became an alderman, and Daniel represented Antwerp and the States of Brabant with the States General. Andries married Suzanne Malapert in 1583: like Andries, she belonged to a merchant family. The Van der Meulens's marriages—both Anna's marriage to François Pierens and Andries's marriage to Suzanne Malapert—served as opportunities to expand the family business.

But the success of the Orangist rebels and the Reformed Protestants in Antwerp did not last. In the early 1580s, the efforts of the Habsburg military general, Alexander Farnese, to reconquer the Low Countries were gaining traction in the south. Brabant sent Daniel van der Meulen to Holland to convince the States to help Brabant, but he was on a mission impossible.[126] During his stay in Holland, Daniel married Hester della Faille: yet another marriage that enabled the Van der Meulens to expand their business network. Andries became increasingly pessimistic about the prospects for Reformed Protestants in Antwerp. The two brothers were—because of their political involvement—well aware of the danger posed by Farnese's advance. As early as September 1584 Andries van der Meulen warned his brother Daniel that, with the rebels' loss at Vilvoorde (just outside of Brussels), Antwerp was at risk. If Holland and Zeeland did not help, he wrote, their enemy would undoubtedly continue gaining victories.[127] During the months that followed, the Van der Meulens monitored events carefully, tried to support the revolt in many ways, and contemplated their own options.

If Farnese's troops succeeded in taking Antwerp, then the religious interests, business strategy, and family loyalty would all shape how the members of the Van der Meulen family decided where to go. During the challenging months of the siege of their city, the Van der Meulens pursued the interests of the revolt as well as their own. As it became increasingly clear that they would have to relocate, they initiated negotiations with Antoine Lempereur in Cologne in addition to their existing cooperation in that city with François Pierens. Lempereur also became their brother-in-law when he married their sister Sara in 1586. The new firm they founded focused on trade between Antwerp and both Frankfurt and Strasbourg, but the Van der Meulens took the liberty of expanding their business to other places as well:

126 Daniel first lived in Haarlem, but in the spring of 1585 Hester and Daniel moved to Delft.

127 Andries van der Meulen to Daniel van der Meulen, September 7, 1584, in RGP 196, ep. 8, 20.

Hamburg, Cologne, Emden, Amsterdam, Middelburg, and London. In the late 1580s, Daniel also partnered with Jacques della Faille (his brother-in-law) to expand their business into the Italian lands.[128] When the conditions of Antwerp's surrender became public, it became clear that the Van der Meulens would have to find a "neutral" place in order to save their property in Antwerp. That is why they could not move to Holland or London.[129] A place near Antwerp would have the advantages of allowing them to closely oversee their ongoing business there.[130] They wanted to continue their normal business, and not every place would allow them to do so.[131] The presence of family members, and the possibility of starting a new "colony" of the family, was another important criterion. And, finally, they wanted a decent house.[132]

After the fall of Antwerp, the family remained as dispersed just as they had been before. Elizabeth Zeghers, Suzanne de Malapert, Sara van der Meulen, and Hanske van den Corput (the son of Anna van der Meulen and Severijn van den Corput) travelled together via Geertruidenberg to Bremen. In Bremen, Sara van der Meulen married Antoine Lempereur, a merchant working in Cologne. After their marriage, Antoine Lempereur returned to Cologne along with his wife, Sara van der Meulen. Daniel van der Meulen went with his wife Hester dalla Faille to Bremen, where he stayed until 1591. In 1589, Antoine Lempereur and Sara van der Meulen moved to Bremen, joining Sara's brothers, Andries and Daniel. Antoine Lempereur, and Sara van der Meulen would later move again: to Utrecht in 1598, to Leiden in 1607, and finally to Amsterdam in 1615. François Pierens and Anna van der Meulen already lived in Cologne, and they stayed there until 1592, when they moved to Bremen. Gommar Govaerts, a cousin, stayed in Frankfurt. Andries van der Meulen went to Bremen after being removed from his duties as an alderman in September 1585. In 1607, he too left Bremen and spent the remainder of his life in Utrecht.[133]

---

128 RGP 196, xl–liv.

129 Jacques della Faille to Hester della Faille, Haarlem, August 12, 1585. RGP 196, ep. 161, 321.

130 Marten della Faille to Daniel van der Meulen and della Faille, Antwerp, September 16, 1585, in RGP 196, ep. 179, 343. Marten della Faille to Daniel van der Meulen and Hester della Faille, Antwerp, September 17, 1585, in RGP 196, ep. 180, 344.

131 Jacques della Faille to Daniel van der Meulen and Hester della Faille, Haarlem, August 22, 1585, in RGP 196, ep. 165, 326. Jacques della Faille made a case for Hamburg instead of Bremen.

132 Jacques della Faille to Daniel van der Meulen and Hester della Faille, Haarlem, September 8, 1585, in RGP 196, ep. 175, 338.

133 RGP 196, xv–cxvi.

During their decision-making process the family tried to balance several, sometimes contradictory, interests. Religion was one interest, but certainly not the only one. Indeed, the Van der Meulens and their correspondents barely mention religion in the letters preceding their migration. A noticeable exception is a letter from Jacques della Faille describing the challenges for Reformed Protestants in Hamburg. Historians have often pointed to the government of Bremen's decision to embrace the Reformed faith for its state church to explain why the Van der Meulens traveled to Bremen. For the Van der Meulens, Bremen's public Reformed church was an asset but not as a decisive factor.[134] After all, the whole family did not go to Bremen: Sara van der Meulen and Antoine Lempereur continued to live in Cologne, which, being a Catholic city, only harbored a clandestine Reformed church.

After Antwerp's reconquest by the Habsburgs, the Van der Meulens continued to do business in a variety of trade centers. Marten della Faille, Daniel's brother-in-law, continued to live in Antwerp; Gommar Govaerts lived in Frankfurt; Anna and Sara van der Meulen and their husbands remained in Cologne; Hans Berwijns—who was married to Vincentia della Faille and whose son Abraham was to become the accountant of Andries van der Meulen—lived in Hamburg along with François Boudewijns, another trusted relative.[135] In Bremen, Andries and Daniel van der Meulen received all the information they needed to make their decisions. The decision of some of the family to move to Bremen was, of course, a direct consequence of Farnese's victory in August 1585; the decision of other family members to live in Cologne, though, had little to do with Antwerp's fall. Pierens and Lempereur were already active as merchants there before the rebels lost Antwerp.[136]

The Van der Meulens were only one among many merchant families who left Antwerp after Farnese's capture of the city. The dispersal of these merchant families had important effects on trade across Europe: other cities benefitted from the relocation of thriving businesses and these Antwerp families continued to use their old networks. Hence, Farnese's victory had a major impact on the location of trade but also on the networks on which trade was based. To a large extent, these trade networks were rooted in kinship. Having kin-based business networks allowed early modern merchants to

134 See, for example, RGP 196, xxix.

135 Jacques della Faille to Daniel van der Meulen and Hester della Faille, Haarlem, August 6, 1585, in RGP 196, ep. 155, 312. Andries van der Meulen to Daniel van der Meulen, Antwerp, August 8, 1585, in RGP 196, ep. 158, 316. See also RGP 196, lv.

136 Thus, our reading of the sources supports Oscar Gelderblom's conclusions about the Van der Meulens' migration, and not Jesse Sadler's recent critique. Sadler, "Family in Revolt," 536; Gelderblom, *Cities of Commerce*, 10–15.

reduce the risk involved in long-distance trade and increased the likelihood of payment.[137] According to Wilfried Brulez, the dispersal of merchant families allowed them to expand their businesses: from a business point of view, the dispersal after the seizure of Antwerp was actually beneficial.[138] Ole Peter Grell has drawn attention to the influence of these international networks of merchants on the Reformed movement of the late sixteenth and early seventeenth centuries. He shows how they became a key network of what he calls "international Calvinism."[139] The networks of merchants and their mobility helped Reformed congregations stay in touch. Hendrik van den Corput, for example, sent letters to Frankfurt via merchants who travelled to Frankfurt's Messe.[140] The networks and financial resources of merchants could help consistories add gravitas to the requests they made to city councils. Nicolas de Malapert (the brother-in-law of Andries van der Meulen), for example, signed several requests to Frankfurt's city council on behalf of the Dutch-speaking Reformed consistory. Moreover, political rulers sympathizing with the Reformed merchants helped the Reformed secure their position in Frankfurt.[141] Merchants were also able to support congregations financially. Jan Matruijt's rental payments for the building in Frankfurt used by the Dutch Reformed for private worship provide a striking example of the dependence of the Reformed community on wealthier members.[142] Because of the financial support merchants could offer, elders of Frankfurt's Reformed church were diligent in ensuring that Dutch-speaking merchants contributed to the Dutch-speaking church and not to the Walloon church: "We have to support our poor."[143] Frankfurt's Reformed consistory called

137 See for a discussion of the relevance of kinship in trade networks: Roitman, *Same but Different?*, 5–21; Monge and Muchnik, *Early Modern Diasporas*, 61.

138 Brulez, "De diaspora der Antwerpse kooplui." See also Gelderblom, *Zuid-Nederlandse kooplieden*, 75.

139 Ole Peter Grell, "Merchants and Ministers: The Foundations of International Calvinism," in Pettegree, Duke, and Lewis, *Calvinism in Europe*, 254–73. See also Grell, *Brethren in Christ.*

140 Hendrik van de Corput to Arent Cornelisz, Dordrecht, August 20, 1581, in WMV 3/2, ep. 22, 162.

141 Frankfurter Ratsprotokollen, November 23, 1592, in Meinert, *Eingliederung*, 487. Supplication of August 4, 1608, in FRH, vol. 1, Beylage CIII, 160–62. In the first request, the Reformed asked for a preacher; in the second request they asked for a church building within the city walls.

142 Frankfurt Consistory records, January 15, 1576, in Meinert and Dahmer, *Das Protokollbuch*, 138.

143 Frankfurt Consistory records, April 8, 1576, in Meinert and Dahmer, *Das Protokollbuch*, 139.

on the merchants when it needed financial support.[144] Floris van Pallandt supported Aachen's Reformed community financially by lending it money. In fact, Aachen's Dutch Reformed congregation was largely dependent on Van Pallandt's generosity.[145] As a result, merchants impacted how Reformed communities organized themselves. When Gommar Govaerts, a business partner of the Van der Meulens, criticized the preaching of Martinus Lydius, the classis strongly urged the minister to improve his sermons.[146]

While the dispersal of merchant families helped to build international firms and furthered Reformed networks, it caused problems, too. The extensive correspondence of the Van den Corput family is replete with the testimonies of parents and siblings who desperately missed each other.[147] As a consequence of their migration, the Reformed Protestants missed major life events in their families. They were absent from each other's marriages, the births of new babies, and the funerals of family members. Anna van der Meulen in Cologne, for example, expressed disappointment that she was not able to visit her brother Andries's new daughter, Suzanna van der Meulen back in Antwerp.[148] Hester della Faille wrote to her new mother-in-law (Daniel van der Meulen's mother), Elizabeth Zeghers, that she regretted that the two were unable to meet in person.[149] Sara van der Meulen was living in Cologne when her mother died in Bremen. Because the journey from Cologne to Bremen was too dangerous, Sara was only able to offer her dying mother words of consolation and comfort in writing.[150] In a letter written in October 1592, Sara testified to her desire to travel to her brother in Bremen: the children of the Van der Meulens were growing older and she wanted them to know each other.[151] People used extensive correspondence networks to soften the absence of friends and family. But, as Coornhert

144 Frankfurt Consistory records, March 23, 1578, in Meinert and Dahmer, *Das Protokollbuch*, 176.

145 Gorter, *Gereformeerde migranten*, 119.

146 Gorter, *Gereformeerde migranten*, 121–22. To be sure: the classis was critical of Govaerts's behavior as well.

147 Schipper, "Across the Borders of Belief," 180.

148 Anna van der Meulen to Sara van der Meulen, Cologne, September 18, 1585, in RGP 196, bijlage 67, 506.

149 Hester della Faille to Elizabeth Zeghers, Haarlem, January 5, 1585, in RGP 196, bijlage 22, 431.

150 Sadler, "Family in Revolt," 545–47.

151 "…dat onse kinderkens die beginnen tot verstande te comen, met u.l. kinderkens als met haer andere nichtkes ende nefkens alhier de lieffde ende vrintschap souden mogen eens ververschen." Sara van der Meulen to Daniel van der Meulen, Bremen, October 1, 1592, DvdM, 295 Brieven van Sara van der Meulen.

testified, a letter could not replace personal contact.[152] Even so, staying in touch via writing was not always easy. Letter writers had to wait for a carrier who was willing and able to deliver their letters, and these highly mobile migrants lost track of each other more than once.[153] Exiles indeed considered it an asset if their new home was one where letters could be easily delivered, and many were the complaints about letters written by loved ones that were never received.[154]

Such feelings of loss were not confined to exiles, of course. Those who stayed at home felt the same. Marten della Faille, for example, was probably unhappy with the decision of his brother-in-law and his sister to move to Bremen. He initially suggested that they move to Aachen since it was closer to Antwerp. But since Hester della Faille and Daniel van der Meulen had already moved to Bremen, he wrote a letter to his sister, urging her to consider returning to Antwerp. He doubted whether Bremen would remain neutral in the confessional politics of the day and felt that the presence of his brother-in-law and his sister was needed to manage the family's properly. But he also explained that his advice was also inspired by brotherly affection.[155]

The migrants we discussed in this chapter had different motives to flee. In some cases, religion was a primary factor; in other cases, political pressure or the miseries of war compelled people to migrate. The tides of refugees were closely connected with the outbreaks of violence in regions of the Low Countries. The iconoclasm and the subsequent crackdown by soldiers of the duke of Alba in 1567–68 pressured many to look for safe harbor elsewhere. The same happened during the military successes of Farnese in the south in the 1580s. Reformed migrants gained an advantage from the experience of early refugees who had fled the Low Countries in the 1540s and 50s, like Jacques de Falais. The small foreign communities that formed in the Holy Roman Empire during these years could provide later waves of migrants with both the information and networks of fellow migrants that would make them less vulnerable. In all the cases we analyzed, Reformed migrants balanced political and religious motives with their personal interests. Before

152 Dirck Volckertsz Coornhert to Frans Volckertsz Coornhert, undated, Coornhert, *Brievenboeck*, ep. 6, 8r.

153 Anthonina van den Corput to Anna van den Corput, Lemgo, November 12, 1567, in CPG 841, 65r. Johanna van den Corput to [Anna van den Corput], Lemgo, November 14, 1567, in CPG 841, 11v. Anthonina and Johanna both wondered where Johan was and whether he was in Basel. On the difficulties of staying in touch, see Schipper, "Across the Borders of Belief," 178–81.

154 Katharina Court to Anna van den Corput, September 16, 1567, in CPG 841, 31v.

155 Marten della Faille to Hester della Faille, DvdM, 274 Brieven Marten della Faille, 45.

they left, they took care to secure their property as much as possible, and in deciding where to go, they carefully considered the respective economic opportunities. Each host community offered different employment prospects that served as pull factors as well. Large trade cities like Cologne and Frankfurt attracted artisans and wealthy merchants, despite the compromises that Reformed Protestants had to make to live there. Migrants leaving the Low Countries after the iconoclasm and during Farnese's victories were often part of larger groups. Groups of migrants from a specific place often headed for one and the same place, effectively preserving the networks they had had at home.

Although historians have often been inclined to equate the decision to migrate with suffering, migration was only an option to those who could afford to travel and could earn their living elsewhere. The Van der Meulens understood that the poor did not have the option to leave. The same went for Reformed Protestants who could not take their occupations with them: like farmers, for example. The number of intellectuals, such as schoolmasters, ministers, doctors, and lawyers, among these migrants is indeed striking.[156] Merchants are also strongly represented among the migrants in our study: their profession was flexible, they were used to moving, and they often had the networks to settle elsewhere. Moreover, the communities along the Rhine River watershed were attractive to many migrants: they were within travel distance of the places migrants came from and the existing travel routes made them easy to reach. The availability of sufficient financial means was but one prerequisite for undertaking a journey. Physical strength was another. Because of the bad roads and because of the means of transportation, travel was often strenuous. Migrants tried to reduce the risks of traveling. They often avoided traveling during the winter and tried to monitor military maneuvers to avoid being looted by troops. Families sometimes also sent one (male) member ahead to prepare the way for the rest of the family.

The social background of migrants had a significant impact on the success or failure of their migration. People with strong networks had a better chance of securing their property back home. Additionally, they used their networks to collect information, arrange housing in their refuge, and plan and organize their travel. People with financial means and extensive networks were less vulnerable than people who lacked money and local insight. A lack of time, however, was an equalizer. When people had to flee suddenly, they lacked the time to activate their networks and take measures to safeguard their property from confiscation. One of the sources of drama in the rebels' unexpected loss of Breda in 1581 was that it left so many migrants destitute. People needed time to plan a migration, and, accordingly, inhabitants

156 For a comparison of the occupational profile of migrants, see chapter 3.

of cities under threat took precautions in case they had to leave. In sum, the way that Reformed Protestants left influenced their migration experiences. Another factor was of course their place of refuge. The context in which they tried to build a new life had a major impact both on their migration experience and how they understood their migration. Once the journey had passed, however, migrants had to navigate life in their new host communities, as we will explore in the next two chapters.

Chapter Two

Foreign Accommodations

The first chapter explored the reasons that Reformed migrants left their homes in the Low Countries and how they chose where they went. The next two chapters explore the relationships they developed with their hosts while living in cities and towns in the Holy Roman Empire. While chapter 3 will explore social relations with local populations, this chapter begins by examining the institutional, political, and ecclesiastical relationships that migrants developed in host communities. Our research emphasizes the importance of the constitutional status of each host community within the Holy Roman Empire, which deeply impacted how local political and religious leaders applied imperial law. As we will see, neither the legal framework nor the religious beliefs and practices permitted by that framework were static. Indeed, their malleability helps explain the arrangements that Reformed migrants developed in order to reside in the Holy Roman Empire.

Many previous studies of the relationships between early modern migrants and their hosts have been primarily interested in understanding the impacts of the migration either on migrants or on the hosts. Those studies focused on the migrants have often depicted diasporic communities as isolated and insular. In such cases, refugee centers look like places where migrants formed tight bonds with one another. In the case of Reformed migrants from the Low Countries, this mode of identity forming has helped historians explain how the movement survived the hardships of persecution as well as the development of a militant, confessional Calvinism.[1] Other work focusing on migrants has been more interested in the opposite: tracking their assimilation into local cultures.[2] In both cases, interest has focused on how the experience of living abroad encouraged migrants to either

1 This work has (often wrongly) described the refugee churches as operating independent from political authority. Klueting, "Obrigkeitsfreie reformierte Flüchtlingsgemeinden." On this point, see Jesse Spohnholz, "Exile Experiences."

2 Spicer, "A Process of Gradual Assimilation"; Greengrass, "Protestant Exiles"; Schilling, *Niederländische Exulanten*, 65–76, 158–59.

become tightly knit groups apart from their host or to fully integrate into the local community.[3]

Other studies have been more interested in describing the migrants' impact on host cultures. Some, for instance, use them to explain how Reformed religious ideas spread into the Holy Roman Empire, though recent research has pointed out that there is little evidence for successful missionary activity among these migrants.[4] Another strand of scholarship emphasizes contributions newcomers made to local economies.[5] Financial considerations certainly shaped why hosts might welcome certain groups of immigrants, but we cannot isolate them from other factors guiding decisions.[6] It would also be impossible to tally up the financial costs and benefits of welcoming refugees. There are too many factors to calculate and too few extant sources to generate accurate numbers. And, if we could, there would be no way of comparing our results to the economic impacts of an alternative reality without refugees. Further, authorities could not simply ignore the legal or religious implications of their decisions, even if financial considerations played a role in their willingness to welcome foreigners, which they surely often did. Finally, even when money featured prominently, the economic considerations do not in themselves explain how people handled the constitutional, social, and religious consequence of migrants' and hosts' decisions to live with their new neighbors.

All of these prior treatments, however, assume that they are describing mutually exclusive ethnic and religious cultures, and they treat the processes of change that emerge through their interaction as linear. Scholars have largely theorized relatively straightforward categorizations of difference that carry assumptions of morphological integrity of confessional or ethnic groups that, when used incautiously, might anachronistically imply the existence of clear political and religious boundaries that map onto modern national or religious identities familiar to readers. As we explained in chapter 1, from the perspective of the migrants, those categories were more

---

3 By contrast, Johannes Müller usefully emphasizes hybrid identities. Müller, *Exile Memories*.

4 Schilling, *Niederländische Exulanten*, 22; Hantsche, "Niederländische Glaubensflüchtlinge." See now Kirchner, *Katholiken, Lutheraner und Reformierte*, 47–48, 377–78; Spohnholz, "Turning Dutch?" Consistories even sometimes urged church members to be cautious about trying to convert others. Meinert and Dahmer, *Das Protokollbuch*, 96–97.

5 Brulez, "De diaspora der Antwerpse kooplui"; Roosbroeck, *Emigranten*, 307–46; Oakley, "Canterbury Walloon Congregation"; Fussel, "Low Countries' Influence." For the seventeenth century, see Wilke, "Der Einfluss der Hugenotten."

6 Arnold, "Migration und Exil."

malleable and permeable. To begin this exploration into how such ambiguities shaped the terms of migrants' stays, then, we must first note four observations.

First, much of the scholarship of the Dutch refugees fleeing into the Empire has assumed that this forced migration constituted a crisis for the hosts. However, managing migration was relatively common in sixteenth-century European cities.[7] Because of high urban death rates, cities needed to import 20–40 percent of their population annually just to maintain their size.[8] To grow, cities needed even more migrants. Half the population of sixteenth-century Frankfurt, for instance, consisted of immigrants. While most of these came from the surrounding region, many came from further afield.[9] Large cities often hosted substantial communities of foreign merchants and artisans as well as substantial diplomatic personnel from faraway lands.[10] People migrated for all kinds of reasons: for work, to find a spouse, for study, or to escape dangers like war, natural disasters, poverty, and religious persecution. Sometimes migrants' motivations overlapped. For many of the travelers in our study, their relocation to the Empire was probably not even their first migration: so many were urban merchants, traders, weavers, and other skilled craftsmen whose lives were already remarkably mobile.[11] Other migrants were lawyers, ex-priests, and other educated people who had also lived mobile lives well before they fled to the communities where we first encountered them.

Host communities also had well-established mechanisms for integrating foreigners, particularly for judging when they became eligible for poor care and guild membership, for instance, as well to perform civic duties.[12] It is true that anti-immigrant rhetoric, protectionism, and xenophobia were common and that immigrants were more vulnerable than people with roots in

---

7 This had been true for centuries. Rubin, *Cities of Strangers*. For educated urbanites, non-migratory travel was also common. See Schunka, *Migrationserfahrungen*.

8 Lucassen and Lucassen, "Mobility Transition Revisited"; Hochstadt, "Migration in Preindustrial Germany."

9 Hochstadt, "Migration in Preindustrial Germany," 203, 215.

10 Subacci, "Italians in Antwerp"; Miller, "Early Modern Urban Immigration"; Gramulla, *Handelsbeziehungen Kölner Kaufleute*.

11 Yves Junot, "Heresy, War, Vagrancy and Labour Needs: Dealing with Temporary Migrants in the Textile Towns of Flanders, Artois, and Hainaut in the Wake of the Dutch Revolt (1566–1609)," in De Munck and Winter, *Gated Communities?*, 61–80. On the demographics of these migrants, see chapter 3.

12 Schunka, "Migrations in the German Lands," 9.

the community.[13] It is also true that civic authorities in the Empire often sought to regulate immigration because they associated itinerancy with disorder.[14] Still, although cities and towns did not have what we might call a coherent immigration policy, they did have regular ways of handling newcomers. New arrivals were expected to attend church in local parishes and could not benefit from local privileges without citizenship or some other indication that they were reputable, stable, and otherwise able to contribute to the community. If migrants begged, stole, or otherwise lived unsettled lives, they could be expelled. While civic leaders often presented their community as an isolated *corpus Christianum*, in practice, immigrants from near and far were a feature of everyday life. Additionally, there existed no legal category of "refugee."[15] Essentially, local officials in the Empire treated Dutch migrants much as they did other migrants.[16]

Second, the arrival of Reformed migrants into Protestant cities was facilitated by the fact that confessional differences among Protestants remained uncertain and contested. By the time the first significant numbers of Dutch Reformed refugees had arrived, in the early 1550s, a legal and ecclesiastical distinction had emerged between adherents of the Roman Catholic Church and those who followed the Augsburg Confession, a statement of faith first presented to Emperor Charles V by evangelical leaders in 1530. But defining who constituted a follower of the Augsburg Confession became confusing, since its author, Philip Melanchthon, continued to revise the text after its original drafting, as he worked to find a phrasing—especially on the question of the Eucharist—that might unify evangelicals. By 1552, four versions of the text existed. Melanchthon also wrote other statements that he considered merely "repetition[s]" of the Augsburg Confession.[17] Some Reformed Protestants rejected any version of the document. However, many—including migrants in our study—were willing to sign Melanchthon's 1540 variation (*variata*) of the Augsburg Confession, which offered more accommodating language on the question of Christ's presence in the bread and wine of the Lord's Supper, but not the 1530 original (the so-called *invariata*), which

13 This was particularly true for immigrant women without substantial family networks. Kamp, "Female Crime and Household Control."

14 Coy, *Strangers and Misfits.*

15 See Geert Janssen's project on the invention of the refugee at http://www.inventionoftherefugee.com.

16 The exceptions being the *Exulantenstädten*, which were formed explicitly to attract Netherlandish migrants. See Kaplan, "Legal Rights of Religious Refugees."

17 Irene Dingel, "Augsburger Religionsfrieden und 'Augsburgerverwandtschaft'–konfessionelle Lesarten," in Schilling and Smolinsky, *Der Augsburger Religionsfrieden*, 157–76.

was more explicit about Christ's Real Presence, and was preferred by those whom historians usually call Lutherans.[18] At the time, the *variata* was still accepted as legitimate by the majority of Protestant states without much controversy. Even after a political consensus of eighty-six Lutheran governments of the empire emerged around the publication of the so-called Book of Concord of 1580, which treated the *invariata* as authoritative, many Lutherans in the Empire and all Reformed remained aloof from this effort to define orthodoxy so precisely.[19] The categories of religious differences among Protestants, that is, remained contested and confused through most of the century, even if partisans often stressed polarizing dichotomies.

Third, imperial laws governing Protestantism were neither static nor consistently followed. The temporary peace treaty ending the Second Schmalkaldic War in 1552 (the Peace of Passau) referred to the "*verwanten der Augspurgischen Confession*" (people who were akin or related—*Verwandt*—to the Augsburg Confession), but provided no clarity regarding that term or its application.[20] A more enduring treaty, the Peace of Augsburg, signed in September 1555, permitted those political entities in the Empire whose autonomy was limited only by their allegiance to the emperor—those with so-called *Reichsunmittelbarkeit* (imperial immediacy)—to determine whether their territory would remain allied with the "old religion" or those "adhering to the Augsburg Confession," whom the text also called *Augsburger Konfessionsverwandten*.[21] However, there was no clear or uniform answer about how to interpret the Peace of Augsburg. As we will see, disagreement soon emerged about which *Reichsunmittelbare* cities (i.e., imperial cities) had the right to pick their own church. Further, an unpublished provision of the Peace granted nobles and cities in ecclesiastical territories (who according to the main text would have to be Catholic) to continue adhering to the Augsburg Confession if they had already been doing so for multiple years. Disputes about the authenticity of that clause arose because it had not been published or officially endorsed by the organs of imperial governance.[22] Many Protestants even argued—sometimes with surprising success—that the Peace of Augsburg granted them freedom of conscience in Catholic territories.

---

18 See also Willem Nijenhuis, "Calvin and the Augsburg Confession," in Nijenhuis, *Ecclesia Reformata*, 1: 97–114.

19 Whaley, *Germany and the Holy Roman Empire*, 1:500–501.

20 Drecoll, *Der Passauer Vertrag*, 113.

21 The text describes "Angehörigen der Augsburgische Konfession," and "die der Augsburgischen Konfessions verwandte Religion," https://ghdi.ghi-dc.org/sub_document.cfm?document_id=4386.

22 Luebke, *Hometown Religion*, 39–42.

Perhaps most significantly, the Peace of Augsburg did not define who counted as *Verwandten*. Some evangelical states—notably representatives of the duke of Württemberg—had argued for adopting a definition of *Augsburger Konfessionverwandten* that explicitly excluded people identified as "sacramentarians," a category that lumped together Reformed Protestants and Anabaptists. Another proposal was to limit *Verwandtschaft* to those territories whose leaders had originally delivered the Augsburg Confession to Charles V in 1530. Both ideas were rejected due to fears that such specificity would only divide the evangelical bloc, leaving them vulnerable to Catholic stratagems.[23] In the end, the politicians and diplomats settled on ambiguity: the text provided little guidance as to whom specifically that term referred.

This result left room to maneuver. At the local level, authorities often had leeway in how strictly to interpret or enforce the law. It was common—at least at first—for Protestant governments not to require that pastors or citizens sign the Augsburg Confession itself but to have a distinct statement of belief drawn up for their specific polity.[24] For them, the logic of *Verwandtschaft* rested on the extent to which those newly crafted statements of faith conformed to, or could legitimately stand in for, the Augsburg Confession. Until recently, conventional wisdom has had it that Reformed Protestantism was excluded from the Peace of Augsburg. Matthias Pohlig and Irene Dingel have helpfully suggested that we reconsider this perspective.[25] The ambiguity of both imperial law and definitions of what it meant to adhere to the Augsburg Confession left Reformed Protestants with several viable paths for securing their stay.[26]

When Dutch Protestant migrants arrived in evangelical cities of the empire, they were often able to use this ambiguity of imperial law and the shifting nature of local ecclesiastical arrangements to their advantage. Still, over time imperial politics put increasing pressure on communities to concretize what it meant to conform to the Augsburg Confession. This process often put an unwelcome spotlight on Reformed Protestants' worship practices and doctrinal statements. As we'll see, the more interpretive layers between a community's local governance and imperial law, the more inventive local interpretations of the Peace could be to facilitate their stay.

---

23 Pohlig, "Wahrheit als Lüge," 148–49.

24 From the perspective of a prince or magistrates, requiring conformity to a confessional statement that they drafted for their policy was about promoting confessional unity under their supervision. On this point, see Atherton, "Power and Persuasion."

25 Pohlig, "Wahrheit als Lüge"; Irene Dingel, "Augsburger Religionsfrieden und 'Augsburgerverwandtschaft'," in Schilling and Smolinsky, *Der Augsburger Religionsfrieden*, 157–76.

26 See also Blum, *Multikonfessionalität im Alltag*.

In practice, the freedom of *Reichsunmittelbarkeit* actually constrained how much latitude localities had in applying the Peace of Augsburg. As such, the rest of this chapter considers the Dutch Reformed migrants' situation in their various host communities: from places where their arrival was the least ambiguous from a constitutional standpoint (Catholic imperial cities) to places where the application of imperial law was the most flexible (small towns in the border territory of Cleves).

Cologne

The situation in the Catholic imperial city of Cologne was unequivocal: local officials were certain that the Peace of Augsburg did not permit Protestants of any kind within their city. Cologne had longed prized its reputation as a regional center of Catholicism, and its leaders presented themselves as refusing to tolerate heresy of any kind.[27] After 1555, no one gave any thought to legalizing Protestantism. Simply because imperial cities held *Reichsunmittelbarkeit*, did they now all have the right to set confessional norms for their local churches? Some Protestants thought so. However, the dominant Catholic answer to this question was that only those imperial cities that had permitted worship for adherents of the Augsburg Confession before 1555 could choose to allow Protestantism after 1555. Cologne's magistrates followed that interpretation; indeed, they believed they had no jurisdiction to rule otherwise.

Thus, Cologne's city council continuously reissued edicts against Protestant worship. Violations could be punished with expulsion or—beginning in the 1580s—hefty fines.[28] From 1562 on, every magistrate had to give an oath testifying to his devotion to Rome. By 1569, all new citizens did too.[29] Additionally, Reformed Protestants were arrested, fined, removed from office, or periodically expelled. The goldsmith Evert van Hattingen, for instance, moved to Wesel after being expelled from Cologne in late January 1567.[30] On November 11, 1571, acting on a tip from a frustrated member of the Reformed congregation, city officials raided a Reformed worship service in a private home. Nineteen people were arrested, tortured, and

27 Bosbach, *Die katholische Reform*; Scribner, "Why Was There No Reformation?"; Klein, "Die Kölner Kirche."

28 Langer, "Die konfessionelle Grenze," 40; Bergerhausen, *Die Stadt Köln und die Reichsversammlungen.*

29 Enderle, "Die katholischen Reichsstädte," 262.

30 Scheffler, *Goldschmiede Rheinland-Westfalens*, 2:1016; Ennen, "Die reformirte Gemeinde in der Stadt Köln," 511; Schwerhoff, *Köln im Kreuzverhör*, 243.

interrogated for information about their illegal activities and networks.[31] Following these arrests, leaders of the church considered shutting down their congregation and transferring all their records to Frankenthal for safety.[32] But the congregation persisted, largely due to the efforts of the elder Jan de Roy. In response to external pressures, expulsions of Protestants also ticked up during the Cologne War (1583–88). A series of Reformed foreigners who had recently arrived from Antwerp in 1584 and 1585 were escorted out of the city by armed soldiers not long after their arrival. In March 1586, Hugo de Buys faced a two-hundred gold guilder fine for baptizing his infant in a Protestant congregation outside the city.[33] The danger religious dissenters faced in this home to Cathedral canons, university theologians, and one of the densest populations of Catholic clergy per capita in the Empire never dissipated.

Considering Cologne's fervent devotion to Catholicism, the city might seem a rather unlikely place for a sustained community of Reformed migrants. And yet Dutch-speaking Reformed Protestants, who arrived in significant numbers in the 1560s, remained in Cologne through the rest of the century.[34] There are two reasons for Reformed Protestants' survival. The first is their successful efforts to keep their dissenting faith from attracting attention. Cologne's Reformed congregations worshipped in secret. Consistory meetings usually rotated through elders' houses. These small affairs, usually consisting of between three and seven people, were probably relatively easy to conceal. Reformed Protestants also tended to reside (along with other dissenters) in a few neighborhoods, especially the *Breitstraße*, where other disreputable activities, such as prostitution, took place.[35] As Ute Langer has noted, keeping a low profile meant that maintaining the trust of acquaintances—especially servants—became extremely important.[36] Protestants in Cologne also learned to prevaricate when confronted. In October 1571, at a synod held in Emden, Cologne's Dutch-speaking Reformed Protestants inquired whether it was permissible to answer questions about whether they were Catholic with a simple "yes" and questions about whether they had disobeyed King Philip with a simple "no."[37] They hoped that such casuistry

31 Gorter, *Gereformeerde migranten*, 75–77.

32 Gorter, *Gereformeerde migranten*, 80.

33 Ennen, "Die reformirte Gemeinde," 519.

34 Chaix, "Die schwierige Schule der Sitten," 231.

35 Ennen, *Geschichte der Stadt Köln*, 806; Monge, *Des communautés mouvantes*, 193.

36 Langer, "Die konfessionelle Grenze," 40.

37 Cologne's consistory sent twenty-four questions to the synod, of which only twelve were answered. This question was among those not addressed. WMV

around the ambiguous meaning of the adjective "catholic" and their claim that Philip could no longer demand obedience because he had broken his oath of office would grant them the safety they sought. When Raymond Rijngold, a Reformed migrant from Brussels, was accused of heresy in 1570, he managed to stay in Cologne by promising his loyalty to the city council.[38] When the Reformed silversmith, Hubert van Coninxloo, also from Brussels, was charged with heresy that same year, he convinced officials that envious merchants had falsely accused him. Accused again three years later, Van Coninxloo brought in a local Catholic friend, Heinrich Faber, to speak on his behalf. Faber told the council that since Van Coninxloo shared a household with a number of Catholics, magistrates had no reason to worry about him.[39]

The second reason for Dutch Reformed Protestants' ability to reside in Cologne was the deliberate inaction of city officials. City leaders surely had both economic and political reasons to turn a blind eye now and again. The city's economy had long depended on its ties to the Antwerp and Flemish markets, such that welcoming foreign merchants with ties to those markets created lucrative opportunities.[40] From 1565 to 1571, the irenical mayor Konstantin von Lyskirchen played a key role in encouraging Protestant immigration.[41] Further, there existed anti-Spanish sentiment in Cologne as well as distaste for the harsh punishments inflicted on dissenters in the Netherlands.[42] Some officials may also have distinguished between the existential danger of an abstract heresy and the less threatening reality of individual migrants whom they knew.[43] In 1578, the city councilor (and diarist) Hermann von Weinberg noted with frustration that "people were not only preaching the condemned doctrine secretly in private homes, but publicly, with open doors, and that many libelous writings and paintings were being published and displayed in the city."[44] However, in 1569 Weinberg seemed rather blasé about discussing matters of faith with his Reformed guest, the pastor at Rheinbrohl John Tonberg.[45] Usually, local officials only took drastic measures against Reformed Netherlanders when external pressure

---

3/5, 14. Rutgers, *Acta*, 90–96. On forms of dissimulation in this era, see Sommerville, "'New Art of Lying'"; Zagorin, *Ways of Lying*.

38 Gorter, *Gereformeerde migranten*, 74.

39 Gorter, *Gereformeerde migranten*, 74.

40 Bosbach, "Köln," 64.

41 Schwerhoff, *Köln im Kreuzverhör*, 243.

42 Schwerhoff, *Köln im Kreuzverhör*, 207–8, 253.

43 For more on this point, see Pollmann, *Religious Choice in the Dutch Republic*.

44 Quoted in Lundin, *Paper Memory*, 22.

45 *Die autobiographischen Aufzeichnungen Hermann Weinsbergs*, April 28, 1579.

compelled them to do so. Such was the case with the raid of November 1571, which followed increased pressure on the city council—from the papacy, the Habsburg government in Brussels, and the archbishop of Cologne—to take sharper action against Reformed Protestants.[46]

Other evidence that the government turned a blind eye to dissent comes from 1582, following a public psalm singing with some five hundred people led by a Reformed preacher just outside the city gates. The city government reacted to this open act of dissent by ordering the expulsion of all non-Catholic migrants from the Low Countries who had arrived since 1566. And yet officials took few actions to enforce this edict.[47] While Cologne's magistrates banished a Reformed elder from Antwerp, Leonard Hoessen, for heresy in August 1582, there is no evidence of any effort to compel his expulsion, and Hoessen remained in Cologne until at least 1594—and probably died there.[48] Moreover, although a series of Reformed Protestant refugees had been escorted out of town with their families and servants by armed guards in 1585, many of then—like the Ghent cloth merchants Anthony Balbiaen and Anthony Lambrecht—soon returned and resided in Cologne for many more years without further issues.[49] And when Alexander Farnese, the governor-general of the Habsburg Netherlands, sent a list of thirty-three names of heretics and rebels who were being tolerated in Cologne, demanding that their asylum be revoked, city officials questioned twenty-three of them but formally expelled only eight (and again, enforcement of this order was lax). In their response to Farnese, they wrote that many of the migrants in question had lived there for years, even decades, without incident, and that even many of the more recent arrivals were peaceful, obedient, and even had passports from the city of Antwerp (or even from Farnese himself!).[50]

We see a similar Janus-faced policy pertaining to Protestants' participation in the economic and political life. From 1583, the city government placed economic restrictions on non-Catholics.[51] From then on, in order to become a citizen or join a Gaffel (i.e., the trade associations that also served

46 Schwerhoff, *Köln im Kreuzverhör*, 243.

47 Schnurr, *Religionskonflikt und Öffentlichkeit*, 75; Bergerhausen, *Die Stadt Köln und die Reichsversammlungen*, 150–52.

48 DNRM-CL-7.

49 Ennen, "Die reformirte Gemeinde," 514. The church elder Anthony Balbiaen and his wife Petronella de Peystere baptized their next child, Sara, in Cologne's underground Reformed church the following year. DNRM-CL-679, DNRM-CL-713. Andries Lambrecht and his wife Anna van Hulle, had twins (Andries and Sara) in Cologne in 1588. DNRM-CL-782, DNRM-CL-1473.

50 Ennen, "Die reformirte Gemeinde," 517–18.

51 The city also hosted Anabaptists, spiritualists, and Lutherans, most of whom were migrants as well, and a Jewish community.

as the basis for political activity), a priest had to vouch for a man's loyalty to Rome.[52] And, while non-Catholics were barred from serving on the city council, at least one Protestant, Ailff von Straelen, sat on the council for forty years![53] Only in 1616 did the city require all citizens to declare loyalty to the Catholic Church, through Protestants still lived in the city and rented property.[54] Thus, as long as religious minorities remained peaceable and quiet, the city council often ignored them or was slow to act—particularly if violations were committed by the wealthy merchants who were the heart of Cologne's Dutch Reformed community. Yet, in a city of roughly forty thousand inhabitants, Protestants made up some 10 percent, and roughly half of those were Netherlanders. Surely, they remained a visible presence.[55] Our point here is not to paint a cheerful picture of a tolerant Cologne. It is, rather, to identify that even in the city where the constitutional situation was the least ambiguous, lax implementation, even in a Catholic bastion, allowed Dutch Reformed migrants to remain in Cologne for decades.

In the early years of their stay in Cologne, Dutch Reformed rarely made arguments legitimizing their stay based on their conformity to the Augsburg Confession. Indeed, there was little reason to think that such an effort would have any success. However, one version of this argument was made at the imperial diet held at Speyer in 1570 to protest the mistreatment of Netherlandish Protestant immigrants in Cologne. On December 9, Protestant princes—including all three Protestant imperial electors—petitioned that these migrants be granted freedom to worship in the Catholic metropolis. At one point, the authors of this letter (which dealt with other matters as well) referred to Netherlanders in Cologne who "confess to the Augsburg Confession" in arguing that these migrants should have free worship, even there.[56] However, the argument that, as *Augsburger Konfessionverwandten*, Reformed Protestants could be granted freedom to worship based on the peace agreement of 1555 was only implicit in this petition. Further, its terms were not accepted by the emperor, Catholic estates, or city leaders in Cologne. The argument was not even accepted by Protestant estates, whose delegates mostly argued that Reformed Protestants did not follow the "true" Augsburg Confession (that is, the *invariata*).

52 Bosbach, "Köln," 63, 73.

53 Herborn, "Die Protestanten," 143; Hsia, *Social Discipline*, 80.

54 Hsia, *Social Discipline*, 81.

55 Bergerhausen, *Die Stadt Köln und die Reichsversammlungen*, 151.

56 Lanzinner, *Der Reichstag zu Speyer*, vol. 2, 1988, 972–80. References are to pages 975–76 and 979. This request came after external pressure convinced magistrates on July 21, 1570 to order the expulsion of Netherlandish refugees by August 13. Bergerhausen, *Die Stadt Köln und die Reichsversammlungen*, 152.

Reformed migrants in Cologne also claimed constitutional protections once in 1582. In a pamphlet defending the psalm singing outside the city walls, described above, the pastor Johannes Christianus claimed that he and his coreligionists were adherents of the Augsburg Confession.[57] At about the same time, in June 1582, wealthy Protestants in Cologne made a similar claim to the city council, which rejected this logic. At an imperial diet held in Augsburg that August, delegates from the city's Protestant congregations made a similar (also failed) supplication to the emperor.[58] Surely, Christianus's reference tried to piggyback on these other efforts.

A more elaborate version of this argument from Reformed Protestants in Cologne came in 1590, after the Reformed pastor Johannes Badius was arrested following another raid of the Reformed congregation. Badius told his interrogators that he supported the Augsburg Confession *variata*, which he explained was also followed in the Electoral Palatinate and elsewhere in the Holy Roman Empire.[59] Though he was soon after expelled (he moved to Aachen), he continued to defend himself from the polemic of a Cologne priest, Kaspar Ulenberg, who claimed that "Calvinists" like Badius hid under the cover of the "Zwinglian Augsburg Confession" (i.e., the *variata* of 1540), rather than what he called the "Lutheran Augsburg Confession."[60] The following year, Badius wrote a pamphlet repeating his support for the Augsburg Confession.[61] In 1591, an imprisoned Reformed pastor Wilhelm Nickel also claimed to interrogators that his congregation was allowed to hold private services because it followed the Augsburg Confession.[62] Of

57 He also stressed that they respected the authority of the emperor, nobles, and the city of Cologne. Christianus, *Summa der Predig, so zu Mechtern vor Colln in der Erbvogtey gelegen, den achten Julii Anno Thausent funffhundert achttzigzwei ist gehalten worden* 1582). Discussed in Gorter, *Gereformeerde migranten*, 84.

58 Schnurr, *Religionskonflikt und Öffentlichkeit*, 74–76.

59 Gorter, *Gereformeerde migranten*, 91–93. The Reformed pastor Johannes Badius claimed in an undated confession of faith to have followed the Augsburg Confession of 1530 when it came to the Lord's Supper. His messaging, however, was contradictory or at least confusing. "*Hiemit stimmet auch ein die lehr der Augpurgischen Confession und deren Apologi, in welcher, da von den Sacramenten und ihrem rechten brauch gehandelt wirdt, also stehet: Denn Sacrament und verheischung gehoret zusamen, und seindt die Sacrament nicht anders, denn nur Zeichen und siegel der verheißung. Nun kan man verheißung nicht anders empfangen denn durch gläuben.*" Rotscheidt, "Confessio D. Johannis Badij," 557.

60 Ulenberg, *Summarische Beschreibung*, 9.

61 On Ulenberg, see Solzenbacher, *Kaspar Ulenberg.*

62 Gorter, *Gereformeerde migranten*, 93.

course, appeals citing the Augsburg Confession had little practical value in Cologne, where Lutheran worship was also banned.[63] It is unlikely that any of these Reformed pastors actually expected this strategy to grant them freedom to worship. They were probably only contributing to an empire-wide effort among Reformed Protestants to broaden what it meant to be *Augsburger Konfessionverwandten*, as well as to link themselves to the protection of the Palatinate.

Aachen

The other leading imperial city of the northwestern empire—Aachen—also had deep political ties to the Catholic Church. Aachen housed the remains of Charlemagne and its Palatine Chapel had been the site of imperial coronations until the Reformation era. Also like Cologne—Aachen had deep social, cultural, and economic ties to the Low Countries, especially to southern cities like Maastricht, which offered the nearest waterway (the Maas River) connecting Aachen to international markets. Following these preexisting commercial routes, Dutch Protestants first arrived in the 1540s, with more significant numbers coming in the 1550s. [64] After the Peace of Augsburg was signed in September 1555, the city remained uniformly Catholic in its public rites. Protestants—including migrants from the Habsburg Netherlands—worshipped covertly before the treaty was signed and continued to do so afterward. There was one significant difference between Aachen and Cologne, however: Aachen's magistrates treated the decision to remain Catholic as theirs to make.

Soon after the Peace of Augsburg was signed, a group of Reformed Protestants from Wallonia petitioned the city council for permission to have legal worship services led by their own pastor. While they made their argument based on the principle that they did not understand German, their request also relied on the assumption that city councilors had the legal competence to grant permission for Protestant services.[65] On January 26, 1556, Aachen's city council explained that they would not permit any worship that deviated from the Catholic Church.[66] Three years later, groups of non-

---

63 In 1582, Lutherans in Cologne—mostly Netherlanders from Antwerp—pled their case at the imperial diet, urging Protestant estates to intercede with the emperor on their behalf, but this effort failed. Simons, *Niederrheinisches Synodal- und Gemeideleben*, 79.

64 Kirchner, *Katholiken, Lutheraner und Reformierte*, 51–53.

65 Schmitz, *Verfassung und Bekenntnis*, 44.

66 Nopp, *Aacher Chronik*, 178.

Catholics again requested permission to hold separate services in accordance with the Augsburg Confession, so long as they promised "to maintain themselves obediently and peacefully" (*sich gehorsamb und still verhalten*).[67] Their requests were accompanied by letters of support from the three Protestant imperial electors—including the Elector Palatine, of course—as well as the city of Frankfurt. A representative from the Palatinate, Wenzel Zuleger, even traveled to Aachen to support this effort. Magistrates quickly responded that they would not approve his request "at this time" (*noch zur Zeit*), implying that they might well reconsider the issue in the future.[68] Meanwhile, pressure to shut down these churches came from Ferdinand, King of the Romans, and Duke Wilhelm of the United Territories. On September 22, 1559, the city government decided that all foreigners who had not yet acquired citizenship had to prove that they were good Catholics or leave the city. Magistrates also issued restrictions on non-Catholics holding city offices.[69] In response to the increased pressure in Aachen, the Dutch and Walloon pastors, Hermes Backereel and Jean Taffin respectively, wrote to Worms requesting permission to reside there, promising to conform to the Augsburg Confession.[70] While magistrates in Worms turned them down, Netherlandish Protestants in Aachen clearly hoped that the Peace of Augsburg provided enough leverage to secure legal privileges in *Reichsunmittelbare* polities of the empire.

It is unclear how many Netherlanders remained in Aachen after 1559, or where the others moved.[71] However, the number of Reformed Protestants did not significantly rise again the crackdown following the iconoclastic riots of 1566, after which new arrivals included a large number of refugees from nearby Maastricht. The Dutch population in Aachen rose to some four thousand people, roughly 15–20 percent of Aachen's population.[72] Like their predecessors, they worshipped covertly, even if their presence constituted an open secret. Meanwhile, Catholic powers from the region, the duke of the United Territories, the emperor, the government in the Habsburg Netherlands and the prince-bishop of Liège, all urged Aachen's city government to crack down on foreign rebels and heretics.[73] This pressure con-

67 Nopp, *Aacher Chronik*, 179; Enderle, "Die katholischen Reichsstädte," 241.

68 Schmitz, *Verfassung und Bekenntnis*, 46–47.

69 Kirchner, *Katholiken, Lutheraner und Reformierte*, 73–74; Heppe, *Geschichte des deutschen Protestantismus*, 1:323.

70 They used the text of the 1540 *variata*. Heppe, *Geschichte des deutschen Protestantismus* , 1:323–24.

71 Some moved to Wesel. SAW A3/52 fols. 45r–v, 46v. EKAW Gefach 6,1,84 fol. 192r.

72 Arndt, *Das Heilige Römische Reich*, 196.

73 Schilling, *Niederländische Exulanten*, 32–33, 73–74; Kirchner, *Katholiken, Lutheraner und Reformierte*, 79, 96–99.

vinced magistrates to order, on April 28, 1572, all refugees from Brabant—as rebels against Philip II—to vacate Aachen (and neighboring Burtscheid, which was part of its jurisdiction) immediately. But they enforced this order. Reformed Protestants were not even deterred from holding a synod in Burtscheid on November 2, 1572.[74] As at Cologne, the Reformed immigrants who remained did so through a combination of secrecy and governmental inaction.

Constitutionally speaking, matters grew more complex in 1574, when there was so much Protestant support among city leaders that magistrates issued an edict allowing *Augsburger Konfessionverwandten* on the city council.[75] In effect, this act granted freedom of conscience (but not freedom of worship) for Protestants. The council seemed to base its authority to make this decision on the Peace of Augsburg, essentially claiming that, as a *Reichsunmittelbare* polity, it could determine religious policy within its jurisdiction. This was also the conclusion of seventeenth-century jurist Johann Nopp, who wrote a history of Aachen.[76] The Reformed congregations—who all claimed to adhere to the Augsburg Confession—no longer had to hide. Still, they did not try to take over Catholic church buildings, but continued worshipping in private homes.[77] The council's decision occasioned a question regarding how the Peace of Augsburg applied in Aachen: did cities that had been Catholic before 1555 have the right to introduce Protestantism after 1555? For Cologne, the answer had been an unambiguous 'no.' For Aachen, the question remained unresolved for decades. Matters escalated in 1581, after citizens elected a majority of Protestants to the city council. The new Protestant-dominated city council (which included Catholic allies) now asserted that it had the right to determine Aachen's religious policies and permitted all adherents to the Augsburg Confession—including Reformed Protestants—to worship freely.[78]

Emperor Rudolf II was furious with Aachen city leaders' claim to possess the authority to make this change. He immediately named an imperial commission that warned that all sectarian preachers and members of banned sects should be expelled from Aachen. His Catholic allies in the region, the prince-bishop of Liège, the duke of Jülich-Cleves-Mark-Berg, and Philip II

74 WMV 2/2, 22–24.

75 Kirchner, *Katholiken, Lutheraner und Reformierte*, 80–81.

76 Nopp, *Aacher Chronik*, 185–86.

77 Kirchner, *Katholiken, Lutheraner und Reformierte*, 268–69.

78 Schmitz, *Verfassung und Bekenntnis*, 122; Enderle, "Die katholischen Reichsstädte," 241–42.

in the Habsburg Netherlands all threatened to interfere on his behalf.[79] A legal case regarding this question made its way through the empire's court system.[80] The matter remained unresolved through the sixteenth century, even as Aachen continued to function as a triconfessional city.

Throughout this period, the city government treated Reformed Protestants as *Augsburger Konfessionsverwandten*, even though there existed a different congregation that professed the *Augustana invariata* (viz., Lutherans). As we'll see, in Frankfurt those who upheld the *invariata* repudiated Reformed Protestants' efforts to claim *Augsburger Konfessionverwandtschaft*. By contrast, in Aachen the two groups found common ground, understanding that the political security of each was tied to their alliance. Supporters of the new government denied that there were any "Calvinists" or other sectarians in the city and insisted that Protestants only accepted ministers who followed the Augsburg Confession—without indicating which version.[81] The new city council made no effort to institute a magisterial Reformation—Catholics kept control of the city's church buildings. But Aachen's city government remained largely confessionally neutral within a triconfessional situation. While Reformed Protestants were free to worship in public, they continued to worship in a private home, the Haus Großerklüppel, which they also used as their schoolhouse.[82] It is not clear whether they kept worshipping this way because of unresolved legal questions making their way through the imperial court system because they lacked funds to construct their own building, feared military interference from an outside power, or because they simply put little value on the physical structure in which their worship took place. But, until a military occupation forced Aachen to once and for all accept the Catholic interpretation of the Peace of Augsburg in 1614, Protestant migrants remained in the city.[83]

---

79 The duke also banned his subjects from trading with Aachen. Kurt Wesoly, "Katholisch, Lutherisch, Reformiert, Evangelisch? Zu den Anfängen der Reformation in Bergischen Land," in Dietz and Ehrenpreis, *Drei Konfessionen in einer Region*, 293.

80 Schmitz, *Verfassung und Bekenntnis*, 134–84.

81 Kirchner, *Katholiken, Lutheraner und Reformierte*, 117. Catholics who resented this situation formed a Catholic government in exile. As Thomas Kirchner has shown, such disaffected Catholics only ever amounted to a minority of loyalists to Rome. Kirchner, *Katholiken, Lutheraner und Reformierte*, 94–95, 248–49.

82 Kirchner, *Katholiken, Lutheraner und Reformierte*, 277–78.

83 Schmitz, *Verfassung und Bekenntnis*, 291–352; Kirchner, *Katholiken, Lutheraner und Reformierte*, 174–218.

Frankfurt

Like Cologne and Aachen, Frankfurt was strategically and symbolically important to the empire. It was home to the Frankfurter Messe, imperial elections, and a strategic bridge across the Main River.[84] Constitutionally speaking, however, the arrival of Netherlanders in Frankfurt posed different questions since it had been officially Protestant since 1533. Initially, its pastors were more oriented toward Swiss and Upper German Reformed brands of Protestantism than toward Wittenberg and Martin Luther. In April 1536, under pressure from the Landgrave of Hesse, the city joined the Schmalkaldic League, the Protestant political alliance. Membership required conforming to the Augsburg Confession. To comply with this requirement, the city adopted the Wittenberg Concord, a confessional statement crafted in May of that year to find a compromise between the divergent Protestant strands.[85] The Wittenberg Concord helped them align their church with the Augsburg Confession (and thus join the Schmalkaldic League) without explicitly adopting the Augsburg Confession.[86] After tensions on this point emerged among the clergy, the Strasbourg reformer Martin Bucer helped Frankfurt officials produce the Frankfurt Concord (modeled on the Wittenberg Concord), which city pastors signed before the council on December 9, 1542.[87]

The Frankfurt Concord remained the official doctrinal statement for the city when the first Reformed migrants arrived in spring 1554.[88] The first to arrive were French-speaking Walloon Protestants led by pastor Valérand

---

84 Scholz, *Strange Brethren*, 6–8; Schindling, "Wachstum und Wandel." On the relationship of Frankfurt to the emperor, see Meyn, *Die Reichsstadt Frankfurt*, 97–103.

85 Johann, *Kontrolle mit Konsens*, 96–97; Schnetttger, "Die Reformation in Frankfurt am Main," 40.

86 Eells, *Martin Bucer*, 206.

87 Johann, *Kontrolle mit Konsens*, 98–99. On the Eucharist, the Frankfurt Concord explains that "the true body and the true blood of Christ are truly and substantially attained and received by those enjoying the Sacrament," but does not explain the nature of Christ's presence in the elements. FRH, vol. 2, Beylage XIII, 42. The document also claimed that Christ sits in heaven, rather than being ubiquitous, which many Reformed also taught.

88 The liturgical standard used in Frankfurt had been updated in 1553, just before the Reformed migrants arrived. The texts used a model of the Lord's Supper, baptism, and marriage, see Arend, *Die evangelische Kirchenordnungen* 9:524–31.

Poullain, who requested permission to live in the city.[89] Poullain flatteringly explained that he "could not think of a better place than Frankfurt" to settle. In fact, he had thought of other places, including Catholic Cologne, where he had been seeking asylum when he happened to meet the powerful Frankfurt merchant Claus Bromm, then returning home from Brussels.[90] Bromm suggested that the migrants might receive a warm welcome in Frankfurt, which was still suffering from a devastating siege during the Second Schmalkaldic War and some costly failed investments in the copper mines of Mansfeld.[91] Poullain decided to give it a go. Poullain's main pitch to Frankfurt's oligarchs was the introduction of a new weaving industry that the migrants would bring to the city.

The pastor explained to city leaders that they were all of "the same religion," but that the French-speaking congregation would need its own church, simply because its members could not speak German.[92] He insisted that they would not interfere with the local church, that they would seek council approval before appointing a new pastor, and that they would submit their confession and liturgy to magistrates for approval.[93] In a meeting with city pastors, Poullain also expressed approval for the Frankfurt Concord (also known as the *Concordia buceriana*).[94] By June 1554, a small group of English-speaking Protestants arrived and received the same welcome.[95] The following spring, the former superintendent for Emden and then for England's stranger churches, Jan Łaski, negotiated the same deal for a Dutch-speaking Reformed congregation.[96] The council allowed the three congregations to share the Weißfrauenkirche (Church of the White Ladies), a former cloister church of the Order of St. Mary Magdalene that had stood

89 Poulain explained that they were drawn to the city primarily because it was a famed commercial center. *FRH*, vol. 1, Beylage I, 1–2. Meinert, *Die Eingliederung*, 3. See Bauer, *Valérand Poullain*.

90 Scholz, *Strange Brethren*, 36–38.

91 Schindling, "Wachstum und Wandel," 229.

92 FRH, vol. 1, Beylage I, 2.

93 Besser, *Geschichte der Frankfurter Flüchtlingsgemeinden*, 9–10. Their liturgy was written by Poullain. Poullain, *Liturgia sacra*.

94 Bauer, *Valérand Poullain*, 293.

95 Meinert, *Die Eingliederung*, 7. Besser, *Geschichte der Frankfurter Flüchtlingsgemeinden*, 43–44; Ebrard, *Die französisch-reformierte Gemeinde*, 66–67.

96 Becker, *Gemeindeordnung und Kirchenzucht*, 26. It is not clear why Łaski and his followers left Emden, which had a public Reformed church and many Dutch migrants. See Scholz, *Strange Brethren*, 44–74.

unused since 1533.[97] Łaski's former London colleague, Marten Micron, who now held a post in Norden (East Friesland), preached the first Dutch sermon in September 1555, while Łaski looked for a permanent pastor for the congregation. He first reached out to Gaspar van der Heyden, a pastor of the underground Dutch Reformed congregation in Antwerp, who turned him down. He then turned to the twenty-four-year-old Petrus Dathenus, a former monk whom he knew from London. Dathenus arrived by November to take his first pastoral position.[98]

The same month that Micron first preached in the Dutch language in Frankfurt, the Peace of Augsburg was signed and quickly ratified by Frankfurt's magistrates. Almost immediately, a few city pastors, led by Hartmann Beyer, complained about the religious deviance of the foreigners.[99] Emboldened by the new imperial law, the city pastors expressed skepticism that the newcomers were *Augsburger Konfessionsverwandten*. The foreign pastors explained that they would be happy to sign the Augsburg Confession but did not clarify which version they meant.[100] Skeptical clergy insisted that the newcomers conform in belief and practice to the 1530 *invariata*. Since 1536, Frankfurt's magistrates' claims to adhere to the Augsburg Confession had been predicated not on its clergy signing either the *variata* or the *invariata*, but on the Wittenberg and Frankfurt Concords, compromise texts designed to promote harmony between those theologically oriented toward Saxony and those oriented toward Upper Germany. In late 1555 and early 1556 the council still referred the newcomers and local pastors to the Frankfurt Concord.[101] Magistrates, that is, still claimed the right to define what it meant to be *Augsburger Konfessionsverwandten*. For them, it seems that the Augsburg Confession served more as a political symbol of support for the evangelical cause than as a fixed definition of theological orthodoxy on whose text all Protestants in the empire needed to agree.

---

97 Dechent, *Kirchengeschichte von Frankfurt am Main*, 1:155. Apparently, sharing this building proved frustrating. In late August 1555, the English congregation requested a separate building for worship. The council turned them down. Besser, *Geschichte der Frankfurter Flüchtlingsgemeinden*, 25. Possibly, they wanted their own space just for practical reasons, but it is worth also noting the high internal discord within the French- and English-speaking congregations. Gunther, *Reformation Unbound*, 158–88.

98 The first evidence of Dathenus's presence in Frankfurt is a letter to John Calvin, dated November 2, 1555, CO 15, ep 2338, 847–48. Schreiber, *Petrus Dathenus und der Heidelberger Katechismus*, 44.

99 Meinert, *Die Eingliederung*, 13.

100 Schreiber, *Petrus Dathenus und der Heidelberger Katechismus*, 48. Besser, *Geschichte der Frankfurter Flüchtlingsgemeinden*, 47.

101 Meinert, *Die Eingliederung*, 18–20, 24–25. FRH, vol. 1, Beylage IX, 151.

Over time, the new imperial law encouraged political leaders to concretize further what it meant to conform to the Augsburg Confession. Local pastors remained unconvinced that the newcomers conformed to the *invariata*'s statement on the Lord's Supper.[102] In defense of the Reformed migrants, Jan Łaski published his *Purgatio ministrorum in ecclesiis peregrinorum Frankfurti* (*Cleaning of the Ministers in the Pilgrim Church of Frankfurt*, 1556), which argued that it was not the Reformed migrants who deviated from the Augsburg Confession, but Frankfurt's pastors.[103] There were some differences in the interpretation of a few passages of the *Augustana*, Łaski conceded, but that was unsurprising given that Melanchthon himself had written multiple versions. Łaski argued that the Reformed immigrants conformed to the Augsburg Confession because their teachings conformed to the *Confessio Saxonica* of 1551. Melanchthon had prepared that text for Maurice of Saxony in advance of the invitation of leading Protestants to the Council of Trent the following year. Not only was this text the work of the same author as the *Augustana*, but Melanchthon had called it a simple "repetition" of the Augsburg Confession, and thus a plausible argument could be made that its signers were *Verwandten* ("kindred spirits"). Finally, the Reformed immigrants could accept the "true and substantial" presence of Christ in the Lord's Supper, since the framing in the document did not also rely on the doctrine of Christ's ubiquity. Łaski's argument highlighted for Frankfurt's magistrates the problem with arguing that conforming to the Augsburg Confession only required signing a statement of faith with which they could plausibly argued aligned with that document.[104] Such a strategy only complicated the question of determining who conformed. By October 21, 1556, the city's patrician leaders shifted their approach to demand simply that the newcomers conform to the Augsburg Confession directly, though they still did not indicate which version.[105]

---

102 *Gegenbericht vnd verantwortung der Predicanten zu Franckfort am Meyn off etliche ungegrundte klagschrifften der Welschen, Das ist, der Frantzösischen vnd Flemmischen Predicanten vnd gemeyn deselbst* … (1563), printed in FRH, vol. 2, Beylage XIV, 407–66.

103 FRH, vol. 2, Beylage XVII, 167–216. Also available in Kuyper, *Johannes à Lasco Opera*, 1:243–68. Gorter, *Gereformeerde migranten*, 34–35; Schreiber, *Petrus Dathenus und der Heidelberger Katechismus*, 51. On May 22, 1556, Łaski also held a colloquium with Johannes Brenz at Stuttgart aimed at finding agreement on doctrine that conformed to the Augsburg Confession and thus to imperial law. Rohls, "A Lasco und die reformierte Bekenntnisbildung," 115–16.

104 Soon after, Łaski left for his native Poland, where he took over leadership of the Reformation under King Sigismund II August.

105 Meinert, *Die Eingliederung*, 36–37.

The local and imperial levels opened another opportunity for the Reformed migrants in the summer of 1557. On June 13, most Protestant princes in the Empire met in Frankfurt to prepare for the upcoming Colloquy of Worms—a meeting of leading Catholic and Protestant theologians scheduled for September to build a theological consensus meant to solve the empire's constitutional problems that had grown out of the Reformation.[106] At this Frankfurt Princely Diet (*Fürstentag*), dozens of theologians and many princely representatives signed a statement agreeing that the foundation of evangelical unity was in a shared Christian doctrine but that this need not be expressed in identical rituals or customs, which could differ according to location. At the event, Frankfurt's foreign pastors presented the *Confessio Saxonica* as their statement of faith.[107] After the meeting, various figures who had attended the princely diet advocated on behalf of the foreign Protestant churches in Frankfurt.[108] There is reason to think that the newcomers' efforts might have had some success. After all, the city council reprimanded Hartmann Beyer for railing against the Reformed migrants in sermons that summer and, on December 8, again urged all citizens to be kind to them (*freundlich und gepurlich zu halten*).[109]

Subsequent events in Worms thwarted the newcomers' strategy. Less compromising Lutherans who had been absent from the Frankfurt Fürstentag were present at Worms, and they were not about to accept the earlier agreement. At the Colloquy, evangelical negotiators broke into open dispute in front of their Catholic counterparts. In March 1558, following that embarrassment, six leading Protestant princes met again in Frankfurt, where they were attending the coronation of Emperor Ferdinand I. There they signed the Frankfurt Recess, written by Philip Melanchthon to satisfy his hardline Lutheran critics, calling for the deposition of any ruler who tolerated deviation from the 1530 Augsburg Confession. The Recess left an ever-smaller window for Reformed Protestants in the empire to argue that they fell under the Peace of Augsburg. Frankfurt's political safety and not just its religious unity increasingly depended on its attachment to the *invariata*. All the Dutch pastor Petrus Dathenus could do in 1560 was write yet another treatise arguing that his church shared "common fundamentals of doctrine"

106 Slenczka, *Das Wormser Schisma*.

107 Dingel, "Augsburger Religionsfrieden und 'Augsburgerverwandtschaft'," in Schilling and Smolinsky, *Der Augsburger Religionsfrieden*, 161.

108 This included Count Georg von Erbach, for instance, as well as Philip Melanchthon. FRH, vol. 2, Beylage XXIII, 279–80 and Beylage XXVIII, 84–86.

109 Meinert, *Die Eingliederung*, 48, 53.

with the Augsburg Confession. [110] He acknowledged differences between himself and some of Frankfurt's pastors, but argued that their different understandings did not mean they fell out outside of Christ's Church.[111] Such arguments may or may not have had intellectual legitimacy, but by 1560 in Frankfurt they lacked the political legitimacy to change city leaders' minds.

By April 28, 1561, Frankfurt's magistrates decided that the Reformed immigrants, whose numbers had been steadily increasing since 1554, would no longer be able to worship publicly unless and until they conceded all disputed matters of faith to the city's clergy.[112] Dathenus felt dark clouds looming over his congregants, for whom he had few kind words. He called them querulous, inflexible, arrogant, and murmuring.[113] His church presented a petition on August 7, 1561 urging that "we are not fanatics [*Schwärmer*], nor violators of the sacrament, not even Calvinists or Zwinglians" as Beyer and his allies had claimed, but "follow the truth as written in Scripture."[114] This claim might be seen as a prevarication or even a lie. However, this perspective misunderstands the situation from the vantage point of 1561, when "Calvinist" and "Zwinglian" were terms of derision, not expressions of identity. Dathenus believed that his faith was the true Christian one, rather than that promoted by any one man, Calvin or otherwise. But members of the city council were unmoved. Interventions from foreign allies—including the powerful Elector Friedrich III of the Palatinate—likewise had no effect.[115] Members of the council did permit them to hold Christmas services in Weißfrauenkirche but then locked up the church again.[116]

---

110 Schreiber, *Petrus Dathenus und der Heidelberger Katechismus*, 192.

111 Schreiber, *Petrus Dathenus und der Heidelberger Katechismus*, 62.

112 Meinert, *Die Eingliederung*, 89. Magistrates' other concerns included theological disputes among the Walloon congregations and the appearance of Anabaptist and spiritualist ideas among the foreign congregations. Gorter, *Gereformeerde migranten*, 38–39.

113 As he expressed in a April 22, 1561 letter to Godfried van Winghen in London. Hessels, *Epistulae et Tractatus*, 2:155.

114 FRH, vol. 1, Beylage XLII, 77. Gorter, *Gereformeerde migranten*, 40.

115 Letters of support also came from Edmond Grindal, the bishop of London, Philip of Hesse, and others. FRH, vol. 1, Beylage XLVII–XLIX, 79–83. Hessels, *Epistulae et Tractatus*, 2:178–80. Meinert, *Die Eingliederung*, 107–10. Godfried van Winghen, the Dutch pastor in London, also traveled to Frankfurt to advocate for the foreign-language churches.

116 Meinert, *Die Eingliederung*, 103–4.

Dathenus made a bid to retreat. He wrote to Emden asking for permission to settle, but the consistory there declined.[117] Early in 1562, the Reformed migrants tried once again, reminding Frankfurt's council that they had signed the *Confessio Saxonica* of 1551 and the Augsburg Confession (they did not say which, of course) and included copies of the French Confession of Faith of 1550 and the recently penned Belgic Confession of 1561.[118] But a majority of the fourteen patricians were unmoved. On March 26, 1562, after a year of back and forth, Dathenus renounced his citizenship and left with a group of about 250 Netherlandish Reformed Protestants for the Palatinate, where they began building a new community at the site of a former Augustinian friary that had been seized by Elector Friedrich III's officials.[119] Other Netherlanders moved to Emden, or back to England, where their former church had reopened under the rule of Queen Elizabeth I.

It is likely that most of the roughly two thousand Dutch-speaking Reformed migrants in the city left in 1562. It's hard to know how many remained.[120] Some who stayed may have started attending services in the city churches, but others joined the Walloon congregation, which started holding French-language services across the street from the Weißfrauenkirche in a barn owned by Peter Gaul, or in a nearby house called *Zur grossen Aunung* on the Mainzerstraße. Their ability to do so probably reflects a high level of bilingualism, though later reports suggest that the Walloons sometimes allowed them to hold Dutch-language services.[121] This was not exactly a

117 Schilling, *Die Kirchenratsprotokolle,* 1:130. Emden's consistory members suggested that Dathenus get letters of support from the Landgrave of Hesse and the Elector Palatine sent to the Lutheran count of East Friesland, which effectively amounted to a refusal. They recommended instead that his congregation move to England. Four and a half years later, when disputes broke out in Emden, the Bürgermeister and city council of Emden warned the consistory to maintain unity in the church, otherwise they would not tolerate foreigners "following the example of Frankfurt." Schilling, *Kirchenratsprotokolle*, 226.

118 FRH, vol. 2, Beylage XXXIX, 335–41.

119 Meinert, *Die Eingliederung*, 107–9. In Frankenthal, Dathenus penned an account of these events, stressing the city pastors' cruelty, professing his conformity to the Augsburg Confession, and ignoring the disputes between Reformed migrants. Dathenus, *Kurtze und wahrhafftige Erzehlung*.

120 On December 17, 1562, the three Protestant imperial electors (Palatinate, Saxony, and Brandenburg) wrote a petition in support of the foreign churches. Meinert, *Die Eingliederung*, 111. That suggests that Reformed Netherlanders were still in Frankfurt during the coronation of the new Emperor Maximillian II, on November 30. Some still lived in Frankfurt the following year. Schilling, *Niederländische Exulanten*, 129.

121 Meinert and Dahmer, *Das Protokollbuch*, 72–73; Gorter, *Gereformeerde migranten*, 43.

fully secret or underground church, but it was a private-house church. After all, in the coming years, city pastors continued to complain about the illicit Reformed services.[122] The Reformed migrants also wrote repeated petitions to the council requesting that they reopen the Weißfrauenkirche for them.[123] In these supplications, they underplayed confessional differences with local clergy and stressed instead the importance of being able to worship in one's native language.[124] They continued to profess that they followed the Augsburg Confession but appealed to the *variata* or the *Confessio Saxonica* as evidence of this claim. Further, since the Reformed immigrants still married and baptized their infants in the city churches—probably to ensure skeptics that they harbored no Anabaptists—their absence at celebrations of the Lord's Supper and other rites was surely conspicuous.[125] For more than two decades, city officials made no serious effort to flush them out.

By 1571, Petrus Dathenus, from the safety of the Palatinate, continued to support the effort to legalize Reformed worship in Frankfurt in his *Bestendigen Antwort* (*Persistent Answer*), which reiterated the unsuccessful argument that the foreigners in Frankfurt conformed to the Saxon church.[126] This time, it was not the *Confessio Saxonica* to which he appealed, but the more recent *Consensus Dresdensis*, a compromise meant to mend the rifts among theological faculty at the Universities of Wittenberg and Leipzig that was proposed that October.[127] Signing the *Consensus Dresdensis*, Dathenus claimed, proved that the Reformed immigrants were *Augsburger Konfessionsverwandten*. He never referred to the specific confessional standards of his own church in Frankenthal (the Heidelberg Catechism and the Belgic Confession of Faith), only vaguely referring to "our church" ("*unserer Kirche*").[128] Frankfurt's preachers grew suspicious of another effort to introduce what they viewed as Sacramentarian heresy with a claim

---

122 FRH, vol. 2, Beylage XLVI, 365–70.

123 FRH, vol. 2, Beylage LX–LXVII, 93–114.

124 FRH, vol. 2, Beylage LXV, 103 and Beylage LXVI, 1–7; Dingel, "Religionssupplikantionen."

125 See Meinert and Mahmer, *Das Protokollbuch*, 212–15. On December 9, 1576, the elders explained to Matthijs Schats, recently arrived from Brussels, that they held marriages and baptisms in the city churches "because the government asks us to do so and to protect the unity of the churches as much as possible, in order to cause no further conflict or to anger the government anymore." Meinert and Dahmer, *Das Protokollbuch*, 151.

126 Dathenus, *Bestendige antwort*. Summarized in Schreiber, *Petrus Dathenus und der Heidelberger Katechismus*, 278–81.

127 Hund and Jürgens, "Pamphlets," 174.

128 Dathenus, *Bestendige antwort*, 12, 18.

that it allied with Saxon policies. Conformity to the *invariata*, they insisted, was a *sine qua non* for public worship in Frankfurt. They also rejected claims that Dutch speakers needed to worship in their own language. They spoke German perfectly well, Frankfurt's pastors explained.[129] Indeed, it's true that many migrants were proficient in German. The pastors argued that foreigners should simply go to services in one of the city's churches. In the end, the council did not grant the Reformed refugees the right to public worship, but neither did it make any effort to close their house churches.

What the council did do was request that the Walloon congregation present a list of all its members in January 1572. Apparently, they were concerned that the Reformed community might become a conduit for Anabaptists to enter the city. At this point, it seems that magistrates did not realize that the Dutch speakers had formed a separate congregation some eighteen months before since it did not ask them for a list as well.[130] That same month, the Dutch pastor Sebastian Matte and an elder Peter Bisschop wrote to theology faculty at the University of Heidelberg for advice about whether they should volunteer a membership list. On the one hand, the Dutch speakers might get in trouble for operating a congregation without permission (further evidence that the Walloons had, in fact, tacit permission for their congregation). On the other hand, they hoped that transparency might ingratiate them to local leaders. Heidelberg's theology professors encouraged them to volunteer the list, advice they subsequently followed. Dathenus also wrote a separate letter to the Walloons, reprimanding them for not being honest with the council about the Dutch members in the first place. The admonishment only embittered the Walloons. Meanwhile, Peter Orth, the senior mayor (*Ältere Bürgermeister*) of Frankfurt, approached Matte and his Dutch-speaking elders, asking them if they "were of a different religion" (*een andere religie waren*), which they explained was not the case.[131] Reformed Protestants were not permitted public worship unless they would conform to the teaching and worship of local clergy, though by 1573 the Dutch began renting a private house in which to hold services separate from the Walloons.[132]

That year, the Elector Palatine also sent a delegation made up of Immanuel Tremellius, Guillaume Houbraque, and Jean Taffin to convince the city council to reopen a public church for Frankfurt's Reformed.[133] The council remained divided on the matter. Many sympathized with the Reformed migrants and wanted to maintain good relations with Friedrich III. Others

129 Gorter, *Gereformeerde migranten*, 45.

130 Gorter, *Gereformeerde migranten*, 167–68.

131 Meinert and Dahmer, *Das Protokollbuch*, 105.

132 Meinert, *Die Eingliederung*, 198. Gorter, *Gereformeerde migranten*, 129.

133 Gorter, *Gereformeerde migranten*, 46.

worried about angering Lutheran and Catholic powers in the region, or that allowing public Reformed services would encourage Anabaptists to infiltrate the city. This time, there appears to have been no discussion of conformity to the Augsburg Confession or concern that the Reformed were themselves heretics or dangerous sectarians. Still, the council rejected the request. In the coming years, as the size of Frankfurt's Dutch Reformed community stabilized and even grew, returning to 2,000 by the mid-1560s and climbing to 4,000—roughly 20 percent of the city's population—by the 1590s.[134] In all this time, some three decades, Frankfurt's patrician leaders made no serious effort to flush out their formally illegal services, even in the face of complaints from city pastors.[135] In October 1577, the Dutch Reformed pastor at Frankfurt, Werner Helmichius, wrote to a colleague in Delft that his congregation was able to remain in the city by keeping quiet (*quiescimus*).[136] As at Cologne and (until 1581) Aachen, city leaders in Frankfurt allowed the Reformed only by turning a blind eye to their private services. Meanwhile, Frankfurt's Dutch Reformed Protestants kept a low profile for their illegal worship services. Just as at Cologne and Aachen, this unofficial coexistence ran on a mix of discretion and inaction.

Frankfurt's patricians seemed relatively content to maintain this informal toleration. They made no serious effort to shutter this illegal church. Indeed, when the pastor Franciscus Gomarus in August 1589 requested permission for his father to live in the city, the city council's scribe referred to him as the "Flemish preacher" without any sense of surprise or disapproval.[137] Of course, one critical reason for the lenience was that wealthy Netherlanders, who made up the core of the Dutch Reformed congregation in Frankfurt, paid taxes and tariffs directly to the city coffers and spurred the local economy by purchasing local goods and services and hiring Germans from the area.[138]

From the late 1570s, Frankfurt's government began limiting immigration, though most of these rules applied to German and Netherlandish migrants equally and did not put any new religious conditions on immigration. In 1578, for instance, the government began demanding that immigrants present attestations from their previous homes.[139] In 1580, Frankfurt's government refused to grant resident alien status to newcomers who could not

134 Schilling, *Niederländische Exulanten*, 52–53.
135 Johann, *Kontrolle mit Konsens*, 44.
136 Cited in Gorter, *Gereformeerde migranten*, 47.
137 Meinert, *Die Eingliederung*, 397–98.
138 Breustedt, "Bürger- und Beisassenrecht."
139 Johann, *Kontrolle mit Konsens*, 48, n.142; Breustedt, "Bürger- und Beisassenrecht," 605, n.48.

present proof of employment.[140] In 1586, another law stipulated that immigrants who became citizens could not marry foreigners.[141] In 1589, magistrates required a new annual "protection fee" (*Schutzgeld*) of 100 guilders for all resident aliens (*Beisassen*).[142] These policies were not aimed at halting immigration or persecuting religious dissenters, but ensuring immigration proved socially stabilized, economically beneficial, and politically harmless. They also did not place *Augsburger Verwandtschaft* at the center of Frankfurt's immigration policies.

When considering the patricians' actions, it is useful to remember just how diverse and dynamic Frankfurt was as a city. It was home to one of the largest Jewish communities in the Empire.[143] Catholics remained free to worship, in accordance with imperial law, and pressure from the powerful imperial elector next door, the archbishop of Mainz, as well as from Holy Roman Emperors ensured that their rights were respected, even if they rankled local Protestants.[144] The Catholic community included religious orders who retained their use of several prominent churches and a foreign Italian merchant community whose members also had permanent alien status.[145] Further, twice a year, Frankfurt played host to the largest trade fair in central Europe, the Frankfurt Messe, welcoming book publishers, jewelers, goldsmiths, and all sorts of international merchants to the city by the thousands.[146] The city also hosted imperial coronations, meetings of foreign princes, and all manner of international diplomatic assemblies. To a remarkable degree, Frankfurt was a cosmopolitan community whose members were accustomed to seeing foreigners and people of other faiths on their streets.

There were certainly efforts to restrict Reformed Protestants from integrating permanently into the city. In 1583, a new law required that Netherlanders have permission from the city government before they purchase a house.[147] And, especially after the arrival of a wave of Netherlanders

140 Breustedt, "Bürger- und Beisassenrecht," 605–6.

141 Meinert, *Die Eingliederung*, 323; Bothe, *Die Entwicklung der direkten Besteuerung*, 244. The 1587 proclamation explicitly targeted Netherlanders, but in 1589 was extended to all citizens. Meinert, *Die Eingliederung*, 348, 394–95. The council sometimes made exceptions for Lutherans, as it did for Jacob de Kaisers in 1592. Meinert, Die *Eingliederung*, 482.

142 Meinert, *Die Eingliederung*, 378–79; Breustedt, "Bürger- und Beisassenrecht," 309.

143 Kasper-Holtkotte, *Die jüdische Gemeinde von Frankfurt/Main*.

144 Schindling, "Wachstum und Wandel," 211–12; Meyn, *Die Reichsstadt Frankfurt*, 235.

145 Breustedt, "Bürger- und Beisassenrecht," 627.

146 Dietz, *Frankfurter Handelsgeschichte*, vol. 2.

147 Bothe, *Die Entwicklung der direkten Besteuerung*, 244.

into the city following Alexander Farnese's conquest of much of the southern Netherlands in the 1580s, efforts to restrict citizenship and resident alien status specifically targeted Netherlanders, even if they also technically applied to other foreigners.[148] Even so, such efforts did not succeed in pushing Reformed Netherlanders out. A census taken in 1588 showed that there were more than eighty men who had been denied citizenship status in Frankfurt—mostly for belonging to the Reformed congregation—who continued living in the city undisturbed for years, including those who held permanent alien status.[149] Even after identifying this discrepancy, the council did not act. Indeed, after the city council revoked the citizenship of Netherlandish baker Matteß de Hameln for religious nonconformity in the summer of 1589, nothing kept De Hameln from remaining in the city until at least 1597.[150]

Starting in 1592, Frankfurt's patricians regulated immigration and religious conformity more strictly. In January of that year, the council banned the Dutch Reformed congregation from appointing a preacher without its permission.[151] That July, it took an even stricter stance, prohibiting Reformed schools and the hiring of "Calvinist" pastors altogether.[152] In 1594, Frankfurt's city council halted Reformed services and banned the Reformed Netherlanders from appointing a new pastor. It also became even stricter in enforcing explicit laws that banned Reformed Protestants from becoming citizens.[153] These new efforts highlight how lax the city government in Frankfurt had been for decades. After this new *volte face*, roughly half of the four thousand Dutch Reformed immigrants left.[154] Initially, the Reformed set up a congregation in nearby Bockenheim, which was ruled by the young Count Philip Ludwig II of Hanau-Münzenburg, under the guardianship of his distant relative, Philipp V of Hanau-Lichtenberg.

In response to this new pressure, Reformed Netherlanders in Frankfurt began a campaign to convince Philip Ludwig's administration to welcome them, describing the deplorable intolerance they faced in Frankfurt. We agree with Maximilian Scholz that these petitions reflected Reformed

148 Breustedt, "Bürger- und Beisassenrecht," 607.

149 Breustedt, "Bürger- und Beisassenrecht," 608.

150 Meinert, *Die Eingliederung*, 463. On October 24, 1597 he was listed as still living in Frankfurt when he visited Frankenthal for his son's marriage. Velden, *Registres de l'Eglise*, 2:37.

151 Meinert, *Die Eingliederung*, 514.

152 Meinert, *Die Eingliederung*, 475, 513–14, 516–19.

153 Meinert, *Die Eingliederung*, 531, 568; Breustedt, "Bürger- und Beisassenrecht," 610.

154 Meinert, *Die Eingliederung*, 576.

Netherlanders' genuine frustration at being denied public worship.[155] However, we also argue that Reformed Protestants in Frankfurt were adopting a strategic gambit: if they could get a genuine invitation from a nearby prince, perhaps they could finally convince Frankfurt's patricians to grant them religious freedom—out of fear of losing revenue from taxes and tariffs should the wealthy Netherlandish community leave. If that is the case, the scheme worked for a time. In 1597, soon after taking the throne and marrying Catharina Belgica (the half-sister of the Dutch Reformed hero Maurice of Nassau), Philip Ludwig founded Neu-Hanau, a new settlement twenty kilometers away that was purposefully designed to attract Reformed migrants from Frankfurt.[156]

By 1601, Frankfurt's patricians realized their mistake. They again permitted Reformed Protestants in the city (though about half had never left), and even allowed the construction of a small church just outside the Bockenheimer Gate (on land owned by Johnn Adolf von Glauburg, a longtime patron of the Reformed migrants). The church burned in 1606, in a case of suspected arson.[157] Reformed Protestants were not again permitted a public church building, probably out of fear that xenophobia might increase. But Reformed Protestants continued to live (and worship) in the city well into the seventeenth century. And during the Fettmilch Uprising of 1612–14, during which Frankfurt's citizens committed a horrific pogrom against the local Jewish community, protestors also complained about restrictions against the Netherlandish migrants who (they said) contributed to the common good just as the other citizens.[158]

Wesel

If constitutional questions prompted by the arrival of Dutch Reformed migrants could be confusing in imperial cities, they were even more so in Wesel, a territorial city in the duchy of Cleves: this is because although it had a Protestant majority, *Reichsunmittelbarkeit* belonged to its Catholic prince. Before the Reformation, ecclesiastically the church had been part of the archdiocese of Cologne, though the duke held extensive ecclesiastical

155 Scholz, "Religious Refugees," 778–79; Scholz, *Strange Brethren*, 8–9, 121–22.

156 See Bott, *Gründung und Anfänge der Neustadt Hanau*. Dölemeyer, "Kapitulations und Transfix." On Count Philip's relationship with House of Orange, see Rauch, "Graf Philipp II."

157 On the investigation into the fire, see Scharff, "Die Niederländische und die Französische Gemeinde in Frankfurt," 287–91.

158 Bothe, *Frankfurts wirtschaftlich-soziale Entwicklung*, 388.

influence in his territories, including the power to conduct parochial visitations.[159] From 1557 on, he even purchased patronage rights in Wesel from a local cloister. In practice, however, starting in 1552, Wesel's city council mostly operated independently in church matters. Following Charles V's loss in the Second Schmalkaldic War that March, Wesel's government abandoned the Augsburg Interim. Within the year, the municipal government adopted a church ordinance that had been drafted in 1543 by the Archbishop of Cologne, Hermann von Wied, in cooperation with Martin Bucer and Philip Melanchthon.[160] That work, *Einfältiges Bedenken* (*Simple Consideration*), was recognizably Protestant but theologically imprecise and liturgically traditional.[161] That is, Wesel's new church norms after the Augsburg Interim were more concerned with promoting liturgical harmony and ecclesiastical unity than clarifying doctrinal orthodoxy. At the same time, Wesel's magistrates also adopted the Augsburg Confession as a way of symbolizing an alliance with evangelicals. At least for the moment, there was little interest or ability at the ducal court to challenge the magistrates' jurisdiction to set church policy.

Only a few weeks later—just as at Frankfurt—English-, French-, and Dutch-speaking migrants arrived from England.[162] Wesel's council's terms were also standard: the newcomers had to conform to the local church and accept the council's authority. English- and French-speakers were permitted to hold sermons in their language but were also required to celebrate the Lord's Supper, baptisms, marriages, and funerals within the parishes.[163] On December 12, 1553, the council also required that immigrants approve the Augsburg Confession, though they did not indicate which version they meant. And, as at Frankfurt, the Peace of Augsburg put increased pressure on the city to concretize what it meant to be *Augburgischer Konfessionsverwandt*. In August 1555, as peace negotiations in Augsburg were wrapping up, Wesel's city council stiffened its policy: anyone who would not hold to the Augsburg Confession was ordered to leave the city within three days.[164] Even after the negotiations, some local pastors

159 Despite the much-cited "*Dux Cliviae est Papa in terris suis*," the archbishop retained considerable ecclesiastical authority in Cleves, and the two often cooperated. Franzen, *Die Kölner Archidiakonate*, 334; Goeters, "Der Katholische Hermann von Wied," 21; Redlich, *Staat und Kirche am Niederrhein*, 83–93.

160 Spohnholz, *Tactics of Toleration*, 34–42.

161 Franzen, *Bischof und Reformation*, 67–73, 118–20; Lurz, "Initiation im Einfältigen Bedenken."

162 Spohnholz, *Tactics of Toleration*, 42–51.

163 The English held sermons in the former Augustinian friary. The French-language sermons were in the Heilig-Geist-Kapelle.

164 Spohnholz, *Tactics of Toleration*, 45.

expressed frustration that the Reformed immigrants still did not conform to the 1530 *invariata*—especially on the Eucharist. In January 1556, news leaked out that the Walloon minister François Perrussel had administered the Eucharist in a Reformed manner. When summoned, he explained that many in his flock opposed clerical vestments and devotional candles and preferred that common table bread be used in the service. Angry magistrates again barred residency for anyone who would not celebrate the Lord's Supper in their churches and accept the Augsburg Confession. The next August, a group of Reformed immigrants was again caught celebrating a secret communion. Magistrates again reissued their ban. In the face of these challenges, by 1557, city leaders clarified that only the *invariata*—with its more direct statement that Christ's body and blood were "truly present" in the Lord's Supper—defined doctrinal orthodoxy in the city. In March, Perrussel and some of his supporters left Wesel for Frankfurt—only to arrive just as the pressure against anyone who deviated from the *invariata* was ramping up there as well.

Over the next few years, three forces stood in a precarious tension in Wesel: liturgical compromise marked by *Einfältiges Bedenken*, doctrinal standards defined by the 1530 Augsburg Confession, and political obedience to their Catholic duke. The city might have maintained this balance if it hadn't been for the arrival of the Reformed migrants. Over and over, the duke fumed against "damned sectarianism" streaming in from the Low Countries, while the council issued repeated ordinances requiring that the migrants conform to the 1530 Augsburg Confession and the "Reformation of Hermann von Wied." During the city elections in March 1561, representatives of the citizenry demanded that the magistrates finally resolve the problem. In response, city leaders asked the pastors to prepare a confession of faith—the Wesel Confession. The new document closely followed the Augsburg Confession of 1530, except that it also included a statement affirming the doctrine of ubiquity as well as an explicit rejection of the premise that Christ's body was only spiritually present in the sacrament. All foreigners were required to sign or leave. Some Reformed refugees in Wesel signed the document. Others refused. Some who initially signed later retracted their names.[165]

In the coming years, Wesel became embroiled in theological debates as local opponents of the Reformed migrants put increasing pressure on magistrates to crackdown on illegal immigration. The town descended into open yelling in the streets. By 1564, the matter had gotten out of hand. In May, representatives of the citizenry asked magistrates to find some means "that the disagreements might be laid aside and the strangers can be tolerated

165 Spohnholz, *Tactics of Toleration*, 51–68.

here."[166] That's exactly what happened. The Wesel Confession quietly disappeared. Migrants still had to attend a local church and at least give lip service to the 1530 *Augustana*, but no one investigated too thoroughly. Meanwhile, the Reformed immigrants established two consistories—one Dutch speaking and one French speaking—that monitored behavior and belief among the Reformed migrants. A critical role of the elders was helping Reformed believers articulate their beliefs in ways that could plausibly conform to the Augsburg Confession. Elders also admonished more enthusiastic Reformed Protestants to temper their zeal and urged pastors to accommodate the preferences of at least some of the Reformed immigrants.[167]

After this, the city council surely knew that many of the new residents strayed from orthodoxy. But so long as the appearance of conformity was maintained, church attendance was robust and uneventful, peace was maintained, and their own political authority was respected, they mostly stayed out of people's business. A *modus vivendi* developed between the city and the duke as well. In 1565 a ducal edict effectively offered freedom of conscience to subjects who follow the Augsburg Confession. While the duke did not grant Protestants the right to open worship—though they had been worshipping openly for decades—in effect his order promised not to punish Protestants who were *Augsburger Konfessionsverwandten*.[168] According to prevailing interpretations, the Peace of Augsburg explicitly banned *Augsburger Konfessionsverwandten* from Cleves. However, in its implementation, the duke interpreted the law as permitting *Augsburger Konfessionsverwandten* as having freedom of conscience, but not freedom of worship. Certainly, as Antje Flüchter has argued, the duke's inaction was a result of his penchant for confessional neutrality, but it was also inspired by the threat of Protestant magistrates in the territory to withhold tax payments.[169]

Following the Diet of Augsburg of 1566, Duke Wilhelm had a series of debilitating strokes that dramatically decreased his ability to rule. More stridently Catholic figures—including delegates representing the duke of Alba in the Netherlands—became leading voices in setting religious policy for the duchy.[170] The threatening presence of the duke of Alba's armies in the region certainly encouraged the ducal government to ramp up pressure on Dutch

166 SAW A3/53 fol. 57r.

167 Spohnholz, "Multiconfessional Celebration."

168 A similar creative interpretation of the Peace of Augsburg prevailed in neighboring Münsterland. Luebke, *Hometown Religion*, 39–40.

169 Flüchter, *Der Zölibat*; Dünnwald, *Konfessionsstreit und Verfassungskonflikt*, 250–62; Spohnholz, *Tactics of Toleration*, 101–4.

170 Keller, "Herzog Alba," 592.

Reformed.[171] Between 1566 and 1572, ducal officials increasingly targeted anyone who had acted as a rebel against the king of Spain, or who was an Anabaptist, Sacramentarian, Calvinist, or sectarian.[172] However, although pressure against rebels and so-called "sectarians" intensified, in principle, the duke's policy with regard to the *Augsburger Konfessionsverwandten* remained remarkably consistent over many years. He never explicitly permitted non-Catholic worship, but he made no efforts to persecute those in Wesel who adhered to the Augsburg Confession.[173] And, so long as the city maintained the outward pretense that its churches adhered to the Augsburg Confession, even Reformed migrants found a degree of protection in Catholic Cleves.

Hometowns in the Duchy of Cleves

Reformed Netherlanders also fled to small hometowns of one or two thousand people just across the border of the Habsburg Netherlands, mostly in the duchy of Cleves.[174] The hometowns focused on here include Goch, Gennep, Kalkar, Xanten, Emmerich, and Rees, though the uneven survival of evidence means that it is impossible to examine them in systematic parallel. In each, Catholics remained the majority. In these smaller and less strategically important towns, the arrival of Reformed Protestants from the Netherlands did not pose the same constitutional questions about how to implement the Peace of Augsburg that we find elsewhere. There are two main reasons for this. The first relates to the porousness of social, cultural, and linguistic borders on the frontier. The second emerges out of the unstable and fluid

---

171 Keller, "Herzog Alba," 594–95; SAW A3/56 fols. 115v–116r.

172 Spohnholz, *Tactics of Toleration*, 72.

173 Elector Palatine Friedrich III wrote to Duke Wilhelm on September 5, 1571, that he had heard that subjects of Cleves who confessed the Augsburg Confession had been threatened with banishment and confiscation of their property. Wilhelm responded that only "damned sectarians" were banned, not those who followed the Peace of Augsburg, who are free in their consciences. Keller, *Die Gegenreformation,* 1:158–59. It may be that Friedrich had falsely understood a rumor. More likely, the two princes had different understandings of who counted as *Augsburger Religionsverwandten*.

174 Schipper, "Across the Borders of Belief." In using the term "hometowns," we are drawing on David Luebke's adaption of a concept introduced by Mack Walker. While Luebke includes Wesel under this umbrella, we leave it out here because its role in Cleves politics was distinct from the duchy's smaller towns. Luebke, *Hometown Religion*; Luebke, "Ritual, Religion, and German Home Towns"; Walker, *German Home Towns*.

ecclesiastical organizations in these small towns. The result was a flexible attitude in these communities toward confessional differences.

In general, one of two ecclesiastical models prevailed in these towns. In Emmerich, Kalkar, Rees, and Xanten, Catholics maintained a monopoly over public worship. In these places, the Reformed congregation was the only Protestant community—there was no competing group claiming to adhere to the Augsburg Confession. Thus, claims to *Augsburger Konfessionsverwandtschaft* allowed Reformed Protestants in these towns to piggyback onto the informal toleration permitted to Reformed Protestants in Wesel. Meanwhile, parish churches in Goch, Gennep and a few other towns in the region adopted accommodationist liturgies that included both Catholic and evangelical elements. Catholics and local *Augsburger Konfessionsverwandt*-Protestants worshipped together using a liturgy that included separate Catholic and Protestant moments. As described by a visitor to Goch and Gennep in 1562, after the bread and wine were placed on the altar, the evangelical minister led his part of the congregation out of the church while the Catholic Mass continued.[175] Afterward, the Protestants returned, and their pastor led his part of the congregation in psalm singing, and then offered an evangelical sermon, from which some Catholics excused themselves. Subsequently, the priest took over the service again (and Protestants who objected again exited). This distinction between two ecclesiastical models hardly does justice to the dynamic situations in these border towns, but it does provide a sense of the structural situations facing Netherlandish migrants when they arrived.

In both ecclesiastical models, most Reformed in Cleves' small towns worshipped in private houses.[176] Goch's congregation kept a list of twenty-five houses that were approved for such uses.[177] However in practice the lines between the supposedly underground Reformed congregations and the public parish churches remained fluid. For instance, Reformed congregations distinguished between full members and those who attended sermons regularly but did not submit to consistorial discipline and who celebrated sacraments in the parish churches.[178] Reformed Protestants even sometimes attended Catholic services when no Protestant pastors were available. Reformed elders and ministers were uncertain about how to handle this matter. In October 1581 attendees of the regional classis meeting debated

175 Van Booma, *Communio clandestina*, 1:58–60. For similar situations in neighboring Münsterland, Luebke, *Hometown Religion*.

176 Van Booma, *Communio clandestina*, 1:20, 22.

177 Van Booma, *Communio clandestina*, 1:127–28.

178 For a similar distinction in the early Dutch Republic, see Kaplan, *Calvinists and Libertines*, 33–34, 68–70.

whether to admit to the Lord's Supper those had who worshipped in Catholic churches because their community had no pastors.[179] In Kalkar as many as forty-five Netherlandish migrants submitted a statement professing their Catholicism in 1569 but were later found to have been Reformed all along.[180] There were also examples of Reformed Protestants who attended Anabaptist services.[181] In some cases, confessional fluidity resulted from the prerogative of individuals, but in others it was enforced from above. In Goch, the town council required that members of the Reformed congregation periodically attend sermons in the city's churches if they were to stay.[182]

Even when they had local elites as members, these congregations remained unstable and vulnerable. They faced pressure when local priests or Catholic officials pursued anti-Protestant policies.[183] Pastors in these towns were particularly at risk when they traveled outside the town, finding themselves vulnerable to discovery by ducal authorities. This proved particularly challenging because of the congregations' meager resources. When communities of believers lacked the funds to pay for a full-time minster, they shared one with other congregations. The enclave of Hörstgen, where a nobleman sponsored a small Reformed church of mostly Netherlanders, sent a pastor to the cathedral city of Xanten for secret underground services.[184] From 1574 to 1578 Reformed congregations in Goch, Gennep, Emmerich, and Rees all shared a pastor.[185] From 1581, the pastor Paschasius Aquensis served the same four towns, as well as small congregations in Kalkar and Zevenaer. The travel that such a post required made the pastors much more vulnerable to capture by Catholic officials. In 1580, Goch's Reformed congregation fired its pastor, Nicholas Pancratius, because the elders deemed it too dangerous for him to be making such trips, following a ducal order that all Reformed pastors should be taken prisoner. Sometimes entire congregations traveled to their pastor rather than him coming to them because that was the safer option.[186] In August 1576, Emmerich's elders invited Reformed Christians from Zevenaer to celebrate the Lord's Supper with them because it was too dangerous for pastor Servatius Wijnants to travel safely to them. The consistory at Goch welcomed Reformed Protestants from the nearby village of

179 Simons, *Synodalbuch*, 560; Schipper, "Across the Borders of Belief," 92–93.

180 Dünnwald, *Konfessionsstreit und Verfassungskonflikt*, 137.

181 Schipper, "Across the Borders of Belief," 93.

182 As noted by elders on October 4, 1570. Van Booma, *Communio clandestina*, 1:176.

183 Schipper, "Across the Borders of Belief," 88–89, 115.

184 Dünnwald, *Konfessionsstreit und Verfassungskonflikt*, 170.

185 Schipper, "Across the Borders of Belief," 128–36.

186 Schipper, "Across the Borders of Belief," 139–40.

Uedem into their eucharistic community because they did not have access to a pastor themselves.[187]

While initially Goch maintained two separate Reformed congregations, they were divided not by geography, language, or culture (as had happened among Reformed congregations in Aachen, Frankfurt, and Cologne), but by ecclesiastical structure. One maintained a consistory and participated in the ecclesiastical structures of the Dutch Reformed Church. The other, supported by the Flemish noblewoman Clara van der Dilft (known as the Lady of Arnhem) did not.[188] The two congregations merged in 1577, but only after considerable debate and with many hard feelings.[189]

When congregations were without a pastor—or when people wanted the social recognition that a public ceremony could confer (for a marriage, for instance)—they traveled to nearby Protestant towns to worship. We find Reformed Protestants from Xanten and Rees, for instance, showing up in Wesel to celebrate baptisms and marriages.[190] Wesel's pastors complained about the practice since it did not offer them the opportunity to monitor the visitors' moral or doctrinal orthodoxy and did not want Wesel to gain a reputation for supporting illegal congregations.

From the perspective of these unstable congregations, debates about whether Reformed congregations were or were not protected by imperial law may have seemed like a luxury. But the Peace of Augsburg was not wholly irrelevant in these borderland regions. Its interpretation became important in negotiations with the duke's officials, particularly since the duke had informally granted freedom of conscience to *Augsburger Konfessionsverwandten*. In May 1562, Goch's magistrates asked the duke for permission to appoint a pastor who endorsed the Augsburg Confession.[191] In January 1567, the Reformed pastor in Xanten, Bruno Bitter, petitioned the city council for free worship according to the Augsburg Confession. When asked if he knew what was contained in the Augsburg Confession, he admitted his ignorance, but claimed that his congregation had heard that it was good and grounded in God's Word.[192] Bitter, that is, seems to have been informed about the document's strategic value but not its content.

---

187 Van Booma, *Communio clandestina*, 1:25, 355, 357; Simons, *Synodalbuch*, 606–8; Schipper, "Across the Borders of Belief," 140.

188 Schipper, "Across the Borders of Belief," 95–108.

189 See chapter 4. For a parallel situation in the city of Utrecht that began shortly after this one ended, see Kaplan, *Calvinists and Libertines*.

190 See Schipper, "Across the Borders of Belief," 142–43; Spohnholz, *Tactics of Toleration*, 204–5.

191 Dünnwald, *Konfessionsstreit und Verfassungskonflikt*, 70.

192 Coenen, *Die katholische Kirche am Niederrhein*, 60; Kessel, "Reformation und Gegenreformation," 17.

At official functions, some Reformed Protestants defended their rights to worship based on their adherence to the Augsburg Confession. This happened at a meeting of representatives of cities with ducal officers in October 1566. A number of Protestant cities of Cleves refused to pay ducal taxes unless the duke permitted worship according to the Augsburg Confession.[193] Protestant delegates to meetings of the duchy's territorial estates (*Landtage*) attempted to persuade ducal officials to recognize worship that conformed to the Augsburg Confession in 1572, 1577, 1580, 1583, and 1592.[194] The duke never granted public worship but instead decided—as he explained in 1580—he would "follow the religious peace to the letter ... and not allow each estate, city, commune or subject freedom, and if the subjects are not happy with the religion of their government [*Overicheit*], that they can leave their government's lands to other places with their wives and children."[195] And yet in practice, managing the arrival of Reformed migrants from the Habsburg Netherlands into the small hometowns of Cleves did not require careful consideration of what was meant by the diplomats who wrote the Peace of Augsburg. Locals in these small towns—so long as they stayed local—maintained considerable freedom to solve problems created by confessional divisions on their own.

Frankenthal

The last type of community that played host to Dutch Reformed migrants in our study comprise the territorial cities in the Electoral Palatinate. Here again, the newcomers' arrival depended on the particularities of how the Peace of Augsburg was applied, but in a wholly different way than in the other cases, because, beginning around the time of their arrival, the Palatinate was officially Reformed. That development turned into an imperial crisis after Elector Palatine Friedrich III abandoned the existing confession of faith and church ordinance for his territory that had been written by Johannes Brenz and instead adopted the Heidelberg Catechism and the Palatine Church order in 1563.[196] Friedrich stretched the limits of what it meant to be *Augsburger Konfessionsverwandt*, particularly because of his new

193 Dünnwald, *Konfessionsstreit und Verfassungskonflikt*, 44.

194 Dünnwald, *Konfessionsstreit und Verfassungskonflikt*, 251–57. Stefan Ehrenpreis, "Die Vereinigten Herzogtümer Jülich-Kleve-Berg und der Augsburger Religionsfrieden," in Schilling and Smolinsky, *Der Augsburger Religionsfrieden*, 262.

195 Keller, *Die Gegenreformation*, 1:257.

196 Wolgast, *Reformierte Konfession und Politik*.

Heidelberg Catechism's Reformed teaching on the Lord's Supper. Friedrich argued that the Heidelberg Catechism agreed with the 1530 *variata*, which he claimed constituted a legitimate interpretation of (rather than an alternative to) the 1540 *invariata*.[197] Friedrich thereby concluded that his territory's church was permitted under the Peace of Augsburg.

Elector Friedrich and Frankenthal's founding pastor Petrus Dathenus quickly realized that their fates were linked by 1562. Friedrich had been among those taking an active role in urging Frankfurt's magistrates to tolerate the Reformed migrants in 1561.[198] When that effort failed, in 1562, Friedrich granted Dathenus and a group of his supporters (made up of about fifty-eight families) a tract of land in the Palatinate at the former Frankenthal cloister, where they established a new community—building by building and road by road—according to Reformed norms without the hiding or constitutional or ecclesiastical compromising seen in the other communities in our study.[199] Frankenthal operated as a kind of small but functional utopian model of Reformed purity. The city adopted the Heidelberg Catechism and the Palatine church order as its doctrinal and liturgical standards. Reformed Protestants crafted a new community—churches, courts, schools—largely free of interference. Anyone moving into the city had to pass an examination of faith, present a written attestation of past behavior, and submit to church oversight in every aspect of their lives.[200] Bailiffs walked house-to-house to make sure no one skipped church, and they levied fines on any truants.[201] Anyone who did not obey orders from the minister or elders was subject to

197 Pohlig, "Wahrheit als Lüge," 154–57; Dingel, "Augsburger Religionsfrieden und 'Augsburgerverwandtschaft'," in Schilling and Smolinsky, *Der Augsburger Religionsfrieden*, 160–61.

198 FRH, vol. 1, Beylage XLVII, 79–90.

199 Becker, "Kirchenordnung und Reformierte Identitätsbildung"; Elisabeth Bütfering, "Niederländische Exulanten in Frankenthal—Gründungsgeschichte, Bevölkerungsstruktur und Migrationsverhalten," in Hürkey, *Kunst, Kommerz, Glaubenskampf*, 37–47; Roosbroeck, "Die niederländischen Glaubensflüchtlinge"; Cuno, *Geschichte der wallonisch-reformirten Gemeinde zu Frankenthal.*

200 In August 1582 Pierre Remu got in trouble for not having his. StAF 1/11/84 fol. 545r. If an attestation could not be supplied an exception could be made in which witnesses could be called to testify to the person's faith and conduct. Such was the case for Amis Reuiert in May 1582. StAF 1/11/84 fol. 526r.

201 StAF 1/11/83 fol. 11v; 1/11/84 fol. 443r. Heinz Günter Steiof, "Alltag in Frankenthal um 1600," in Hürkey, *Kunst, Kommerz, Glaubenskampf*, 65.

secular punishments.[202] Here, Reformed migrants were not forced to compromise with locals, for the simple fact that there were no locals.

In the security provided by Frankenthal, Dathenus recast his position on the Augsburg Confession. In a letter to Heinrich Bullinger, Dathenus now explained that in Frankfurt he had never defended nor approved the Augsburg Confession. He explained to his colleagues in Zurich that the "true doctrine of the Eucharist" could not be found in the Augsburg Confession.[203] While in Frankfurt, Dathenus had complained about his fellow Reformed causing conflict. Now he placed all the blame for the clashes there on the city pastors' ignorance of the Gospel and fractious spirit.[204] The intellectual freedom and political security of Frankenthal allowed Dathenus to emerge as a leader of the Dutch Reformed movement. While there, he published Dutch translations of the Heidelberg Catechism and Palatine church order and a Genevan-inspired version of the psalms.[205] He also engaged in a theological disputation that more clearly defined the Reformed movement against Anabaptism.[206]

At the imperial level, questions about whether the Heidelberg Catechism conformed to the teaching of the Augsburg Confession remained a topic of significant debate. Some Protestant princes—including Duke Christoph of Württemberg and Count Wolfgang of Palatine-Zweibrücken—stressed that its Reformed views on the Lord's Supper were excluded by the Peace of Augsburg. Others, including the powerful Elector August of Saxony, worried that such inflexibility would weaken a united Protestant front against Catholics. Meanwhile, Elector Friedrich of Palatine always insisted that his territory's church conformed to the Peace of Augsburg. No unambiguous decision on this point was ever achieved in the sixteenth century.[207] Yet, from the vantage point of Frankenthal, there was no ambiguity at all. The town remained a haven for persecuted Reformed Christians seeking freedom to worship according to their consciences.

Frankenthal, however, never thrived, but remained relatively small and unimportant. By 1573, the town had only grown to about five hundred people. Many thousands more Reformed refugees were fleeing to locations where their faith was illegal, semiclandestine, or at least legally disputed,

---

202 See, for instance, the case of Hans van Vasterscauen, from May 31, 1582. StAF 1/11/84 fol. 356r.

203 Van Schelven, "Petrus Dathenus," 333–34. See also Ruys, *Petrus Dathenus*, 50–52.

204 Dathenus, *Kurtze und Wahrhafftige Erzehlung.*

205 Spohnholz, *Convent of Wesel*, 52–58.

206 *Protocoll, Das ist, Alle handlung des gesprechs zu Frankenthal.*

207 Pohlig, "Wahrheit als Lüge," 162–65.

than ever came to Frankenthal, which was the only place where their faith maintained an undisputed religious monopoly. That immigration proved less robust than expected is shown in the conditions of a second treaty (*Kapitulation*) defining the city's rights and responsibilities from May 9, 1573, which reduced the fee required for residency by half and offered a full reimbursement for those who chose to depart within their first year.[208] These efforts were in vain. Records from the church in Frankfurt suggest that some migrants who had opted to move from there to Frankenthal, changed their mind and returned to the imperial city where they had to worship either in Lutheran churches or underground. We have found forty such cases, including that of Jan Claerboue, who escaped anti-Reformed sentiment in Frankfurt for Reformed Frankenthal in 1567, only to return to the Lutheran imperial city soon after.[209] It is likely many found they could not make a living in this small town with little infrastructure or preexisting commercial networks.

Conclusion

Our examination of the constitutional situations facing both hosts and migrants presents four main conclusions. First, in each, the migrants developed strategies to secure their survival based on how the logic of the imperial constitution applied locally. Making this work required a combination of skillful argument, discreet connivance, and cultivation of political allies. Second, the ambiguity of the Peace of Augsburg left substantial avenues for Reformed Protestants to find a home in the Holy Roman Empire. While considerable scholarship has maintained that "Calvinism" was excluded from the Peace, Reformed Protestants often leveraged the various ambiguities in the interpretation of imperial law to their advantage. Third, support from the Electoral Palatinate proved critical for the Dutch Reformed to find safety in any of these communities.[210] Electoral patronage worked most explicitly in Frankenthal, where the migrants had written permission from Friedrich III to build a Reformed colony. The elector also frequently intervened on behalf of Reformed Netherlanders in Frankfurt, Cologne, Aachen, and in the duchy of Cleves. And his muddying of the constitutional waters surrounding how to interpret the Peace of Augsburg also enabled creative applications of the law that, in several instances, allowed Dutch Reformed to argue that

208 StAF 1/1/B.

209 DNRM-FL-1433.

210 For another example of how Friedrich's patronage protected Reformed Protestants, Blum, *Multikonfessionalität im Alltag*, 57–93.

imperial law protected their faith. Lastly, more institutional steps between imperial immediacy (*Reichsunmittelbarkeit*) and the Reformed migrants meant more opportunities to interpret the Peace of Augsburg in ways that permitted Reformed Netherlanders to find political cover for their stay in the Holy Roman Empire.

Chapter Three

Strangers and Neighbors

While the previous chapter examined how the diverse and unstable constitutional situations of host cities contributed to dynamic and diverse conditions for the Dutch-speaking migrants, this chapter shifts to an examination of social experiences within host communities. While previous scholarship has sometimes accepted the differences between "Dutch" migrants and "German" hosts as stable and self-evident, our research suggests that more nuance is needed. Of course, historians have long recognized that the legal relationship between the Holy Roman Empire and the Habsburg Netherlands was ambiguous and variable.[1] Political identities in these lands were too.[2] Language distinctions between Dutch and German were just as messy and did not match political boundaries.[3] In addition, the social and linguistic profile of each of these Dutch Reformed communities was remarkably different relative to each other as well as to those of their local host community. We can use these differences to understand the mutual comprehensibility of hosts and migrants native tongues.[4] Taken together with occupational profiles, information about city and region of origin can also

1 Arndt, *Das Heilige Römische Reich*, 154.

2 Duke, "Elusive Netherlands"; Poelhekke, "Het naamloze vaderland"; Tilmans, "De ontwikkeling van een vaderland-begrip"; Groenveld, "'Natie' en patria'"; Robert von Friedburg, "'Lands' and 'Fatherlands': Changes in the Plurality of Allegiances in the Sixteenth-Century Holy Roman Empire," in Stein and Pollmann, *Networks, Regions, and Nations*, 263–82.

3 Cornelissen, *Kleine niederrheinische Sprachgeschichte*; Tervooren, "Sprache und Sprachen am Niederhrein"; Giesbers, "Dialecten op de grens"; Bakker and Van Hout, "Twee vrienden: jij en ik?"; Mihm, "Rheinmaasländische Sprachgeschichte," 143–44; Peters, "Mittelniederdeutsche Sprache."

4 On confessional migration and language, see Majérus, "What Language Does God Speak?"; Murphy, "Exile and Linguistic Encounter"; Van de Haar, *Golden Mean of Languages*, 194–246; Christiaan Ravensbergen, "Language Barrers to Confessional Migration: Reformed Ministers from the Palatinate in the East of the Netherlands (1578)," in Soen, Soetaert, Verberckmoes, and François, *Transregional Reformations*, 333–61.

help us understand just how socially and culturally different migrants were from their hosts.[5] Beyond the simple binaries of political, cultural or ethnic belonging, lies a more complicated sixteenth-century reality that played a critical role in shaping relations between migrants and hosts.

Perhaps unsurprisingly, the further away the migrants traveled, the more likely their community was to be culturally, socially, and ethnically distinct from their hosts. Thus, while we organized chapter 2 around the host community's relationship to the imperial constitution, this chapter is organized geographically. We begin with those host communities along the border, tracing increasing social differentiation between migrants and hosts in terms of language, social status, and cultural difference as we move further away. The chapter then shifts to a discussion that compares—insofar as sources allow—patterns of legal and social integration of migrants into their host communities. While scholarship sometimes treats the assimilation of migrants into local communities as a one-way, natural, or inevitable process, our approach suggests that it was highly variable, multidirectional, and shaped by a variety of local and nonlocal factors.[6]

Aachen

The surviving evidence suggests that, socially speaking, Dutch Reformed migrants traveling to Aachen had much in common with their hosts. Firstly, a large number (37 percent) of Netherlanders whose territory of origin we can identify (n=96) came from cities and towns in neighboring Limburg. Of these, 54 percent came from Maastricht, the nearest large city (only thirty kilometers away), which had a long history of economic and cultural exchange with Aachen. People in this region had less of a distinct Netherlandish identity (which was stronger in the Burgundian heartlands), and more of a regional identity across the Limburg-Liège-Aachen area.[7] 40 percent of the immigrants came from nearby Brabant as well, including Antwerp, which had long-established regular trade routes in textiles,

5 Some scholars have noted the demographic specifics of individual migrant communities. Fagel, "Immigrant Roots," in Goose and Luu, *Immigrants*, 43–56.

6 See the special issue of *Church History and Religious Culture* 100, no. 4 (2020) on "Rethinking the Refuge." For heterogeneity in diasporas, see Muchnik and Monge, "Fragments d'exils"; Monge and Muchnik, *Early Modern Diasporas*, 167–92.

7 Lejeune, *Land zonder grens.*

food, and dry goods to Aachen.[8] Almost no immigrants to Aachen came from elsewhere in the Low Countries. In Aachen, most of the newcomers spoke basically the same dialect of sixteenth-century Dutch (east Franconian *Limburgic,* or a closely related dialect), which allowed them to be easily understood by locals.[9] We have uncovered no mention of any significant language barriers for Dutch migrants living in Aachen. Indeed, in many ways, Aachen's Reformed community was not so much a subcommunity of aliens but a mix of people from Aachen and its neighboring regions, including the Overmaas (part of eastern Brabant), Limburg, and the duchy of Jülich. Their migration was also in some ways the continuation of a longer tradition of people from the region moving to the city for work.[10]

Aachen's Dutch Reformed Protestants did not dramatically stand out in terms of their socioeconomic profiles either. The majority (57 percent of those whose occupation is known) were artisans and craftsmen. They were not, however, dominated by members of the cloth weaving industries (as Dutch Reformed migrants elsewhere in the empire) but comprised an assortment of bakers, carpenters, locksmiths, tailors, cobblers, and cloth makers. Aachen also hosted Dutch merchants, but those who moved to Aachen were not particularly wealthy or well-connected to international markets; they were tied to regional markets. The newcomers also joined Aachen's trade associations without sparking noticeable unease among locals. The immigrants did not stand out from their hosts in terms of either wealth or poverty, and there is no evidence of significant economic tensions between these immigrants and their hosts. While some Catholics resented the arrival of foreign Protestants, most locals seem to have welcomed migrants from the Netherlands without comment. There is no record of a crisis or significant cultural conflict that emerged as the result of their arrival. Confessional differences appeared in the city, of course, but they were not markedly shaped by parallel ethnic or linguistic divisions. Instead, they were usually aggravated

---

8 Harreld, *High Germans in the Low Countries*, 161; Poettering, *Migrating Merchants*, 215. The Aachen-Antwerp trade was frequent but relatively low value compared with Antwerp's high value trade with Cologne and Frankfurt. For this chapter, people from Mechelen are treated as coming from Brabant, though the city belonged to the *Heerlijkheit* Mechelen, an enclave surrounded by the duchy of Brabant.

9 Aachen and Maastricht stood on opposites sides of the Benrath Line, though they were on the same side of the Uerdinger Line and were so close to one another that linguistic and cultural variations were minor. For a linguistic map, see Hantsche, *Atlas*, 67; Schützeichel, "Rheinische und Westfälische 'Staffel'/'Stapel'-Namen."

10 For one example, Asten, "Religiöse und wirtschaftliche Antriebe."

by outside political actors, such as the duke of Jülich-Cleves-Mark-Berg, the archbishop of Cologne, or the Habsburg government in Brussels.[11]

Neither did binary linguistic and political divides define the ecclesiastical institutions developed among Reformed Protestants in Aachen. The earliest foreign Reformed congregations that we have evidence for were ephemeral and localized. The first, starting in 1544, was made up of a group of about thirty families coming from Artois and Flanders. The second consisted of a small congregation that arrived from Antwerp in 1558 but was not permitted to remain.[12] The third congregation moved—seemingly *en masse*—from nearby Maastricht. It functioned separately from Aachen's local Reformed congregation from 1567 to 1579. During the period when two Reformed congregations overlapped—one local and one from Maastricht—new members could choose which congregation they would join. By 1579, the same year that a new wave of refugees fleeing Maastricht arrived in Aachen, the local and Maastricht congregations merged.[13] It seems that the local congregation had already been financially supporting the poorer congregation of Maastrichters for years. It may be that the merger aimed to strengthen the Reformed-Lutheran alliance against those Catholics who opposed all Protestantism in the city. Whether this decision played a role or not, two years later, an alliance of Reformed, Lutheran, and those Catholics who were willing to tolerate Protestants gained the majority on the city council, which managed a triconfessional coexistence in Aachen through the end of the century. While confessionalism shaped social relations, German-Netherlandish linguistic, cultural, ethnic, or political divides did not form a significant part of this story. Among Aachen's Reformed Protestants, it hardly makes sense to separate "Germans" from "Netherlanders" as discrete political, social, or ethnic categories.

Hometowns in the Duchy of Cleves

The situation was similar in the borderland towns in the duchy of Cleves. We have been able to identify sixty-six individuals in these towns who had migrated from the neighboring Netherlands and joined Reformed congregations. More than 70 percent came from small- and medium-sized

11 Kirchner, *Katholiken, Lutheraner und Reformierte.*

12 See chapter 2. Older historiography suggested that Dutch immigrants introduced Reformed ideas to Aachen. Schilling, *Niederländische Exulanten*, 97–98. This conclusion has recently been challenged. Kirchner, *Katholiken, Lutheraner und Reformierte.*

13 Molitor, "Reformation und Gegenreformation," 190–91.

towns across the border in the eastern Netherlands not far away, mostly in Guelders, eastern Brabant, and Limburg. Kleverlands, the local Lower Franconian dialect, was a form of sixteenth-century Dutch that was closer to the dominant Brabantine form than to either the Middle Low German spoken in the Hanseatic cities or the High German spoken further to the south and east.[14] The high proportion of migrants from Guelders should not be surprising, since residents there were more culturally, politically, and socially oriented to the Holy Roman Empire than they were to the Burgundian heartlands of the Low Countries.[15] Most adults in Guelders had also already lived under the rule of Duke Wilhelm of Jülich-Cleves-Mark-Berg, who had also held the duchy of Guelders from 1538 to 1543. These individuals from the Netherlands often migrated within family networks, such as the group around Ernst Witten, from Harderwijk, who fled his home late in 1568 and moved eighty kilometers southeast to Emmerich. Migrants also sometimes had relations—and in the case of nobles, even property—in and around these towns, as was the case of the Van Randwijck family who moved from Nijmegen to Gennep—a "migration" of only seventeen kilometers.[16]

In terms of their occupations, too, the Dutch Reformed migrants in Cleves' hometowns were not significantly different from their hosts. An astonishingly high percentage of those whose occupation can be identified were ministers (35 percent)—a result of the fact that unsafe conditions in Catholic-majority communities caused high turnover among Reformed pastors, and the congregations themselves were small. Outside of that, most migrants with known occupations did not make up a uniform group: they were a motley assortment of bakers, cobblers, clockmakers, soldiers, cloth bleachers, and boat pilots. For a short time in the 1570s, Emmerich had a few printers, though these operations were never large.[17] Professionally as well as linguistically, the Dutch immigrants in Goch, Gennep, Kalkar, Emmerich, Xanten, and Rees tended to resemble their neighbors.

---

14 High German spread relatively slowly and nonlinearly in Cleves. Tervooren, *Van der Masen tot op den Rijn*, 316–25. There was greater linguistic distinction in government documents than in society because scribes and notaries were often trained to write in forms of Dutch and German used by government chancelleries, whose members were often educated at Leuven or Cologne. Cornelissen, *Kleine niederrheinische Sprachgeschichte*, 34–52.

15 Aart Noordzij, "Against Burgundy," in Stein and Pollmann, *Networks, Regions and Nations*, 111–29; Raingard Esser, "Upper Guelders's Four Points of the Compass: Historiography and Transregional Families in a Contested Border Region between the Empire, the Spanish Monarchy, and the Dutch Republic," in De Ridder, Soen, Thomas, and Verreyken, *Transregional Territories*, 23–41.

16 Schipper, "Across the Borders of Belief," 42–47.

17 See Valkema Blouw, *Dutch Typography*; Pettegree, Emden, 87–108.

The Reformed congregations that developed within these towns cannot be called "foreign" or "Dutch" churches in any straightforward sense, as scholars have sometimes done.[18] All constituted a mix of locals and migrants. The Bürgermeister of Goch, Peter von Hegenrath, even served as an elder for the Reformed church.[19] City judges were also members of Goch's church. In the Cathedral city of Xanten, three *Gemeinsfreunde* (a local office charged with representing citizens' interests) were members of the Reformed congregation in 1581.[20] Two leaders of the Rees congregation, Johannes von Altena and Dietrich von Ryswick, came from important Clevish patrician families, while a leader of that church from Utrecht, Gilles Spaens, was one of its few Netherlanders.[21] In Emmerich, Bürgermeister Johan Maschap was a member of a mixed local/migrant congregation in 1588. His influence probably explains how it came to be that the supposedly secret church managed to worship in the city hall.[22] With local benefactors and considerable social ties linking them across the border region, linguistic, social, and cultural divisions were not central to these congregations.[23]

Wesel

The situation was different in the duchy of Cleves' largest city, where fleeing Netherlanders sparked a legitimate refugee crisis. As a port along the Rhine River, Wesel had long-standing economic ties throughout the Rhine-Maas-Scheldt Delta region. While the bulk of Antwerp's high-value trade with the Holy Roman Empire in the sixteenth century took the overland Cologne Highway (*Keulse baan*), Wesel's merchants sent a regular but more modest exchange of wine, wool, timber, and grain to Antwerp and brought back cured fish, salt dry goods, and textiles, which were sold in the area or transferred to flat-bottomed barges for shipping up the Lippe River.[24] From

18 Van Booma, *Communio clandestina*; Van Schelven, *De nederduitsche vluchtelingenkerken*, 301–8; Kipp, *Landstädtische Reformation.*

19 Kessel, "Reformation und Gegenreformation," 71.

20 Kessel, "Reformation und Gegenreformation," 74.

21 Kessel, "Reformation und Gegenreformation," 70; Schipper, "Across the Borders of Belief," 47–50.

22 Kessel, "Reformation und Gegenreformation," 37, 70–71.

23 Dutch Catholics fleeing places that had been captured by Protestant rebels integrated into local Catholic parishes in Emmerich, Kalkar, and Kevelaer. Janssen, *Dutch Revolt and Catholic Exile.* On the multiconfessionalism in Cleves, see Fuchs and Reitmeier, "Konfession und Raum."

24 Christian Reinicke, "Der Weseler Rheinkran im 16. und frühen 17. Jahrhundert," in Prieur, *Wesel*, 49–81; Harreld, *High Germans in the Low*

1559, a regular market ship traveled from Wesel to Nijmegen, carrying goods down the Rhine-Maas Delta to Antwerp.[25] Beginning in the 1540s, but especially after 1566, Reformed Protestants fleeing persecution followed these trade routes across the border to Wesel, where a combination of extensive civic autonomy, widespread support for Protestantism, and an eagerness to bolster the local economy with new industries contributed to their mostly positive reception. By 1571, market ships regularly connected Wesel to Antwerp, now also carrying textiles produced in Wesel.[26] By the early 1570s, newcomers had doubled Wesel's population. At the peak of immigration, refugees slept in the streets and camped outside the city gates. There was no way to ignore them or for them to blend into the local population.[27]

Dutch migrants to Wesel were also more distinct demographically from the local population than the migrants to Aachen or nearby towns in Cleves. We have identified 880 Reformed Netherlanders in Wesel in the second half of the sixteenth century. Some 35 percent of those whose origin is known came from Brabant (40 percent of whom came from Antwerp) while 21 percent came from Flanders. Fifteen percent came from neighboring Guelders. Significant numbers came from Zeeland, Limburg, and Overijssel as well. Basically, every region of the Low Countries was represented in Wesel. This diversity encouraged the Dutch Reformed consistory there to assign elders to supervise coreligionists according to the province (*natie*, or "nation") of their origin, rather than the more common Reformed practice of dividing up elders by neighborhood. Initially, there were four "nations"—Brabant, Flanders, Holland (which included migrants from Zeeland and Utrecht), and Guelders (which included migrants from Drenthe and Friesland).[28] In 1577 and again in 1581 these "nations" were reorganized as the demographics of the community changed to include fewer Netherlanders and more Reformed Protestants from nearby locations lands of the Empire.[29]

In accordance with their diverse origins, the Dutch Reformed migrants in Wesel spoke a diverse array of dialects. They included the Low Franconian dialects of sixteenth-century Dutch that were mutually comprehensible but noticeably distinct, including Flemish (and its relative Zeeuws), Brabantic,

---

Countries, 159–68; Lesger, *Rise of the Amsterdam Market*, 37–38.

25 SAW A3/52 fol. 19r.

26 SAW A3/56 fol. 82r; Münker, *Die Weseler Schiffahrt*, 20–22.

27 Spohnholz, *Tactics of Toleration.*

28 Spohnholz, *Tactics of Toleration*, 76.

29 In 1577, the nation of Guelders became the nation of Guelders and Jülich. In 1581, the nations of Flanders and Holland merged, and a new nation was created for Jülich and Cleves. EKAW Gefach 72,2 fols. 62v, 217r. By 1586, these regional organizations had been replaced by city districts.

Hollandic, and Limburgic, but also the Lower Saxon dialects of German spoken in Overijssel, Drenthe, and parts of Guelders and Groningen.[30] Likely the most important touchstone that they shared in the early years was a shared antipathy for both Catholicism and the Habsburg government in Brussels. But there is little reason to think that most migrants from the Low Countries arriving in Wesel imagined themselves as a single people, despite William of Orange's attempts to present them as such in the propaganda produced by Wesel's printing presses.[31]

While Dutch migrants to Wesel clearly stood apart from their hosts, the ethnic and linguistic boundaries were still blurrier than any simple German-Dutch distinction recognizes. In Wesel, the local dialect of Kleverlands, as noted earlier, was more closely related to Brabantine Dutch than dialects of German used further south and east. As a member of the Hanseatic League, many Weselers also communicated regularly in Middle Low German, the trade language of the league used by merchants from Deventer to Riga (in present-day Latvia). While High German was beginning to influence Wesel's printed language, fluid and uneven linguistic mixing in Wesel remained common in all parts of society, both formal and informal.[32] As a result, the dialects spoken by migrants from the Low Countries to Wesel were largely comprehensible to locals and vice versa. There was enough of a difference that one married Dutch couple explained that they were returning to Leiden in August 1581 because "they could not understand the German language [*de Duytsche sprake*] of our church's ministers."[33] But the fact that they were the only Netherlanders to ever make this claim suggests that this was not a common problem. Mutual comprehensibility in Wesel made it realistic for city officials to require Dutch-speaking migrants to attend the local church and difficult for migrants unsatisfied with this arrangement to argue that they should hold separate services because of language differences (as happened

30 In printed publications, Brabants Dutch and High German were both spreading in the sixteenth century, though scribal and oral languages changed at different speeds and sometimes in different directions.

31 See, for example, Orange, *De verantwoordinge*. For printing in Wesel, see chapter 5.

32 Tervooren, "Sprache und Sprachen," 30–38. The shift toward High German in the region was not linear but depended on political and economic developments relative to the Dutch Republic and central German lands. This change took place faster in Catholic areas than Protestant areas. Meanwhile, multilingualism remained common among social elites. Mihm, "Rheinmaasländische Sprachgeschichte," 146–48.

33 EKAW Gefach 72, 2 fol. 240v. The adjective *Duytsche* could refer to a range of Germanic tongues and does not reflect the modern distinction between German and Dutch.

in Frankfurt). Such social interactions also meant that, over time, migrants and hosts influenced one another's language.[34] Thus migrants to Wesel were relatively similar to locals even though, as a group, they were more diverse than migrants to neighboring towns in Cleves or Aachen.

In terms of wealth and status, Dutch migrants to Wesel looked a lot like residents of Wesel, a river town dominated by regional merchants and whose economy depended on the small-scale production of goods. The dominant industries were wool weaving, furriery, and armor making; the city also had an assortment of other artisans and craftsmen common in early modern cities. Roughly 43 percent of the Dutch-speaking migrants to Wesel were also artisans and craftsmen. However, the kinds of work they did proved to be different. Most artisans, craftsmen, and merchants who came to Wesel were involved in textile production, especially the so-called new draperies, lighter and mixed cloths popular among northern Renaissance elites.[35] The newcomers established factories in Wesel, producing silk-velvet blends, silk-wool blends, cords, edgings, belts, buttons, and other similar products. Taxes collected on per-unit production of cloth goods skyrocketed during Wesel's time as a refugee center.[36]

Merchants made up 24 percent of the Dutch Reformed population in Wesel—about twice the percentage in the local population. In Wesel, though, the most important trade was in locally produced wool, Rhenish wine, and lumber brought in on flat-bottomed barges along the Lippe River from further inland and transferred to river boats at the city's docks for shipment down the Rhine to the Rhine-Maas-Scheldt Delta.[37] Wesel's traders returned with herring and salt for local and further inland distribution. By contrast, Dutch merchants in Wesel mostly traded in higher value, locally produced "new draperies" at factories primarily owned by the merchants themselves. These luxury fabrics were intended for distant markets in Italy, England, or elsewhere. Meanwhile, educated professionals—like ministers, schoolteachers, doctors, lawyers, and printers—made up another 28 percent of the Reformed migrants—roughly the same percentage as Wesel's population. Thus, Netherlanders fleeing to Wesel were not dramatically wealthier than the local population, but they did stand out. They brought new skills,

34 Hassall, "Dialect Focusing and Language Transfer."

35 These numbers are slightly different than those presented in Spohnholz, *Tactics of Toleration*, 186. The difference reflects additions of new prosopographical data added to the database since that original project and the fact that earlier numbers included Lutheran and Anabaptist migrants from the Netherlands, whom we excluded for this project. On the "new draperies" see Coleman, "An Innovation and its Diffusion."

36 Spohnholz, *Tactics of Toleration*, 186–87.

37 Münker, *Die Weseler Schiffahrt*, 40–41.

new trade connections, and new sources of local revenue, and their numbers were large enough that their social and economic impacts were dramatic.

In several ways, then, Wesel's Dutch Reformed migrants more clearly constituted a refugee community than did the immigrants from the Low Countries moving to other areas in our study. Because they had a separate consistory, education, and system of poor relief, they also had some clear institutional markers that separated them from their hosts. Netherlanders in Wesel faced higher degrees of poverty as well. Their arrival in this river town was more driven by push factors (e.g., fleeing persecution) than pull factors (e.g., following economic opportunities or family connections). Indeed, there was little drawing them to Wesel except its convenient location along the Rhine River—it was the closest major settlement upriver from Habsburg territory—and the willingness of its Protestant-dominated city government to welcome them.

Cologne

Further up the Rhine River watershed, in Cologne and Frankfurt, greater economic, linguistic, and cultural differences separated the Dutch migrants from their hosts. In our research we have identified 780 discrete Dutch Reformed migrants who lived in Cologne, one of the largest and most cosmopolitan cities in the Empire.[38] Of these, we have information about their province of origin for 546, and city of origin for 520. A full 68 percent came from Brabant, with 90 percent of those coming from either Antwerp (70 percent) or Brussels (20 percent). Eighteen percent came from Flanders (mostly from Bruges, Ghent, and Oudenaarde). Only 14 percent came from the other regions of the Habsburg Netherlands combined. That is, Cologne's Dutch Reformed population constituted a rather homogenous population: these people largely came from urban backgrounds in the densest and most cosmopolitan parts of the Low Countries. They were thus more likely than migrants in Wesel to have preexisting social networks from back home within their new congregations. We get indications of this in cases like Hugues Sohier and Anna Saye who married in 1581 while they were living in Antwerp, but then in 1593 served as godparents for the child

38 Not all of these individuals were full members of the Dutch-speaking church. For the following numbers, we have excluded the relatively few Dutch-speaking Reformed congregation members who came from the Empire or French-speaking Walloon regions. Their presence only reinforces the extent to which modern political and cultural categories cannot adequately capture the nature of this community.

of Aernout van Gerwen and Martha van Uffel, who had recently arrived from Antwerp.[39] It seems that they had begun their friendship in Antwerp and continued it in Cologne. Because Antwerp and Brussels were vibrant European hubs of political, economic, and cultural exchange, those Dutch migrants coming to Cologne were also more likely to be cosmopolitan in outlook than migrants coming from the provinces further north and east.

Their more shared origins also meant that linguistically and culturally they were also more similar to one another than members of Wesel's migrant community. At the same time, their Brabantine and Flemish dialects of sixteenth-century Dutch were further afield from the dialect of High German spoken in and around Cologne (called *Oberländisch*).[40] Surely, many residents of Cologne could communicate in Middle Lower German, the *lingua franca* for the Hanseatic League (of which it was a member), and the city's earlier dialect, Ripuarian "Kölsch," included loans from Middle Dutch and other similarities along the Rhenish linguistic continuum. In any case, a blend of Germanic dialects was probably used in the streets.[41] Meanwhile, among the Dutch migrants, multilingualism was common. In any case, we learn of no significant barriers to communication between the Dutch immigrants and their hosts. However, the linguistic differences were more striking than in Aachen or the duchy of Cleves and, indeed, some individuals might not have understood one another across the language barriers.

Dutch Reformed in Cologne stood out from their hosts in other ways as well. Cologne's Dutch Reformed community was dominated by a group of wealthy social elites. Of the 136 for whom we have evidence of their occupation, 28 percent were educated professionals (doctors, ministers, schoolteachers, or government officials) or artists (engravers, painters, jewelers, and goldsmiths).[42] Meanwhile, merchants made up as much as 43 percent of the Dutch Reformed in the city. These were among the wealthiest international traders in Europe, including members of the famed Van der

---

39 Sohier and Saye were originally from Mons and Tournai, respectively. DNRM-CL-2442. DNRM-CL-2443.

40 Mihm, "Spache und Geschichte am unteren Niederrhein"; Elmentaler, "Die Schreibsprachengeschichte des Niederrheins"; Tervooren, *Van der Masen tot op den Rijn*, 331–34.

41 WMV, 2/5, 345–46; Mihm, "Sprachwandel in der frühen Neuzeit." For a comparable situation in Hamburg, see Poettering, *Migrating Merchants*, 132.

42 Our choice to categorize goldsmiths with these professions, rather than with artisans like weavers and smiths, resulted from the fact that most of Cologne's goldsmiths were masters who produced expensive artistic works, not middling journeymen. See Briels, "Zuidnederlandse goud- en zilversmeden"; Muylaert, "Accessibility of the Late Medieval Goldsmith Guild."

Meulen, Thijs, Van Geel, Boel, Perez, Van Uffel, and Del Prato[43] families from Antwerp. These wealthy merchants often had agents working for them in Antwerp, Bremen, Hamburg, Amsterdam, La Rochelle, Venice, Lisbon, Seville, London, and elsewhere, connecting them to vast global trade networks and giving them access to sugar from the Azores, as well as spices, diamonds, and other valuables from the Indian subcontinent.[44] They were more similar in profile to Dutch communities in Venice and Hamburg than to those in Wesel or Aachen.[45]

Indeed, Cologne and Antwerp had long maintained robust trade relations, mostly along the so-called Cologne Highway (*Keulse baan*) that ran through Brabant, Liège, and Jülich.[46] Cologne shipped products for the international market through Antwerp, especially Rhenish wine, while Antwerp supplied dry goods, textiles, and foods to the region. The Cologne-Antwerp trade was far more voluminous than the Wesel-Antwerp trade and more than twice as valuable per shipment.[47] Cologne was also one of Antwerp's most important trading partners because it was a key transfer point across the Rhine for luxury goods transported further inland to Frankfurt and then to Nuremberg, Augsburg, Venice, and Prague.[48] As a result, many large merchant firms in one city had agents in the other. When conditions deteriorated for Protestant merchants in Antwerp, Cologne presented an attractive alternative. In Cologne, Reformed merchants moving from Antwerp maintained their extensive international ties, including to other centers of Catholicism in

43 The Del Prato family was originally from Pesaro, Italy, but had long worked in Antwerp. Baumann, *Merchants Adventurers*, 295.

44 Before 1585, Dutch merchants in Cologne mostly engaged in Italian trade through deals with Italian merchants living there. As Italians left in the late 1580s, Netherlanders began trading with Italian cities directly. Gramulla, *Handelsbeziehungen*, 202–41. See also Gelderblom, "Governance of Early Modern Trade."

45 Van Gelder, *Trading Places*, 99–130; Poettering, *Migrating Merchants*.

46 Harreld, *High Germans in the Low Countries*, 29–32, 61, 106; Van Houtte, *Die Beziehungen zwischen Köln und den Niederlanden*, 6–14.

47 Harreld, *High Germans in the Low Countries*, 129–30. Until war in the Netherlands collapsed this overland route to Cologne from 1577, after which Rhine River traffic increased. Harreld, *High Germans in the Low Countries*, 181.

48 Harreld, *High Germans in the Low Countries*, 29–32, 195. Puttevils, "Ascent of Merchants," 119–20. Most trade between Antwerp and Venice traveled on land (via Cologne) until the 1590s, when sea routes came to dominate. Van Gelder, *Trading Places*, 41–66.

Spain and Italy.[49] Those wealthy men often belonged to merchant firms with a global reach.

Because 7 percent of the Dutch Reformed living in Cologne were servants or maids, one might wrongly conclude that a substantial part of the community was poor. However, these men and women mostly served well-off Dutch families. They thus lived more stable lives than the destitute refugees arriving at Wesel's city gates. The relatively high proportion of domestic workers actually serves as an indication of the overall wealth in the community, not a sign of its poverty. Meanwhile, a relatively small proportion of the population whose occupation is known were ordinary craftsmen and artisans (15 percent), even though elsewhere these groups made up the largest part of Reformed migrant populations.

In all, Cologne's Dutch Reformed community looks surprisingly like the foreign expatriate communities common to large cities in sixteenth-century Europe. Cologne also hosted Portuguese, Italian, and Dutch Catholic communities, and the Jewish community across the Rhine in Deutz did the bulk of its business in the city.[50] Given this profile, the willingness of Reformed Protestants to move to this Catholic citadel on the Lower Rhine makes more sense. In this sense, the "pull factors" of Cologne's markets, financial services, and travel opportunities help us understand the demographics of Cologne's Dutch Reformed community more just than the "push factor" of religious persecution.[51] The relative wealth of this foreign community also helps us understand local officials' occasional willingness to turn a blind eye to their religious dissent.

Cologne is the first host community where we find Reformed Protestants formally and institutionally dividing themselves according to ethnic or linguistic lines. Initially, in the late 1560s, the German and Dutch speakers shared a single small congregation, though by 1571 they separated permanently.[52] However, with high levels of multilingualism and high mobility, determining who belonged to which congregation posed a challenge. The institutional division did not simply reflect clear-cut ethnic divisions between local "German" and immigrant "Dutch" Protestants. Consider the arrests of nineteen individuals captured in a raid of an illegal worship service in November 1571. Though the congregation that was interrupted was

49 Gramulla, *Handelsbeziehungen*, 219–22; Thimme, "Der Handel Kölns"; Sadler, "Family in Revolt."

50 On foreign merchant communities in Cologne, see Gramulla, *Handelsbeziehungen*; Thimme, "Der Handel Kölns," 450.

51 See also Gelderblom, *Zuid-Nederlandse kooplieden*, 72–74.

52 It's not clear what prompted the divide, except that it arose from some kind of dispute. Gorter, *Gereformeerde migranten*, 75.

the so-called Dutch-speaking church of Cologne, only six of those arrested were from the Netherlands, while the majority seemed to come from the Empire.[53]

Neither did the linguistic division between these two congregations encourage greater ethnic division. By 1575, the two congregations adopted an agreement regarding who would belong to which church. The boundary, they decided, should be the Maas River.[54] If a coreligionist came from lands west of the Maas, they would join the Dutch-speaking church, and if they came from east of the river, they would join the German-speaking church. That meant that people who had come from eastern regions of Limburg, Luxembourg, and Guelders joined the German-speaking church, including Jacob Boenen, from Maaseik (Limburg), who became an elder of that congregation in 1592 and 1593.[55] Given the instability of political boundaries during this era, selecting a relatively stable geographical boundary seems prudent, even if they had to make exceptions from time to time. Such was the case with Guiljame Gammerslach who was from Xanten (thus east of the Maas River), but who requested to join the Dutch-speaking church on the basis of the many years he had lived in Rotterdam. Thus, Gammerslach likely understood sixteenth-century Dutch (including the Kleverlands dialect spoken in his native Xanten) better than the *Oberländisch* German spoken in Cologne.[56] However, some Dutch speakers preferred to join Cologne's German-language church, despite the 1575 agreement. Such was the case with Herman Schonk. In 1578, after elders confronted him about this decision, he claimed that he worshipped with the Germans because his family preferred it. Elders skeptically noted that he had attended the German language services for two years, even before he had married into his new family.[57] Perhaps Schonk's choice to join the German-speaking church had been motivated by his desire to build personal ties within the local community. If that's the case, his marriage into a Cologne family may have been the successful outcome, rather than cause, of his decision to join the German church. Additionally, according to a mutual agreement between the congregations in 1586, those individuals who spoke both French and Dutch should join the congregation that matched the language of their

---

53 Gorter, *Gereformeerde migranten*, 77; Ennen, "Die reformirte Gemeinde," 527.

54 WMV 2/2, 85.

55 Simons, *Kölnische Konsistorial-Beschlüsse*, 462–63.

56 WMV 1/3, 345–46.

57 WMV 1/3, 117–18.

previous church. If this was their first Reformed congregation, they were free to choose which language they preferred.[58]

In practice, there may have been other reasons for people to join churches whose language did not match their native tongue, since we have identified twenty-five people in the Dutch-speaking congregation who—according to the agreement—should have joined the German-speaking church and fifteen who should have joined the French-speaking church. Maria Fassinck, from the French-speaking city of Liège, had been a member of the German-speaking congregation until she transferred to the Dutch-speaking congregation in 1592 after marrying one of its members, Christianus Quintin.[59] Perhaps personal choice or marriage decisions explain these differences, though Peter Gorter has demonstrated that questions about church membership were also influenced by the efforts of congregations to attract wealthier members so that consistories might benefit from their charitable gifts.[60] In March 1587, an elder of the Dutch-speaking congregation asked the elders of the French-speaking congregation why Barbara Machelit (the wife of Aernout Dragon), who had been born in Antwerp and did not understand French well, joined their congregation instead of Cologne's Dutch-speaking church.[61] Their answer is not recorded, but the question suggests there was substantive social interaction across the Dutch-, French-, and German-linguistic divides, and that although congregations were organized around those divides, the divisions were not rigid.[62]

We have found almost no evidence of any interaction, however, between the Dutch Reformed refugees and the parallel community of Dutch Catholic refugees in Cologne. As Geert Janssen has shown, from about 1577 the "holy city" played host to Catholic exiles fleeing Protestant-controlled areas in the Low Countries. This population included clergy and members of religious orders whom Cologne's vast ecclesiastical infrastructure could absorb. A Jesuit college and a vibrant Catholic printing industry meant that Cologne could become what Janssen refers to as "the intellectual powerhouse" of the Dutch Catholic exile community.[63] Such exiles played key roles in providing valuable intelligence to the government in Brussels.[64] The two immigrant groups must have known of each other's existence; the fact that Protestant

---

58 WMV, 1/3, 230. WMV 3/5, 102–104.

59 DNRM-CL-1165.

60 Gorter, *Gereformeerde migranten*, 165–66. Such was the case in Emden as well. See Fehler, "Coping with Poverty."

61 WMV 1/3, 258–59.

62 For ecclesiastical cooperation across these divides, see chapter 5.

63 Janssen, *Dutch Revolt and Catholic Exile*, 65.

64 Marnef, "Een Gentse proost in Keulen."

and Catholic merchants often did business with one another in the city meant that they certainly had mutual acquaintances. They would also have recognized familiar accents when passing on the street. But we have seen no evidence of direct interactions. On the other hand, that also means that there is no evidence of militant, angry, or violent interactions. While confessional rhetoric did erupt in the city—especially before and during the Cologne War (1582–88)[65]—the hostilities of war in the Low Countries that forced both groups to flee to Cologne did not spill over into open conflicts between groups of Dutch-speaking migrant communities. It may well be, as Janssen has argued, that the experience of living in exile radicalized Dutch Catholics, but that radicalization seems to have been targeted at Protestants in the Netherlands rather than the Dutch Protestants who lived alongside them in Cologne.

Frankfurt

As in Cologne, Frankfurt's Dutch Reformed community functioned in many ways as a foreign expatriate community. That is, this too was a community dominated by migrants from a few wealthy, cosmopolitan cities in the southern Netherlands. We have collected demographic data from 536 Dutch Reformed who resided in Frankfurt in the second half of the sixteenth century. Of those whose territory of origin is known, 86 percent came from either Brabant (38 percent) or Flanders (48 percent). Of those from Brabant whose city of origin is also known, 78 percent came from the great trade city of Antwerp. Only 14 percent came from the rest of the Low Countries. That is, Frankfurt's Dutch Reformed community was even more homogenous than Cologne's. These people largely spoke the same dialect, were familiar with the same cities back in the Low Countries, and primarily came from the same social circles. Many understood themselves to be operating within an international network of trade, information, and politics that included Nuremberg, Madrid, Lisbon, and Venice, as well as places further afield, such as Brazil and India. While Frankfurt saw far fewer shipments from Antwerp than Cologne did, those shipments were more than twice as valuable. Wagons arriving from Antwerp (and transported through Cologne) brought sugar, spices, lace, embroidery, and belts to the wealthy Renaissance elites in Frankfurt and the surrounding regions—and thence to elsewhere in German-speaking lands up the Rhine and further east as well as

65 Schnurr, *Religionskonflikt und Öffentlichkeit.*

to Bohemia and Italy.[66] Further, with one of Europe's largest and most well-connected Jewish communities, communities of English and Italian traders, and foreign merchants arriving in massive numbers for the city's famed trade fairs, Frankfurt's Dutch migrant community may have stood out from their hosts, but they also constituted a regular part of the city's diverse fabric.[67]

In socioeconomic terms Frankfurt's Dutch Reformed population also resembled Cologne's. Twenty-six percent were educated professionals (pastors, lawyers, printers, doctors, etc.) or involved in the arts (jewelers, goldsmiths, and painters). Twenty percent were merchants. The Dutch merchants in Frankfurt, however, were some of the wealthiest residents of the city, with extensive international ties throughout the German-speaking lands, to the Low Countries and beyond.[68] Toward the end of the sixteenth century, almost 50 percent of the wealthiest residents in Frankfurt were migrants from the Low Countries.[69] Meanwhile, 26 percent of the Dutch Reformed population of known occupation were servants, most of whom worked for wealthier members of their own community. This is a far higher percentage than in Cologne, though it may be that this number reflects differences in recording the names of servants rather than different rates of wealthy elites hiring help. Frankfurt's Dutch Reformed community had a higher proportion of craftsmen and artisans than Cologne (26 percent versus 15 percent), about 70 percent of whom worked in the "new draperies." The prospect of introducing new weaving industries to Frankfurt had helped convince magistrates to welcome Valérand Poullain's congregation in 1554.[70] And the strategy worked; Frankfurt's clothing-related industries spiked with the arrival of the migrants.[71] This profile meant that overall, the Dutch Reformed were wealthier and more tied to lucrative trades than the local population.[72] With the exception of the kerfuffle that ended with the closing of the Weißfrauenkirche in 1562, Frankfurt's patricians often

66 See Harreld, *High Germans in the Low Countries*, 129–30. Thus, as at Cologne, land trade was more important than river trade. Meyn, *Die Reichsstadt Frankfurt*, 134–36.

67 On Frankfurt's Jewish community, see Kasper-Holtkotte, *Die jüdische Gemeinde von Frankfurt/Main*. On the English merchant community, Baumann, *Merchant Adventurers*, 170–73. On the role of foreign traders in Frankfurt, see Dietz, *Frankfurter Handelsgeschichte*, 2: 48–67.

68 Dietz, *Frankfurter Handelsgeschichte*, 2:41.

69 Brulez, "De diaspora der Antwerpse kooplui," 292–93.

70 See Poullain's petition to the city government from March 1554, printed in Ebrard, *Die französisch-reformierte Gemeinde*, 156–58.

71 Baumann, *Merchant Adventurers*, 67–69.

72 Only 3 percent of Frankfurt's population were merchants, while most were artisans and craftsmen. Jütte, *Obrigkeitliche Armenfürsorge*, 64–66.

sought to attract new industries and wealthy traders, even if that meant dealing with complaints from local pastors and guild leaders. The newcomers were looking for a safe place with access to secure and profitable travel routes, stable banking, and investment opportunities. They may have been fleeing their homes because they refused to embrace Catholicism, but—for those who stayed at least—they were not so inflexible that they refused to accommodate themselves to life in a semiclandestine church.

There was also a significant linguistic gap between the Brabantine or Flemish versions of sixteenth-century Dutch spoken by Frankfurt's Dutch Reformed community and the Hessian-style High German spoken in Frankfurt. Mutual incomprehensibility seems to have been taken for granted by Dutch and German speakers alike. Initially, linguistic differences had been a justification for allowing separate congregations for Dutch, French, and English speakers.[73] In later years, Dutch Reformed migrants repeatedly cited linguistic differences as the reason that they could not worship in local churches.[74] The "push factors" of religious persecution may have driven them from the Low Countries, but the "pull factor" of access to international markets and banking convinced them to move to Lutheran Frankfurt. In that sense, Frankfurt's Dutch Reformed community was more like Cologne's than Aachen's or Wesel's. As in Cologne, there was some ethnic blurring in Frankfurt's Dutch-speaking Reformed congregation, though it was of a substantively different nature. Thirty-seven migrants from elsewhere in the Empire joined the Dutch-speaking congregation, since there was no German-speaking alternative, and most of these did not arrive until the 1590s, often from Reformed territories in the Empire, like the Palatinate, Moers, Nassau, and Hanau-Münzenberg. Meanwhile, we have only identified ten people who came from the Walloon provinces of the Netherlands who joined the Dutch-speaking congregation instead of Frankfurt's larger, French-speaking Reformed congregation.

Frankenthal

Of all the Dutch migrant communities in the Holy Roman Empire during the sixteenth century, Frankenthal's was the most distinct from the local population. Of course, this was because there was no host population—the Netherlanders were given a recently emptied tract of land where a cloister had once stood. Demographically, Frankenthal's residents also looked like

73 Meinert, *Die Eingliederung*, 4. As Poullain claimed in 1554, FRH, vol. 1. Beylage, I, 2.

74 As for instance in 1592, FRH, vol. 2, Beylage LXXIX, 121–22.

a largely homogenous settler colony, relatively distinct from the Germans living in the nearby villages and towns. Thus far, we have collected demographic information from 784 Netherlanders who lived in Frankenthal, all of whom were Reformed. The vast majority of residents whose origin we have been able to identify came from Flanders (49 percent) and Brabant (39 percent). That's not surprising, since almost half had moved to Frankenthal from Frankfurt, which had a similar profile. Many of those came from individual family networks in Bruges, Ghent, Ypres, Antwerp, Brussels, Steenwerck, and Oudenaarde. We see this in the De Carmer and Schoubroeck families from Oudenaarde, the Notemans and Van Orlei families from Brussels, as well as the Van Conninxloo family from Antwerp. While some of them had probably experienced the broad cosmopolitanism of places like Antwerp or Brussels, once they settled Frankenthal, their personal networks, news sources, and economic connections became, necessarily, more limited.

The Netherlanders who came to Frankenthal also spoke a wholly different language than the Palatine dialect of High German used in surrounding villages.[75] As the linguist Meredith Hassell found, the Brabant and Flemish dialects of sixteenth-century Dutch used by the immigrants became more similar after they began living together in Frankenthal, but the immigrants' dialects did not start influencing or being influenced by the local dialect, as happened in Wesel.[76] German- and French-speakers moving to Frankenthal were initially required to learn Dutch. Dutch continued to be used in Frankenthal into the seventeenth century, if we can judge by the language used in church records.[77] Indeed, mutual incomprehensibility was the main reason that later German-speaking immigrants to Frankenthal petitioned for a separate church in 1582.[78] That's not to say that the native German-, Dutch-, and French-speakers could not communicate. Multilingualism was fairly common in Frankenthal. However, it seems that language groups formed subcommunities that shared an identity and recreated networks that deeply shaped social life in the town.

The occupational profile of migrants to Frankenthal was remarkably limited—and hardly even capable of sustaining a working town. A small pipeline of individuals with family and business ties seems to have made up the

75 For this language barrier for Palatine German ministers moving to the Low Countries, see Ravensbergen, "Language Barrers," in Soen et al., *Transregional Reformations*, 333–61.

76 Hassall, "Dialect Focusing and Language Transfer."

77 In 1578, with the arrival of Walloons from Lutheran-run Heidelberg, the elector forced the Dutch speakers to permit French-language services.

78 Cuno, *Geschichte der wallonisch-reformirten Gemeinde zu Frankenthal*, 11–12.

leading source of Frankenthal's population.[79] Twenty-nine percent of the population whose occupation is known were just goldsmiths, painters, and tapestry makers, often from Brussels and Oudenaarde. Tapestry weavers from Oudenaarde were of particular importance to Frankenthal, and indeed they made it a new center for artistic production.[80] About 10 percent of the population of Dutch Reformed in the town were merchants—the lowest proportion in our study except in the small towns of Cleves. Some of these merchants later returned to Frankfurt or moved to Neu-Hanau, another community specifically established in 1597 to attract Dutch Reformed migrants but was closer to Frankfurt. Among the 40 percent in Frankenthal who were artisans and craftsmen (and this number does not include the goldsmiths, painters, and tapestry makers noted above), more than half made fancy clothes for export. In all, Frankenthal was mostly an outpost of Dutch-speaking artists, artisans, and educated urbanites who were left to build a colony largely on their own.

Measuring Social Integration

As we noted in the introduction to this book, uneven survival of sources in the communities studied here has occasionally made comparisons difficult. Yet surviving evidence reveals some patterns about various modes of social integration of Dutch Reformed migrants who lived in the Holy Roman Empire in the late sixteenth century. Many studies of interactions between migrants and hosts have focused on theological, political, or economic conflicts that developed between them. There are good reasons for this. After all, as we saw in chapter 2, religious and political contests could be central to shaping the terms of the migrants' welcome.[81] However, there are good reasons to go beyond these conflicts too. First, theological debates in these congregations were often led by a small group of educated elites who did not necessarily represent the migrant community as a whole. That's why, for example, the heated theological debates that emerged in Frankfurt in the later 1550s have received so much attention while Netherlanders' experiences there in the 1570s and 1580s have received so little. Second, conflicts produce many more sources than quotidian realities. Finally, surviving

79 On the role of personal networks in shaping early modern migration, see Lesger, "Informatiestromen."

80 Erik Duverger, "Bildwerkerei in Oudenaarde und Frankenthal," in Hürkey, *Kunst, Kommerz und Glaubenskampf*, 86–96. Oudenaarde had been the center of Netherlandish tapestry production. Vanwelden, *Productie van wandtapijten*.

81 Pettegree, "London Exile Community"; Scholz, *Strange Brethren*.

sources often do not provide useful windows into many aspects of daily interactions between migrants and hosts. The Dutch Reformed's internal records, like consistory records, tend to focus on their own members' behavior, while city records, like civil court records, usually do not identify the origin of individuals.

Some of the sources give us useful glimpses here and there. There are good records of the social tensions that resulted when large numbers of foreigners arrived. Pretty much everywhere that Dutch migrants showed up, locals complained about their arrival. They complained about rising rents and food prices, or that newcomers stole property, generally promoted disorder, even that they intended to take over.[82] However, it's important to recognize that locals expressed such concerns generally about all newcomers in the early modern era, so we should not assume that such concerns were specific to the confessional, linguistic, or demographic profile of this migrant movement in particular.[83]

There are also indications that some Dutch migrants also developed more positive relationships with locals, even across confessional lines. Certainly, the ability to worship alongside hosts who subscribed to non-Reformed belief systems without widespread conflict is some indication of stable social relations. In Wesel, worshipping together was required by law, so we cannot treat such a practice as a sign of friendship or mutual respect. However, the fact that migrants and locals with different confessional allegiances celebrated the Lord's Supper, baptized children, and attended sermons together without widespread social conflict or violence is remarkable in the context of the confessional hostilities tearing apart other communities in the late sixteenth century. In Frankfurt, too, from the late 1560s to the late 1590s, Dutch Reformed migrants were required to wed and baptize in the city's Lutheran churches. The fact that no hostilities erupted over those ceremonies can be taken as evidence of a degree of stable coexistence, if not mutual respect.

More surprisingly, we also see some Dutch Reformed migrants attending services in Catholic churches as well. We have records of such activities because Reformed elders worked to monitor this practice and to punish errant members. But it is also relevant to point to the positive social relations that must have developed for such behaviors to take place. Reformed migrants, for instance, attended the funerals of their Catholic friends.[84] Those who defended the practice argued that it marked one's respect for

82 Meinert, *Die Eingliederung*, 43–44; Witzel, "Gewerbgeschichtliche Studien," 181; Schilling, *Niederländische Exulanten*, 54–56, 60; Spohnholz, *Tactics of Toleration*, 43; Pettegree, *Foreign Protestant Communities*, 283–85.

83 Coy, *Strangers and Misfits*; Selwood, *Diversity and Difference*.

84 For a discussion of debates about this practice, see chapter 4.

one's neighbors. While conflicts produce more documentary evidence than peaceful coexistence, such incidents point to a possible wealth of unrecorded quotidian interactions that sometimes produced relationships, and even friendships, built on trust, mutual interest, or respect.

There are other indications that some Dutch Reformed migrants maintained substantive and peaceful relationships with their neighbors. When Hubrecht van Coninxloo was accused of heresy in Cologne in 1573, a German Catholic roommate, Heinrich Faber, spoke to the city council on his behalf.[85] In 1565 and 1567, Dominicus Pettitpas similarly relied on the testimony of his neighbors Martin Schneider and Ambrosius Meies as to his honor and good relations to save him from accusations of heresy.[86] Elders in Frankfurt reprimanded the Reformed cloth shearer from Maastricht, Melchior de Coninck, for socializing with Catholics in the early 1570s.[87] In 1590, Reformed silk merchants from the Low Countries in Cologne also signed a petition along with Italian Catholic silk merchants to advocate for their shared business interests. The following year, the Antwerper Jan Doussaert agreed to teach Italian-style silk weaving and dyeing to local citizens' children.[88] Dutch migrants participated in Cologne's Gaffeln, which required annual feasts, rites of mutual support, and extensive political and economic cooperation.[89] Our point is not to ignore that members of Cologne's Dutch Reformed community lived under regular threat of being arrested and expelled for heresy. Surely suspicious neighbors also sometimes informed authorities of Reformed migrants' illegal activities.[90] But it is also important to recognize that neither were they a wholly isolated or universally marginalized group.

Another way to examine social interactions might be to look at conflicts between ordinary migrants and hosts. For this examination, Wesel offers useful insights. There was periodic violence between migrants and Weselers, especially at the high point of confessional tensions in the early 1560s. On May 12, 1562, for instance, a group of local Lutherans walked through the city streets shouting "blasphemous words and songs" to protest a local ministers' willingness to tolerate Reformed migrants. When the pastor chastised this immodest behavior, he became the target of verbal abuse. However, the worst conflicts were between Dutch immigrants of opposing confessional orientations, not between locals and migrants. In July 1564, a fight that

85 Gorter, *Gereformeerde migranten*, 74.

86 Monge and Muchnik, *Early Modern Diasporas*, 188.

87 DNRM-FR-612.

88 Koch, *Geschichte des Seidengewerbes in Köln*, 76.

89 See chapter 2.

90 Monge and Muchnik, *Early Modern Diasporas*, 184–88.

broke out in a tavern between Dutch Lutherans and Dutch Reformed seems to have been limited to verbal abuse. In 1570, an argument between Dutch Lutherans and Dutch Reformed turned to violence after someone drew a sword, resulting in a bystander losing a couple of fingers.[91] Direct hostilities between locals and migrants were a rarity in Wesel. However, we do see evidence of judicial conflicts between Netherlanders and Weselers. Since complete court records from sixteenth-century Wesel are lacking, we are left only with more serious infractions that had to be taken to the city council for adjudication. Of these, during the period of the greatest social and religious tensions between newcomers and their hosts—in the 1560s and early 1570s—most lawsuits were either between locals or between migrants. That is, because members of the two groups were largely doing business among themselves, when they show up in legal disputes, it was mostly the result of contractual and financial disputes that emerged from those day-to-day exchanges, as was the case after wine was damaged when Arndt de Beyer hired Otto de Man to transport it for him in 1577.[92] But into the 1580s, we see an increase in legal disputes between Dutch migrants and Weselers over matters like business disputes, property rights, and access to church pews.[93] Rather than seeing such lawsuits as evidence of social tensions, it is wiser to see them as symptoms of a broader pattern of stable social interaction.

Examining residency patterns can be another useful measure of social interaction, even if it cannot tell us much about the quality of those interactions.[94] When migrants moved in down the street or next door to locals, there were certainly more opportunities for conflicts, especially if locals were hostile to the newcomers' religious convictions. But living in close proximity also provided opportunities for peaceful interactions, social integration, and cross-cultural fertilization. At the same time, of course, when immigrants lived in more homogenous neighborhoods, there was the possibility of building stronger ethnic and confessional identities among themselves.

As it turned out, the more socially, culturally, and linguistically similar the migrants were to their hosts, the more likely the Netherlanders were to live in streets and neighborhoods throughout the host community. While we do not have evidence from residency patterns for the smaller towns in Cleves, evidence from tax collections in 1568 and 1582 in Wesel suggests that Netherlanders lived in houses, apartments, and rented rooms that were well

---

91 Spohnholz, *Tactics of Toleration*, 188.

92 SAW A3/59 fol. 11r.

93 Spohnholz, "Calvinism and Religious Exile," 9–10.

94 See also Pettegree, *Foreign Protestant Communities*, 21, 83–83; Esser, *Niederländische Exulanten*, 137–50; Spicer, *French-speaking Reformed Community*, 150–51; Monge and Muchnik, *Early Modern Diasporas*, 148–66.

distributed throughout the town and its suburbs.[95] Indeed, migrants lived in all city districts in roughly the same proportion as locals. They lived on practically every street. And hardline Lutheran critics of Reformed Protestants lived right next to Dutch Reformed migrants for years, without any evidence of interpersonal conflict. Such was the case with the Reformed migrants Hans Boots and Jan Fijch, who lived next door to Jan Bremer, Heinrich van School, and Lannert van Bellinckhoven, three leading anti-Reformed Lutherans. The Reformed elder Goert van Wesick also lived next door to the fervently anti-Reformed Johann van Heshusen. That's not to suggest that tensions from this situation did not arise; but Reformed migrants and their hosts seem to have managed daily coexistence without widespread conflict or violence.

Meanwhile, in Cologne and Frankfurt, Reformed Netherlanders tended to live in tight-knit neighborhoods next to one another. In Cologne, most Dutch Reformed lived in a couple neighborhoods around the *Breitestraße* and *Glockengasse* in the center of town, or further north around the *Machabäerstraße*.[96] In Frankfurt, Dutch Reformed clustered around the spinning workshops, jewelry-cutting businesses, and dyeing operations that popped up between *Alter Mainzer Gasse* and *Roßmarkt*, close to their house church near the *Weißfrauenkirche*.[97] Such proximity might have been prompted by the hostility they felt from local Catholics and Lutherans, respectively. But living together also had practical benefits. In cities where some did not speak the local language, where they shared close business relationships and friendships from back home, where they were responsible for caring for their own poor and sick, and where they had to arrange underground worship, living close together simply made life easier.

Frankenthal was the most extreme example of residential isolation. Residents there moved to a former friary granted to them by the Elector Palatine, and began building new houses in an undeveloped expanse of land with hardly any interactions with local Germans. Social interactions did start taking place after German immigration increased some twenty years after Frankenthal's founding. But in that case, it was the Germans who had to find housing among the migrants. Initially, Netherlanders who migrated to Frankenthal made the explicit choice to move to an all-Dutch colony in which social interactions with people of other faiths, who spoke other languages and shared other cultures, were largely unnecessary.

---

95 The following summarizes from Spohnholz, *Tactics of Toleration*, 191–94.

96 Monge, *Des communautés mouvantes*, 193; Ennen, "Die reformirte Gemeinde," 514.

97 Schindling, "Wachstum und Wandel."

Citizenship might be thought of as another relatively straightforward measure of integration of migrant families into host communities, but the reality proved remarkably complex. Host governments often encouraged wealthy immigrants to acquire citizenship because they would be more likely to stay. Such permanence, local authorities hoped, might encourage economic stimulus, including raising tax payments, providing locals with jobs, attracting other highly skilled migrants, and increasing contributions to local charities. Local governments also sometimes restricted citizenship for poor or unskilled immigrants so that they did not become eligible for local charity institutions.[98] Attaching an expensive fee to citizenship, or even to a residency permit, was one way that local governments discriminated based on economic ability, as was the case in Wesel, where citizenship fees could be exorbitant for those of means.[99] Prospective citizens also had to be cautious before making any commitment at the outset, because many communities charged expensive departure fees (*Abzugsgeld*) for those who later renounced their citizenship.[100] When host communities wanted to encourage immigration, they sometimes waved such departure fees.[101] Fears of heresy also encouraged local officials to restrict new citizens only to those willing to publicly profess allegiance to the city's official church. There were such policies in place in all the cities of our study—and across the Holy Roman Empire—even if enforcement varied widely and the regulations did not always have the intended effects.[102]

From a migrant's perspective, acquiring citizenship often lowered the tariffs that businessmen paid to local coffers for production or trade in goods, opened the way for guild membership, gave migrants and their families access to local charity institutions, and/or offered the opportunity to vote in local elections or hold municipal offices. Even when governments tried

98 In Frankfurt, new citizens even had to promise not to claim poor relief from municipal charity institutions within the first four years of their residency, even though all residents were technically eligible for poor relief. Jütte, *Obrigkeitliche Armenfürsorge*, 214–17; Breustedt, "Bürger- und Beisassenrecht," 607.

99 Spohnholz, *Tactics of Toleration*, 289 n. 15. In contrast, Frankfurt had a set fee for new citizens but from 1578 set a minimum amount of property a new citizen had to possess. Breustedt, "Bürger- und Beisassenrecht," 606–7.

100 Breustedt, "Bürger- und Beisassenrecht," 604.

101 As at Frankenthal, see Kaller, "Wallonische und niederländische Exulantensiedlungen," 339; Dölemeyer, "Kapitulations und Transfix," 48.

102 De Meester, "Keeping Immigrants." For England, Esser, "Citizenship and Immigration," 237–52; Lien Luu, "Natural-Born versus Stranger-Born Subjects: Aliens and their Status in Elizabethan London," in Goose and Luu, *Immigrants*, 57–75; Spicer, *French-speaking Reformed Community*, 140–48.

to encourage migrants to become citizens, however, some foreigners had no interest in acquiring citizenship. Even those who were firmly ensconced in the community could be disinclined to acquire citizenship if they retained hopes of returning home. Immigrants who had lived relatively mobile lives sometimes saw acquiring citizenship as unnecessarily restricting their options.[103] Being a citizen of another city might bring certain liabilities as well; a citizen living elsewhere might be held responsible for political acts or economic obligations of the city where they held citizenship.[104] While in chapter 2, we treated citizenship within the framework of the legal parameters for the migrants' stay in host communities, in this chapter we ask about the extent to which the decision to become a citizen of their host communities reflected Dutch Reformed migrants' social integration.

In Catholic refugee centers, few Reformed migrants ever became citizens because their beliefs were deemed heretical and illegal according to local, territorial, and imperial laws. However, Catholic authorities proved willing to overlook such restrictions from time to time. We have identified five Dutch Reformed migrants who acquired citizenship rights in Cologne. Jan Dibbout did so only months after arriving from Antwerp.[105] Christianus Quintin also took citizenship seemingly immediately upon arrival.[106] Paul Mondekins from Oudenaarde became a citizen in 1581 even though he served multiple times as an elder on Cologne's Dutch-speaking Reformed consistory.[107] Meanwhile, Francois and Hubert van Coninxloo (from Brussels) were members of the *Himmelreich Gaffel*, one of the trade organizations central to the city government.[108] Citizenship was not required for *Gaffel* membership, but *Gaffel* membership was required for citizenship.[109] The Reformed merchants from Antwerp, Simon le Bruin and Anton Morneau, were members of the *Buntwartern Gaffel*.[110] Dominicus Petitpas, the merchant from Antwerp (and later church elder), also became a member of the *Windeck Gaffel*.[111] Of the seventy Netherlanders who took citizenship in the Cleves town of Emmerich, we have confirmed that Berndt Eijckelbom

103 Esser, "Citizenship and Immigration"; Poettering, *Migrating Merchants*, 46, 48.

104 Prims, *Antwerpse stadsschulden*; Puttevils, "Ascent of Merchants," 366.

105 WMV 1/3, 336, 352.

106 DNRM-CL-716.

107 The other two were A. Gyer and H. van Remscheid.

108 DNRM-CL-36. DNRM-CL-123. See Militzer, "'Gaffeln, Ämter, Zünfte.'"

109 Jütte, *Obrigkeitliche Armenfürsorge*, 328–29.

110 DNRM-CL-1954. DNRM-CL-1956. There are also examples of Anabaptists who were members of a Gaffel. Monge, *Des communautés mouvantes*, 209.

111 Monge, "Communautés et indivus à Cologne," 126 n. 34.

from Doesburg (Guelders) and Thomas Vogel from Eeklo (Flanders) were full members of the Reformed congregation there. Eijckelbom was even an elder of this church.[112] Especially in the case of Reformed elders becoming citizens, drawing attention to their religious deviance might put the entire congregation at risk. It seems that they felt confident that becoming a citizen would not do so.

A lack of surviving sources in other Catholic towns in our study has left us unable to determine whether there are similar examples elsewhere. But clearly, local authorities periodically allowed exceptions to restrictions on non-Catholic citizenship. At the same time, fear of attracting unwanted attention to their dissent probably discouraged Reformed Protestants from seeking citizenship status in Catholic communities, keeping these numbers low. But many Dutch Reformed migrants were probably not interested in gaining citizenship in Catholic cities in any case. After all, if citizenship and public recognition of social standing had been all that important to these people, they probably would not have moved to Catholic-majority communities where their religion was banned.

Dutch Reformed who moved to officially Protestant cities in our study acquired citizenship in greater numbers. A comparison between Dutch Reformed who became citizens in Wesel and Frankfurt proves instructive regarding the complex forces that shaped this kind of legal integration. For Wesel, we have identified 127 Dutch Reformed who became citizens between 1542 and 1600.[113] Nearly half (44 percent) of these were merchants—about twice the percentage as in Wesel's Dutch Reformed population overall. In Wesel, Dutch merchants were never recognized as a foreign "nation" with special tax exemptions, as happened in larger trade cities.[114] In this case, exemptions from excise taxes offered by citizenship proved an enticing lure to merchants.[115] Meanwhile, Wesel had a relatively weak guild system before the waves of migrants came, and citizenship was not required for guild membership.[116] As a result, craftsmen and artisans immigrating from the Low Countries did not have as much pressure to take on

112 DNRM-EM-118. DNRM-EM-77.

113 These numbers are smaller than those in Jesse Spohnholz's earlier study of Wesel because they are limited to only those Netherlanders who we can confirm as Reformed Protestants. We have also updated these numbers based on new research. The trends remain the same. Spohnholz, *Tactics of Toleration*, 188–90.

114 Harreld, *High Germans in the Low Countries*; Poettering, *Migrating Merchants*.

115 Sarmenhaus, *Die Festsetzung*, 22.

116 By the end of the sixteenth century, guilds were becoming stronger in Wesel, largely encouraged by Dutch immigrants. Sarmenhaus, *Die Festsetzung*, 47–60.

citizenship, as was the case for immigrants elsewhere.[117] Further, except for a brief time in the early 1560s, confessional restrictions on citizenship were applied more flexibly than other migrant centers.[118] Still, most Reformed migrants lived for years in Wesel without acquiring citizenship status. These people were not marginalized within the community; they attended church regularly, worked in crafts and trades openly, shopped at local markets, and otherwise participated in the city's socioeconomic life. Thus, in Wesel, citizenship cannot be used as a measure of social integration of Dutch Reformed migrants within the larger urban community. The newcomers had lived alongside their hosts for years, and at some point in time, some opted to become citizens. But why?

Political and military events taking place outside the city walls convinced some migrants to make that move. The first uptick in Netherlanders acquiring citizenship in Wesel came in 1569 as the duke of Alba's Habsburg army restored Catholic hegemony across the Netherlands following William of Orange's failed rebellion of late 1568. At the same time, the city was rapidly building new fortifications to protect residents, should war spread to Cleves.[119] It's no surprise then that some, like the goldsmith and Reformed elder from Ypres, Jacques Matte, became a citizen in 1569 after having lived in Wesel for six years, or that Hans de Bloem, the Reformed cloth merchant from Antwerp, did the same. After all, that year, Protestants and rebels in both men's home cities were being subject to brutal repression at the hands of Alba's soldiers. A second uptick seems to have been sparked by a Habsburg military campaign in the Netherlandish civil war following the collapse of the Pacification of Ghent in 1578 and the failure of the peace talks in Cologne in 1579, which made it clear that the Habsburgs were not going to abandon their strict anti-Protestant policies.[120] Thus, Derick van den Berg, a tailor from Leuven (which had been captured by Habsburg forces in 1577) who had lived in Wesel for over a decade, became a citizen in 1579. So too did the merchant Wouter Buyssen, from 's-Hertogenbosch, which had just abandoned the States General and aligned itself with the Habsburg government.

The spark for the largest spike in Dutch Reformed becoming citizens in Wesel—between late April and early June 1583—was surely Alexander

117 Ogilvie, *European Guilds*, 96–100.

118 Even during the period with clearly-defined confessional restrictions, from October 1561 to January 1565, Reformed Protestants became citizens either through ambiguity or strategic silence and inaction. Spohnholz, *Tactics of Toleration*, 52–55, 188–90.

119 Dieter Kastner, "Johann Pasqualini und die Anfänge der Festung Wesel—Der Bau des Flesgentorbastion im Jahre 1568," in Prieur, *Wesel*, 83–121.

120 Arnade, *Beggars, Iconoclasts, and Civic Patriots*, 166–211.

Farnese's rapid string of military victories capturing cities across Flanders and Brabant in 1582 and 1583.[121] Refugees from those regions living in Wesel now faced grim hopes that they might ever return to their homes. To make matters worse, in January 1583 rebel-held Antwerp faced a bloody attempted coup by the rebels' supposed ally and "Protector of the Liberty of the Netherlands," Francis, the duke of Anjou. By July, William of Orange's decision to withdraw from Antwerp in favor of security in Holland may have dashed the hopes of refugees from Antwerp that they might ever return to their former homes.[122] At the exact same time, changing politics in Wesel incentivized refugees to become citizens. Twice in 1582, delegates from Wesel and the ducal court met to debate an order from Duke Wilhelm to expel all foreign Reformed Protestants. Wesel's officials refused to pay their taxes if the prince interfered in local matters and warned that such expulsions would only spark the kind of unrest befalling the war-torn Netherlands. By the end of the year, the duke agreed not to compel anyone's conscience.[123] To be sure, some of these new citizens were recent arrivals from cities captured by Farnese's troops. But at least eighteen others were already elders and deacons of the local Reformed consistory and over a dozen more were long-time cloth merchants in the city. They included the Antwerp merchant Hans Six as well as the weaver from Ypres, Jan Ginnebar, the latter of whom had lived in Wesel for almost twenty years. These men were already socially and economically integrated into the city. Their decisions were not centrally about new policies adopted to attract wealthy immigrants. Neither were they the result of the immigrants' desire for guild membership, a reduction in taxes, or access to civic charity institutions. Instead, becoming a citizen was a calculated move aimed at increasing their political and social security during a time of intense instability.

After 1585, few Dutch Reformed migrants became citizens in Wesel. By then, it seems, nearly all who had wanted to had become citizens, and likewise nearly all who preferred to move away had done that. In any case, we cannot treat acquiring citizenship as an inevitable or natural process of social and cultural assimilation alone. Rather, dramatic changes in the politics at home and in migrants' host communities combined to shape their decision to acquire citizenship. Evidence in the following years—that Netherlanders began to purchase funeral markers in Wesel's parish churches and hold civic offices—suggests that this level of social engagement continued in other

121 Langhans, *Die Bürgerbücher der Stadt Wesel*, 146–47.

122 Arnade, *Beggars, Iconoclasts, and Civic Patriots*, 311–19.

123 Spohnholz, *Tactics of Toleration*, 102–4; Dünnwald, *Konfessionsstreit und Verfassungskonflikt*, 256–60.

areas of life as well, at least among migrants of higher financial means and social status.[124]

The situation was rather different in Frankfurt. We have identified forty-seven Dutch Reformed immigrants who gained citizenship in Frankfurt between 1554 and 1600.[125] Of course, after 1562, becoming a citizen in Frankfurt was riskier for Dutch Reformed than in Wesel. But the key difference lay less in different laws than in the variable enforcement of similar laws. In both cities, residents were required to give formal profession of support for the city's church and conformity to the beliefs articulated in the Augsburg Confession. In Wesel, however, councilors and pastors proved flexible about what it meant to conform to the Augsburg Confession, so long as migrants were clear about obeying local political and ecclesiastical authorities. By contrast, after 1562, Frankfurt's clergy and oligarchs treated conforming to the Augsburg Confession *invariata* as an expression of obedience to local political and ecclesiastical authorities. In that situation, it is hardly surprising that the overall number of Dutch Reformed who become citizens in Frankfurt was smaller. In addition, some immigrants instead requested the status of resident alien (*Beisass*), which offered them some legal protections and increased access to poor relief but did not require abandoning citizenship status back home.[126]

Almost half the Dutch-speaking Reformed refugees we have identified as having gained citizenship—nineteen—did so in the years between the first arrival of Netherlanders in the city, in March 1554, and the large-scale departures of 1562. This number is likely much larger since, in all, over four hundred migrants from the Low Countries became citizens in these years, many of whom must have been Reformed Protestants. Meanwhile, the council never increased citizenship fees to exorbitant levels to reduce these numbers. While that period saw increasing confessional tensions, until 1560 the council proved remarkably willing to offer Dutch migrants citizenship. Since in Frankfurt citizenship was required for guild membership, and guild

124 Spohnholz, "Calvinism and Religious Exile."

125 Most of these we have identified from city council minutes. Making such identifications can be tricky, however, since city officials often used German spellings for Netherlanders. Thus, that number was likely larger. Meinert, *Die Eingliederung.* These numbers are also smaller than those discussed by Georg Witzel, who covered 1554 to 1562, because Witzel examined migrants from across the Low Countries (instead of Dutch speakers) and regardless of confessional orientation (instead of only who can be verified as Reformed). Witzel, "Gewerbgeschichtliche Studien," 137–38.

126 Breustedt, "Bürger- und Beisassenrecht"; Jütte, *Obrigkeitliche Armenfürsorge*, 214–17. On nonresident citizenship in the Low Countries, see Decavele, "De Gentse poorterij en buitenpoorterij."

membership was required for participation in most trades, the council had to open the citizenship rolls widely if it hoped to encourage the Netherlanders to bring new business to the city.

In earlier studies, much has been made of the opposition from Frankfurt's guilds to the Netherlanders' arrival during these years.[127] Some guilds did indeed complain about Dutch craftsmen claiming to be too impoverished to pay the guilds' entrance fees and thus working outside the guild system. However, some guilds that successfully forced the foreigners to pay the fees—the tailors, cabinetmakers, bakers, brewers, and cobblers—were among the strongest in Frankfurt and their trades were practiced by relatively few migrants.[128] Meanwhile, for a trade strongly represented among the immigrants—wool weaving—Netherlanders unable to pay membership fees or produce proof of birth (a so-called *Geburtsbrief*) were able to negotiate (with some mediation from the city council and the Dutch-speaking Reformed consistory) a one-year reprieve in 1556. This rule was not strictly enforced even after that deadline had passed.[129] Meanwhile, some Dutch workers faced no local opposition because they worked in trades that had no preexisting guild to oppose (like the tapestry weavers and passementerie makers) or because the newcomers paid the guild's membership fees without complaint (like the linen weavers).[130]

We do not believe that guild opposition was a central factor in limiting the numbers of Reformed migrants who became citizens of Frankfurt. No guild ever adopted laws requiring an oath to the Augsburg Confession *invariata*. Neither did any guild adopt policies that restricted entry to Netherlanders as such. Frankfurt's guild ordinances look much like those of other large cities of the day. They regulated the quality and quantity of the production of goods; defined procedures for becoming an apprentice, journeyman, and master; and explained how migrants could join a trade.[131] Guild leaders

---

127 Schilling, *Niederländische Exulanten*, 52–59, 123–33. Guilds could be more welcoming to foreigners than scholars once suggested. Muylaert, "Accessibility of the Late Medieval Goldsmith Guild"; Maarten Prak et al., "Access to the Trade." Guilds' anti-immigrant policies should not simply be explained as knee-jerk xenophobia but also as an expression of their sense of the moral economy. Ulrich Niggemann, "Craft Guilds and Immigration: Huguenots in German and English Cities," in De Munck and Winter, *Gated Communities?*, 45–60.

128 See Witzel, "Gewerbgeschichtliche Studien," 149–50.

129 Witzel, "Gewerbgeschichtliche Studien," 148–53. The worsted wool weavers, who organized separately, got an even better deal. Witzel, "Gewerbgeschichtliche Studien," 159–65.

130 Witzel, "Gewerbgeschichtliche Studien," 178.

131 Schmidt, *Frankfurter Zunfturkunden*, vol. 1.

did complain about Netherlanders who violated guild rules, but they also complained about locals as well as Italian and Portuguese immigrants who did so.[132] It was not guild restrictions that limited the ability of Reformed immigrants to become citizens. It was the fact that—from 1562—the council required conformity to the *Augustana invariata* for citizenship. The fact that citizenship was required for guild membership meant that the magistrates' decision limited Netherlanders' ability to join local guilds. But guild opposition played no direct role here. The lower citizenship rates among Dutch immigrants in Frankfurt compared to Wesel was largely an outcome of religious disputes about Christ's presence in the Lord's Supper, which resulted in the requirement of conformity to the Augsburg Confession for citizenship. By contrast, guilds were primarily focused on ensuring that they retained control over their crafts.

In fact, guilds were the primary draw for Dutch Reformed who became citizens of Frankfurt. Here, too, timing is a useful guide. In forty of forty-two cases we have identified, Dutch Reformed migrants became citizens within a year of the first record we have identified of their living in Frankfurt. Their speedy decision stems from the citizenship requirement for guild membership. Further, thirty-four of these men had occupations—merchants, wool weavers, goldsmiths, diamond cutters, and/or jewelers—whose guilds proved especially welcoming to newcomers. We have identified no spikes in Dutch Reformed taking citizenship around specific dates relating to external military or political developments in the Habsburg Netherlands or in or around Frankfurt. We don't see many cases of refugees living peacefully in Frankfurt for years only to have some later event trigger a decision to become a citizen, as often happened in Wesel. For the most part, it seems, they made the choice soon after arriving, and those who did tended to have occupations that made it easier to do so.

After 1585, some of the Dutch Reformed migrants were marrying the widows or daughters of Frankfurt citizens to acquire citizenship. By January 12, 1589, concern that this practice was being used to undermine citizenship laws convinced the city council to ban the practice; at the same time, Frankfurt's oligarchs banned citizens from marrying women from outside the city (on pain of losing their citizenship).[133] The concern seems to have been inspired by the large influx of immigrants following the consolidation of Habsburg authority in the southern Netherlands after 1585. By the 1590s,

132 Meyn, *Die Reichsstadt Frankfurt*, 203; Schilling, *Niederländische Exulanten*, 61 n.83. Max Scholz agrees, for different reasons. He argues guilds were not that powerful in Frankfurt, and patrician leaders usually did not respond to their pressure. Scholz, *Strange Brethren*, 76.

133 Bott, *Gründung und Anfänge*, 35; Gorter, *Gereformeerde migranten*, 51.

anti-immigrant sentiment led to increasingly restrictive measures. A turning point came in 1594, when the city expelled the Dutch Reformed pastor Franciscus Gomarus—himself a citizen of Frankfurt—for violating the 1589 law against marrying a woman from outside the city.[134] While his expulsion has sometimes been depicted as an act of intolerance on the part of city magistrates, the fact that they recognized his role as the "Flemish preacher" for years before this suggests that city leaders were aware of and willing to tolerate his illegal preaching and officiating at the Lord's Supper, so long as he obeyed local citizenship laws. It was his violation of Frankfurt's marriage laws—and not his violation of laws against non-Lutheran worship—that triggered city oligarchs to expel Gomarus. In any case, such pressure encouraged many Reformed migrants to leave for Neu-Hanau, a new settlement not far up the Main River built by Count Philip Ludwig of Hanau-Münzenberg, to attract Reformed Netherlanders. By 1597, he convinced a sizeable population to move to Neu-Hanau, though the financial opportunities offered by the larger imperial city meant that a sizeable Dutch-speaking Reformed congregation remained in Frankfurt.[135]

The difference between Wesel and Frankfurt with regard to patterns of Dutch Reformed migrants gaining citizenship is the result of a combination of geographical realities, political incentives, and economic structures shaping the two cities. Wesel was closer to the Low Countries. That means that it was less of an investment to move there (or to return) and easier to get news from home. Meanwhile, its weak guild system and accommodating ecclesiastical system made it easy for migrants to live there without making much of a commitment. Dutch Reformed migrants could participate in the city's religious, cultural, and social life—which took place in a mutually comprehensible dialect—to the degree that they felt comfortable, whether the male head of household had citizenship or not. As a result, the decision to become a citizen was more a function of that man's sense of immediate security and his hopes for the future. By contrast, refugees moving to Frankfurt had traveled much further away from home to a place where people did not understand their language, did not legally permit their form of worship, required submitting to guild regulations to ply a craft or trade, and required citizenship for guild membership. Simply put, moving to Frankfurt demanded more from a Dutch Reformed migrant. There were stricter rules about conforming to the local church, stronger guild oversight of the trades, and confessional requirements for citizenship status. In such a situation, questions about citizenship were indeed questions about how

134 Gorter, *Gereformeerde migranten*, 52–53.

135 Bott, *Gründung und Anfänge*; Kaplan, "Legal Rights of Religious Refugees"; Gorter, *Gereformeerde migranten*, 53–55; Müller, *Exile Memories*.

willing migrants were to integrate socially, religiously, and politically into the city. By contrast, citizenship in Wesel remained largely untethered from occupation or confession. In such a situation, the choice to become a citizen was more a function of political developments outside the city walls.[136]

In addition to looking at residency patterns and forms of legal integration to host communities, we have also looked for patterns of family life that might provide a sense of how Dutch Reformed migrants situated themselves within their host communities. To conclude this chapter, we examine the choice of whom to marry and what to name one's children. There are two reasons for this: first, we have relevant sources with which to compare multiple communities and, second, because those choices are intimate, connected to religious belief, and expressive of the production and reproduction of social and familial networks. Let's start with marriage patterns. Previous studies have largely looked for patterns in endogamy or exogamy of Dutch Reformed as a measure of assimilation. For the most part, such endeavors have treated the political, linguistic, and ethnic lines between "Dutch" and "German" as self-evident and stable.[137] For this project, we not only explored broader marriage patterns but also more nuanced understandings within these broad categories.

First, and least surprisingly, Reformed migrants seem to have married endogenously along confessional lines. Whether they lived in Reformed-, Lutheran-, or Catholic-majority host communities, Dutch Reformed Protestants married other Reformed Protestants. Certainly, pastors and elders promoted such confessional endogamy.[138] We have found a few examples of members of Reformed congregations who came from local families marrying other locals from different churches in Goch.[139] But we have not found any examples of those migrants who moved into these communities from the Netherlands marrying across confessional lines. Indeed, among

136 For a comparison to Dutch migrants in England, see Fagel, "Immigrant Roots," in Goose and Luu, *Immigrants*, 41–56.

137 Spohnholz, *Tactics of Toleration*, 199–205. See also instance, Spicer, *French-speaking Reformed Community*, 153. On migrants' marriages in the early Dutch Republic, see Van Nierop, "De bruidegoms van Amsterdam," 136–60, 329–44. For the linguistic impacts of intermarriage of immigrants in the Republic, see Hendriks, "Immigration and Linguistic Change."

138 EKAW Gefach 12,5 fol. 54r. Gorter, *Gereformeerde migranten*, 151.

139 In November 1583, elders in Goch investigated Trijnken van Sonssbeck for getting engaged to "an unbeliever." Van Booma, *Communio clandestina*, 1:348. See also Van Booma, *Communio clandestina*, 1:374. In February 1591, Derick van Eilst, a member of Goch's Reformed congregation from the neighboring village of Uedem, wanted to marry a non-Reformed woman in February 1591. Van Booma, *Communio clandestina*, 1:331–32.

the Dutch migrants in our study—including the 363 married couples we have identified in Cologne, the 314 married couples we have identified in Wesel, the 122 married couples in Frankfurt, or the 1,172 married couples in Frankenthal—we have not found any people marrying across confessional borders. This result is not surprising. In Cologne, Reformed congregations were illegal in the first place; so marrying outside one's confession posed a threat to oneself and one's entire church community. The same was true after 1562 in Frankfurt, except that here migrants married in city churches, rather than in their own congregations. Meanwhile, in Wesel, migrants were more integrated into the local community and all Protestants worshipped in the same churches. If cross-confessional marriages were taking place, they might not have been recorded as such. Still, the fact that no one complained about mixed marriages—even as many complained about multiconfessional communion and baptisms—suggests that they were not a concern.[140] Finally, in Frankenthal we have yet to identify a non-Reformed resident of the town, so there could be no confessionally-mixed marriages there. Thus, while the religious, social, institutional, and legal situations were distinct in each community, the pattern of endogamous marriage was the same. We cannot state with confidence that mixed marriages took place—some might feasibly have been celebrated in Catholic or Lutheran parishes and thus be invisible to us today. However, given that we have found no complaints from pastors, elders, or spouses' relatives about this practice, we feel confident in concluding that confessional endogamy remained the rule.

The examples that come closest to cross-confessional weddings relate to Reformed Protestants involved with Anabaptists. Willem de Deckenmaker, a Reformed Protestant living in Emmerich, had a wife who attended Anabaptist services for several years. By October 1577, however, she joined the Reformed congregation.[141] A case from Cologne involves Joos van de Scheuren and his wife Anna who had moved from Antwerp sometime after Alexander Farnese's 1585 conquest of their home city. After ten years as a member of Cologne's Reformed congregation, Joos joined an Anabaptist congregation (it seems that Anna remained with the Reformed).[142] However, these exceptions only prove the general trend of confessional endogamy. Given the deep anxiety of sixteenth-century church officials regarding the dangers of mixed marriages for seducing the faithful away from the true church and the conflicts between families that confessionally

140 On mixed marriage in Wesel, see Spohnholz, *Tactics of Toleration*, 199–201.

141 DNRM-EM-36. DNRM-EM-88.

142 WMV, 3/1, 239, 252, 258, 296–97, 369, 373, 383. DNRM-CL-380.

mixed marriages often spawned elsewhere, it seems unlikely that such marriages were taking places without leaving any record.[143]

For the most part, Dutch Reformed migrants also married people who came from the same city or region as themselves in their new homes. For Wesel, we have identified the geographical origin for both bride and groom among Dutch Reformed who married in Wesel in fifty-one cases. Of those, twenty (39 percent) originated from the same city. That number is pretty high considering the diverse geographical origins of Wesel's migrant community. It suggests a preference among many to reproduce preexisting social networks and identities while living abroad. Of the remaining marriages, only three others married someone who came from their region, but not their hometown. There seems to have been a preference for marrying people who came from the same social circles in the same hometowns. But barring that, Dutch Reformed migrants living in Wesel made no distinction between marrying people from their region and those from far-flung territories, including French-speaking regions or parts of the Holy Roman Empire. A migrant to Wesel from Antwerp was more likely to marry someone else from Antwerp, but if they did not, they were just as likely to marry someone from Harderwijk, Delft, Lille, or Kleve. Thus, those migrants who did not re-create connections to their hometown in marriage demonstrated no preference to re-create territorial or regional identities, to marry among people who spoke like them, or to re-create any kind of preexisting regional, "Dutch" or even "Netherlandish" ethnic or political identity.

The pattern is even more pronounced for Cologne, where we have identified the geographical origin for both bride and groom of 113 couples who married in the Dutch-speaking Reformed congregation. Of those, fully 61 (54 percent) came from the same home city in the Netherlands (mostly Antwerp). For them, marriage re-created the social networks of their hometowns. The wealthy merchant families in Cologne, the Van Uffel, Heymas, Boel, d'Ablaing and others largely intermarried among people of similar social status and place of origin while living abroad. Of the rest, however, couples in Cologne's Dutch-speaking congregation were just as likely to marry someone from a different region entirely as to marry someone from a town nearby their own place of origin. Only nine couples married someone from the same territory as themselves but a different city (including one couple who came from the duchy of Jülich). And if a potential spouse was not from one's home city, they were just as likely to marry someone from a distant territory, including from French-speaking regions or the Empire, as they were someone from a city or town near where they had grown up. Among the eleven Netherlanders who married people from the Empire, ten

143 Kaplan, "Integration vs. Segregation"; Freist, *Glaube - Liebe - Zwietracht*.

spouses were from Jülich, Cleves, Aachen, or the archbishopric of Cologne, and only one grew up in Cologne. Marriage choice was not a way of expressing or reproducing regional "Dutch" or "Netherlandish" identities. Marriages between people of diverse geographical origins also contributed to ethnic diversity within the Dutch-speaking Reformed congregation. Take, for instance, the example of Anna Benoit, from Brussels, who married Gillis Andries, a migrant to Cologne from Burtscheid (near Aachen) in 1597, who joined Anna's Dutch church.[144] The Walloon migrant from Tournai, Michiel du Bouraigne, married Geertken Kocks, a woman from the duchy of Jülich in Cologne's Dutch-speaking Reformed congregation.[145] Such marriages only reinforce the conclusion that Cologne's Dutch-speaking Reformed congregation was not neatly defined by linguistic, political, or ethnic boundaries. But it also suggests that once individuals married beyond existing networks from their hometowns, they made little distinction about whether that their marriage partner shared a dialect or native language, political allegiance, or regional identity.

Marriage patterns in Frankenthal differed significantly, where we have identified the geographical origin of both partners who married in the Dutch-speaking Reformed congregation in 287 cases. In those cases, only 4 percent of marriages (11) were between people who hailed from the same hometown. Of the rest, the majority (55 percent) came from the same territory—either both from Brabant or both from Flanders—but different cities. Meanwhile, we found sixty cases (22 percent) in Frankenthal in which two migrants from the Empire married in the Dutch-speaking church, even after a separate German-speaking congregation was established in 1583. Of those cases, only two involved partners from the same territory (in both cases, they were from different towns in the Palatinate). German-speaking migrants came to Frankenthal not only from villages in the Palatinate but also from Hesse, Saxony, Württemberg, Ansbach, Strasbourg, and elsewhere, and they built new families of German-speaking migrants with no preference for the origin of the spouse. Meanwhile, few Dutch speakers ever married German-speaking immigrants. Of the eight cases where someone from the Netherlands married a migrant from the Empire in Frankenthal's Dutch-speaking church, seven involved one person from the Netherlands where German dialects dominated (like Luxembourg) or from regions in the Empire where Dutch dialects were prominent (like Cleves). In a few other cases, German pastors in the Palatinate married Dutch women in Frankenthal

144 DNRM-CL-1287.

145 DNRM-CL-1259. DNRM-CL-1260.

and brought them back to their hometown.[146] However, those cases indicate nothing of social integration in Frankenthal, since the couple never lived in Frankenthal together. Meanwhile, although Frankenthal developed a substantial French-speaking population (and from 1578 a French-language congregation), we have only identified eleven cases of someone from the Walloon provinces or France marrying into the Dutch-speaking population. The general pattern is clear. Unlike in Cologne and Wesel, Frankenthal was more clearly socially divided between three language groups: a Dutch-speaking population, a German-speaking population, and a French-speaking congregation.[147] That is, in contrast to Wesel and Cologne, in Frankenthal, a shared "Netherlandish" or "Dutch" identity was indeed being reinforced by marriage patterns.

By the 1590s, the preference among the Dutch-speaking population of Frankenthal to retain its linguistic and cultural coherence in the face of increasing immigration from German- and French-speaking lands encouraged them to create a transregional Dutch marriage market. That is, families in the Netherlands and throughout the Dutch Reformed diaspora sent brides and grooms across vast distances to Frankenthal to create new marriage partnerships. Reformed Protestants in Cologne maintained a particularly vibrant relationship with Frankenthal over the years and, by the 1590s, were regularly supplying marriage-eligible women to men in Frankenthal. Such was the case when Christiana Kael, moved from Cologne's Reformed congregation in 1598 to marry the widower Adriaen van Avoorde.[148] The following year, the daughter of Guillaume Wijmout, a refugee from Antwerp and deacon for his current congregation, moved from Cologne to Frankenthal to marry goldsmith and city councilor Pieter de Meier, who likewise belonged to the Antwerp diaspora.[149] By the end of the century, Reformed families living in Dutch Republic also supplied Frankenthal's transregional marriage market. In April 1598, for instance, Janneken Aelbrecht moved from Middelburg to Frankenthal to marry Maillaert van der Meersch, whose family had fled Middelburg a generation earlier.[150] The previous September, Margriet Comans made the same move from Middelburg to Frankenthal to

146 Such was the case in December 1586, when the pastor at Nierstein, a village forty kilometers to the north, Conradus Arnoldi, married Beiken s'Ridders. Velden, *Registres de l'Eglise*, 2:15.

147 It is not clear whether French and Walloon migrants—who shared a congregation—in Frankenthal intermarried extensively. In Southampton, the two communities remained endogamous despite sharing a congregation. Spicer, *French-speaking Reformed Community*, 154.

148 Velden, *Registres de l'Eglise*, 2:40.

149 Velden, *Registres de l'Eglise*, 2:42.

150 Velden, *Registres de l'Eglise*, 2:39; Van Vloten, *Onderzoek van 's Koningswege*.

marry Adam Strijckhout, a second-generation Netherlander living there.[151] These migrants were not refugees escaping persecution but part of a diasporic social network that maintained their family ties across long distances well after the danger they faced as Protestants had passed. It's not clear why Roeland Hendrix moved from the small Overijssel village of Wanneperveen to marry Elisabeth van den Bosch in the summer of 1597, but their families probably had some preexisting connections.[152]

Another useful look into how the immigrants situated themselves within the community can be gained by examining the names they gave their children. After all, naming practices are inherently an expression of social identity and positioning.[153] During the early modern era, choosing a baptismal name for a newborn could be a way of expressing one's faith, status, or values but also of extending the implications of that decision throughout the child's lifetime, even after the parents were gone.[154] As Renaissance humanism spread across Europe, some educated European elites began adopting classical Greek and Roman names for their progeny, such as Alexander and Hercules for boys and Diana and Helena for girls.[155] Scholars of the Reformation have noted that Reformed Protestants often favored names from the Old Testament, such as Abraham and Isaac for boys and Sara for girls.[156] For a parent, the latter decision not only entailed a self-conscious rejection of saints' names and an embrace of biblicism but also identification with the ancient Israelites, God's chosen people.[157]

The practice of expressing new religious identity through naming stood in tension with other naming practices that promoted conservativism from medieval pools of names. First, was naming one's infant after a godmother or godfather. Such a practice strengthened the relationship of fictive kinship and conferred honor on the godparent who might be responsible for the care and Christian education of an orphaned child.[158] In addition, many families had a tradition of alternating first names between generations, a practice that was more common for boys than girls, given its symbolic role

---

151 Velden, *Registres de l'Eglise*, 2:36.

152 Velden, *Registres de l'Eglise*, 2:35.

153 Aldrin, "Choosing a Name = Choosing Identity?"

154 Wilson, *Means of Naming*, 185–214; Spierling, *Infant Baptism*, 224.

155 We chose those examples because they appear in the migrant communities in our study.

156 Benedict, *Christ's Churches*, 505–6; Benedict, *Rouen*, 104–6, 256–60.

157 Kist, "De Synoden," 146; Leibring, "Given Names," 206; Spierling, *Infant Baptism*, 141.

158 Spierling, *Infant Baptism*, 116, 144. Some Reformed rejected godparentage because it has no biblical precedent. That view, however, never became dominant.

in emphasizing patrilineality.[159] Finally, minorities whose religious commitments put them at risk may have had strategic reasons to choose names for their children so they would not stand out.[160] Studying naming patterns thus allows historians to explore the ways in which migrants might have tried to blend in or stand apart from their hosts. Before proceeding, it is useful to note the uneven nature of the sources. Our most important sources for naming practices were baptismal registers, though they were supplemented by references to children in consistory protocols and correspondence. There exists a comprehensive baptismal register for Frankenthal, the only host community in which the Dutch Reformed operated an independent public parish church throughout the period of their stay. We excluded the names of those immigrants who came from the Empire. We were left with 1,281 names. We also have relatively good records from Cologne's Dutch-speaking congregation, which operated independently (though covertly). However, in Cologne, many parents had their infants baptized in enclaves in nearby Reformed territories. There, too, we excluded the small number of individuals whom we have identified as migrants from the Empire. For Cologne, we counted 670 names. For Wesel's multiconfessional church there are comprehensive baptismal lists from the 1570s, but those lists do not indicate whether the parents submitted to the discipline of the Dutch-speaking consistory or which parents were immigrants from the Low Countries or elsewhere. Thus identifying the geographical origin or confessional orientation of parents required matching names with other sources, such as consistory records. We were able to use our database to cross-reference those to identify 178 names. The other communities in our study lack comprehensive baptismal registers, so for this part of our study, we limited ourselves to Wesel, Cologne, and Frankenthal.

In all, a minority of Dutch Reformed migrants distinguished themselves from their hosts through their choice of baptismal names. The majority of names were common in the late Middle Ages and into the sixteenth century in Catholic and Protestant regions in the Low Countries and throughout the Empire. Many of these names derived from the New Testament (versions of Jan, Peter, and Maria, for instance), while others were Germanic names that had been popular from the Middle Ages (like versions of Willem or Janneke). Still others derived from biblical names but also deep connections to saints that made them popular in the Middle Ages and in Catholic territories, so that their confessional association remained ambiguous (such as

159 Leibring, "Given Names," 207.

160 In Rouen, France, after the St. Bartholomew's Day Massacre, Reformed Protestants' use of Old Testament names declined as they sought to keep a lower profile. Benedict, *Rouen* 149.

Elizabeth and Jacob). The higher frequency of saints' names for girls (especially versions of Catherine) than for boys is also common across Europe and probably reflects the heightened importance of Germanic patronymics for males, a result of patrilineal inheritance patterns. Regardless, most names assigned within these Dutch-speaking migrant congregations were what Etienne François called "confessionally neutral."[161] In some cases, the names used might have signaled an ethnic or linguistic identity—Wilhelm versus Willem. However, it is hard to make much of these patterns since a scribe could choose a spelling familiar to them, and individuals frequently used multiple versions of the same name.[162]

Table 3.1. Six most common first names for children belonging to Wesel's Dutch Reformed sub-congregation, 1550–1600.

Boys (n=91)	Girls (n=87)
Hans/Jan/Johannes (16%)	Elisabeth (10%)
Abraham (7%)	Catharina/Cathalyne (10%)
Cornelisz (6%)	Maria/Marie/Marij (8%)
Derrick/Derich (6%)	Sara/Sarah (8%)
Gerrit (6%)	Hillikem (7%)
Jacob/Jacques (6%)	Janneken (6%)

Table 3.2. Six most common first names in Cologne's Dutch-speaking Reformed Congregation, 1566–1600.

Boys (n=357)	Girls (n=313)
Hans/Jan/Johannes (12%)	Catharina/Cathalyne (15%)
Abraham (8%)	Sara/Sarah (14%)
Jacob/Jacques (7%)	Anne/Anna (13%)
David (5%)	Maria/Marie/Marij (11%)
Frans/Francois (5%)	Susanna (7%)
Peter/Pieter/Petrus or Cornelius (5%)	Elisabeth (6%)

161 François, *Die unsichtbare Grenze*, 167–79.

162 Common examples of the latter group include linguistic variants (as Jacques versus Jacob) or full names and hypocorisms (for example, Catherina versus Trijn).

Table 3.3. Six most common first names for children in Frankenthal's Dutch-speaking Reformed Congregation, 1562–1590.

Boys (n=655)	Girls (n=626)
Hans/Jan/Johannes (21%)	Maria/Marie/Maiken (17%)
Jacob/Jacques (9%)	Susanna (13%)
Peter/Pieter/Petrus (9%)	Catharina/Cathalyne (9%)
Abraham (8%)	Sara/Sarah (8%)
David (5%)	Anna/Anneken (7%)
Frans/Francois (3%)	Janneke/Janneken or Esther/Hester (6%)

There is a noticeable and confessionally distinct use of Old Testament names among the Dutch-speaking Reformed migrants. Such names, especially Abraham for boys and Sarah for girls, were largely unknown among Christians in pre-Reformation Europe or among Catholics in the post-Reformation era. By the mid-sixteenth century, Reformed Protestants began using such Old Testament names. Scholars have identified such patterns in Geneva, Rouen, Neuchâtel, and other centers of Reformed Protestantism.[163] As Guido Marnef has demonstrated, it was also true at Antwerp, which had previously been home to many of the migrants in our study.[164] We should therefore not be surprised to find these Old Testament names being adopted by the Reformed migrants who traveled to the Empire. Such choices set them apart from Catholics and Lutherans, but in these naming choices they likely also sought to invoke their status as the new Israelites.

However, what is most notable about the naming patterns in these three Dutch-speaking Reformed communities is not the frequency of these previously unused Old Testament names, but their *relative infrequency* compared to other Reformed communities. Among boys, Abraham and David are the only Old Testament names that might be considered distinctly Reformed to appear with any frequency (8 percent and 4 percent, respectively) during this era. Other distinctly Reformed boys' names used among Reformed Protestants elsewhere—Isaac, Moses, Noah, Samuel, and Benjamin—remained uncommon or absent in all three communities. Among girls, Susanna and Sarah were generally popular among Reformed Protestants. Such confessionally distinctive Hebrew names were more common for girls than for boys (at least in Frankenthal and Cologne). This trend might reflect the fact that boys' names tended to change more slowly because of their connection to patrilineal inheritance. However, while several Old Testament or

163 Benedict, *Christ's Churches*, 505–6; Benedict, *Rouen* 105–6.

164 Marnef, *Antwerp*, 199–201.

Hebrew names for girl were popular with Reformed Protestants generally—Susanna, Sara, Esther, Rachel, Judith, and Rebecca—such names appear in only 23 percent of cases in Cologne, 28 percent of cases in Frankenthal, and only 14 percent in Wesel. This frequency of Old Testament and Hebrew girls' names was noticeably more common than comparable names for boys. Still, most Dutch-speaking Reformed parents opted for confessionally neutral names.

Further, it seems that a subset of parents was responsible for a disproportionately large number of the Old Testament names that do appear. Jan Claerbout, a tailor from Brussels who lived in Frankenthal (and Frankfurt), had children named Abraham, Rebecca, Jacob, Daniel, and Sarah. Jelis van der Abel, a Netherlander who became a citizen of Wesel in 1591, had sons named Abraham, Isaac, and Jacob. And Pieter van Dillenburg, the hatmaker who belonged to the Dutch-speaking congregation in Cologne, had children named Abraham, Isaac, and Hester. Concentrations of Old Testament names among certain families might suggest powerful connections these parents felt to the ancient Israelites, but it also underscores the fact that most parents adopted confessionally neutral names. Overall, parents did not primarily appeal to a personal connection to the ancient Israelites of the Old Testament in expressing identity. As Mirjam van Veen and Inge Schipper have argued elsewhere, invocations of an identity with the ancient Israelites belonged to a wider repertoire of intellectual resources to which Dutch Reformed referred in making sense of their experiences, and it was not necessarily the central component thereof.[165]

It is also useful to note the significantly lower number of confessionally distinct naming practices for girls in Wesel (14 percent) than for Cologne (23 percent) and Frankenthal (28 percent). This difference stands in contrast to boys, where between 15–16 percent of names were confessionally distinct names in all three communities. We have already suggested why this difference appears for girls rather than boys, that is, patrilineage meant that fathers' names tended to stay in the family, often skipping a generation. Thus, naming a daughter offered greater opportunity to express nonfamilial forms of identity, including religious identity. However, why Wesel saw such lower expressions of confessionally distinct naming patterns for girls than the other two communities remains to be explained.

The key difference between Wesel and the other two congregations likely relates to the larger social integration into other arenas of life that we have seen among Reformed migrants in Wesel. In Frankenthal, Reformed migrants from the Low Countries were free to use baptismal naming as an

165 Van Veen, "'Reformierte Flüchtlinge"; Schipper, "Across the Borders of Belief," 214–24. See also chapter 6.

expression of confessional identity, like naming their daughters Susanna or Sarah. After all, they were under no pressure to conform to preexisting social norms or expectations. By contrast, migrants in Cologne were under tremendous pressure to conform to preexisting social norms and expectations. Flouting the city's Catholicism could get them expelled and their property confiscated. But because they worshipped clandestinely, they did not face those pressures at the baptismal font in the public church. It's true that the name would get out once the infant left the birthing chamber, however, since they mostly lived in the same neighborhoods, and their illegal faith was largely a public secret, social pressures to conform in this way did not seem to dramatically affect naming patterns. In Wesel, however, Reformed migrants shared a language and a congregation with local Lutherans, and even some local Catholics, and they lived and worked beside them on a regular basis. Dutch-speaking elders spent considerable energy tamping down confessionally distinct behaviors that might endanger the city's hospitality. Further, the baptismal ceremony took place in front of the entire multiconfessional congregation, such that social pressures promoting confessionally ambiguous behavior included the baptismal rite. These reasons may explain why we see higher levels of confessionally ambiguous naming patterns in Wesel than in Cologne and Frankenthal.

Conclusion

Clearly, measuring the social integration of early modern migrants is a complex task. First, people could integrate into the local community in one arena of life while maintaining a distinct identity in another. Second, the significance of decisions that might indicate social integration (like becoming a citizen) depended on local circumstances. Third, understanding patterns that indicate the re-creation or transformation of social networks requires that we carefully consider the categories we use. We cannot research Dutch migrants with the assumption that they shared either a preexisting autochthonous "Netherlandish" or "Dutch" identity or that they developed such an identity as result of shared experiences. However, our examination of the social profiles of the migrants and their integration into host communities has revealed three important conclusions, contributing to a deeper understanding of these migrations.

First, even in the most hostile environments, Dutch migrants were never simply cowering victims moving from hardship to hardship. They maintained vibrant economic lives, spoke up for themselves, built friendships among themselves and with their hosts, built and rebuilt social networks depending on local circumstances, nourished local alliances, adapted to local conditions, and sustained stable lives alongside their new neighbors. The strategies by which they achieved this depended not only on local conditions but also on their own demographic profiles.

Second, geographical distance from the Netherlands plays a key role in understanding the vastly different experiences of Dutch Reformed living in the Empire. Close proximity meant more linguistic and cultural similarities between newcomers and their hosts. It meant that these new relationships were built on stronger preexisting regional connections and identities. Moving farther afield meant that migrants were more linguistically and culturally distinct from their hosts and often had to make more radical compromises to manage their stay abroad, whether that be worshipping underground or building a community from scratch. Moving farther away also meant greater isolation and resultant limitations, like fear of expulsion in Cologne or lack of access to markets in Frankenthal. But the relative isolation in Cologne and Frankenthal also brought greater freedom to express identities within their Dutch Reformed community than in places like Aachen or Wesel, where confessional, cultural, or linguistic boundaries were blurrier.

Third, while scholars have often treated all Dutch migrants equally as "refugees," such generalizations can no longer be maintained. Of all the locations in our study, Wesel was most unambiguously a "refugee community." The city roughly doubled in size as forced migrants fled the violence and warfare taking place across the Netherlands. These refugees moved just across the border, hoping to return home when conditions allowed and willing to compromise until that happened. Migrants in the small towns of Cleves and in Aachen were more difficult to distinguish from their hosts. Some fled as refugees, but the German-Dutch distinction hardly makes sense in describing the relationships that developed there. Frankfurt and Cologne operated much more as expatriate communities formed around wealthy merchants and businessmen with deep ties to the commercial metropolis of Antwerp. They worshipped in underground or semiunderground churches, but their economic utility to their host city provided them a degree of protection, even in the face of hostility from confessional adversaries or complaints from economic competitors. Finally, Frankenthal was a kind of utopian colony of migrants seeking to build a Dutch Reformed settlement from scratch in the wilderness, only to find that it lacked sufficient "pull factors" to achieve that dream. Here, Netherlanders developed the most distinctly Dutch identity and the most overtly Reformed one. Of course, the migrants of these diverse communities shared a commitment to the Reformed faith, regardless of whether they worshipped openly. In the following chapter, we will explore just how they lived and practiced their faith.

Chapter Four

Managing Worship

The features described in the previous chapters—both constitutional arrangements and social interactions—allowed Dutch Reformed to exist in the city and towns in our study. The distinct combination of these factors in each city or town, however, meant that the terms of their stay varied. How migrants worshipped in each asylum also differed. This chapter considers patterns in religious worship—focusing on baptisms, weddings, funerals, and communion—across host communities in the Empire. For each, the implications of specific theological views certainly shaped liturgical practice, as did the constitutional and demographic questions discussed in chapters 2 and 3. However, it also proves fruitful to distinguish those rituals that served as rites of passage—baptism, marriage, and funerals—from the Lord's Supper, which served as a symbolic ritual that expressed an understanding of the communal nature of the church and the process of salvation.[1] Rites of passage involved a transition of an individual from one stage of life to another. They also have strong social implications in terms of, for instance, inheritance claims and civic status. The key factors shaping ritual practice with regard to rites of passage did not neatly align with totalizing confessional categories. Rather, the Protestant-Catholic divide—and for baptism, the believer's baptism-pedobaptism divide—proved more important than distinctions between Lutherans and Reformed in places where the local church was Protestant. In situations where the local church was Catholic, Dutch Reformed migrants preferred to travel to nearby Protestant churches to marry and bury, though they always recognized the legitimacy of baptism, marriages, and funerals that took place in Catholic churches. Meanwhile, Dutch Reformed migrants baptized, married, and buried their loved ones in Protestant churches without issue, regardless of whether the church followed the Augsburg Confession *invariata* or even whether Reformed Protestants were legally recognized in that community.

---

1 Here, we are drawing on Luebke, *Hometown Religion*. See also Muir, *Ritual in Early Modern Europe*.

By contrast, the Lord's Supper, as a rite of community, offered a symbolic expression of the body of the church (in the sense of *ecclesia*), which played a role in communal and individual salvation. In all of the communities of our study, Reformed migrants only celebrated the Lord's Supper within their own congregations. In situations when it became too dangerous to do so, they preferred to celebrate the sacrament in private or to forgo it altogether rather than cross over to a different territory or a different confession. While the stakes of rites of passage could be high—property claims, permission for residency, and social belonging—the stakes of the Lord's Supper were purely soteriological: they involved how believers reconciled with Christ. As David M. Luebke helpfully put it, when it came to the Eucharist, "reciprocities between belief and ritual" were more difficult to evade than rites of passage.[2] As a result, while they often had to compromise on standards of worship in exile, these Reformed Protestants refused to compromise on ensuring that they only celebrated the Lord's Supper with fellow believers within their own congregation.

Weddings

The most important criteria for Dutch Reformed migrants in the Holy Roman Empire when it came to weddings was whether they took place in a public church that was officially recognized by governing authorities. This priority thus ensured that marriages were administered by a legally ordained clergyman whose legitimacy would be recognized by local secular officials and, if necessary, officials in a future place a migrant might call home. Less important was whether the couple belonged as full members of that public church or adhered to the theological teachings or liturgical practices of said church, although these were also relevant criteria. In officially Catholic cities and towns, Reformed migrants either crossed the confessional boundary to marry in a Catholic church or—preferably—crossed the political boundary to marry in a nearby Protestant church in another territory. Meanwhile, in Protestant cities and towns, even when Reformed Protestantism was not officially tolerated, they married in local churches. In all these cases, then, pastors and elders on the Dutch Reformed consistories played, at best, minor roles in overseeing weddings. As a result, no one ever questioned the legitimacy of migrants' marriages.

In Catholic Cologne, almost three quarters of recorded marriages between Reformed couples took place outside the city walls. The most common locations for these weddings were the city of Elberfeld (in the duchy

2 Luebke, *Hometown Religion*, 78.

of Berg, forty-four kilometers north-northeast) or Neukirchen (in the county of Moers, sixty-nine kilometers north-northwest), both of which had functioning Protestant churches from the late 1560s.[3] Other Reformed Protestants traveled even further afield to marry, often to small *Herrschaften* and *Unterherrlicheiten* ruled by Adolf von Neuenahr, a nobleman with close ties to the Netherlands and to the Palatinate.[4] Such weddings would be less likely to raise questions about the legitimacy of the union from Catholic authorities—who recognized lawfully performed weddings celebrated in Protestant churches the pastors of which were apparently quite willing to cooperate—than ones celebrated clandestinely.[5] Traveling to marry had the benefit of guaranteeing both legal recognition of the union and ensuring that the service took place within a true church of God. To some degree, however, the reliance on clergy elsewhere to officiate weddings for their church weakened the consistory's authority over congregants. They tried to compensate by closely monitoring whether couples had approval from parents and the congregation for their union. On March 1, 1587, for instance, elders in Cologne admonished their counterparts in Frankfurt for permitting the marriage of Caspar Bynoit and Barbara de Costere there (while they were visiting the Frankfurt Messe) without getting permission from their home consistory.[6] The frequency of traveling for marriage also meant that there existed no central archive documenting the weddings of people in this congregation. This fact makes it harder for historians to trace these migrants, just as it made it harder for pastors and elders to do so at the time.

Some Reformed Protestants also married in Cologne's Catholic churches, perhaps to avoid drawing attention to their nonconformity. The consistory fined this behavior, though some church members may have been willing to pay the cost if it helped them avoid being expelled from the city as religious dissidents.[7] The consistory always recognized weddings in Catholic churches, of course, just as Protestants across Europe did. While Protestants did not believe that marriage was a sacrament, neither did they want to garner a

---

3 On Elberfeld, see Bonterwek, "Die Reformation im Wupperthal." On Neukirchen, Heiner Faulenbach, "Hermann, Graf zu Neuenahr und Moers," in *400 Jahre Bedburger Synode*, 82, 86.

4 Gorter, *Gereformeerde migranten*, 151–53; J. F. G. Goeters, "Die Herrschaft Bedburg und ihre kirchliche Verhältnisse zur Zeit der Reformation," in *400 Jahre Bedburger Synode*, 58–60. In Dutch, the Neuenahr noble family's name is spelled Nieuwenaar.

5 Protestants and Catholics shared anxieties about clandestine marriages or couples living together outside of marriage. Harrington, *Reordering Marriage*, 48–100.

6 WMV 3/5, 108–9. Gorter, *Gereformeerde migranten*, 152.

7 Langer, "Die konfessionelle Grenze," 41.

reputation for promoting fornication or clandestine weddings.[8] Indeed, during the sixteenth century, Protestants and Catholics alike increasingly required weddings to take place in church buildings in front of a congregation. These factors meant that elders left Reformed couples relatively free to decide how they would marry.

In the years when Aachen's Reformed congregations operated covertly and under exclusively Catholic rule (1544–1559 and 1566–1574), presumably similar patterns emerged, though we do not have evidence for those years.[9] But the same seems to have been the case in officially Catholic communities in Cleves. Consistories encouraged members to travel to nearby Protestant cities to marry. On December 4, 1580, the consistory in Goch concluded that its members should only marry "in a public church that practices proper Christian discipline."[10] Wesel's marriage registers periodically indicate that couples came from a nearby town to wed. Such was the case with Catharina Weltschuit and Gerrit Haeth in 1578 and Gertgen Hanssen and Evert ohn gen Guim in 1589, each of whom came to Wesel from Xanten to marry. The same was the case with Neesken Mercators and Wilhelm de Raed, who came from Goch for their wedding in 1590.[11] Social pressure or political danger probably encouraged some to marry in parish churches. Though parish records might indicate that this practice did not survive, the fact that church members attended other rituals in Cleves's Catholic churches suggests that it probably did happen.

In Protestant cities and towns, Reformed migrants from the Netherlands married in parish churches without incident or controversy, regardless of whether local authorities recognized their congregation or Reformed migrants attended sermons or celebrated communion in the public churches. In Frankfurt, the Dutch Reformed consistory rarely interfered in matters of marriage among its church members, leaving arrangements to the city's pastors. The service in the Lutheran churches was recognizably Protestant, and

8 The nonsacramental status of marriage for Protestants also sometimes encouraged them to legalize divorce. Kingdon, *Adultery and Divorce*. In practice, though, divorce remained extremely uncommon even where it was legalized. Watt, "Divorce in Early Modern Neuchâtel." Spousal abandonment proved a more common method of ending an unhappy marriage. Burghartz, *Zeiten der Reinheit*, 214–18. For cases in refugee communities, Spohnholz, "Instability and Insecurity."

9 Aachen's government issued no marriage ordinances and did not let the city's Catholic churches create universal rules on marriage. Kirchner, *Katholiken, Lutheraner und Reformierte*, 337–38.

10 Van Booma, *Communio clandestina*, 1:238.

11 EKAW Mathenakirche Trauregister, 1578, 1589, 1590.

contained nothing likely to spark controversy for Reformed Protestants.[12] Of course, this willingness to stay out of overseeing matrimony is precisely what angered Cologne's elders in the case of Caspar Bynoit and Barbara de Costere, described above. In December 1578, Frankfurt's elders explained to one church member, Philips Pehij, that he would not have to travel to the Netherlands to get his parents' approval to marry Tanneken van Wechele and, if a letter he requested from his parents did not arrive in time, that it would not be a problem for the wedding to take place in Frankfurt.[13] Marrying in Frankfurt's city churches probably ensured clarity of property inheritance for the largely well-to-do Dutch Reformed community, provided a symbol of their community engagement, and allowed them to earn civic confirmation of their matrimonial bond. In 1588, the elders even refused to intervene on behalf of a member of their congregation who was having difficulty getting approval from the city pastors and magistrates to marry.[14] In 1590, Frankfurt's elders also explained that couples did not even need to notify them when they announced the banns.[15] Reformed migrants' willingness to marry in Frankfurt's city churches also suggests a mutual recognition on the part of city pastors and Reformed migrants alike of some degree of shared faith, despite the heated confessional polemics in other matters. The fact that none of them saw marriage as a sacrament probably made this cooperation easier.

In Protestant Wesel, too, Dutch Reformed elders who ran the consistory left wedding oversight to the city pastors.[16] The consistory there had approved the decisions of the synod held in Emden in 1571, which required that church members get the elders' approval before marrying.[17] Elders never recorded giving such permission.[18] It's impossible to prove from

12 The 1589 marriage service included far more theological content than the 1553, however. But none of it was likely to provoke disputes. Arend, *Die evangelische Kirchenordnungen*, 9:529–30, 554–56.

13 Gorter, *Gereformeerde migranten*, 150; Meinert and Dahmer, *Das Protokollbuch*, 183–84.

14 Gorter, *Gereformeerde migranten*, 48.

15 That was probably a response to increase government oversight over who migrants could marry, aimed at encouraging integration into the city. Gorter, *Gereformeerde migranten*, 150. On this point, see chapter 3.

16 In the case of a man who wanted a divorce from his wife in 1581, they forwarded the matter to city pastors. EKAW Gefach 72,2 fol. 234r. Yet they regularly involved themselves in reconciling unhappy marriages.

17 EKAW Gefach 72,1, fol. 12v.

18 In one case from 1578, a couple failed to get parental consent from the bride's parents. The elders did not get involved but did recommend that the groom write a letter to his father-in-law in Jülich, asking forgiveness. EKAW Gefach

this absence that elders did not require their approval for marriages, however Reformed Protestants in Wesel disregarded those decisions made at Emden that proved irrelevant or impossible to implement in their local situation.[19] Wesel's wedding ceremony, which was traditional but recognizably Protestant, was conducted by city pastors in one of the two parish churches, where the banns were also declared for three weeks before the ceremony.[20] No Reformed Protestant ever gave any indication of concern with the ceremony or questioned the pastors' role in officiating.[21]

Evidence suggests that Wesel's confessional neutrality concerning weddings was more nuanced in practice. It turns out that Reformed migrants sometimes married in the Mathena church, even when they lived in the Old Town, and were formally required—according to a rule known as *Pfarrzwang* in German and *bannus parochialis* in Latin—to marry in St. Willibrord's church. Such was the case with Gerhardt Hesseling, a Reformed migrant from Limburg in 1567, the Brabantine button maker Jan Boisot in 1577, the deacon Peter van Wassenberg in 1575, as well as for the three marriages of Jan de Becker. Their actions probably reflect a preference for Mathena's pastor, Johannes Heidfelt, who proved more welcoming of Reformed migrants, over St. Willibrord's Gerhard Veltius, who expressed resentment about the activities of the Reformed consistory in the city.[22] We do not know whether migrants in Frankfurt may have attempted a similar kind of maneuver, but given the acrimony that had developed between Reformed migrants and those ministers who defended the Augsburg Confession *invariata*, it seems plausible to think that Reformed migrants there might have approached more sympathetic pastors for their own weddings.

Wesel's pastors proved less willing to officiate weddings for the Reformed migrants living in other towns in the duchy of Cleves. In August 1574, they urged Jan Dogewerdt, a widower living in Emmerich and Yttgen van den Bosch, a widow residing in Goch—both members of the semiclandestine Reformed congregations in those towns—to live in Wesel for at least three months before they celebrate their union. They explained that they were

---

72,2 fol. 84r, 105r. In another case, a father asked the elders to urge a woman to marry his son, but they refused to get involved. EKAW Gefach 72,2 fol. 14r.

19 Matters on which Wesel's church differed include procedures for the calling of pastors, the administration of poor relief, and the administration of Christian discipline. On this point, see also chapter 5.

20 Wied, *Einfältiges Bedenken*, 173–79.

21 There are two cases of couples traveling to Frankfurt to marry, but there is no indication of the reason. It's possible their parents disapproved of the unions. Spohnholz, *Tactics of Toleration*, 204.

22 Spohnholz, *Tactics of Toleration*, 79, 85, 97–98, 105.

concerned that Catholic officials of the duke might threaten their city if Wesel gained a reputation for casually permitting residents of other cities to marry within its walls.[23] Yet in later years, Reformed residents of nearby towns married in Wesel without any fuss. Elders in Xanten or elsewhere never recorded any concern regarding members of their congregation marrying in Wesel. They were content, and even supportive, of members of their congregation marrying in public Protestant churches, even those that were not part of the Dutch Reformed ecclesiastical system. Indeed, even when members of these semiclandestine congregations married in Catholic churches, while elders expressed concern about the idolatry their decision might promote, they never questioned the legitimacy of the marriage.

Funerals

A central question about funeral celebration focused on the honor conferred on deceased relatives and their families by a public funeral. When the deceased was buried in a city cemetery—or even under the church itself—they remained part of the community in a physical way. An honorable burial thus symbolized the membership of the deceased person—and their living family—in the community. Another distinction in funerals when it came to managing religious coexistence was the Catholic belief that churches and cemeteries were sacred ground that should not be polluted with heresy. Whether for social or theological reasons, whenever foreigners clearly stood apart as a separate subcommunity within the wider urban fabric, there were more restrictions on honorable burials. Elsewhere, migrants were afforded honorable burials without ado.[24]

Because of Catholic teachings about holy ground, Protestants were not permitted to be buried in the consecrated cemeteries in either Cologne or Aachen. In Cologne, until 1578, Reformed Protestants buried their dead outside the city walls in an unmarked field. It is also possible that a few were interred in the so-called *Elendenfriedhof* (cemetery of the wretched), designated for foreigners (*cimiterium alienorum*), at the parish church of St. Johann the Baptist. Some wealthy Protestants seem to have been buried

---

23 Spohnholz, *Tactics of Toleration*, 205.

24 On cemeteries elsewhere at this time, see Harding, *Dead and the Living*. On shared cemeteries in multiconfessional France, see Luria, "Separated by Death?"; Penny Roberts, "Contesting Sacred Space: Burial Disputes in Sixteenth-Century France," in Gordon and Marshall, *Place of the Dead*, 131–48.

there, though we have found no evidence that any Dutch migrants were.[25] In 1576, the noblewoman Ursula Goor (a daughter of the imperial chamberlain Ailf von Wyenhorst) from Kaldenbroek in Limburg, donated a piece of land just outside Cologne's city wall to serve as a formal Protestant cemetery. The cemetery eventually became known as the Beggars' Cemetery (*Geusenfriedhof*), because of the association of Reformed Protestants with Dutch rebels in the civil war in the Low Countries.[26] Cologne's three Reformed congregations (Dutch-, German-, and French-speaking) shared the Beggars' Cemetery with Lutherans and Anabaptists living in Cologne. No confessional tensions appear to have developed around the use of this extramural cemetery.[27]

In Aachen, too, Reformed Protestants and Lutherans alike buried their dead in a field outside the city gates or in unconsecrated ground within the city walls. Starting in 1582, when the Protestant-dominated city council legalized Protestantism, all three Protestant congregations buried their dead in the cemetery at St. Jacob's Hospital, which had fallen into disuse decades earlier.[28] The Dutch Reformed immigrants could now be buried honorably within the city walls. Reformed funerals in both Aachen and Cologne sparked no significant controversy, probably because they took place outside the city walls or away from consecrated ground.[29]

In the Catholic towns of Cleves, however, Reformed Protestants seem to have been buried in city cemeteries without commotion until the early 1590s. Take, for instance, the case of the infant Jacob van Randwijk, the first son of a nobleman from eastern Brabant, who was born in Xanten early in 1573. Because his parents, Floris van Randwijk and Mechteld van Boekholt, were members of the underground Reformed congregation, they took their infant son Jacob to the nearby Protestant town of Büderich for baptism. However, when Jacob died only a few days later, he was buried in Xanten's city cemetery without any record of complaint.[30] Catholic officials may have periodically raised objections, but there is no indication that burying Protestants—immigrants from the Netherlands or otherwise—caused serious problems in Goch, Xanten, Kleve, Kalkar, or Rees. The Catholic duke

25 Abt and Vomm, *Der Kölner Friedhof Melaten*, 14; Gorter, *Gereformeerde migranten*, 154–55.

26 On the term "beggars," see Van Nierop, "Beggars' Banquet."

27 Langer, "Die konfessionelle Grenze," 49.

28 Gorter, *Gereformeerde migranten*, 156–57.

29 In Cologne, funeral regulations become confessionalized in the seventeenth century. Langer, "Die konfessionelle Grenze," 46–47.

30 Schipper, "Across the Borders of Belief," 144, 148.

barred the practice, but local officials paid little heed to this order.[31] In 1583, knowing the duke's orders full well, representatives from Rees, Kleve, and Xanten at the territorial diet (*Landtag*) even asked for explicit permission to bury Protestants in city cemeteries.[32] As in the hometowns in the neighboring Catholic prince-bishopric of Münster, studied by David M. Luebke, Reformed laypeople seemed to prefer burial in the city cemeteries of officially Catholic towns.[33] While Goch's Reformed elders sent church members to nearby Protestant towns for baptism and marriages, they left no record of sending families away for burials.[34] Meanwhile, Catholics' defended consecrated ground sporadically at best. A couple of incidents in which Protestant bodies were disinterred from Catholic cemeteries in Rees and Kalkar, occurring after the intensification of Catholicization in the 1590s, stand in contrast with the apparent normalcy of such burials in the preceding decades.[35] It was only after these cases that we find evidence of Reformed Protestants moving corpses to Protestant cities for burial.[36]

In Protestant cities, Reformed Protestants from the Low Countries buried their dead in city cemeteries, regardless of whether their congregation was legal or whether they worshipped regularly in the parish churches.[37] In Wesel, burial in the city cemetery was permitted to everyone, regardless of confession. By treating funerals as a civic obligation owed to all Christians, rather than a confessional marker, residents reduced conflicts over the treatment of the dead.[38] The fact that Protestants denied that the cemetery was sacred space certainly made this compromise easier. When Wesel's government expanded the cemetery in the Mathena suburb in 1582, the city received contributions from the Walloon and Dutch Reformed communities as well as the "Heshusians," a reference to supporters of the stridently

---

31 Keller, *Die Gegenreformation*, 1:224.

32 Schipper, "Across the Borders of Belief," 147 n.728; Dünnwald, *Konfessionsstreit und Verfassungskonflikt*, 170.

33 Luebke, "Confessions of the Dead."

34 Elders also complained about being barred from baptisms and marriages but never mentioned funerals. Van Booma, *Communio clandestina*, 1:248, 249; Schipper, "Across the Borders of Belief," 149.

35 Teschenmacher, *Annales Ecclesiastici*, 251–52.

36 Schipper, "Across the Borders of Belief," 148.

37 French-speaking Protestant migrants in the English city of Southampton also shared the city cemetery. Spicer, *French-speaking Reformed Community*, 126.

38 For Catholic funerals, see SAW A3/56 fols. 25r–26r. An example of an Anabaptist who received an honorable burial is Herman Barbier's wife in 1585. EKAW Gefach 37,6 fol. 1231. Spohnholz, *Tactics of Toleration*, 208.

Lutheran Tilemann Heshusius, who had been expelled from the city in 1564 for his anti-Reformed vitriol.[39]

After a generation of living in the city, starting in the 1580s Reformed Netherlanders began requesting funeral tolling, even though Reformed theologians elsewhere rejected the practice as superstition because it suggested that the ringing might affect the outcome of the dead person's soul.[40] These men and women had not abandoned their religious convictions—they included devoted Reformed deacons and elders. Around the same time, the first Reformed Netherlanders also began purchasing church graves as markers of social status.[41] In such cases, migrants were adopting markers of civic honor and communal membership in funeral observance. While we have less detailed evidence for Frankfurt, it seems that Reformed immigrants were permitted to bury their dead in the city cemeteries—though they were only permitted dishonorable night burials—and there is no evidence of any conflicts raised by this limitation.[42]

Since they rejected the concept of holy ground, Reformed migrants often proved willing to bury their loved ones in Catholic or Protestant cemeteries. To them, the greater risk came from attending Catholic funerals, because of their concern around the temptations of the supposed idolatry associated with crucifixes, bell ringing, holy water, incense, and clerical vestments.[43] The elders at Goch, in September 1590, reprimanded Jacob Kop for attending the funeral of an Augustinian canon at the Windesheim monastery in nearby Gaesdonck, which they noted "would not have happened

39 SAW A3/60 fol. 70r. On Heshusius, see Spohnholz, *Tactics of Toleration*, 64–66; Barton, *Um Luthers Erbe*.

40 These results were previously published in Spohnholz, "Calvinism and Religious Exile," 246–47. Elsewhere, frustrated Reformed ministers also fumed against this practice, but only where governments were supportive of their agenda was funeral tolling abolished. Van Deursen, "Kerk of parochie?"; Spicer, "'Rest of their bones'."

41 EKAW Gefach 37,6 *Willibrordi Kirchenrechnungen*, 1581 fols. 1014–1015; 1584, fol. 1235. On this practice in general, Daniell, *Death and Burial*; Samuel Cohn, "The Place of the Dead in Flanders and Tuscany: Towards a Comparative History of the Black Death," in Gordon and Marshall, *Place of the Dead*, 17–43. Reformed preachers fought against this tradition fiercely, with mixed results. Spicer, "'Rest of their bones'," 167–83; Andrew Spicer, "'Defyle not Christ's Kirck with your Carrion': Burial and the Development of Burial Aisles in Post-Reformation Scotland," in Gordon and Marshall, *Place of the Dead*, 149–69.

42 Gorter, *Gereformeerde migranten*, 157–58.

43 Karant-Nunn, *Reformation of Ritual*, 170–86; Koslofsky, *Reformation of the Dead*.

without superstitious and idolatrous ceremonies."[44] The pastor of the Dutch Reformed Church in Cologne, Herman Faukelius, and the delegates at the classis meeting at Bedburg in 1580, urged Cologne's Dutch-speaking consistory to limit the presence of Reformed Protestants at Catholic funerals. In response, elders of the congregation, who were mostly wealthy merchants, insisted that skipping the funeral of one's neighbor would cause annoyance and confusion. They only urged that members make their concerns known about what they described as the superstitious parts of the ceremony, by which they presumably meant the priest's surplice, crucifixes, incense, bell ringing, and holy water.[45] In March 1587, Raymond Rijngold—an elder of Cologne's Dutch-speaking congregation—even participated in the funeral procession of the Dutch Catholic merchant Simon de Decker. Aachen's Reformed consistory took a similar perspective, allowing its members to attend Catholic funerals, so long as they did not embrace external signs of Catholic piety they considered superstitious.[46] From March 1574 until October 1584, delegates at the classis meeting held in Aachen adopted this more lenient approach.[47] Later, the classis again banned attending Catholic funerals in 1587, though it is unlikely that this rule was enforced.[48] In 1597, Aachen's Reformed consistory reconsidered the question again, yet scribes did not record any new resolution.[49] As late as 1609, the Reformed in both cities argued that attending funerals was a Christian act as well as a civic act that marked one's respect for one's neighbors, and that friends and relations should attend funerals regardless of confession.[50] Delegates from the Reformed congregations in the classis of Cleves debated whether Reformed Christians could attend Catholic funerals in October 1575, April 1576, October 1582, October 1592, and May 1597.[51] The fact that ministers and elders kept returning to the issue suggests that the answer was far from clear to them, but it also suggests that members of their churches kept attending Catholic funerals. From a Protestant perspective, this ambivalence might be

44 Van Booma, *Communio clandestina*, 1:328.

45 For differences in funeral traditions, see Karant-Nunn, *Reformation of Ritual*, 138–89.

46 Kirchner, *Katholiken, Lutheraner und Reformierte*, 345–47.

47 WMV 2/2 35, 94, 118.

48 Gorter, *Gereformeerde migranten*, 156.

49 Gorter, *Gereformeerde migranten*, 156.

50 Cologne's Walloon Reformed in the city rejected this argument as tolerating papistry, but they did little to halt the practice. Langer, "Die konfessionelle Grenze," 48–50.

51 Simons, *Synodalbuch*, 514, 522, 577, 597, 607; Van Booma, *Communio clandestina*, 1:22, 23, 339, 342.

understandable. Funerals were civic rites, not sacraments.[52] Their chief concern was to avoid the temptation of "idolatry," though in truth living in a Catholic city probably meant that dealing with Catholic ornamentation and rituals was an unavoidable daily experience, not one limited to funerals.

Meanwhile, similar cases were not recorded in Frankfurt and Wesel, since Catholics were small minorities in both cities.[53] However, elders did warn members of their congregation against attending Lutheran funerals that included "superstitious" ritual elements that betrayed what Reformed Protestants described as Lutherans' half-finished Reformation. Thus, in July 1577, the Dutch Reformed consistory in Frankfurt banned church members from attending Lutheran funerals because the local practice of carrying a cross at the head of the procession was simply too close to what they described as Catholic idolatry.[54] Meanwhile in Wesel, Reformed elders reported in the autumn of 1581 that many Reformed refugees disparaged the traditional burial practices followed by locals.[55] One specific concern was the use of funeral wreaths (*verheuen kranssen*), which family members laid on the graves of their deceased relatives. Elders not only warned their own members to avoid this practice but asked the town pastors to discourage it. Unsurprisingly, magistrates refused to accept any limitations on the practice.[56] As with marriage, official uniformity coexisted with informal representations of difference.

52 Luebke, *Hometown Religion*, 168–93.

53 On Catholics in Wesel, see Spohnholz, *Tactics of Toleration*, 161–76. On Catholics in Frankfurt, see Schindling, "Wachstum und Wandel," 211–12; Meyn, *Die Reichsstadt Frankfurt*, 235.

54 Gorter, *Gereformeerde migranten*, 157–58. On this concern elsewhere, Koslofsky, *Reformation of the Dead*, 123. A few years earlier, in 1572, members of the consistory also debated whether to introduce sermons to their funerals, which was becoming a Lutheran practice, not a Reformed one. There is no record of a decision in this matter. Gorter, *Gereformeerde migranten*, 157 n.14. On Reformed views on this topic, Van den Broeke, "No Funeral Sermons"; Karant-Nunn, *Reformation of Ritual*, 185. Consistories at the synod held at Aachen, which included delegates from Cologne, permitted their own church members to use crosses as funeral markers. WMV 2/2, 119; Gorter, *Gereformeerde migranten*, 158.

55 EKAW Gefach 72,2 fols. 236r, 242r.

56 SAW A3/61 fol. 81r.

Baptism

Theologically, Reformed Protestants viewed baptism—like the Lord's Supper—as a sacrament, the proper administration of which constituted a mark of the true church.[57] Baptism signified the remission of sin and a believer's entrance into the true church. As such, we might have expected their views about baptism relative to their hosts to be significantly less compromising than they were regarding marriages and funerals, which they regarded as civic rituals of no particular soteriological significance. In their behavior, however, they treated baptism much as they did other rites of passage.

Particular to the case of baptism, though, was the anxiety felt about those Christians who professed the so-called believer's baptism, whom English-language scholars usually refer to as Anabaptists.[58] Reformed Protestants needed to demonstrate their commitment to infant baptism first, as a way of distinguishing themselves from the near-universally reviled Anabaptists. This proved a challenge at times. Indeed, Reformed Protestants proved especially anxious about the dangers of being cast as akin to Anabaptists. This is in part because their theological critique of the Catholic and Lutheran ritual systems substantially overlapped with Anabaptist critiques but also because the absence of Reformed from the baptismal font might wrongly imply that they were Anabaptists themselves.[59] Catholic and Lutheran debaters repeatedly lumped Reformed Protestants and Anabaptists together into a single dangerous category of sacramentalist heresy.[60] But the matter was more than a rhetorical one. Reformed consistories routinely found people with Anabaptist ideas or who attended Anabaptist services within their own congregations. This nagging problem only reinforced their sense of danger.[61] Thus, whether their welcome in cities or towns of the Holy Roman Empire

57 In the Belgic Confession, Cochrane, *Reformed Confessions*, 210–11. See also Gootjes, *Belgic Confession*. In the Heidelberg Catechism, Noll, *Confessions and Catechisms of the Reformation*, 149–51. See more generally, Spierling, *Infant Baptism*; Karant-Nunn, *Reformation of Ritual*, 43–71.

58 See Monge, *Des communautés mouvantes*; Hill, *Baptism, Brotherhood, and Belief*, 98–135.

59 Mirjam van Veen, "Calvin and the Anabaptists," in Holder, *John Calvin in Context*, 364–72.

60 Scholz, *Strange Brethren*, 77–79; Spohnholz, *Tactics of Toleration*, 58–66. On Lutheran anti-Reformed polemic more generally, see Nischan, *Lutherans and Calvinists*.

61 Spohnholz, "Overlevend non-conformisme"; Schipper, "Across the Borders of Belief," 93–95; Gorter, *Gereformeerde migranten*, 89–90; Pettegree, "Struggle for an Orthodox Church."

was formal or informal, warm or begrudging, Reformed Protestant migrants in the Empire needed to ensure with absolute certainty that no one confused them with Anabaptists.

As a result, the stakes could be high if new Dutch Reformed parents failed to show up at their local parish to baptize their infant. They might be arrested (and expelled or executed), their congregation might gain a reputation for harboring Anabaptist heresies or, if they chose to travel elsewhere for the rite, they risked the newborns dying en route. Pastors, elders, and parents navigated these perils as best they could. The result was a wide variety of options for how and where Dutch Reformed living in these migrant communities baptized their children. Their order of preference generally went as follows. The best-case scenario was to baptize newborns safely in the presence of their own congregation according to a Reformed baptismal liturgy. The next best option was to baptize in a local, recognizably Protestant church, even if it was not Reformed. The third option was to travel to a Protestant church elsewhere. Their fourth best option was to have the infant baptized in a local Catholic church. This diversity of options also meant that Dutch Reformed consistories often proved unable to keep track of the baptisms of children born within their congregations. There were simply too many jurisdictions and too many clergymen who might have been involved to keep it all straight.

In Cologne, of course, baptisms were required by law to take place in a Catholic church. Reformed Protestant parents put themselves into considerable danger if they failed to appear at the baptismal font in one of the city's nineteen parish churches soon after a new birth.[62] When Peter van den Eynde, the Reformed elder from Mechelen, failed to show up in a parish church to baptize his newborn twins (Peter and Katline) in 1572, city officials arrested him for suspected Anabaptism. After two weeks of detention, he was banished from Cologne.[63] In 1580, the Reformed Netherlander Herman Schonk was also arrested when officials noticed his absence from the Catholic baptismal font following a recent birth. When questioned, Schonk explained that he had baptized his child in Bedburg, where the nobleman Hermann von Neuenahr maintained a Reformed pastor in his *Unterherrschaft* within the archbishopric of Cologne, because (he explained) Cologne's priests do it wrong.[64]

62 See Monge, *Des communautés mouvantes.*

63 Gorter, *Gereformeerde migranten*, 138.

64 Gorter, *Gereformeerde migranten*, 139. On the legal and ecclesiastical situation for Neuenahr's *Unterherrschaft* within the archbishopric of Cologne at the time, see Goeters, "Die Herrschaft Bedburg," in *400 Jahre Bedburger Synode*, 49–71. On the these kinds of noble inholdings as centers of Protestantism, see

Cologne's Dutch Reformed elders also sometimes urged new parents to hurry up with the baptism, probably anxious not only for the parents' safety but for that of the whole congregation. They visited Anna Sauvage in July 1577 because she had waited three months to baptize her son.[65] In August 1585 they similarly urged Jan Flagelet to speed up the baptism of his newborn.[66] Elders gave the same push to Hans Claessens in January 1587. They urged Andries Lambrecht to hurry up with the baptism of his children—presumably twins—in April 1588.[67] This effort was about keeping up appearances, lest their Catholic neighbors suspect them of harboring Anabaptists. But it was more than that. In seventeenth-century France, Reformed parents sometimes delayed the baptism of their children for long periods, as a self-conscious rejection of the Catholic teaching that infants who died before baptism were damned to hell.[68] But of course, such parents were unlikely to be suspected of Anabaptism, which barely existed in that country. Elsewhere, Dutch Reformed pastors did urge parents to avoid emergency baptisms to sickly infants, based on the same rejection of Catholic doctrine, but instead to wait for upcoming Sunday worship services for the baptism.[69] But in Cologne, fear that Anabaptism might be lurking risked the reputation of the parents but also that of the entire congregation. Thus, the consistory's main concern was speeding up, not slowing down, the pace of baptism as a matter of combating the spread of heresy from within.

Cologne's Dutch Reformed elders also sometimes arranged baptisms in nearby Protestant polities, just as they did for marriages. In the spring of 1575 a Reformed woman traveled to Hückelhoven, part of another small *Unterherrschaft* ruled by Count Hermann von Neuenahr within the archbishopric of Cologne.[70] In May 1586, they prepared an attestation for Lisbeth de Beekers (Lijsbeth die Backersche) to baptize her child in Oberwinter ("Wynteren"), a small *Herrlichkeit*, 46 kilometers up the Rhine where the local lord also supported a small Reformed congregation.[71] In November 1587, the elder Jan Castelyn met with the new mother Yngel

---

also Gillner, *Freie Herren, Freie Religion*. The Neuenahr lands also provided sanctuaries for Anabaptists. See Monge, "Überleben durch Vernetzung."

65 WMV 2/2, 107.

66 WMV 2/2, 221.

67 WMV 2/2, 297.

68 Benedict, *Huguenot Population*, 23–28.

69 Alastair Duke, "The Reformation of the Backwoods: The Struggle for a Calvinist and Presbyterian Church Order in the Countryside of South Holland and Utrecht before 1620," in his *Reformation and Revolt*, 263; Evenhuis, *Ook dat was Amsterdam*, 2:50–53.

70 Goeters, "Die Herrschafft Bedburg," in *400 Jahre Bedburger Synode*, 63–64.

71 WMV 1/3, 237.

Tobias to advise her on where she could travel to baptize her infant.[72] In some cases, members of Cologne's Dutch Reformed consistory also helped organize baptisms for members of their congregation with Protestant pastors from outside the city. In 1578, the pastor Johannes Christianus came to Cologne (where he had earlier served as pastor in 1572) from the *Herrlichkeit* of Bedburg, another Protestant noble enclave within the archbishopric of Cologne, to baptize the first born child of a young Reformed couple.[73] The situation was probably similar in November 1587, when Cologne's Dutch Reformed elders gave permission for the wealthy merchant Wouter van der Meersch (i.e., Gualtero del Prato) to arrange for a minister from elsewhere ("*eenen vrembden Dienaer*") to baptize his infant son.[74] But elders did not appreciate it when members of the congregation arranged for private baptisms on their own. On October 13, 1578, they admonished the recent widow Anna van Venlo for organizing a private baptism of her newborn without consistorial approval.[75] In January 1587, they sent one of the elders, Hans Castelyn, to investigate whether there was a "foreign minister in the city in order to baptize children."[76] Whatever intelligence they had must have been solid because in November they admonished Jan Flagelet for having an outside minister baptize his children there without permission.[77] Elders' chief concern seems to have been not that baptism was performed by another congregations' minister specifically, but that it had happened without the knowledge and support of Flagelet's home congregation.

Occasionally, fear of being associated with Anabaptists encouraged some Dutch Reformed migrants in Cologne to baptize their infants in the city's Catholic churches.[78] Jan van Laer, for instance, was temporarily suspended from the Lord's Supper for having his infant baptized by one of Cologne's priests in 1573.[79] In 1580, the new mother Anna, wife of Jan Sauvage, similarly confessed her guilt before the congregation for having her newborn

---

72 WMV 1/3, 282.

73 Goeters, "Die Herrschafft Bedburg," in *400 Jahre Bedburger Synode*, 60.

74 WMV 1/3, 285–86; Gorter, *Gereformeerde migranten*, 139.

75 WMV 1/3, 120.

76 WMV 1/3, 251.

77 WMV 1/3, 285; Gorter, *Gereformeerde migranten*, 139. This Jan Flagelet may be the son of the previous man mentioned with the same name, because in the intervening years, the elders begin to mention the widow of Jan Flagelet in their records, for example, WMV 1/3, 269.

78 Gorter, *Gereformeerde migranten*, 109.

79 WMV 1/3, 60. For a similar case about the same time in the Reformed church for those from east of the Maas (i.e., the "German" Reformed congregation), see Simons, *Kölnische Konsistorial-Beschlüsse*, 51.

baptized in one of Cologne's Catholic churches.[80] In September 1588, the Dutch Reformed consistory at Cologne wrote to a synod (which one is not clear, since that word had multiple meanings at the time) to ask what they should do if they were unable to dissuade someone in their church from baptizing his children "in papistry."[81] Similar to burials, elders' central concern was the possible temptation to idolatry associated with holy water, crucifixes, clerical vestments and the like, not the validity of Catholic pedobaptism. While there is no comparable evidence from Aachen during the years when Protestantism remained underground, we can surmise that the situation there was similar.

In the small hometowns of Cleves, the same basic pattern emerged. In some cases, particularly if the Reformed community had a strong local patron, arranging for a baptism in the presence of their own congregation proved relatively easy. But when they did not, baptisms could attract unwanted attention. In April 1576, elders in Emmerich asked the delegates at the classis of Cleves whether they could baptize children only in their presence, rather than in front of the whole congregation, to avoid risking unwanted attention. The classis approved of this but only if such a practice was done "with discretion," and not if this was permitted only to wealthy members of the congregation.[82] And in June 1576, the pastor officiating a baptism in Emmerich warned attendants not to discuss their presence at the rite with others.[83] Reformed migrants in Xanten sometimes traveled to Wesel or other nearby locations with a Protestant church for baptism. In early 1573 Floris van Randwijk and Mechtel van Boeckholt took their son Arnold to Wesel to be baptized.[84] As mentioned earlier, the baby died soon after making the journey and was buried in Xanten. When they had their next child, in 1574, they decided to move to Wesel for the birth so that they would not have to travel with a fragile infant. In Rees, too, parents often took infants to Protestant towns for baptisms.[85] While Rees's Reformed elders may have encouraged parents to make the trip, their arrival in the

---

80 660WMV 1/3, 141–42, 146, 147. It is not clear that this is the same person as Anna Sauvage, mentioned earlier, though this is possible. The previously mentioned woman was married to Guillaume Wijbaut, while this one is only listed as Jan Sauvage's wife. They may be the same woman or related.

81 WMV 1/3, 310. On diverse meaning of synods, see chapter 5.

82 Simons, *Synodalbuch*, 522. Elsewhere, Protestants did not support private baptisms because they failed to convey the communal principle of the sacrament. Karant-Nunn, *Reformation of Ritual*, 55.

83 Schipper, "Across the Borders of Belief," 91.

84 Schipper, "Across the Borders of Belief," 144–45.

85 Dünnwald, *Konfessionsstreit und Verfassungskonflikt*, 157–58; Schipper, "Across the Borders of Belief," 145.

community to which they traveled sometimes worried locals. In June 1574, Wesel's Reformed elders wrote a letter to their colleagues in smaller towns around the duchy of Cleves asking them to stop sending members of the congregations to baptize newborns in Wesel, warning of the "disunity and division that would arise from this."[86] Apparently, Weselers feared that the city would get a reputation with ducal officials for violating *Pfarrzwang* or supporting sacramentarian heresy in the duchy.

In the hometowns of Cleves that relied on itinerant pastors or shared pastors splitting their time between multiple congregations, parents sometimes had to wait for the sacrament. In November 1576, the elder at Goch noted to new parents that their shared pastor, Servatius Wijnants (from Weert, in neighboring Guelders) could not safely make it to Gennep to baptize their newborn, and they could not get to the noble enclave of Hörstgen, ruled by the Reformed Myllendonk noble family. They recommended that the parents instead travel with their infant to Goch, on the condition that they not tell anyone in Gennep the reason for their journey.[87] The fact that Reformed believed that salvation did not require baptism, which constituted an external sign of the inward sacrament, meant that parents did not have to worry that newborns might suffer eternal damnation if they died before baptism could be administered.

The threat of punishment convinced some Reformed Protestants in Cleves hometowns to baptize their infants in Catholic parish churches as well.[88] Social pressure could also convince parents to compromise on this point. In 1577, the wife of Bernd de Snyder explained that she had promised to neighbors who had helped her in childbirth that she would let Goch's Catholic priest baptize her twins.[89] Apparently her husband agreed, since they did not have the money for a trip to Wesel, a forty-two-kilometer journey that required crossing the Rhine. When the elders warned Bernd not to take this step, he reminded them that they too had been baptized in the Catholic Church and had not been rebaptized when they left Rome. Elders were appalled and disgusted that Bernd would so easily "sacrifice his children to Satan." He went ahead and baptized his infants in the city church with, as the elders complained, five or six "godless papists and enemies of the congregation of Christ" as godparents. We only know the details of the

86 EKAW Gefach 72,1 fols. 35v, 36r. Spohnholz, *Tactics of Toleration*, 179.

87 Van Booma, *Communio clandestina*, 1:221; Schipper, "Across the Borders of Belief," 145.

88 While we don't have surviving evidence about whether any Reformed Protestants asked Lutheran clergy to baptize their newborns, the fact that some had priests administer infant baptisms makes this likely.

89 Schipper, "Across the Borders of Belief," 94.

story because Bernd later repented. But he was not alone. The Reformed Protestant Thies de Bommeler baptized his newborn in Goch's Catholic Church in 1591.[90] In Kalkar, too, some Reformed Protestants baptized infants in the local Catholic Church.[91] Those who received permission to attend sermons in Reformed congregations but did not submit to disciplinary oversight of the elders, probably also baptized infants in Catholic parish churches in Cleves hometowns.[92]

In Protestant asylums, baptism was a far less fraught matter for Dutch Reformed migrants. This might seem unsurprising, given most Protestants' shared critiques of Catholic sacramental theology.[93] And yet, Lutheran-Reformed conflicts on the sacraments, including baptism, could be intense. At times, the polemical chasm seemed as intractable as any other religious conflict of the Reformation era. Reformed Protestants especially mocked those Lutherans who retained exorcisms as a part of the rite, which they saw as a superstitious holdover from Catholicism.[94] They also criticized Lutherans' willingness to accept emergency baptisms, performed by a midwife or other layperson, in the case of justified fear that the infant might die before getting to a church. Such a view, Reformed critics countered, implied that the external actions of the rite itself were required for salvation and not merely God's grace.

Heated conflicts between Protestant camps emerged in the mid-1550s over both exorcisms and emergency baptisms, including in Wesel.[95] And yet, once the initial confessional hostilities died down, most Reformed Protestants baptized their newborns in one of Wesel's two parish churches without incident. Compromise helped make this possible since the city's church ordinance included exorcisms and recognized emergency baptisms.[96] A surviving liturgical book from the late sixteenth century includes the *Einfältiges Bedenken* (*Simple Consideration*) of Hermann von Wied, but also the Württemberg church ordinance of 1565 and Veit Dietrich's guide for pastors from 1543. Next to the passage on baptism in the Württemberg church ordinance, which did not include the exorcism in its rite, is a

90 Van Booma, *Communio clandestina*, 1:331.

91 Ehrenpreis, "Die Vereinigten Herzogtümer Jülich-Kleve-Berg," in Schilling and Smolinsky, *Der Augsburger Religionsfrieden*, 263.

92 See Van Booma, *Communio clandestina*, 1: 34–35.

93 Karant-Nunn, *Reformation of Ritual*, 66–71.

94 Nischan, "Exorcism Controversy." See also Raitt, *Colloquy of Montbéliard*, 137–47.

95 Spohnholz, *Tactics of Toleration*, 46, 52. See also Nischan, "Exorcism Controversy," 31–51.

96 Lurz, "Initation im Einfältigen Bedenken," 294–95; Spohnholz, *Tactics of Toleration*, 39–40.

marginal note from one of Wesel's pastors, Johannes Havenberg, "If it is pleasing, read from the form of the Archbishop [Hermann von Wied]," which included the exorcism.[97] The note indicates some measure of choice as to whether baptismal exorcism was used or not. Given that Wesel's pastors allowed congregants to choose for themselves how to receive the bread and wine in celebration of the Lord's Supper, it seems reasonable to conclude that the choice referenced here was not made by pastors but offered to parents. The fact that even Lutheran defenders of baptisms regarded exorcisms as an indifferent matter (*adiaphoron*) made this option less controversial. Further, the fact that Reformed elders, like Jacques van der Haghen in 1581, and deacons, like Bernt Mensing in 1578 and 1589, baptized their newborns in Wesel's churches probably served as a model for other Reformed Protestants to follow.[98]

Some Reformed Netherlanders in Wesel, however, were not content to baptize their infant in a congregation so tainted by "superstition." In August 1575, Matthijs Schaets, a Reformed refugee from Oudenaarde, explained to elders that he and his wife would have to move elsewhere before the birth of their next child because Wesel's formula of baptism offended their consciences.[99] Similarly, in the summer of 1579, Nicholas Muller, a Reformed Protestant from Brussels, refused to baptize his child in one of Wesel's churches.[100] We have found no specific examples of parents traveling for baptisms to more "pure" Reformed congregations that operated in secret elsewhere in the duchy.[101] However, in April 1580 the classis of Cleves permitted church members to skip the baptisms of others if they objected to the exorcisms used by "the Lutheran preachers."[102]

Ironically, it was supporters of the 1530 Augsburg Confession *invariata*—Lutherans—who raised a louder objection to baptizing children in Wesel's churches because they resented the heretical contamination that the Reformed Protestants represented within their congregation. Further, unlike Reformed Protestants, they felt entitled to make their discontent known. Thus in 1562, Antwerp Lutheran Philip van Wesenbeke caused a scandal when he hired a Lutheran chaplain from the village of Mehr, fifteen

---

97 EKAW Gefach 21,1 Kirchenordnung in Fürstentum Wüttemberg, fol. 6r.

98 These are among the 151 Reformed Netherlanders Jesse Spohnholz identified in the surviving baptismal lists from 1578 to 1582 for St. Willibrord's parish in Wesel. Spohnholz, *Tactics of Toleration*, 79.

99 EKAW Gefach 72,2, fol. 8r.

100 Spohnholz, *Tactics of Toleration*, 79.

101 This claim corrects one made in Spohnholz, *Tactics of Toleration*, 79.

102 EKAW Gefach 12,5 fol. 43r.

kilometers down the Rhine, to baptize his child.[103] In 1564, Johann von Pruit, a Weseler, appeared before the pastor who openly supported the Augsburg Confession *invariata*, Thomas Plateanus, rather than going to his neighborhood parish. As he explained when he got in trouble for the transgression, he "held himself to the pure Augsburg Confession and not to other sects. He did not want to anger any pious Christians and he suspected the faith of [his pastor Nicholas] Rollius."[104] In 1578, the Lutheran Stephen Zemmemeister, brought his pregnant wife to Essen so that their newborn could be baptized in a church that taught the Augsburg Confession *invariata*.[105] In 1590, an anti-Reformed song circulated in manuscript form among Wesel's hardline Lutherans, lambasting the "poisonous Calvinists," who "reject the Holy Baptism … Reject the exorcism / Insult the churches and altars / Storm all images [and] / will not tolerate a baptismal font."[106]

Matters were fairly similar in Frankfurt. From 1554 to 1562, when Dutch-speaking Reformed Protestants had permission to worship in the Weißfrauenkirche along with English- and French-speaking migrants, they celebrated baptism as they saw fit, according to Reformed tradition.[107] After the city council closed the Weißfrauenkiche in 1562, infants born in Frankfurt were required to be baptized in city churches. Frankfurt's two Dutch Reformed ministers disagreed on how to respond. Gaspar van der Heyden wanted to refuse to baptize Reformed newborns in Frankfurt's churches. He justified his position by citing the city pastors' refusal to accept his congregation as part of the true church, but he also objected to the "papist opinion" that tolerated emergency baptisms.[108] His colleague, Petrus Dathenus, countered that Frankfurt's pastors' doctrine of baptism did not fundamentally deviate from Reformed teachings. Further, the fact that exorcism was not practiced in Frankfurt made the city's baptisms less objectionable for Reformed migrants. As Dathenus explained, the requirement that parents and godparents reject Satan during the ceremony in place of exorcism was unnecessary, but it was not godless.[109] With regard to the

103 Spohnholz, *Tactics of Toleration*, 61.

104 SAW A3/55 fol. 65v.

105 The child died upon his return, which prompted Zemmemeister to protest because he felt the pastor's willingness to tolerate heresy was the cause of the tragedy. The pastor Gerhard Veltius blamed Zemmemeister for his contempt for the local church. Spohnholz, *Tactics of Toleration*, 129.

106 EKAW Gefach 65,2,2 fol. 4v. Spohnholz, *Tactics of Toleration*, 133.

107 On these three refugee groups together, see Scholz, *Strange Brethren*.

108 Gorter, *Gereformeerde migranten*, 141–42.

109 As he explained in his letter to John Calvin, dated April 28, 1562. CO 19, ep. 3777, 396–97. For Frankfurt's 1554 formula of baptism, Arend, *Die evangelische Kirchenordnungen*, 527–39. The 1589 revision was largely the same but

Lord's Supper, Dathenus had vitriolic words for Frankfurt's church and its pastors.[110] But on baptism, he saw no reason for confessional polemic. As it turned out, the two pastors' disagreement was moot, since both men left Frankfurt after the closure of their church.

After another Dutch-speaking Reformed congregation reemerged in Frankfurt in 1570, Reformed Netherlanders baptized their children in Frankfurt's city parishes without much ado. In 1575 city pastors reported to Frankfurt's patricians that some Reformed had expressed reluctance about taking their newborns to the city church for baptism, but in general they complied.[111] We see no evidence of controversy emerging about this practice, either among local Lutherans or within Frankfurt's Dutch-speaking Reformed congregation. Indeed, the elders focused on ensuring that they did not spark the wrath of magistrates by openly repudiating the local baptism rite.[112] As at Cologne, it seems likely that an eagerness not to appear to be Anabaptist played a role in encouraging Reformed to accept baptism according to practices used in Frankfurt's Lutheran churches. Overall, there seems to have been widespread agreement among Dutch Reformed migrants across the Holy Roman Empire with regard to baptism: baptisms in non-Reformed churches should be avoided if possible but not rejected if they occurred.

Starting in the 1590s, elders and pastors in Dutch Reformed migrant congregations in majority Catholic communities expressed new concerns that laypeople in their churches not have Catholics serve as godparents for their children or serve as godparents for Catholic children. Cologne's Dutch Reformed elders warned Gillis Zeghers in March 1592, for instance, that he could only have members of his own church serve as godparents for his children.[113] They told Hans Mannaert the same later that year.[114] Their concern is understandable: if something happened to Zeghers or Mannaert, it would not be clear whether the children would be raised in the Reformed tradition. Elders also insisted that Reformed Christians not serve as godparents for children being baptized in the Catholic church. Elders at Goch admonished Willemken Luvendals for serving as a godparent at a Catholic

---

includes instructions for how to conduct an emergency baptism. Arend, *Die evangelische Kirchenordnungen*, 547–51.

110 See his Petrus Dathenus, *Kurtze und warhafftige Erzelung.*

111 Meinert, *Die Eingliederung*, 382.

112 Gorter, *Gereformeerde migranten*, 43–44; Scharff, "Die niederländische und die französische Gemeinde," 259–60.

113 WMV 1/3, 272–73.

114 WMV 1/3, 284.

baptism "over the Maas River" (*over der Masen*) in October 1593.[115] It's not clear whether this new concern reflected the frequency of cross-confessional friendships, described in chapter 3, a more intense patrolling of confessional boundaries by ministers and elders at the end of the century, or a combination of both.[116]

The Lord's Supper

In all the cities and towns that hosted Dutch Reformed migrants in our study, practicing rites of passage often required crossing either a political boundary—traveling to a territory elsewhere to worship—or a confessional boundary, which meant worshiping periodically or even regularly in a church outside the Reformed tradition. By contrast, the celebration of the Lord's Supper can better be understood as a ritual of community, which Reformed Protestants treated as an expression of their understanding of the church (*ecclesia*) and the process of salvation. As a result, Reformed migrants nearly always celebrated communion within their own congregation (*gemeente*), which they viewed as a part of the invisible community of saints. We find little evidence of traveling to neighboring territories to celebrate the Lord's Supper in a public Reformed church elsewhere or celebrating the sacrament in a congregation of a different confession, whether Catholic or Lutheran. The one possible exception to this rule—in Wesel—is only an exception insofar as it requires a more nuanced definition of what we mean when we talk of the relationship between church (*ecclesia*) and congregation (*gemeente*).

The Lord's Supper stood out as the most important ritual of sacred community for both migrants and their hosts. But there were competing understandings of its meaning and purpose. On the one hand, particularly from the perspective of leaders of the cities and their parish churches, the celebration of the Eucharist represented a social act as much as an individual one. Since the Middle Ages, the rite had stood as a symbolic representation of the Christian community itself, beyond its purpose in reconciling an individual with Christ.[117] The Eucharist simultaneously symbolized the universal *corpus Christianum* and the spiritual unity of the participants' own sacral

115 Van Booma, *Communio clandestina*, vol. 1, 347, 348; Schipper, "Across the Borders of Belief," 59.

116 As happened elsewhere in the region. Spohnholz, *Tactics of Toleration*, 230–40; Ehrenpreis, *Lokale Konfessionskonflikte*; Luebke, *Hometown Religion*.

117 Bossy, "Mass as a Social Institution"; Rubin, *Corpus Christi*; Wandel, *Eucharist in the Reformation*, 14–93.

community, which they presented as a kind of *corpus Christianum* in miniature.[118] This dual feature of the Lord's Supper is a key factor in why disputes about the Eucharist were among the most heated of the Reformation era—they were not simply about individual salvation but also about protecting the Christian community itself.[119] Threats to communion constituted visceral danger to the social and political order and to the salvation of the entire civic community. Protecting the religious unity of a eucharistic community could be cast as a defense of the universal Christian church.

The Lord's Supper also took on a distinct valence in the Dutch Reformed tradition. Reformed Protestants defined their church and the congregations that belonged to it around the eucharistic community, which constituted the pure assembly of the faithful.[120] They worried about dangers to the individual but also to the community in partaking of the Supper in a state of sinfulness. To ensure the purity of the Lord's Supper, Reformed Protestants put considerable emphasis on self-examination before the sacrament but also gave a key role to elders in monitoring the worthiness of church members for the sacrament. Critical to Reformed understandings of the church was that individuals had to make a choice to profess their faith and a promise to live according to the standards of the church in order to join a congregation. This often meant, necessarily, that the body of the faithful could not include all members of the civic community.[121] The congregation could constitute a local expression of the true church, but it no longer coincided with the social body of the civic community, in the medieval sense.

Because of their understanding of the church, Reformed elders worked hard to ensure the purity of the Lord's Supper. As Wesel's Reformed elders wrote,

> just as no house or society, no matter how small, can exist without discipline and order [*disciplin ende tuchordening*], so also the church of God cannot be without it. Because just as doctrine is the aim of the church, so also is discipline the sinews in the body, in order to tie and bind members to each other through love, peace, and unity.[122]

118 James, "Ritual, Drama, and Social Body"; Muir, *Ritual in Early Modern Europe*, 166–90. Of course, such rhetoric was often rhetorical more than real and hid all kinds of divisions, hierarchies, and resentments. Hsia, "Myth of the Commune"; Roper, "Common Man'."

119 Spohnholz, "Multiconfessional Celebration."

120 On the relationship between the Lord's Supper and Christian discipline in the Dutch Reformed tradition, see especially Roodenburg, *Onder censuur*.

121 Roodenburg, *Onder censuur*, 82–85.

122 EKAW Gefach 72,1 fol. 11r. See also Davis, "Sacred and the Body Social," 65; Mentzer, "'*Disciplina Nervus Ecclesiae*'."

In accordance with these views, pastors and elders used disciplinary procedures to ensure that no one gained access to the Lord's Supper in a state of moral compromise or doctrinal error. Elders also sought to keep people who were in a state of conflict or anger from polluting the spirit of Christian peace and unity expressed in the sacrament.[123] Joining a congregation required submitting oneself to the disciplinary oversight of the consistory in all matters of life. Guy de Bres's 1561 *Belgic Confession*, which all the Dutch Reformed migrant communities in our study accepted as an expression of their faith, even made discipline one of the marks of the true church.[124] For Dutch Reformed, the Lord's Supper needed to be celebrated by members of their congregation, and only members of their congregation.[125]

For the rites of passage discussed earlier, there were important reasons that the act be public, even if that meant crossing confessional or political boundaries. There were practical reasons for this—they all had important civic implications that promoted social honor, defined legal status, and ensured property claims. There were also theological reasons. In the minds of Reformed Protestants, marriage and funerals had no sacramental status and, while baptism did, they emphatically rejected the believer's baptism promoted by Anabaptists. Reformed Protestants thus recognized the legitimacy of any of these three rites of passage in Catholic and Lutheran churches, and vice versa. None of this was true of the Lord's Supper. It need not be public. It could not be administered by secular authorities. Taking Holy Communion in another church was not acceptable. The celebration of the Eucharist became a symbolic act that defined one's congregation (*gemeente*), one's membership in the church (*ecclesia*), and one's commitment to a Reformed moral and spiritual order.

Surviving protocols of consistories for Dutch Reformed congregations in the Holy Roman Empire testify to the centrality of church discipline to their understanding of the nature of the church. For each congregation, elders visited all members before the celebration of the Lord's Supper, which usually took place four times per year, inquiring into their beliefs, lifestyle, and personal relationships, and encouraging them to prepare themselves for the sacrament. During the rest of the year, Reformed elders responded to concerns from church members about the transgressions of other church members and investigated suspicious conduct themselves. They usually

123 Roodenburg, *Onder censuur*, 348–50.

124 "The Belgic Confession of Faith, 1561," in Cochrane, *Reformed Confessions*, 210–11.

125 See also Parker, "Moral Agency"; Wandel, *Eucharist in the Reformation*, 139–207; Mentzer, *Sin and the Calvinists*; Mentzer, Moreil, and Chareyre, *Dire l'interdit*.

admonished violators, first discreetly at home. If necessary, they summoned the person for a more formal reprimand. The only punishment at the disposal of pastors and elders was limiting a church member's access to the Lord's Supper—thus, cutting them off from the congregation, the local embodiment of Christ's church. In Frankfurt, Aachen, and Cologne, elders also submitted to the *censura morum*, a kind of mutual investigation into one another; there is no evidence whether the other congregations in our study used this practice.[126]

We have a general sense of how communion services went. We know that the Dutch-speaking Reformed congregations in Cologne, Frankfurt, and Frankenthal used the liturgy of the Electoral Palatinate.[127] Members sat together around a table. The services include a sermon, an exhortation about the meaning of the sacrament, and then prayer and psalm singing. During the ceremony, elders distributed ordinary table bread (rather than unleavened wavers), which they broke during the ceremony to symbolize that Christ was not present in the bread, but at God's side in heaven, as well as wine.[128] Communicants also placed their bread into their own mouths to symbolize their active role in embracing Christ. We have learned of no controversies over the form of the ritual or significant debates within the congregations about its meaning. As a result, we know little about the ritual of communion in practice beyond the liturgical guides.

The celebration of the Lord's Supper in these Reformed congregations emphasized congregational unity. When necessary, congregations tried to be discrete so as not to anger their non-Reformed neighbors. Thus, in places

126 Gorter, *Gereformeerde migranten*, 111. On the *censura morum*, see Becker, *Gemeindeordnung und Kirchenzucht*, 90–92.

127 Sehling, *Die evangelischen Kirchenordnungen*, 383–88. For a general summary of Reformed liturgies of communion, Mentzer, "Reformed Liturgical Practices." We don't know much about the form of communion in Aachen or the small semi-clandestine congregations in Cleves. Goch's congregation seems to have used the French Ecclesiastical Discipline (Discipline ecclésiastique) from 1559, since a Dutch translation, apparently from 1570, can be found in the congregation's extant records. However, this document does not discuss the eucharistic rite. Van Booma, *Communio clandestina*, 1:53–58; Quick, *Synodicon in Gallia Reformata*, xlvii–xlix.

128 See, for instance, *Kirchenordnung, Wie es... inn der Chur und Fürtlichen Pfalz bey Rhein*, 42. Among Dutch Reformed Protestants, Petrus Dathenus was an early advocate for the centrality of bread breaking as a Reformed ritual, which he may have taken from Jan Łaski in London. He practiced this rite in Frankfurt, Frankenthal, and Heidelberg. See also on this point, Spohnholz, *Convent of Wesel*, 50–51, 53. On breaking of the bread, see Nischan, "'Fractio Panis'"; Olson, "'Fractio Panis'."

where their version of Holy Communion was banned, they rotated locations for communion celebrations, often in an elder's house, a barn rented specifically for that purpose, or another inconspicuous location. Sometimes they also celebrated the sacrament in small groups to avoid drawing attention to themselves.[129] When it seemed too dangerous to celebrate the Lord's Supper, they canceled or postponed the service, and there is no evidence of protest or anxiety about this decision.[130] The celebrations were designated for members of that congregation's eucharistic community alone. In April 1582 the classis of Cleves allowed elders to travel to the town of Orsoy to celebrate Holy Communion in the town of Baerl, in the county of Moers, "to help build the congregation there."[131] But this exception required explicit approval to ensure that extracongregational communion helped build Christ's church in times of need rather than undermine the Christian discipline.

There were some people—notably in the confessionally ambiguous terrain of Cleves' small hometowns—who affiliated with the Reformed tradition but did not put Christian discipline at the center of their understanding of the church. These included those with express permission to attend Reformed sermons but would not submit to the discipline. These individuals were excluded from the Lord's Supper. For the most part, they seem to have celebrated the sacraments in local parish churches, whether they were Catholic or mixed Catholic-Lutheran. Some also traveled to Wesel, where the Protestant communion was more inclusive. Elders from Xanten complained about this practice in April 1579 and April 1581.[132] Starting about mid-1570, the Flemish noblewoman Clara van der Dilft (known as the Lady of Arnhem) had hired a pastor, Gerhard Loeffs, who maintained a Reformed congregation separate from the Reformed congregation that was part of the classis of Cleves (and thus the Dutch Reformed ecclesiastical system). Records about this alternative church are unclear, but Inge

129 In Frankfurt, the Dutch Reformed worshiped openly in the Weißfrauenkirche from 1554 to 1562, during which time their method of celebrating the Lord's Supper sparked enormous controversy and became the chief reason for the closure of their church in 1562. Except for Frankenthal, this was the only case in our study in which Reformed Protestant migrants worshipped openly in a church building designed specifically for that purpose.

130 Though Reformed Protestants reopened a Dutch-speaking congregation in Frankfurt in 1570, they postponed celebrating the Lord's Supper for eighteenth months out of caution. Gorter, *Gereformeerde migranten*, 146–47.

131 Simons, *Synodalbuch*, 572; Schipper, "Across the Borders of Belief," 138. For a similar case involving travel outside the duchy, see Simons, *Synodalbuch*, 569.

132 Simons, *Synodalbuch*, 520, 521, 557, 563, 564, 573, 578; Schipper, "Across the Borders of Belief," 143–50.

Schipper has pieced together a reasonable picture.[133] The Lady of Arnhem's church allowed Christians to take part in the Lord's Supper without subjecting themselves to any disciplinary oversight. We have no record of Van Arnhem's religious views or evidence of her motivations. The only surviving evidence stems from the efforts of elders in Goch's other Reformed congregation to close her church. By April 1577, they succeeded. It's not clear how many Reformed Netherlanders joined the Lady of Arnhem's congregation. But since the main difference seems to have been about the practice of consistorial discipline, it seems likely that those who did had a more inclusive understanding of the eucharistic community.[134] However, the antagonism that Van der Dilft and Loeffs proved among the elders across town only further underscores how important church discipline was to their understanding of the church.

Meanwhile, magistrates and city pastors in (almost) all the host communities in our study—whether in Catholic Cologne, Lutheran Frankfurt, or in confessionally mixed Goch—remained centrally committed to the premise that their city or town constituted a sacral community, and having a single public rite was essential to upholding peace and unity (under their oversight). That is, they were uncompromising on keeping the civic and ecclesiastical systems united. Heterodox worship thus remained illegal overall. Accordingly, where congregations of other confessions operated, they did so only discreetly, out of open view.[135] The period in which the Reformed operated the Weißfrauenkirche in Frankfurt, from 1554 to 1562, is no exception to this rule. Magistrates only permitted a public church because the Reformed newcomers claimed to not understand the German used in the local church but insisted that they shared the faith of the local congregation. Once it became clear that their congregation followed incompatible doctrinal and liturgical norms—and thus constituted a separate church and not just a separate congregation—magistrates shut it down.[136]

The striking exception is Wesel, where both celebrations—communion as an expression of sacral communalism of the city and a Reformed sacrament that only those under consistorial discipline partook of—*happened at the same time in the very same ritual.* As we have seen, Wesel's magistrates made attendance at the Lord's Supper in the parish churches compulsory. Authorities reacted with alarm when they learned that newly arrived

133 Schipper, "Across the Borders of Belief," 95–108.

134 In this sense, her church bore some similarity to the so-called libertine church led by Hubert Duifhuis starting in 1578 (who was living at the time in Cologne). Kaplan, *Calvinists and Libertines*, 68–110.

135 On this phenomenon, more broadly, see Kaplan, "Fictions of Privacy."

136 See Scholz, *Strange Brethren*, 101–4.

Reformed Protestants wanted to form a separate eucharistic community.[137] "If they want to come here on account of God's Word," the city council had ordered in January 1554, "they should experience the common prayer and the distribution of the sacrament in the church."[138] By 1564, as a way of calming the hostilities that broke out around this question, magistrates focused their attention on preserving unity in peaceable praxis, rather than in doctrine or liturgy. That is, they required Lutherans, Catholics, and Reformed to celebrate communion together.[139] How pastors, magistrates, and ordinary citizens—to say nothing of members of Catholic religious orders—understood the theology of this ritual act is unclear. But when anyone spoke of the matter, they used the language of promoting "peace and unity" in the city and in the church.[140]

But parallel to this shared celebration of Holy Communion, and subsumed within the larger civic celebration, Reformed Protestant migrants in Wesel maintained the system of Reformed ecclesiastical discipline largely as it was practiced elsewhere. Reformed Protestants could submit to Christian discipline overseen by the elders, who determined whether they could attend the Lord's Supper in one of the city's two parish churches. While magistrates and pastors never officially recognized the consistory or its authority to discipline those under elders' supervision, they unofficially permitted it to function. The elders' authority thus remained informal—those who disagreed with their judgment could simply attend the Lord's Supper in the city's churches just as ordinary city residents did. The elders' leverage here thus depended on Reformed Protestants' internal commitment to self-examination as a precondition for the sacrament and, perhaps, to their hope that elders might one day write them a letter of recommendation should they move elsewhere.[141]

In the service, congregants assembled not around a table—as happened in the other congregations in our study—but before an altar. The liturgy followed the structure of the Catholic Mass, but the content of the sermons, prayers, psalms, and Bible readings was all clearly Protestant. During the distribution of the two forms of the Eucharist, Wesel's pastors, dressed in

---

137 Spohnholz, *Tactics of Toleration*, 44.

138 Quoted from Wolters, *Reformationsgeschichte*, 155. The original archival records of council minutes from this period no longer exist, but Wolter's other transcriptions have been verified as accurate.

139 Spohnholz, "Multiconfessional Celebration."

140 On similar language of "good order" used by political officials in the region, see Wilhelm Janssen, "'Gute Ordnung' als Element der Kirchenpolitik in den Vereinigten Hertzogtümern Jülich-Kleve-Berg," in Dietz and Ehrenpreis, *Drei Konfessionen in einer Region*, 33–48.

141 On these so-called letters of attestation, see chapter 5.

clerical vestments, used an unleavened wafer instead of the ordinary bread that the Reformed elsewhere preferred.[142] The ritual, that is, in many ways looked like a standard Lutheran communion service. However, there are indications that the pastors tried their best to help the Reformed migrants feel more comfortable participating. The surviving liturgical handbook from St. Willibrord's church includes a marginal note indicating alternative language that pastors might use to avoid conflict on the controversial question of the nature of Christ's presence in the Eucharist. The original text, from the church ordinance of Württemberg, reads: "that You have nourished [*gespeisst und getrenkt*] us with the holy flesh and blood of Your only son." The handwritten commentary on the side offers a possible substitute: "that You have nourished us with the holy sacrament of the body and blood of Your only son."[143] This more ambiguous language skipped right over the question of the presence of Christ's body and blood in the Eucharist. In 1578, the chief pastor at St. Willibrord's also stopped using provocative language with regard to Christ's presence in the bread and wine in a hymn sung by the congregation during the communion service.[144] In addition, pastors granted Reformed communicants other options during the service to help ease their discomfort. Worshippers could choose whether to put the wafer in their mouths themselves, as the Reformed preferred, or to have the clergyman place it there, as Catholics and Lutherans practiced.[145]

Only a few Reformed in Wesel proved unwilling to accept Wesel's multiconfessional communion. In 1571, a group of Reformed migrants requested permission to hold separate communion services in a Reformed manner. The city council refused, citing the conflicts that had erupted in the early 1560s over just this issue, which brought "great unrest and no small amount of trouble."[146] This was the last time any Reformed Protestant ever tried to separate their "pure" Reformed eucharistic community from the larger civic ritual. After this, those who were unhappy with this state of affairs simply stayed home. Elders visited these truants to convince them to join with the rest. In January 1574, when questioned about his truancy, Thomas de Hoymaker explained that he doubted whether Christian discipline even existed if it did not apply "generally over the whole body of the congregation" [*over het gansscher corpus der gemeynte*].[147] In 1578, Nicolas Muller, from Brussels, refused to attend the Lord's Supper because he resented

142 For a summary, see Spohnholz, *Tactics of Toleration*, 41–42.
143 EKAW Gefach 21,1. Spohnholz, *Tactics of Toleration*, 141.
144 Spohnholz, *Tactics of Toleration*, 141.
145 EKAW Gefach 72,1 fol. 39r–v.
146 Spohnholz, *Tactics of Toleration*, 73–74.
147 These three cases are also cited in Spohnholz, *Tactics of Toleration*, 81.

Wesel's use of an unleavened wafer instead of ordinary table bread. Multiple threats of excommunication never convinced him to put aside his objections. Similarly, in 1580, Peter Hasevelt, from Aalst, also skipped communion because his conscience rejected "some ceremonies and adiaphoral practices used here."

What's interesting about these cases is that the Reformed elders—the very men who carefully monitored those under their discipline for sin and false belief—now worked tirelessly to ensure that the Lord's Supper symbolized not only the purity of the true church but also a broad civic unity. Ironically, church discipline was working in reverse: elders utilized their power to excommunicate not just to protect the pure eucharistic community but also to compel individuals to participate in a sacrament they critiqued as impure. Of course, the subtext to this role reversal was the elders' central concern to maintain the immigrants' reputation and to keep criticisms of the local church that might threaten their welcome out of public notice.

The one case in which we see Dutch Reformed Protestants leaving Wesel to worship in another congregation comes from 1575. That year, Wesel's elder Jan de Poerck, learned from Gillis Spaens, an elder in Rees, that some residents of Wesel had celebrated the Lord's Supper in the smaller town some twenty-two kilometers downriver during the previous Pentecost. The matter went to the classis of Cleves, which promptly banned anyone from attending the Lord's Supper in any congregation other than their own without express permission from their own consistory.[148] We never hear of such a violation again.

In a way, Reformed Protestants living in Wesel participated in two different forms of church (*ecclesia*) at the same time, one that was tied to the invisible community of saints and the other that reflected the sacral unity of the civic community. Wesel's "church within a church" functioned for nearly half a century—nearly the entire time that the city served as a refugee center for Dutch Reformed Protestants.[149] The example of Wesel was more institutionally complicated than the practice of the Lord's Supper in the other Dutch Reformed congregations in our study. And yet, in another way, it only confirms the pattern that, when it came to Holy Communion, Reformed migrants in the Holy Roman Empire only worshiped within their own congregations and did not travel to neighboring Reformed

148 EKAW Gefach 72,2 fol. 7v. EKAW Gefach 12,5 fol. 10r. Simons, *Synodalbuch*, 513–14, 20–21.

149 The system broke down fully in 1612. In 1598–99, too, during a Spanish occupation of Wesel, only Catholic services were permitted. Spohnholz, *Tactics of Toleration*, 235. Evocative stories of violence committed by soldiers during this period can be found in Funke, "Religion and the Military."

polities or reluctantly attend Catholic or Lutheran rites, as they so often did with rites of passage.

Frankenthal

Before concluding our discussion of religious worship, it is necessary to mention Frankenthal separately. We have not included Frankenthal in the previous discussion of how Dutch Reformed migrants managed worship in the Holy Roman Empire for two reasons. First, and most importantly, consistory records from Frankenthal's church have not survived. The best surviving sources from the Dutch settlement in the Upper Rhine are city council and courts records, combined with extensive baptismal and marriage lists, as well as agreements with the central government in Heidelberg, and property and tax lists.[150] Those are all valuable records, but they tell us little about worship in Frankenthal. We know that they used the Palatine liturgy, followed the Heidelberg Catechism, and used Petrus Dathenus's translation of the Psalms. But beyond that, we are left with silence in the sources.

The second reason we did not discuss Frankenthal in this chapter until now is that, unlike the rest of the communities in our study, the town was officially Reformed and faced no barriers to managing its worship services as the Dutch Reformed migrants preferred. Dutch Reformed migrants in Frankenthal did not need to compromise on religious practice at all. Residents of Frankenthal did not cross political or confessional boundaries for rites of passage. And they maintained the universality of both the Lord's Supper as a symbolic expression of both the confessional purity of their congregation and the social unity of their civic commune. Frankenthal existed as a kind of ideal of Reformed purity, guaranteed by its powerful Reformed prince. But what it gained in purity it lacked in a powerful economic base to attract and sustain Dutch Reformed migrants in large numbers. The town remained small and relatively marginal both to the Palatinate and the Dutch Reformed movement as a whole.

---

150 City council and court minutes, StAF 1/11/82–91. Baptismal and marriage lists, StAF 1/10/47, printed in Velden, *Registres de l'Église*. Agreements with the government in Heidelberg, StAF 1/1/1–6, 13. Property and Tax Records StAF 1/3/34, 1/52/466–68.

Conclusion

With the exception of Frankenthal, then, worship required some degree of compromise for Dutch Reformed migrants living up and down the Rhine watershed in the second half of the sixteenth century. As this chapter has shown, members of these congregations were more willing to compromise when it came to rites of passage than to the central rite of community of their faith: the Lord's Supper. By way of conclusion, however, it is useful to note that their willingness to compromise depended not only on which ritual they intended to perform but also which confessional boundary they were being asked to cross. They were extremely careful not to cross lines that required mingling with Anabaptists. Of course, Anabaptists were nearly universally reviled across Europe after the Münsterite Rebellion of 1535 showed that group—in the eyes of most sixteenth-century observers—to be politically rebellious, socially deviant, and even sexually perverse.[151] Given that many Reformed Protestants had supported revolts against governments in France and the Netherlands in the 1560s, they had an especially strong reason to want to avoid this stigma. That problem became more difficult because Anabaptist and Reformed theological challenges to late medieval understandings that the sacred could take material form in this world were so similar, a point that encouraged Reformed polemicists to sharpen their polemic against Anabaptists.[152] And because members of these congregations periodically expressed Anabaptist ideas, the threat that others would see them as sympathetic to Anabaptism was felt strongly by pastors and elders attuned to the dangers.[153]

Dutch Reformed migrants were also extremely reluctant to compromise with Catholics, though their incentive here was spiritual: they did not want to promote what they saw as the "idolatry" and "superstition" of the sensorially rich and materialist characteristics of Catholic worship. However, in situations where Catholic political and ecclesiastical control threatened their survival, they sometimes found themselves accepting compromise. Reformed migrants had a harder time forgiving the voluntary attendance of Catholic worship than when their fellow believers reluctantly baptized, married, or attended funerals to avoid dangers that might otherwise arise.

151 Haude, *In the Shadow of "Savage Wolves"*; Waite, "From Apocalyptic Crusaders to Anabaptist Terrorists."

152 Van Veen, "Reformed Polemic"; Van Veen, "Calvin and the Anabaptists," 364–72.

153 Spohnholz, "Overlevend non-conformisme, " 89–109; Schipper, "Across the Borders of Belief," 93–95; Gorter, *Gereformeerde migranten*, 89–90; Pettegree, "Struggle for an Orthodox Church," 45–59.

Meanwhile, although previous scholarship has stressed that these migrations engendered remarkable conflict between Reformed migrants and Lutheran hosts,[154] when it came to rites of passage at least, the migrants proved remarkably willing to compromise. Migrants who asked to wed and baptize their infants in Lutheran churches and bury their dead in Lutheran cemeteries seem to have done so without sparking serious conflict. Those other scholars are not wrong to have highlighted the conflicts—they were heated and real. But our broader comparative approach shows that they were not totalizing. Of course, as Petrus Dathenus pointed out, with regard to baptizing in Frankfurt in 1562, the theological disagreements on these points were less stark than those shaping Reformed objections to Anabaptists and Catholics. And yet, Dathenus's colleague Gaspar van der Heyden disagreed with him. At least for baptism, Lutheran-Reformed polemics could be heated.[155] But the point is that they did not always need to be. There were moments when both sides could turn down the temperature to accommodate a cautious and reluctant coexistence.

The celebration of the Lord's Supper required compromise too; but never one that involved crossing confessional boundaries. Instead, when faced with restrictions on the celebration of Holy Communion, Dutch Reformed migrants worshipped in members' homes, in houses purchased for the purpose, in barns, or in fields outside of city walls, or they just put off the sacred sacrament until conditions allowed it. The unusual compromise regarding the celebration of the Lord's Supper at Wesel only proves the point. Reformed migrants there were willing to satisfy the most difficult requirement for their stay—worship in the city's multiconfessional communion services—only because they retained control over ecclesiastical discipline and thus who belonged to the invisible community of saints that made up Christ's true church. Like the last two chapters, this chapter has demonstrated just how valuable it has been to compare the experiences of different migrant communities through a variety of lenses. The next chapter, though, asks what kinds of relationships they developed with coreligionists back home in the "fatherland" and across the wider international Reformed diaspora.

---

154 Works that emphasize conflicts include, Scholz, *Strange Brethren*; Pettegree, "London Exile Community"; Schilling, *Niederländische Exulanten.*

155 Nischan, "Exorcism Controversy."

Chapter Five

Living in Diaspora

While the previous three chapters have examined the diversity of constitutional, social, and religious experiences of Netherlandish migrants covered by this book, this chapter looks at the transnational, transregional, and regional networks that members of these congregations developed to sustain a sense of community and mutual fellowship in the face of the social fracturing created by forced migration. In our usage here, *transnational* refers to links among the Dutch-speaking Reformed diaspora across the Low Countries, England, and the Holy Roman Empire.[1] By contrast, *transregional* networks refer to long-distance connections developed across political borders within the Empire, especially between the Lower Rhine and Upper Rhine regions.[2] By *regional*, we mean communities located in a variety of polities that were bunched together around nodes of activity. These communities might be separated by as up to eighty-five kilometers, but they were close enough to make recurring personal visits feasible. As we will argue, while historians have often stressed the importance of transnational networks among the Dutch Reformed diaspora, the transregional and regional networks proved much more important among the congregations in our study.

Before proceeding, it is helpful to reflect on two kinds of past scholarship on this topic. First, many scholars of Reformed Protestantism have stressed that the experience of persecution and exile encouraged a distinctly international or transnational identity that some scholars refer to as "international Calvinism."[3] For many, the internationalism of the Reformed tradi-

1 A useful model is Grell, "Creation of a Transnational, Calvinist Network." We recognize that the concept of 'transnational' might anachronistically imply the existence of nation-states. However, we find it useful, to contrast the connections across regions of the Empire to the broader diasporic connections that we mean when we use this word.

2 On transregionalism, Soen et al., "How to do Transregional History." We recognize that this distinction does not match Violet Soen's exactly, but we find it useful for our study.

3 Robert M. Kingdon, "International Calvinism," in *Handbook of European History*, Brady Oberman, and Tracy, vol. 2, 229–45. See a correction in Mack

tion distinguished it from other religious traditions.[4] As scholars have rightly shown, intellectual, personal, and political ties bound Reformed Protestants together over vast distances. However, historians have sometimes been taken in by the unifying rhetorical strategies of the actors of the texts they are reading, which can belie more complicated pictures.[5] Additionally, as recent scholarship has stressed, Catholics, Lutherans, and Anabaptist traditions also had their own substantive international networks binding people together across vast distances, multiple languages, and diverse polities.[6] In a world in which most people grew up in the medieval Christian church, which embraced an international—even universal—identity, the presence of transnational religious networks across vast distances should perhaps not surprise us. After all, it was tying one's faith to a specific polity that was the novelty of the sixteenth century, not the internationalism of religious networks and identities. In that sense, the transnationalism of Reformed Protestantism was very much the rule. A focus on International Calvinism also risks prioritizing one form of identity over others. As Johannes Müller has argued, migrants developed multiple, overlapping identities without any sense of contradiction or disorientation.[7]

Rather than measuring transnationalism of this Reformed diaspora using malleable categories like identities, in this chapter we examine the networks of mutual association that Reformed Protestants developed among themselves as well as with other coreligionists in the Holy Roman Empire and the Netherlands. Thus, our approach, much like that adopted by Johannes Arndt, treats Reformed Protestantism as a kind of social network defined by interactions among the individuals who led and belonged to these congregations.[8] One advantage to this approach is that it is capable of recognizing multiple identities, as well as integrating ambiguities, tensions, and flexible adaptions within these networks. Moreover, while this chapter privileges the perspective of pastors and elders, this approach does not assume a top-down model of causality or assume that the efforts of church leaders had any necessary effects among congregations or others. Finally, this method has the

---

Holt, "International Calvinism," in Holder, *John Calvin in Context*, 375–82.

4 Grell, *Brethren in Christ*; Graeme Murdock, *Beyond Calvin*, 2; Prestwich, "Changing Face of Calvinism," 144.

5 Muchnik and Monge, "Fragments d'exils"; Pohl, "History in Fragments." See also Van Veen, "'Reformierte Flüchtlinge."

6 Clossey, *Salvation and Globalization*; Hsia, *World of Catholic Renewal*; Rublack, *Reformation Europe*, 64–66; Monge, *Des communautés mouvantes*, 154.

7 Müller, *Exile Memories*. See also Onnekink, "Models of an Imagined Community"; Muchnik and Monge, "Fragments d'exils."

8 Arndt, *Das Heilige Römische Reich*, 26–28.

potential to identify how local conditions—like those explained in chapters 2 through 4—shaped relationships across transnational, transregional, and regional networks.[9]

A second body of scholarly literature relevant to this topic has been written by historians of the Dutch Reformation, who have emphasized the transnationalism of Reformed Protestantism to explain the role of Dutch Reformed refugees in providing personnel, ecclesiastical models, and printed propaganda for promoting the evangelical cause and otherwise providing the foundation for the construction of the Dutch Reformed Church starting in the 1570s.[10] According to this understanding, living abroad not only bound migrants together in an international community whose members shared the experience of persecution. It also stressed that they developed a shared goal of building Christ's Church in the fatherland. Recently, Silke Muylaert has countered that from 1560, foreign congregations in England were more focused on supporting one another and preserving a good relationship with English political authorities than they were on building Reformed churches in the Low Countries. Muylaert also points out that the Dutch-speaking congregations in England were often roiled by disagreements and demographically unstable, so that such coordinated action would have been challenging, even if that had been their primary goal.[11] Our findings for the congregations in the Holy Roman Empire largely support Muylaert's conclusions. Our study of the international ecclesiastical networks developed by these congregations suggests that, rather than imagining them as living primarily as foreign staging grounds to build an imagined Dutch Reformed Church, their leaders also aimed to build multilingual, regional, and transregional communities of support among the faithful, often prioritizing more immediate local and regional needs.

This chapter proceeds in four sections. The first examines the ecclesiastical institutions in which these Dutch Reformed congregations in the Empire participated across the diaspora. Here we see a developing tension between efforts to create a new Dutch-language Reformed church that might serve as the public church for the rebel-held territories of the Low Countries starting in 1572 and the creation of multilingual, regional ecclesiastical institutions in the Empire. The second section looks at the role of migrant congregations in providing pastoral care for coreligionists both in the Netherlands and across

9 On this point, see also Poettering, *Migrating Merchants.*

10 Andrew Pettegree, "Coming to Terms with Victory: The Upbuilding of a Calvinist Chruch in Holland," in Pettegree, Duke and Lewis, *Calvinism in Europe*, 160–80; Fitzsimmons, "Building a Reformed Ministry." Janssen, "Verjaagd uit Nederland."

11 Muylaert, *Shaping the Stranger Churches.*

the diaspora. Here again, we see a tension developing between the needs of local and regional congregations and the interests of the churches in the rebel-held regions of the Low Countries. The third section examines charitable efforts across the diaspora. We find that the Reformed congregations in our study were more oriented toward aiding one another across a transregional network of congregations in the Empire than they were at interacting with churches in the emerging United Provinces of the Netherlands. The fourth section examines written correspondence between congregations, especially focusing on letters of attestation for church members migrating from one place to another. Here we find the strongest evidence for transnational networks binding congregations together across the Low Countries, England, and the Empire. However, as we will see, in practice, letters of recommendation proved far less important than often imagined in holding communities together or monitoring migrants moving across the diaspora. The chapter ends with a brief consideration of two other forms of transnational ties that other historians have examined—support for the Protestant military cause and the spread of Reformed printed literature—both of which played a very minor role in the activities of the congregations in our study. In sum, this chapter shows that the religious networks of Dutch Reformed migrants were weaker and less focused on supporting the Dutch Reformed Church than previously understood. Instead, they adapted to serve local, regional, and transregional needs, including helping one another in cooperation with French- and German-speaking coreligionists in their area.

Ecclesiastical Institutions

Before 1568, there were no serious efforts to build up transnational ecclesiastical associations among Dutch Reformed Protestants. Instead, we see regional nodes of organization emerging around Antwerp, London, and Emden.[12] However, the ecclesiastical institutions remained separate. No transnational ecclesiastical system existed that might facilitate formal coordination across the diaspora operated until 1571. The first effort to develop such an organization took place in 1568, following the launch of William of Orange's 1568 military campaign against Habsburg rule in the Netherlands. This effort to organize Reformed Protestants across the diaspora into a single

12 Antwerp's underground Reformed congregations organized a series of underground synods for congregations in Flanders and Brabant between 1562 and 1567. Hooijer, *Oude kerkordeningen*, 1–23. Knetsch, "Ortsgemeinden und Synoden." On Emden and London, see Becker, *Gemeindeordnung und Kirchenzucht*; Pettegree, *Emden*; Muylaert, *Shaping the Stranger Churches*.

church system seems to have been led by Petrus Dathenus and Herman Moded. In November 1568, its organizers began circulating 122 articles in manuscript form proposing a church structure in migrant communities in the Empire and England. The intention of the organizers of this project seems to have been to promote a church model that looked similar to those used in the Palatinate, Geneva, and among Huguenots in France. This proposal was laid out in Latin, not Dutch, and its signers included native Dutch, French, and German speakers, including at least two who had never even visited the Low Countries.[13] In the end, though, the articles failed to garner attention, let alone enthusiasm.[14]

Soon after, the efforts of Netherlandish congregations across the diaspora picked up steam. Again the vision seems to have been of a multilingual, internationalist vision for these Reformed churches. Discussions about the strategic benefit of such an organization seem to have begun among Dutch Reformed in the Palatinate (probably including Dathenus) as well as coreligionists in England.[15] A key promoter of this effort was Philip van Marnix, Lord of St. Aldegonde, a Reformed nobleman who had participated in political protests and scheming against Habsburg rule in 1565 and 1566.[16] Marnix's own vision for the Reformed church at this point, as demonstrated by Alisa van de Haar, was one of multilingual unity.[17] In spring 1569, Marnix helped to develop alliances between Elector Palatine Friedrich III, leading Netherlandish Reformed pastors in the Palatinate like Petrus Dathenus, and William of Orange, now the undisputed leader of anti-Habsburg resistance in the Low Countries.[18] The following year, Orange hired Marnix as a propagandist and political advisor capable of earning Orange support among Reformed leaders suspicious of Orange's

13 The Walloons were Henricus Michael and Adrianus Vossius. There is no evidence that the Germans Gerhadius Venradius and Philip Raesfeld ever visited the Netherlands. Another German, Caspar Coolhaes, had lived in Deventer for a year, but the rest of his life thus far had been spent in the Holy Roman Empire.

14 This effort was re-remembered fifty years later as a large and successful meeting that significantly contributed to the construction of the Dutch Reformed Church. Spohnholz, *Convent of Wesel.*

15 Muylaert, *Shaping the Stranger Churches*, 197; Jelsma, *Frontiers of the Reformation*, 113.

16 Weis, *Philipp de Marnix et le Saint Empire*; Weis, "Philip of Marnix and 'International Protestantism'."

17 Van de Haar, *Golden Mean of Languages*, 202–06.

18 Spohnholz, *Convent of Wesel*, 95–96.

intentions.[19] One necessary precondition for this, in Marnix's view, was to promote greater coordination across the Netherlandish Reformed movement. By March 1570, Marnix and the pastor at Frankenthal, Gaspar van der Heyden, cowrote a long letter addressed to coreligionists across the diaspora recommending that they build institutions capable of tracking migrants between the disparate and poorly connected congregations and organize some means of raising funds to support the hiring of pastors in underserved congregations.[20] In the next year, Marnix worked hard to build transnational ecclesiastical institutions that could help coordinate the Reformed and Orangist causes.

In the summer of 1571, Marnix helped organize a meeting of Reformed Protestants in the town of Bedburg, an *Unterherrschaft* of the Neuenahr noble family that operated as a feudal dependency (*Lehnsabhängigkeit*) from the archbishop of Cologne, a small Reformed enclave within the duchy of Jülich.[21] Marnix used this meeting to promote greater coordination between the congregations and to try to convince Reformed migrants to approve the Augsburg Confession, to build support among *Augsburger Konfessionsverwandt* princes in the Empire against Catholic officials in the Netherlands.[22] He also hoped to build an alliance with French Reformed Churches, which had recently secured limited freedom to worship in the Peace of Saint-Germain-en-Laye of 1570.[23] The meetings at Bedburg took

19 Dankbaar, "Marnix van St. Aldegonde," 41–85; Frijhoff, "Marnix over de opvoeding"; Alastair Duke, "Dissident Propaganda and Political Organization at the Outbreak of the Revolt of the Netherlands," in Benedict, Marnef and Venard, *Reformation, Revolt and Civil War*, 133–48.

20 Philip van Marnix and Gaspar van der Heyden, "Rondgaande brief, namens de gemeenten te Heidelberg en Frankenthal, aan de verstrooide gemeente der vluchtelingen in Engeland en Duitschland," in Van Toorenenbergen, *Philips van Marnix van St. Aldegonde*, 3–38.

21 Herbert Frost, "Ablauf und kirchenrechtsgeschichtliche Bedeutung der Bedburger Synode vom 3. und 4. Juli 1571," in *400 Jahre Bedburger Synode*, 25–48. This essay contains useful information, but also some speculations that go beyond the evidence. On the role of Neuenahr's princely holdings in supporting regional Reformed congregations, see Goeters, "Die Herrschaft Bedburg," in *400 Jahre Bedburger Synode*, 49–71.

22 As in a letter from July 24, 1571 Hessels, *Epistulae et Tractatus*, vol. 2, 378–87. See also WMV 2/2, 6–7.

23 On connections between the French Wars of Religion and the politics of the Empire, see Van Tol, *Germany and the French Wars of Religion*. On connections between the Dutch Revolt and the politics of the Empire, see Arndt, *Das Heilige Römische Reich*. On connections between the Dutch Revolt and the French Wars of Religion, see Holt, *Duke of Anjou*.

place on July 3 and/or 4.[24] We don't have a complete list of attendees and, besides the surviving articles, we know little about what took place.[25] However, two features of the meeting are clear. First, the meeting only had a handful of attendees and largely came to nothing. The organizers agreed to further consult on how to form an alliance with the "churches of the Augsburg Confession," but such aspirations found no traction. The idea of creating a common fund to help support the training of pastors and developing a system to monitor migrants between congregations also never resulted in any concrete action either. Neither were any significant steps taken to coordinate with the Reformed churches in France. The only meaningful outcome seems to have been that Marnix, Van der Heyden, and their allies organized another meeting in Emden later that year. Second, its organizers did not see the meetings at Bedburg as an exclusively "Dutch" matter. Representatives of German Reformed congregations came from the surrounding area, including Aachen and Cologne, but also the villages in Meil (near Rheinbach, also held by the Neuenahr family) and Laurensberg (in the jurisdiction of Aachen). Reports were written in both Dutch and German. The records do distinguish between "*Duytschlandt*" and "*Nederlandt*," but they treat Reformed Protestants from both places as sharing a common cause. The gathering at Bedburg suggests that Reformed in the diaspora imagined a multilingual alliance of congregations that was not limited by their ties to the Netherlands.

Later that year, Marnix was closely involved in a larger and more successful effort. He helped organize a synod in the East Frisian city of Emden, which included twenty-nine attendees who met over the course of ten days in October 1571 to write a proposal for a provisional church order in fifty-three articles and twenty-five statutes.[26] Organizers had invited representatives from Netherlandish Reformed congregations located in the Netherlands; the duchy of Cleves; the Palatinate, England; and the imperial cities of Aachen, Frankfurt, and Cologne; they were asked to send questions about issues of concern or for advice.[27] Perhaps the most novel decision

24 The German-language records report that the meeting was on July 3. The Dutch-language records indicated that the meeting lasted two days, July 3 and 4. Some have speculated that the Dutch speakers may have held separate meetings on the second day, though there is no clear evidence for this. Frost, "Ablauf," in *400 Jahre Bedburger Synode*, 30.

25 WMV 2/2, 3–7.

26 Nauta, Van Dooren, and De Jong, *De Synode van Emden.* Nauta, "Wesel (1568) en Emden (1571)"; Van Meer, *De synode te Emden.*

27 Organizers tried to convince Friedrich III, Elector Palatine to send representatives of his court in Heidelberg to the meeting in Emden, but the prince declined to do so. Ruys, *Petrus Dathenus*, 103–04.

made at Emden was to recommend a transnational ecclesiastical structure with periodic assemblies to which congregations would send delegates to resolve thorny questions and discuss matters of common interest. The Netherlandish Reformed congregations would be divided into nine regional groupings—delegates used the Latin word *classis* ("group")—that would meet regularly to consult.[28] The recommended groupings of congregation were Palatine/Frankfurt; Jülich/Cologne/Aachen/Limburg; Cleves, Emden, England, Brabant, Flanders, the Walloon provinces; and Holland/Overijssel/West Friesland.[29] Less frequent and more expansive assemblies would meet at regional synods (called "provincial synods," though they did not all correspond to a specific province or territory) and at the broadest "general synods." While this presbyterial-synodal structure drew on French Reformed churches for precedents, coreligionists in France only included congregations operating *in France*, while the Netherlanders imagined a transnational, multilingual diasporic organization operating in the Low Countries, England, and the Holy Roman Empire.[30]

In terms of understanding the connections across the Reformed Netherlandish diaspora, three points are worth making about the synod held at Emden. First, while delegates came from a broad swath of congregations, the meeting was not comprehensive in scope. The churches in England selected delegates but were barred from attending by the English government, which insisted they fell under the jurisdiction of the Church of England, not a foreign institution.[31] The city church in Emden declined to attend, probably for fear of similarly running afoul of Count Edzard of East Friesland, but perhaps also because leading members of the church disagreed on key matters with its organizers.[32] No one came from Frankfurt either. The only consistory in the duchy of Cleves that sent delegates was that in Wesel. Many regions within the Low Countries had no representatives either. Second, considerable disagreements emerged at Emden on key issues, including which doctrinal statements to adopt and how narrowly to draw the lines of acceptable belief.[33] These debates had theological implications as well as political ones, including whether the Reformed might get support from French Huguenots, German Lutheran princes, William of

28 For a history of the classis, see Van den Broeke, *Een geschiedenis van de classis*. See also Van Deursen, *Bavianen en Slijkgeuzen*.

29 Rutgers, *Acta*, 59–61.

30 On the French example, see Sunshine, *Reforming French Protestantism*.

31 Hessels, *Epistulae et Tractatus*, 2:150, 391.

32 Pettegree, *Emden*, 178.

33 Willem Nijenhuis, "Synod of Emden, 1571," in his *Ecclesia Reformata*, 2:101–24.

Orange, and the Elector Palatine.[34] Third, delegates were building a multilingual ecclesiastical system. Native Dutch, French, and German speakers all attended, and the records were written in Latin. The articles did distinguish between the "foreign" churches (meaning congregations made up of Netherlanders living abroad) and "Netherlandish" churches (those located in the Low Countries), but the word used to refer to the location of their common origin—*Belgium*—referred broadly to the multilingual lands of the Low Countries.

In the year after the synod held at Emden, some congregations in the diaspora began to meet in their regional classis groupings. But while the synod of Emden had envisioned a transnational ecclesiastical system operating in support of Reformed Protestantism in the Low Countries, that is not what happened outside the Netherlands. In some cases, pastors and elders in the diaspora built entirely separate ecclesiastical structures. Such was the case with the congregations in England and East Friesland, for example, which never joined the Dutch ecclesiastical system.[35]

For the eleven congregations in our study, the regional classis organizations proposed at Emden proved extremely important. Very soon after the synod, three classes formed, geographically centering around the duchy of Cleves, the duchy of Jülich, and the Electoral Palatinate. Those institutions focused the bulk of their attention on serving the multilingual Reformed congregations in their region, not providing cooperation across the Dutch Reformed diaspora or providing support for the building of the Dutch Reformed Church. All three maintained ties to the emerging Dutch ecclesiastical system but did not invest much of their attention either in providing leadership for congregations in the Netherlands or in seeking guidance from church leaders in the Netherlands.

The classis centered in the duchy of Cleves was not simply a foreign or diasporic appendage to the Dutch Reformed ecclesiastical system but a multilingual hybrid institution. The heart of the classis was the Dutch-speaking Reformed consistory in Wesel, made up of eight elders elected by members of the congregation. Classis meetings probably took place at the house of

34 J. J. Woltjer, "De politieke betekenis van de Emdense synode," in Nauta, Van Dooren, and De Jong, *De synode van Emden*, 22–49.

35 The English congregations formed organizations they called the coetus and colloquy, which shared some of functions of classis, but coreligionists elsewhere remained frustrated that they never formed a parallel institution. Becker, *Gemeindeordnung und Kirchenzucht*, 458–62; Muylaert, *Shaping the Stranger Churches*, 64–65, 75–78. East Friesland had already long had a so-called *coetus* (a Latin word for a meeting), at which Reformed pastors met to discuss matters of common interest. Jürgens, *Johannes a Lasco in Ostfriesland*, 304–11; Becker, *Gemeindeordnung und Kirchenzucht*, 40, 110–11.

one of Wesel's elders.[36] Wesel's Walloon congregation, whose pastor held French-language services apart from the city church, joined the classis too. The classis also included the mixed, local-migrant Reformed congregations at Goch, Xanten, Gennep, Rees, Emmerich, Kleve, and Kalkar. Reformed congregations in the Clevish towns of Duisburg, Zevenaer, and Orsoy also belonged, as well as those in the small enclave lordships of Hörstgen and Alpen. These last groups of congregations were made up of mostly locals, not migrants from the Low Countries. Such was also the case for the Reformed congregations in neighboring territories, including Rheinberg (in the archbishopric of Cologne), Bocholt (in the prince-bishopric of Münster), and Hamm (in the county of Mark). The classis of Cleves thus constituted a multilingual, regional ecclesiastical body. What the congregations who belonged to it shared—besides proximity—were their experiences as clandestine or semiclandestine Reformed congregations in the region, which was dominated by Catholic rulers, as well as a dependence on the powerful Protestant city of Wesel, including the Reformed elders in the city, for support and advice. Most classis business focused on recommendations for best practices for managing worship within majority Catholic communities, including traveling to services elsewhere and limiting the influence of Catholics and Anabaptists on their congregations.[37]

The classis whose geographical center lay in the duchy of Jülich—usually called the classis of Cologne—similarly constituted a multilingual body whose orientation remained regional.[38] The congregations in Cologne and Aachen provided the bulk of classis leadership. That included the Dutch-speaking congregation of Cologne, the displaced Maastricht congregation that had moved to Aachen[39] (until it merged with the local Reformed church in 1579), but also, later, a new congregation that had formed in Maastricht, which thus lay within the Low Countries.[40] French-speaking

36 The classis of Cleves was also called the classis of Wesel. In September 1580, Wesel's elders instructed delegates coming from out of town to go to the house of the elder Hans van der Clocken, where they would be informed about what to do from there. EKAW Gefach 72,2 fol. 200v.

37 These records are at EKAW Gefach 12,5. For a modern printed edition, Simons, *Synodalbuch*.

38 The classis was also sometimes called the "classis of Jülich."

39 In the classis minutes, that congregation was variously called, "*der kercken van Maestricht, nu binnen Aken gevlucht zijnde*," "*der kercken van Maestricht (binnen Aken zijnde)*," "*der Maetsterychtse ghemeyndte tot Aken*", and "*de ghmeynte van Maestricht binnen Aken*." WMV 2/2, 9, 12, 31, 44.

40 Until 1579, Maastricht formally stood under co-dominium of duke of Brabant and the prince-bishopric of Liège, but its government operated autonomously in most matters and magistrates claimed the right to appeal to the imperial

congregations in Cologne and Aachen were also part of the classis. The majority of its churches were not made up of people from the Netherlands, however, but Reformed Protestants from the Empire. That included the German-language Reformed congregation in Cologne and—from 1579—the merged Dutch-German Reformed congregation of Aachen, and the German-language congregation in Burtscheid, which lay within the city of Aachen's jurisdiction. It also included many German-speaking congregations in the duchy of Jülich and the archbishopric of Cologne—places like Sittard, Düren, Neuss, Euchen, Gladbach, Bonn, Susteren, Oberwinter, Warden, and those in noble enclaves, like Bedburg and Bedburdyck. Attendees seem to have spoken a mixture of German, Dutch, and Latin at their meetings.[41] As was the case with the classis of Cleves, most meetings of the classis of Cologne centered on delegates providing advice and support to congregations worshipping underground in Catholic territories and helping to ensure that all the congregations in the region had godly worship and limited the impact of Catholics and Anabaptists on their flocks.[42]

The classis based in the Electoral Palatinate similarly constituted a multilingual organization more oriented toward nurturing the faithful of the region than building God's church in the Netherlands.[43] Leadership largely came from the Dutch congregation at Frankenthal. It also included the Dutch-speaking congregations in Frankfurt and (from 1594) in Neu-Hanau. However, *most* of the churches represented in this body were French speaking. Those included Walloon congregations in Otterberg, Frankenthal, Schönau, and St. Lambert, in the Palatine, as well as that of Neu-Hanau. From 1586, it also included the Walloon congregation in the free imperial city Wetzlar, which welcomed some sixty Walloon families fleeing the Spanish siege of Wesel.[44] Meetings of the classis focused on local matters, including solving conflicts between Dutch and French speakers in the region.[45]

Soon after the synod held in Emden, we see the first evidence of a tension developing between these multilingual regional institutions and the emerging Dutch Reformed Church. The first place we see this is in the uncertain authority of the articles adopted at Emden. It took two years for Wesel's

---

Reichskammergericht. Geurts, "Maastricht tussen Brabant en het Rijk," 26–65. In 1579, it was captured by Habsburg troops, and thus formed part of the Spanish Netherlands until 1632.

41 Gorter, *Gereformeerde migranten*, 170.

42 WMV 3/5. Gorter, *Gereformeerde migranten*, 156, 158, 170.

43 The classis was also sometimes called the Highland (*Oberland*) classis.

44 Cuno, *Die pfälzischen reformierten Fremdengemeinden*, 22–23.

45 Gorter, *Gereformeerde migranten*, 54, 169–70.

elders to approve the articles passed at Emden, despite the fact that three members of their church had attended.[46] Thereafter they largely treated the decisions made at Emden as authoritative. In late 1573, for instance, they chastised members of the Reformed congregation at Duisburg for failing to follow the synod's standards for writing letters of attestation by failing to interview housemates of those seeking an attestation.[47] Others remained unsure. Immediately after the synod, in November 1571, the elders of the German-speaking Cologne congregation declined to sign the Emden articles, even after repeated insistence from the pastor of the Dutch congregation in that city, Cornelis Walraven, the elder Adriaen van Coninxloo, and others over many months.[48] Elders of Cologne's Dutch-speaking congregation wrote to Aachen to inquire if there were similar problems there.[49] We do not know what answer they received, but we do know that at the meeting of the Cologne classis held at Bierkesdorf (just north of the city of Düren) on December 17, 1571, there was no recorded discussion about signing the Emden articles.[50] There appears to have been some support for the articles among from non-Netherlanders, since at the next classis meeting, held on March 3, 1572 in Bedburg, delegates permitted the congregation at Neuss to make a copy of the articles approved at Emden for themselves at their own expense.[51] Still, delegates asked at the following classis meeting whether a pastor might offer a sermon on the content of the Emden articles.[52] A couple of weeks later, on March 15, leaders of Cologne's Dutch-language congregation sent Johannes Christianus, then serving as pastor in Bedburg, to urge his colleagues to sign the articles. Leaders of Cologne's Reformed congregation said that they would respond at the next classis meeting.[53]

The next gathering of the Cologne classis took place that summer, on July 7, 1572, in the town of Venrath, in the duchy of Jülich. Johannes Christianus began with a sermon based on the decisions of the synod held at Emden.[54] The matter appeared to be resolved when delegates ordered members of Cologne's German-language consistory to sign the Emden articles "because they were recognized as right and Christian."[55] But apparently

46 EKAW Gefach 72,1 fols. 10r, 11r–19r.
47 EKAW 72,1 fol. 50r.
48 WMV 1/3, 11, 19, 20–21; Simons, *Kölnische Konsistorial-Beschlüsse*, 36.
49 WMV 1/3, 13, 20–21.
50 WMV 2/2, 8–11.
51 WMV 2/2, 12.
52 WMV 2/5, 11–12. WMW 2/2, 11–12.
53 WMV 1/3, 24–25.
54 WMV 2/5, 16.
55 WMV 2/5, 17.

resistance continued because at the meeting that November in Burtscheid, which Cologne's German-language congregation did not attend, Christianus was asked to write to Caspar Olivianus, theologian at the University of Heidelberg, and Gaspar van der Heyden, pastor at Frankenthal, for advice about the Cologne congregation's unwillingness to sign the articles.[56] We have not yet found such a letter, but the matter seems to have been ignored at the next classis meeting the following spring.[57] When the classis convened again on July 4, 1573, Cologne's German-speaking congregation, for the second time, did not send a delegate. The delegates present again admonished that congregation for its unwillingness to sign the articles.[58] After that, the controversy was simply dropped. In the coming months and years, Cologne's German-language Reformed congregation still participated collegially in classis business, without any sign of lingering acrimony. But its leaders never approved the articles of the Emden synod.[59]

Three years later, some members of the Reformed church at Susteren, also in the classis of Cologne, similarly refused to approve the articles from the synod at Emden. However, they did not bring the controversy back to the classis. Instead, members of the consistory wrote to the Dutch Reformed elders in Wesel—in a different classis altogether. Elders there recommended that Susteren's Reformed Protestants follow the example proposed at Emden, because it is "good enough and has been signed by many wonderful congregations."[60]

We never get any explicit explanation about what aspect of the Emden articles caused concern, though it is notable that only Germans appeared hesitant. We seem to be tracing some kind of strain within the Cologne classes, which was both part of the ecclesiastical structure of the Dutch Reformed Church *and* a multilingual, regional Reformed institution operating in support of the broader evangelical cause in their region of the empire. While similar tensions did not emerge in the classes of Cleves and the Palatinate, the dual function was the same for all three. All three classes included underground, semiclandestine, and public congregations across a range of types of states. They all included German, Dutch, and French speakers. None of

56 WMV 2/5, 23. Leaders of Cologne's German Reformed congregation explained that they did not attend because of the dangers of Catholic troops in the area, though Cologne's Dutch- and French-speaking congregations sent delegates without incident. WMV 3/5, 65–67.

57 WMV 2/2, 24–27.

58 WMV 2/2, 27.

59 In later years, they discussed recommendations made at Emden in their deliberations, but they never recognized them as binding. Simons, *Kölnische Konsistorial-Beschlüsse*, 124.

60 EKAW Gefach 72,2 fols. 45r–46r.

them provided an especially robust support for the Netherlandish Reformed churches before 1572, and none took their cues exclusively, or even primarily, from the Dutch Reformed ecclesiastical system that began forming in 1574. And while Reformed Protestants in the Netherlands were developing ever more standardized terminology and procedures for their classes and provincial synods, members of these classes never developed anything like a provincial synod and did not even standard terminology to describe the classes.[61]

For the most part, meetings of all three classes took place regularly, although uncertain circumstances sometimes forced delays and cancellations. The classes of Cleves and Cologne met twice yearly, except when military threats made such meetings dangerous.[62] The classis of the Palatinate met only once per year but canceled these annual meetings thirteen times between the first assembly in 1572 and the end of our project in 1600.[63] The attendance of individual congregations could also be patchy. The Dutch congregation in Frankfurt, the largest in its jurisdiction, rarely attended the Palatine classis, though it is not clear whether that was disinterest or a strategic decision to avoid drawing attention.[64] Reformed congregations in the small towns of Cleves frequently missed classis meetings because of the threats within their towns or the danger of travel, or because they lacked a pastor.[65] In Cologne, the consistory similarly skipped the classis meeting in 1590 and 1591 because of the dangers of freebooters or capture by "the

61 They were called, variously, "*classische bijencomsten*," *classische versamelinge*," "*classici conventus*," "*classensche synodis*," "*synodus*," "*quartier versammelinge*," and "*quartierkonsistorien*." WMV 2/2, 1, 25, 27, 34, 37, 42, 75, 83. Simons, *Synodalbuch*, 491, 495, 552. The congregations in Aachen also had a body called a *coetus* that involved ministers of the city's three Reformed congregations consulting. It was thus more limited in scope than the bodies with the same name in England and East Friesland. Gorter, *Gereformeerde migranten*, 164. See above, n. 35.

62 In July 1572, members of the classis of Cologne admonished those in the classis of Cleves because they were not meeting at least every three to six months, as recommended by the synod of Emden. WMV 2/2, 17–18. The classis of Cleves did not meet again until January 1574. Simons, *Synodalbuch*, 491–500. After that, it met twice yearly until 1583, when it started meeting only annually. After the May 1586 gathering, the classis of Cleves stopped meeting for six years due to warfare in the duchy. Initially, the classes of Cologne met three times a year, but it decreased to twice yearly in 1575. It cancelled meetings in 1583 and 1588, due to military activities during the Cologne War.

63 Cuno, *Die pfälzischen reformierten Fremdengemeinden*, 22–23.

64 Gorter, *Gereformeerde migranten*, 169–70.

65 See, for example, Simons, *Synodalbuch*, 491.

prince of Jülich's men," who made the road to Aachen unsafe.[66] During the Cologne War (1583–1588), the Dutch consistory of Cologne frequently skipped classis meetings due to unsafe road conditions, "for he who loves danger" they wrote to their colleagues meeting in Aachen in April 1586, "will perish in it."[67] More mundane reasons also led to absences. The Dutch-speaking consistory of Cologne, for instance, skipped its classis meeting in 1589 because it conflicted with the Frankfurt Messe.[68]

A similar tension emerged in 1578, when church leaders in the rebel-held Netherlands organized a large-scale Reformed church meeting planned for that summer to be held in Dordrecht. Frictions emerged because organizers including Petrus Dathenus, Gaspar van der Heyden, and Arent Cornelisz referred to the planned assembly as a "national" synod. Van der Heyden wrote to invite delegates from across Brabant, Holland, Zeeland, and Flanders as well as from the diasporic Dutch-speaking Reformed congregations in the Empire and England. However, he did not send similar invitations to the French- and German-speaking congregations in the classes of Cologne, Cleves, and the Palatinate. As the pastor in Cologne, Cornelis Walraven, pointed out in his response to the invitations, there was no mutually agreed upon explanation for how this new term "national synod" might compare to the "general synod of all Netherlandish churches" recommended at the synod of Emden in 1571.[69] Accordingly, we must ask: Who did organizers of this meeting understand as belonging to their church organization?

It is worth pausing to consider the meaning of the word "national" in a sixteenth-century context.[70] In Dutch, the word *natie* did not hold a single meaning. In general, it referred to a group of people who came from the same place and had a common heritage. However, the term had three more specific connotations. Many sixteenth-century Netherlanders understood their "nation" to be the *territory* they came from, that is, the duchy of Brabant, the county of Flanders, the county of Holland, or otherwise. That is how Netherlandish migrants moving to Wesel organized themselves.[71] That is, in the sixteenth-century Low Countries, regional identities were often more important than countrywide identities.[72] "Nation" could also refer to members of a shared language group, as the Dutch speakers in

66 WMV 1/3, 366.
67 Gorter, *Gereformeerde migranten*, 84–85.
68 Gorter, *Gereformeerde migranten*, 86.
69 Rutgers, *Acta*, 59, 310–13.
70 On this question for the Netherlands generally, Van Sas, *Vaderland*.
71 Spohnholz, *Tactics of Toleration*, 76–77.
72 Duke, "Elusive Netherlands."

Frankfurt who distinguished those of "their nation" from the Walloons.[73] This also appears to be how the pastor of the Dutch-speaking congregation in London, Simeon Ruytinck, meant the term in his 1618 book, the *History and Proceedings That Primarily Concern the Lower German Nation and Congregations Living in England, and in particular in London.*[74] Most inclusively, "nation" could be used to refer to all people with origins in the Netherlands. In Hamburg, the "Netherlandish nation" included Dutch and Walloon speakers who held specific legal and economic privileges in the city.[75]

What did it mean, then, when organizers of the synod to be held in Dordrecht in the summer of 1578 planned a "national synod"? The answer is complicated. The official proceedings claim to be the records of a "National Synod of the Netherlandish Dutch and Walloon churches, both domestic and foreign."[76] There was certainly a sense that they were building on the expansive vision of the synod held in Emden in 1571. They asked delegates, for instance, to consult and approve the articles from that meeting or to suggest changes to the proposed church structure. Surely, Walloon delegates from Hainaut, Artois, and Liège viewed the synod's decisions as applying to them.[77]

And yet, by 1578, there was a growing sense that ecclesiastical organization would be divided by language.[78] Gaspar van der Heyden, in preparing for the meeting, called it a gathering of "*de nederlandtsche duytsche kercke.*"[79] The Walloons also recognized that the synod was for the "Flemish churches," and only selected delegates who spoke "the Flemish language."[80] In their response, the congregations in England also describe the event as being for congregations of the "*Neder-duydschen sprake.*"[81] At the event

73 Meinert and Dahmer, *Das Protokollbuch*, 140–41.

74 Ruytinck, *Gheschiedenissen ende handelingen.*

75 Poettering, *Migrating Merchants*, 53–54, 242–43.

76 Rutgers, *Acta*, 234.

77 They made a French translation of its decisions. *Livre synodal*, 1:43–65. See also Kist, "De Synoden," 184–88.

78 It's possible that this change reflected the fact that so many Dutch elders of the new consistories in the Netherlands lacked the multilingualism common in the migrant communities.

79 Rutgers, *Acta*, 284.

80 See "*Advis du Synode sur les articles resolues à Emden pour estre communiquez à compaignie (assemblée des Eglise flamenge (1)): Afin qu'il en soit arresté au Synode general,*" printed in Kist, "De Synoden," 189. Rutgers, *Acta*, 303. On this point, see Knetsch, "National Synod of Dordrecht." See also Nauta, "De Nationale Synode van Dordrecht."

81 Rutgers, *Acta*, 304–5.

itself, the discussions were held in Dutch, and all records were written in Dutch. There had been a small meeting of the three French-language congregations in Holland and Zeeland the previous year, so there was already some sense that French speakers would organize separately.[82]

The trend toward separating along linguistic lines raised questions for congregations in the trilingual classes of Cleves, Cologne, and the Palatinate. A year before, the Dutch congregation at Frankfurt had also submitted questions to a synod of Walloon congregations held in Dordrecht in 1577, without realizing that the meeting was not intended for them; pastors in the Netherlands simply held the letter until it could be addressed by Dutch-speaking delegates at the next year's "national" synod.[83] The Palatine classis made no mention of any incongruity in their reply to the invitation to the synod of Dordrecht, though they did send, as one of their representatives, Engelbert Faber, a church superintendent in the Palatinate who neither hailed from the Netherlands nor served in a Dutch-speaking church.[84] The classis of Cleves sent, along with the Dutch-speaking pastor Servatius Wijnants, Cornelius Rhetius, an elder of Wesel's Walloon congregation, to represent what elders referred to as the "*duytscher ende walscher gemeijnten*" of the classis at the 1578 synod.[85] There's no evidence that classis leaders meant for the appointments of Faber and Rhetius to represent a critique of the synod. But the contrast provides a useful indication that the three classes operating in the Empire continued to function as multilingual institutions, even if the churches' rebel-held territories were developing a more language-based definition of their church and their activities understandably focused more on matters within the Netherlands.

Members of the classis of Cologne were more explicit in their resentment of the new approach taken by their coreligionists in the Low Countries. As they explained in a sharply written letter, they resented the very concept of a "so-called national synod" (*eens Synodi, ghenoemt nationael*). The idea of a "national synod," explained a frustrated Cornelis Walraven on behalf of the classis, needed justification. The planned assembly at Dordrecht was not really a synod at all, he explained, but just an "extraordinary meeting" (*bysonder versamlung*), since it did not look like one of the three tiers of the hierarchy of synods—general, provincial, classical—recommended at the

82 Knetsch, "National Synod of Dordrecht."

83 Meinert and Dahmer, *Das Protokollbuch*, 164; Knetsch, "National Synod of Dordrecht," 59–67.

84 On Faber, see Schatorjé, "Kirchengeschichtliche Hintergründe," 134–37.

85 Like the other Walloon delegates, Jean Taffin and Guillaume Feugueray, Rhetius spoke and wrote Dutch perfectly well. Rutgers, *Acta*, 308–9.

synod held at Emden.[86] Walraven, then pastor at Cologne, also explained that his classis included not only his own Dutch-speaking congregation but also the French- and German-speaking congregations in Cologne and Aachen, as well as churches across the duchy of Jülich. "We have not yet heard of anyone who has approved such extraordinary meetings," which would meet without representatives of his classis's French- and German-speaking congregations, "but now that we see that those of the Dutch [*Nederduytsche*] or Flemish language follow such an example, we can no longer stay silent about it."[87] Walraven thus painted such a Dutch-language-centered approach as running counter to the multilingual, transnational spirit shared at the synod in Emden.

Meanwhile, in response to their invitation to the "national" synod to be held in Dordrecht, leaders of the Cologne classis replied that they did not possess copies of the articles of the synod of Emden and so could not comment on them. There is reason to be suspicious about this claim.[88] As noted above, members of Cologne's classis disagreed about whether to adopt those articles. We also know that at least one congregation, at Neuss, had a copy of the articles made for their use, and we know that Christianus had preached on them at the classis meeting. Thus, it seems likely that some members of the Cologne classis were familiar with the content of the articles. They may have been prevaricating to hide their unwillingness to accept the authority of the synods in the first place. Regardless, after the "national" synod of Dordrecht, as before, the three classes continued to operate as multilingual bodies, unaffiliated with any political entity.

There were two more "national synods" of the Dutch Reformed churches in the sixteenth century, one at Middelburg in the spring of 1581 and another in The Hague in the summer of 1586. At both, domestic concerns dominated while the foreign congregations played a minor role.[89] At Middelburg in 1581, the only delegate from any of the congregations in the

86 Rutgers, *Acta*, 310–11; Gorter, *Gereformeerde migranten*, 172–73; Knetsch, "National Synod of Dordrecht," 54–55. This question was also raised in the fiercely particularistic city of Gouda, which refused to allow delegates to attend synodal meetings. Hibben, *Gouda in Revolt*, 105.

87 Rutgers, *Acta*, 311.

88 Leaders of the stranger churches in England made the same claim, although Petrus Dathenus had sent a copy of the articles to the Dutch church of London in April 1572. Hessels, *Epistulae et Tractatus*, 2:294–96. But the English churches also declined to come to Dordrecht, given their deference to the bishop of London. Rutgers, *Acta*, 304–6.

89 Rutgers, *Acta*, 339–643; Van Dooren, *De nationale synode te Middelburg*; Hibben, *Gouda in Revolt*, 105–11.

Holy Roman Empire was Johannes Badius from Cologne.[90] Wesel's French- and Dutch-speaking congregations explained that they would not be able to attend, but they did ask for advice.[91] Their request that all responses should be written to them in both Dutch and French provides another reminder that they remained multilingual in their orientation.[92] While Wesel's elders certainly respected the synod's decisions, they did not treat those decisions as the last word. In 1578, Wesel's elders had asked delegates at Dordrecht whether it might be appropriate to use an unleavened wafer instead of table bread in the celebration of the Lord's Supper.[93] Even after receiving an answer, they debated the issue into the following year.[94] Wesel's elders had also asked delegates meeting in Middelburg whether it was permissible to continue appointing women as deaconesses.[95] After they were instructed to stop the practice, they began calling women who performed the same roles "overseers" (*opsienderesse*) or "caretakers of the sick" (*krankenpleegsterssen*), but soon reverted to appointing women deacons.[96] None of the congregations in our study sent delegates to the synod that met in The Hague in 1586; neither did that synod deal with matters brought forward by congregations in the Holy Roman Empire.

In retrospect, the transnational ecclesiastical networks of support that connected the sixteenth-century Dutch migrant communities in the diaspora to coreligionists in the Low Countries were not only relatively weak but also short lived. They began at Emden in 1571, and we can see their last flickers at the synod in Middelburg ten years later. Even during this year, the foreign classes of Cleves, the Palatinate, and Cologne played a relatively small part in the larger story of the Dutch Reformed church, either as leaders or as followers. But they played key roles in supporting the multilingual regional networks of Reformed Protestants in the Empire.

90 The classis of Cologne intended to send an elder from the joint German-Dutch Reformed congregation at Aachen, but there's no indication that happened. WMV 2/2, 99–100.

91 Rutgers, *Acta*, 417, 427–28, 429–30, 457–60.

92 EKAW Gefach 72,2 fol. 229v–230r.

93 Rutgers, *Acta*, 271.

94 EKAW Gefach 72,2 fol. 148.

95 EKAW Gefach 12,5 fol. 42r. Rutgers, *Acta*, 417, 437.

96 Spohnholz, "Olympias and Chrysostem." In 1574, Goch's Reformed congregation named a deaconess, but by 1580 explained that deaconesses were unnecessary because poor people were cared for by "our deacons and other well-meaning women." Van Booma, *Communio clandestina*, 1:231.

The Supply of Pastors

The situation was similar regarding the calling of pastors. It's true that a number of pastors living in Emden were sent to serve the faithful in the rebel-held Netherlands.[97] However, the story looks rather different when we look elsewhere for four reasons. First, we need to understand the supply for Reformed pastors not just in the context of refugee churches supporting the cause back home but also as part of the politics of the Electoral Palatinate. Second, Dutch pastors recruited to serve new Reformed congregations in the rebel-held Low Countries sometimes emerged as opponents of Reformed orthodoxy. Third, congregations in the diaspora also sometimes resented and successfully blocked the recruitment of their pastors to serve new pastorates in the Protestant-controlled Netherlands. Finally, the Dutch Reformed congregations in the Empire spent more time searching for qualified pastors for congregations in their own region than they did helping to staff pulpits back in the Netherlands. In this section, we'll address each of these points.

First, it's true that some pastors in rebel-held Reformed areas in the Netherlands were recruited from positions in the diasporic congregations in the Empire. The three most influential of these, Petrus Dathenus, Gaspar van der Heyden, and Arent Cornelisz, deserve attention. All three men had served in the Dutch church at Frankenthal, and later became key reformers in Ghent, Antwerp, and Delft, respectively. Dathenus and Van der Heyden had been collaborators well before working together in Frankenthal: they served as pastors of the Dutch congregation in Frankfurt for four years before the closure of the Weißfrauenkirche in 1562 convinced them to move to the Palatinate.[98] In 1566–67, both men had actively preached and organized in Flanders and Brabant until the arrival of the duke of Alba forced them to return to Frankenthal. After fleeing the Low Countries, both remained among the most active organizers (along with Philip van Marnix) in promoting coordination among the churches across the diaspora between 1568 and 1571. Van der Heyden (1530–86) ministered in Frankenthal from 1567 to 1574, when he returned to the Low Countries to help organize a synod of congregations in Holland and Zeeland that met in Dordrecht that year. He later became pastor of Middelburg (1574–78) and Antwerp (1578–85) before fleeing the Habsburg reconquest of the southern Netherlands for the Palatine, where Johann Casimir gave him an appointment in 1586

---

97 Pettegree, *Emden*, 71–74; Fitzsimmons, "Building a Reformed Ministry."

98 Gorter, *Gereformeerde migranten*, 141–43. Van der Heyden's presence in Frankfurt goes unmentioned in Scholz, *Strange Brethren*.

in Bacharach, where he died soon after.[99] After organizing in Ghent in 1566/67, Dathenus (c.1531–88) escaped to Frankenthal until 1570, when he became an advisor to the Elector Palatine in Heidelberg. He returned to Ghent in 1578 after the orthodox Reformed took over that city but fled back to Frankenthal the following year after his brand of hardline reform fell out of favor. He returned to Ghent in 1583–84, until again forced to flee following the collapse of Ghent's Reformed republic.[100] For both men, Frankenthal served as a kind of staging ground to build ties between the Dutch Reformed movement and the Palatinate, to find safe harbor in preparation for their next organizing activity, and to provide pastoral care for fellow Dutch refugees.

The profile of Arent Cornelisz (1547–1605) was rather different. Sixteen and seventeen years younger than Van der Heyden and Dathenus, respectively, Cornelisz did not leave for the Holy Roman Empire because of any danger to his life but to pursue an education at the University of Heidelberg in 1565.[101] When the Reformed demonstrations broke out in summer 1566, rather than returning home to preach and organize, he continued his studies abroad, moving to study at the Genevan Academy from 1568 to 1570. When he took his first pastoral post in Frankenthal in 1570, alongside Van der Heyden (after Dathenus began working for Elector Friedrich in Heidelberg), he was again moving from one safe and supportive environment to another. Two years later, on a trip to his hometown of Delft, soon after Orangist victories there allowed the creation of a Reformed church, he became pastor there and retained that post until his death in 1605. While the older Van der Heyden and Dathenus had been refugees multiple times, forging new lives for themselves over and over again, Cornelisz led a more stationary existence. He lived most of his life in his hometown, except when he was getting a university education (which the two other men lacked). He also played a critical role in the first two "national" synods in the Netherlands, and basically every provincial synod in southern Holland until his death. Dathenus and Van der Heyden represented the fluid, mobile, multilingual, and transnational character of the Netherlandish Reformed movement up until the mid-1570s. Cornelisz, by contrast, was part of a growing trend toward domesticating the Netherlandish Reformed movement as a "Dutch" enterprise centered on the United Provinces of the Netherlands from 1572,

99 Cuno, *Die pfälzischen reformierten Fremdengemeinden*, 16–25; Van Lennep, *Gaspar van der Heyden*.

100 Ruys, *Petrus Dathenus*; Van Schelven, "Petrus Dathenus." For the tragic end to his life, see Janssen, "Petrus Dathenus." On Ghent's Reformed republic, see Decavele, *Het Eind van een rebelse droom*.

101 For Cornelisz's early life and education, see Jaanus, *Hervormd Delft*, 94–100.

even if he still understood himself as a part of the European-wide Reformed movement.[102]

What Dathenus, Van der Heyden and Cornelisz did have in common, though, was their time in the Palatinate. Indeed, no other home for Dutch Reformed migrants in our study supplied so many influential pastors for the new Reformed churches in the rebel-held Low Countries. In this respect, it was Cornelisz whose experience is the most representative for pastors in the early Dutch Republic, not his elder colleagues, because he had not fled as a refugee but had studied at the University of Heidelberg. It was that university's training of Reformed pastors, not the refugee churches' role in staffing Dutch pulpits, that proved most influential for Dutch Reformed church building. From 1550 to 1600, some 529 Netherlanders studied at the University of Heidelberg, many of whom returned to the Low Countries to staff churches.[103] The majority of those came, like Cornelisz, in the 1560s or the 1580s. They included prominent Dutch reformers, including Mathaeus de Lannoy, Werner Helmichius, Peter van Aelst, Thomas van Thielt, Jacob Barlaeus, Reginaldus Donteclock, Hendrik van den Corput, Hendrik de Smet, Hugo Donellus, Franciscus Gomarus, and many more. Meanwhile, the migrant congregations in our study had a relatively small impact on staffing of the churches in the early Dutch Republic. Wesel's Reformed community supplied four pastors to churches of the Dutch Republic.[104] Aachen's only supplied two. Five former pastors in Cologne later worked in the Netherlands, though three of these also studied at Heidelberg (and one other was soon dismissed for bad behavior). Nine former pastors in Frankfurt later worked in the Republic, but eight of these had also studied at the University of Heidelberg or worked elsewhere in the Palatinate.[105]

Germans who studied at the University of Heidelberg also later became pastors in the Low Countries, including ten men from the Palatinate identified by Fred van Lieburg, as well as twelve recruited by Johann Casimir to serve in Guelders identified by Christiaan Ravensbergen.[106] Van Lieburg does not provide complete numbers for those who studied theology at the

102 We will discuss this further in chapter 6.

103 De Wal, *Nederlanders, studenten te Heidelberg.* On this university as an international center of Reformed learning, see Christoph Strohm, "Die Universität Heidelberg."

104 Martinus Janssen (who became pastor in Delft), Lieven Massis (who later became pastor in Middelburg), Abraham Musenhole (who took a post in Breda), and Pierre Moreau (who served as pastor of the Walloon congregation at Delft).

105 Gorter, *Gereformeerde migranten*, 187–88, 190–91.

106 Van Lieburg, *Profeten en hun vaderland*, 226; Ravensbergen, "Language Barrers," in Soen, Soetaert, Verberckmoes, and François, *Transregional*

Figure 5.1. Dutch students at the University of Heidelberg, 1550–1600.

University of Heidelberg, but he identifies ninety-one German pastors who served in Dutch Reformed parishes from 1572 to 1599, many of whom surely studied at Heidelberg.[107] Language barriers sometimes proved a barrier to this transnational supply of pastors. But in many cases the Germans were able to provide much needed spiritual care to vastly understaffed parishes in the Low Countries, especially after the death of Elector Friedrich III; the succession of his Lutheran son Ludwig VI in 1578 meant that the job market collapsed for Reformed pastors in most of the Palatinate.

The Palatinate also provided theological training for pastors in the migrant congregations in our study. More than half of the pastors who served Cologne's and Frankfurt's Dutch Reformed congregations had been trained at Heidelberg, or at the Casimirianum, founded in Neustadt in 1578 by Johann Casimir after his Lutheran brother became Elector Palatine.[108] Thus, while previous historians have stressed the role of refugee churches in helping to staff the newly opened Reformed congregations in the United Provinces, far more important was the role of the University of Heidelberg. And most of the students at Heidelberg were not refugees but more conventional participants in the *peregrinatio academica*.[109]

Second, some of the pastors who moved from Dutch migrant centers to take pastoral positions in the newly independent United Provinces emerged as central critics and thorns in the side of orthodox reformers. We have previously noted that this was the case for Hubert Duifhuis, who had fled to Cologne; Herman Herberts, who worked as a pastor in a civic parish in Wesel from 1571 to 1577; and Caspar Coolhaes, who fled Deventer for the Empire in 1567, serving as pastor in Essen and Mönsheim. All three men became prominent "libertines" in the early Dutch Republic and had public conflicts with leading Reformed pastors.[110] It was also true for Petrus Bloccius, who had served as a pastor in Niedermörmter (a noble enclave within the duchy of Cleves), had lived in Wesel and Rees, and later became pastor in Lier, Brabant. Like Duifhuis and Herberts, Bloccius was a spiritualist

---

Reformations, 354–55. Some financial aid to support these pastors came from the Lutheran landgrave of Hesse-Kassel. Ruys, *Petrus Dathenus*, 123.

107 Van Lieburg, *Profeten en hun vaderland*, 198.

108 Gorter, *Gereformeerde migranten*, 187–88.

109 On this tradition in the German-speaking lands, see Irrgang, *Peregrinatio academica*. Because there were so few Reformed universities, the *peregrinatio academica* was particularly common for sixteenth-century Reformed Protestants. Murdock, *Beyond Calvin*, 41–45.

110 Van Veen and Spohnholz, "Calvinists vs. Libertines." For Duifhuis, see Kaplan, *Calvinists and Libertines*. For Herberts, see Van den Berg, "Herman Herberts"; Plaizier, *Herman Herbers*; Hibben, *Gouda in Revolt*. For Coolhaes, Kooi, *Liberty and Religion*.

who rejected requiring the signing of confessional statements, which he saw as a hindrance to true faith, not a path toward it.[111] Others in these migrant communities who spread spiritualist views included the minister of Goch, Godfried Loeffs, and the elder in Wesel, Pieter de Zuttere, both of whom promoted the ideas of Sebastian Franck and other radical authors.[112] In 1574, De Zuttere moved to Rotterdam to take a pastoral position, but he was soon run out of town by orthodox reformers.[113] In some cases, migrant centers were not seedbeds for orthodoxy, but petri dishes of religious heterodoxy, as Nicole Grochowina has argued was the case for Emden.[114] To be clear, most Reformed pastors and elders in these migrant communities strove to eliminate Anabaptist, spiritualist, and anti-Trinitarian ideas from within their ranks. But it would be wrong to conclude that preachers coming from these Dutch migrant communities always promoted the spread of Reformed orthodoxy. In some cases, they did the opposite.

Third, at times migrant churches even opposed efforts to recruit pastors for the United Provinces from their ranks (a point we will return to in chapter 6). In 1574, when Dordrecht's consistory proposed hiring the Dutch schoolmaster in Wesel, Gerardus Larenius, Wesel's elders refused, explaining that their need for Larenius's work was greater than the need in Holland.[115] Soon after, Wesel's elders helped Larenius take a pastoral position in a newly formed congregation in Emmerich.[116] In October 1576, the Reformed congregation in Gorkum, in southern Holland, asked that Maastricht's exiled church in Aachen send their pastor, Johannes Huckelum, to help them build their congregation in the "fatherland."[117] Members of the church at Gorkum appealed to article thirty-five of the synod at Emden (actually they appealed to article thirty-four, but they got their numbering off), which suggests that "pastors who originate from the Netherlands" (*Ministri Belgio oriundi*) who have taken positions abroad (*exteris*) should heed calls to serve the churches in the Netherlands.[118] But the Reformed Protestants in Aachen declined. In his letter refusing this request on behalf of his classis, Johannes

111 In the nineteenth century, Bloccius was romanticized as representing the tolerant "Dutch" spirit. Kist, "Petrus Bloccius."

112 Van Booma, *Communio clandestina*, 1:231; Sepp, *Drie evangeliedienaren*, 81–122.

113 Rogghé, "Pieter Anastasius de Zuttere"; Ten Boom, *De reformatie in Rotterdam*, 162–63.

114 Grochowina, *Indifferenz und Dissens*.

115 EKAW Gefach 72,1 fol. 55r–v.

116 Schipper, "Across the Borders of Belief," 129, 155.

117 Gorter, *Gereformeerde migranten*, 174–75.

118 Rutgers, *Acta*, 74.

Christianus argued that Aachen's Reformed community was larger and growing and needed to maintain pastoral care for its members. He also argued that it was inaccurate to describe Huckelum as originating from the Netherlands, since he was born in the duchy of Guelders *before* it became part of the Habsburg Netherlands under the Treaty of Venlo in 1543.[119] Aachen's Reformed Protestants had supported needy coreligionists as needed, Christianus argued. But this request simply went too far. The Palatinate was sending pastors to help staff Dutch churches, but even the pious Elector Friedrich III would not abandon his own congregations to do so![120]

The next year, we find two more cases. In the first, the church at Dordrecht hired Servatius Wijnants from under the nose of the five small congregations he was serving in Cleves.[121] Originally, in October 1577 the classis of Cleves had just loaned Wijnants to the Reformed congregation in Eindhoven.[122] Since he was already in the Netherlands, the classis also encouraged him to attend the synod held in Dordrecht in July 1578.[123] Wijnants never returned to Cleves. Instead, immediately following the closure of that assembly, he took a permanent position in Dordrecht.[124] Wesel's elders grew angry. Not only had Dordrecht hired Wijnants without consulting the classis of Cleves—as Wesel's elders put it, "not without great scandal and shame"—the congregation at Emmerich had funded his journey to Brabant and Holland in the first place. They called for the return of Wijnants, or at the very least repayment of his travel costs.[125] That same year, the Reformed congregation at Brussels asked the Dutch-speaking congregation at Frankfurt to send Werner Helmichius "to strengthen those brothers" and to "help plant the Word of God among them." But Reformed elders in Frankfurt said they would refuse the request unless their coreligionists found a replacement and a means to pay the substitute's salary. After all, they argued, they could not reasonably sacrifice the spiritual care of their own congregation.[126] The following year, Dathenus found a replacement, Martinus Lydius, and the elders in Frankfurt agreed to loan Helmichius out. This may not have been the best deal for them, however, because Helmichius never returned. And as, within a year, Lydius had moved to Amsterdam, Frankfurt's Dutch Reformed congregation was again in search of a new pastor.

119 Simons, "Ein rheinisches Synodalschreiben."

120 Christianus had no way of knowing that Friedrich III had died two days earlier.

121 Schipper, "Across the Borders of Belief," 110, 111, 129.

122 EKAW Gefach 72,2 48r. Simons, *Synodalbuch*, 533.

123 Rutgers, *Acta*, 308–9.

124 Jensma, *Uw Rijk kome*, 114, 116.

125 EWKA Gefach 72,2 fols. 155v–156v.

126 Gorter, *Gereformeerde migranten*, 173–74.

A final case emerged in 1578, after the newly appointed stadholder of Guelders, Count Johann of Nassau-Dillenburg requested that Johannes Badius—then pastor of Cologne's German-language Reformed congregation and like his predecessor Christianus, a native of Jülich—become his court preacher.[127] For Count Johann, Badius was a sensible option. The deeply Reformed prince needed a Reformed pastor who spoke High German, since Johann spoke no Dutch. Badius was one of several German pastors trained at Heidelberg whom Johann had recruited to serve in Guelders. However, Cologne's congregation declined to give up their pastor to the Nassau prince.[128] Clearly, when it came to pastoral staffing the Dutch Reformed congregations in the Empire did not primarily envision themselves as refugee congregations seeking to build up Christ's true church in the "fatherland."

The Dutch Reformed congregations and classes in the Empire spent more of their attention trying to staff their own congregations and those in their region. Wesel's elders, for instance, devoted considerable attention to helping nearby congregations secure pastoral care. After the small congregations who shared the pastor Nicolaus Pancratius fired him in 1579 because his travel was gaining too much attention, elders in Wesel tried to hire a German minister trained at the University of Heidelberg, Erasmus Lauterbach, to replace him.[129] The following year, they found a pastor to serve congregations at Büderich, Orsoy, and Xanten, though congregants at Xanten did not approve of the candidate, and the other towns could not afford his salary on their own.[130] In 1581, Wesel's elders successfully arranged for a new minister, Paschasius Aquiensis to come from Aachen to serve congregations in Goch, Gennep, Emmerich, Rees, Kalkar, and Zevenaer.[131] More than once Wesel's elders urged smaller congregations in Cleves to put up with a pastor they did not approve of, in part because finding a replacement proved so challenging.[132] When Pieter Hazaert complained in May 1588 at the classis of Cleves about the lack of pastoral care in his community, the elder in Wesel, Gillis van Musenhole, promised to send his son Abraham to serve that role.[133] Similarly the Dutch-speaking congregation in Cologne was often

---

127 Nauta, "De Nationale Synode van Dordrecht," 47.

128 Rutgers, *Acta*, 332–33; Ravensbergen, "Language Barrers," in Soen et al., *Transregional Reformations*, 341 n.32.

129 EKAW Gefach 72, 2 fols. 222r–223v. Instead, Lauterbach took a post in Werth, in the prince-bishopric of Münster. Luebke, *Hometown Religion*, 125.

130 EKAW Gefach 72,2 fol. 180v.

131 EKAW Gefach 72,2 fols. 235r–v.

132 EKAW Gefach 72,2 fol. 217r, fol. 254r–v. Schipper, "Across the Borders of Belief," 131–32.

133 His son never arrived in Emmerich, though he later served as a pastor in Frankenthal. Cuno, *Geschichte der wallonisch- und französisch-reformirten*

on the hunt for a new pastor, given the risks inherent to that job.[134] The German- and Dutch-speaking Reformed congregations at Cologne often had to share pastors, which could lead to disagreements about finances.[135] The same was true between the French- and Dutch-speaking congregations at Frankfurt.[136] Aachen's Reformed congregation also loaned a pastor to serve fellow believers in Cologne in 1572.[137] Congregations tried to spread the Gospel in other communities, but their priority was not necessarily the Low Countries. At the meeting of the Cologne classis at Birkersdorf (in the duchy of Jülich) in 1573, delegates sent the pastor Cornelis Walraven to help set up congregations in Düsseldorf and Essen "where many good people are who do not want to find themselves in superstition."[138] In all, these congregations did not play major roles in supporting or building up the Reformed churches in the Netherlands. Instead, they spent more time protecting their congregations in unstable and uncertain conditions and supporting coreligionists in their regions.

Charitable Giving

We see a similar focus on local and regional concerns in these Dutch migrant congregations when it came to charitable giving. These congregations tended to support one another and others in their regional and transregional networks within the Empire, while—insofar as we can tell—they never received charity assistance from congregations in the Netherlands, where congregations remained short staffed and under-resourced. Cologne's Dutch-speaking congregation, which included many wealthy merchants, often took the lead in providing financial assistance to others in the Reformed diaspora. On October 29, 1571, pastors of Cologne's Dutch congregation urged church members to give generously (*liberalich*) to support poor coreligionists in Wesel.[139] While congregations proved unable to collect a substantial sum that year, due to difficulties faced by their own congregation, the following year, Cologne's congregation sent a generous 25 *daler*.[140] In

---

Gemeinde zu Wesel, 24. On the theological career of Gillis's son, see chapter 6.

134 WMV 1/3, 13, 19, 25, 40. Gorter, *Gereformeerde migranten*, 80.

135 WMV 2/2, 30. Simons, *Niederrheinisches Synodal- und Gemeideleben*, 56; Gorter, *Gereformeerde migranten*, 165–66.

136 Gorter, *Gereformeerde migranten*, 167–68.

137 WMV 2/2, 14.

138 WMV 3/5, 79; WMV 2/2, 30; Gorter, *Gereformeerde migranten*, 169–70.

139 WMV 1/3, 10.

140 WMV 3/5, 26, 55–57.

December 1577, Wesel's elders wrote to the Dutch-speaking congregation of Cologne for another gift and asked whether the German-speaking congregation there might give some too.[141] In January 1579, they again wrote to Cologne's Dutch-speaking congregation to get help supporting impoverished Reformed refugees there.[142] Cologne's Dutch congregation responded by sending three Hungarian ducats, two Portuguese half real coins, two sovereign crowns, four royal *daler*, and one imperial *daler*.[143] In November 1587, the Dutch Reformed in Cologne gave yet another gift of thirty-seven gold guilders to their comrades in Wesel—then suffering a more than year-long siege. As they wrote:

> Because we believe in a community of the Saints, who together are members of one body under one head, Jesus Christ, that calls to a common father in heaven, who are in one church, who are baptized with one baptism, who are governed with one spirit, like members of one body with one soul.[144]

Peter Gorter estimates that Cologne's Dutch congregation spent two-thirds of its charity expenditures on other Dutch Reformed congregations in the diaspora, including at Wesel, Frankfurt, Aachen, and Frankenthal.[145] The only time that Cologne's Dutch congregation ever sought financial support was in 1586, when it faced the twin crises of the Cologne War and floods of refugees fleeing Alexander Farnese's conquest of Antwerp. In March of that year, that consistory wrote to Frankenthal for help "during this sorrowful and dreadful time."[146]

By contrast, Wesel's Dutch Reformed community proved to be the largest charitable receiver in our study. Besides cash, Cologne's Dutch congregation sent other provisions, including food, clothing, and firewood, at the request of Wesel's Reformed elders. As they wrote to their coreligionists in Cologne in March 1579, "Because our poor are still numerous and the most prominent of our church have left, we have little means to care for our poor."[147] At that time, Wesel's consistory also requested charity from coreligionists in Frankenthal, Hamburg, London, and Stade.[148] Frankfurt's Dutch Reformed congregation similarly held collections for Wesel in 1572 and again during

141 EKAW Gefach 72,2 fol. 72r.

142 EKAW Gefach 72,2 fol. 124r–v.

143 WMV 3/5, 90.

144 WMV 3/5, 123. EKAW Gefach 72,3 57.

145 Gorter, *Gereformeerde migranten*, 177; WMV 1/3, 40, 73, 241; WMV 3/5 53–55, 83–84, 87–88.

146 WMV 3/5, 95.

147 Quoted in Spohnholz, *Tactics of Toleration*, 92.

148 EKAW Gefach 72,2 fol. 27r.

the siege of that city in 1587 and 1588.[149] Wesel's elders and deacons drew financial support for their needy from well beyond the Dutch migrants congregations in this study. On a few occasions, they received financial support from stranger churches in England. In November 1571, Southampton's French-speaking congregation sent £3 to help Wesel's impoverished refugees.[150] In 1577, the Walloon congregation in Canterbury sent £5 to Wesel to alleviate the poverty there.[151] Far more often, though, they turned to sympathetic nobles in the region around Wesel, including Hermann von Neuenahr (count of Moers), Walburgis von Neuenahr (countess of Alpen), and Gotthard of Myllendonk (Lord of Goor).[152] In September 1575, they received a generous gift to the poor and needy of Wesel from the church of Bedburdyck, a small noble enclave within the duchy of Jülich belonging to the Neuenahr family.[153] By contrast, the only charitable gift Wesel's consistory ever recorded receiving from the Netherlands did not come from a congregation but from an individual living in Dordrecht, who had probably once lived in Wesel, who left money for Wesel's poor in his will in 1574.[154] Wesel's consistory clearly understood that they were part of a community of giving as well as receiving. In March 1579, just as Wesel's elders were writing desperate letters asking for assistance as refugees were streaming into the city following a string of Habsburg military victories in the Netherlands, they also send one hundred *daler* to Aachen's church for assistance as refugees from Maastricht who were also fleeing into that city.[155]

The Habsburg army's siege of Wesel from 1586 to 1590 led to a wave of contributions to that community. As the second year of the siege began, Wesel's elders wrote impassioned pleas for charity in the face of a massive death toll due to plague and hunger. In March 1587, they wrote to churches in Amsterdam, Dordrecht, and Leiden, as well as to the diasporic congregations in Emden, Bremen, Cologne, Frankfurt, and elsewhere.[156] While they did not receive responses from the Dutch Republic (for reasons yet unknown), gifts poured in from across the diaspora in the Empire. As noted before, donations arrived from Cologne late in 1587 and from Frankfurt in

149 Gorter, *Gereformeerde migranten*, 177.
150 Spicer, *French-speaking Reformed Community*, 129.
151 Muylaert, *Shaping the Stranger Churches*, 209.
152 EKAW Gefach 72,2 fols. 41r, 47v, 48r–v 65v–67v, 70r–71v, 93r, 163v, 165r–v.
153 EKAW Gefach 72,2 fol. 10r.
154 EKAW Gefach 72,1 36v.
155 EKAW, Gefach 72,2 157r. Van Booma and Van der Gouw, *Communio et mater fidelium*, 80–81. For examples of similar collections among stranger churches in England, see Spicer, *French-speaking Reformed Community*, 113.
156 EKAW Gefach 72,3 15–19, 20–21.

1587 and 1588.[157] Hamburg's Dutch Reformed community also sent an impressive three hundred *daler* in 1589, two-thirds of which was earmarked for the Dutch-speaking consistory and one-third of which was designated for Wesel's Walloons.[158] The Reformed church at Stade, just outside Hamburg, also provided a charitable contribution to Wesel's Reformed community in 1589.[159] Elders also sought assistance from wealthy individuals who had once lived in their community, including the longtime elders Jacques van der Haghen and Steffen Wolters.[160] After the devastating siege ended, elders wrote to the Dutch-speaking church of London for more help dealing with all the hungry people and orphaned children.[161]

Dutch Reformed congregations also collected funds for coreligionists across Europe, including in France, Switzerland, the Empire, and the Netherlands. Between 1571 and 1591, Frankfurt's Dutch-speaking congregation held collections for coreligionists facing hardship in Antwerp and Brussels but also Sedan, Geneva, and Wetzlar. During that same period, Cologne's Dutch-speaking congregations collected for coreligionists in Brussels, Antwerp, and Maastricht, but also Neuss, Geneva, and Roermond.[162] That is, while they did see themselves as part of a family of the faithful that included coreligionists in the Netherlands, that family was part of a universal community of Christians, not one limited to the "fatherland."

This generosity was not limitless. In 1573, when the Reformed congregation in Antwerp asked the Dutch-language congregation at Cologne for financial support for impoverished members and to pay the church's debts, the elders in Cologne did not hold a collection but instead simply forwarded their request to the German-speaking congregation in the city and the one in Duisburg. Frankfurt's consistory did not respond to the same request.[163] In 1580, five years after Wesel's refugees received a generous gift from the

157 EKAW Gefach 72,3 57. Gorter, *Gereformeerde migranten*, 176–77.

158 Spohnholz, *Tactics of Toleration*, 92; Norwood, *Reformation Refugees*, 10.

159 EKAW Gefach 72,3 131–32. Another gift arrived from some source whose name is undecipherable. Gefach 72,3 135–36.

160 EKAW Gefach 72,3 120–22.

161 EKAW Gefach 72,3 159–61.

162 Gorter, *Gereformeerde migranten*, 178. On parallel collections in England, see Charles Littleton, "The Strangers, their Churches and the Continent: Continuing and Changing Connextions," in Goose and Luu, *Immigrants*, 185–87; Muylaert, *Shaping the Stranger Churches*, 191, 219.

163 Meinert and Dahmer, *Das Protokollbuch*, 23; WMV 1/3, 58; Simons, *Kölnische Konsistorial-Beschlüsse*, 62. Three years later, Cologne's German-speaking congregation did make a collection to support Antwerp's Reformed community. Simons, *Kölnische Konsistorial-Beschlüsse*, 108–9, 125. For cases of the English stranger churches refusing to support requests for aid from coreligionists

congregation at Bedburdyck, the pastor there declined to provide further support.[164] In 1593, Antwerp's congregation wrote to Frankfurt's Dutch-speaking congregation to ask them to support the theological training of future ministers. Frankfurt's consistory turned them down but suggested that the congregations in Aachen and Hamburg might prove willing to help.[165] There are no indications that these rejections reflect hostility, mistrust, or a lack of support. But they do underscore the fact that the migrant congregations had priorities that they had to balance. It's also critical to remember that sharing charity across the diaspora was not just a matter of exchanging economic resources, but also a symbolic and performative act that reinforced mutual bonds of allegiance between givers and receivers.[166]

Dutch Reformed migrant congregations in the Empire supported one another not only financially but also by providing direct care for orphans. In December 1571, the elder in Cologne, Gillis de Schepper, brought recently orphaned children of his congregation to Wesel, to be cared for by deacons of the Dutch-language community there.[167] Two weeks later, the consistory sent the children of Joris de Greve, a tapestry maker from in or around Oudenaarde, thirteen-year-old Francijnken and seven-year-old Antoonken, to Frankenthal to be cared for by another tapestry maker, Everard van Heist from Brussels.[168] After Peter Eckberg died in the Spanish siege of Maastricht in 1579, his wife and children fled to Aachen. When his wife died the following year, Aachen's Reformed congregation sent them to live with their grandmother in Wesel.[169] In February 1590, Wesel's elders asked the church in Frankenthal to care for two sixteen-year-old orphaned girls whose parents had likely died as a result of starvation or disease during the siege of Wesel.[170] The following year, Wesel's Dutch Reformed elders coordinated moving another orphan to Cologne, though this time Cologne's Dutch-speaking elders reprimanded them because the child seems to have been badly disabled, and thus care would be both expensive and make it harder for members of Cologne's clandestine congregation to hide from Catholic

on the continent, see Muylaert, *Shaping the Stranger Churches*, 198; Spicer, *French-speaking Reformed Community*, 129–30.

164 EKAW Gefach 72,2 fol. 231v–232v.

165 Gorter, *Gereformeerde migranten*, 174.

166 Monge and Muchnik, *Early Modern Diasporas*, 72–78.

167 WMV 1/3, 17.

168 WMV 1/3, 17–18. The records do not indicate that Joris de Greve was deceased, but that seems likely in this case.

169 After the grandmother died, Wesel's Reformed deacons found local caretakers for the children. Spohnholz, *Tactics of Toleration*, 93.

170 EKAW Gefach 72,3 133–34. Spohnholz, *Tactics of Toleration*, 93.

authorities.[171] Cologne's elders made it clear that Wesel's elders should not take advantage of offers of mutual assistance, "because it is not an appropriate custom that one church should send the burden of their poor to another, but that each [church] should take good care of their own poor." Their response reminds us that historians should be careful about only emphasizing congregations' generosity and mutual aid, at the risk of romanticizing the bonds of "international Calvinism."

Despite the chastising tone of Cologne's Dutch Reformed elders, in fact they did rely on other congregations to care for orphans within their own ranks. They sent orphans to Wesel and Frankenthal, for instance.[172] When, in March 1574, they sent the orphaned son of Peter de Zee to be cared for by the Dutch-speaking congregation in Frankfurt—they provided some indication of how they understood this situation. They explained that the boy misbehaved badly and openly in the streets, which brought unwanted attention to their congregation. At Frankfurt, they reasoned, because the Reformed congregation was safer, guardians would be able to "punish such bad behavior with words and also with rods."[173]

Attestations and Correspondence

A fourth way to understand networks that developed among these diasporic congregations is to examine their correspondence. Letters allowed ministers and elders to give and receive advice and to exchange information, money, and goods to help the poor or build up Christ's church. The surviving correspondence from these communities—the most robust collection of which comes from Wesel—reveals extensive regional, transregional, and transnational coordination across the diaspora. Consistory members wrote many letters to pastors and elders in the Netherlands, the Empire, and England, for instance, seeking to hunt down husbands who had abandoned their wives, or otherwise to inquire into the behavior and misbehavior of migrants.[174] They sought advice on all manner of subjects. Leaders in the largest congregations used correspondence to organize classis meetings or, as noted above, to hire pastors. They also resolved conflicts within and between regional congregations, as Wesel's elders did with a congregational schism surrounding the noblewomen Clara van der Dilft (i.e., the Lady of Arnhem) in Goch from

171 WMV 3/5, 130–33.

172 Gorter, *Gereformeerde migranten*, 176.

173 WMV 3/5, 81.

174 For example, EKAW Gefach 72,2 fols. 96v–97r, 115r–v, 219r, 146v. Spohnholz, "Instability and Insecurity."

1570 to 1577.[175] Elders also offered informal advice to one another on specific matters.[176] And, as we have seen, they exchanged letters with local noblemen and noblewomen who served as their patrons. Elders and pastors in the congregations in our study participated in transnational religious networks that included the Netherlands, as well as other areas of Europe. But they were just as engaged regionally, with the congregations of their classes, and transregionally, among the networks that developed between diasporic churches in the Empire.

Written attestations of a believer's true faith and Christian conduct became a critical form of correspondence for elders across the diaspora. Ministers and elders would write to certify the faith and behavior of a church member who was moving, explaining to the home community the reason for that migration and describing specific circumstances relating to their case. Developing such a system of tracking individuals across the diaspora, recall, had been a chief motivating factor for Philip van Marnix and Gaspar van der Heyden to start organizing transnational cooperation in 1570, efforts that led to the synod in Emden the following year. At that meeting, delegates recommended:

> in order to reduce the heavy burdens on the churches that grow larger daily from the recklessness of those who too easily move from place to place ... that in each and every church it is proclaimed that those who leave from there... have an attestation or testimonial about how they conduct themselves in belief and conduct in the church that they are coming from.[177]

Attestations should include the traveler's name, hometown, occupation, reason for traveling, and the proposed length of stay. The danger that primarily concerned delegates at Emden was not just the contamination of the church of God with unbelievers, but that unfaithful migrants would pretend to be godly in order to get charity, thereby "draining off alms for the faithful [*huysghenooten des Gheloofs*]."[178] From the perspective of migrants, such attestations acted as letters of reference of their godliness, smoothing over their incorporation into a Reformed community. From the perspective of pastors and elders, attestations constituted a system of coordination across the diaspora, ensuring the spiritual, fiscal, and communal integrity of

175 Schipper, "Across the Borders of Belief," 95–108. Wesel's elders also intervened to resolve disputes that plagued the congregations at Hörstgen in 1576 and Xanten in 1581. EKAW Gefach 72,2 49r, fols. 231r–v.

176 Emmerich's elders wrote to Wesel in March 1578 to ask whether it was permissible for a certain widower to marry his brother-in-law's widow. EKAW Gefach 72,2 fol. 84v.

177 Rutgers, *Acta*, 81.

178 Rutgers, *Acta*, 81.

their ecclesiastical system of church discipline. Andrew Pettegree explained that, for the Reformed congregation at Emden, using attestations in this way ensured that the strict system of ecclesiastical discipline so valued by Reformed Protestants could be maintained among migrants, "since without a valid letter of recommendation ... they would not be able to join the Church in any other Reformed community."[179]

Considering how mobile members of these communities were, of course, such monitoring proved helpful for elders. Consider, for example, Jan Mondekins, a Reformed Protestant from Oudenaarde, who fled to Aachen in 1558. Within two years, Mondekens had moved to Frankfurt. Two years after that, he moved to Frankenthal. He stayed in Frankenthal until at least April 1574. In January 1577, he was living in Cologne, but this is where we lose track of him.[180] With such mobile lives, elders struggled to keep track of whether new members had properly married or baptized their children, submitted to consistorial discipline, or whether they had a reputation for trustworthiness and piety. When Gillis Vogelsank and his wife Sibille moved from Frankfurt to Wesel in the autumn of 1581, they got a recommendation from their former pastor, Gilich Ubrecht. After reading the letter attesting that they were properly married and upstanding members of their former congregation, Wesel's elders accepted the couple as full members without further questions.[181] Conversely, elders also refused to write attestations when they could not provide a positive assessment of a person's belief and conduct. In May 1576, for instance, Wesel's elders refused Peter Zeebeke's request for an attestation because he had lived there for such a short time that they could not honestly speak for his faith.[182] They also denied Jan van Erkelens an attestation in December 1587 because no suitable witness could testify to his godly belief and behavior.[183] To further improve the effectiveness of their monitoring, Wesel's elders also decided, in September 1576, to collect all the attestations that newcomers brought to them in a book, which could then be consulted when writing attestations if that person moved again.[184]

In practice, however, letters of attestation seemed to have worked differently. When newcomers did not have an attestation, consistories might write back to their former home or try to find someone locally who could speak

179 Pettegree, *Emden*, 49–50.
180 DNRM-AC-148. DNRM-FR-828. DNRM-FL-62. DNRM-CO-146.
181 EKAW Gefach 72,2 246v.
182 EKAW Gefach 72,2 21r.
183 EKAW Gefach 72,3 52.
184 EKAW Gefach 72,2 fol. 36v.

on their behalf.[185] In other cases, it was consistory members who did not live up to the ideal. In the summer of 1574, Frankenthal's elders admonished the Dutch elders in Cologne for not preparing a letter of attestation for one of their church members, Adriaen de Brienen, from Brussels, who moved to Frankenthal.[186] In November 1573, Wesel's elders wrote to the Reformed congregation in Duisburg, explaining that they could not accept an attestation that elders there had written for Jan van Maele because it was not written according to the standards required by the synod of Emden.[187] Four years later, Wesel's elders warned the consistory in Dordrecht that they should no longer accept anyone moving from Wesel to that city without an attestation from them.[188] In 1580, elders in Cologne's Dutch Reformed congregation investigated how Wilhelm Krayen, formerly a member of their church, managed to marry in the Reformed congregation of Aachen without getting an attestation from them.[189] It is also important to admit that, even with all good intentions, congregations might have proved unable to exchange letters due to the risk of Catholic political authorities capturing them and thereby endangering the congregations themselves.

The best records we have of attestations for our project come from the records of the Dutch Reformed consistory in Wesel, which included transcriptions of elders' correspondence, including 130 attestations written between November 1573 and November 1590.[190] We cannot be confident that this list is comprehensive, of course. After all, there are cases in which the consistory's scribe failed to record the arrival or departure of someone in the community.[191] Still, this is the most comprehensive collection of attestation letters of any of the migrant congregations in our study, providing a useful window into the monitoring of belief and behavior across the diaspora.

The first thing to notice about these letters of attestation is that there were three different kinds of documents. The first were those written to the

185 For people arriving without attestations, see below, for example, in Frankenthal, Edgard J. Hürkey, "Kunst, Kommerz, Glaubenskampf—Frankenthal um 1600," in Hürkey, *Kunst, Kommerz, Glaubenskampf*, 12.

186 WMV 1/3, 69.

187 Wesel's elders expected that Duisburg's elders should have interviewed one of Van Maele's housemates. EKAW Gefach 72,1 fols. 50r–51r.

188 EKAW Gefach 72,1 fol. 34v.

189 WMV 1/3, 140.

190 There are no surviving records from the consistory before this point, and none for the years 1583, 1584, or 1585.

191 That is why it is inappropriate to estimate membership size by lists of attestations for departing members and mentions of new members, as in Dünnwald, *Konfessionsstreit und Verfassungskonflikt*, 115–20. On this problem in consistory records, see Pollmann, "Off the Record."

consistory of a specific community to which a migrant intended to move, just like those recommended by delegates at the synod of Emden—our research found a total of fifty-seven such letters. Fifteen (25 percent) of these were sent to other Dutch congregations in the Empire. The remaining forty-two letters of this type were for Netherlanders moving to the provinces of Holland and Zeeland (mostly in the early 1570s) and to the provinces of Brabant and Flanders (mostly in the late 1570s and early 1580s). These kinds of letters offer elders the greatest measure of oversight of migrants' behavior and belief. After all, once the migrant left Wesel, he or she could not change destinations without raising suspicions. Often these letters also provided valuable information about the reason for travel, such as the letter that Wesel's elders wrote on behalf of Jan Kools, from Leuven, to travel to Antwerp in October 1578, hoping to earn a better living as a silk weaver.[192]

A second kind of letter consisted of open-ended letters from Wesel's elders to wherever a migrant might end up—our study included forty-nine such letters. These letters served a somewhat different purpose. A church member might bring one with them to a variety of locations, and thus the document might prove useful so long as the paper and ink maintained their integrity. These letters were often more general in nature, usually attesting to a person's church membership and good conduct but less likely to indicate the reasons for travel. Thus the attestation for Jan van Nuce from May 3, 1580, only states that he was "a member of our church, pure in the faith, upright in his comportment and in his work," without indicating where he might be heading or why.[193] Similarly open-ended is the letter from May 1589 for the carpenter Willem Pauwels and his wife, "who have lived here for a long time and have carried themselves as members of the church" but are "of the opinion to leave here."[194] These letters helped ensure the integrity of the Christian community across congregations with very mobile populations, but they granted more flexibility to migrants as to where and how they might use such recommendations.

The third type of letter of attestation was written for short-term trips. The three surviving letters of this sort were not written to help the traveler integrate into a new home but served as a kind of safe-conduct passport (though only for those few authorities who recognized Wesel's Reformed consistory as legitimate).[195] One example is the recommendation written for Henrich

192 EKAW Gefach 72,2 fol. 111. Van Booma and Van der Gouw, *Communio et mater fidelium*, 402–3.

193 EKAW Gefach 72,2 183r. Van Booma and Van der Gouw, *Communio et mater fidelium*, 494.

194 EKAW Gefach 72,3 114.

195 On passports (letters of passage) and safe-conduct, see Scholz, *Borders*.

van Bijpen, a merchant heading to Emden to buy cheese and butter in the summer of 1574. The consistory testified to his piety and honesty—and that he had never acted against "the honorable prince of Orange." Such letters would not have proven useful for Van Bijpen within the duchy of Cleves, but may have helped down the Rhine in Dordrecht, where he probably planned to get sea transport to Emden.

There are strong indications, however, that the vast majority of Reformed migrants neither received nor sought an attestation when moving and that this was normal and uncontroversial (the complaints mentioned above notwithstanding). First, consider what we know about 187 individuals who joined Wesel's Reformed congregation as full members after moving to the city from elsewhere during the same period as the attestations we analyze (November 1573 and November 1590). Of those, only forty (22 percent) came with an attestation. For the rest, elders usually only noted that they "made a confession of faith" (or used similar language) before being accepted into the community. The statement of faith that elders used to determine orthodoxy was the Belgic Confession of Faith, written in 1561 by Guy de Bres.[196] However, members were not expected to have memorized all thirty-seven articles of this document to gain church membership. On July 30, 1576, for instance, elders indicated that one of them read aloud the confession of faith to Hans van Mechte and his wife Sybille van Bergingen—recently arrived from Mechelen—which they approved.[197] In September 1577, after Faes Fryssen arrived from Linter (a small town in Brabant), elders explained that one of them held up their church ordinance before him and then presented the content of "our discipline" to him. He was asked whether he could conform to these, to which he answered "yes" before being received with a handshake by the brothers.[198] The next month, when Jan Kools requested to join, because he had formerly been an Anabaptist in Leuven, elders first made sure that he was instructed on their church's teaching on baptism, the incarnation of Christ, the swearing of oaths, and obedience to secular authorities "so that he knew enough." After that, the elders read aloud "the articles of faith," which he confirmed with a "yes."[199] Such examples suggest that joining Wesel's Reformed community did not require an attestation and that becoming a full member of the church was not an especially onerous or intrusive process (even if being subject to consistorial oversight could be). Such a perspective indicates that we might need to rethink the role of attestations as tools of coordination across the diaspora.

196 EKAW Gefach 60,7,18; Gefach 72,1 fol. 10r.

197 EKAW Gefach 72,2 fol. 32r.

198 EKAW Gefach 72,2 fol. 4.

199 EKAW Gefach 72,2 fol. 64v.

A useful perspective can be gained by asking what kinds of people received letters of attestation in the first place. Here again, the extensive surviving letters from Wesel prove helpful. Of the 130 letters that elders sent and the 40 records they made of receiving attestations, four categories of people are prominent. It's hard to say what we might make of the largest group who received attestations: working-aged single men (32 percent). In many cases, such attestations mentioned the man's occupation and testified to his having financial reasons for moving. Single men might well want to avoid suspicions that they were thieves or miscreants. However, it was fairly common for male apprentices and journeymen of good repute to travel for work in sixteenth-century Europe.[200] These men made up a high proportion of migrant communities in general. There is simply no reliable indication about whether single working men were overrepresented or underrepresented among those asking for attestations. Thus, it's probably impossible to make any useful conclusions about this group.

The other prominent groups offer more useful clues. First, a relatively high proportion (18 percent) of letters were written on behalf of men who had served a church or other public office. These men could use the document to provide testimony of their past service, perhaps to facilitate integration into those same social circles in their new homes. Second, there was a relatively high percentage of attestations (22 percent) for women traveling alone, including widows, wives separated from their husbands, and women who had never been married. In such cases, attestations may have protected the women from suspicion that they were thieves, beggars, or prostitutes. After all, given the dependency of women on social networks for financial and social stability, marginalized women were pushed into migrant lives that combined begging, work as a servant, domestic theft, and prostitution.[201] Thus women traveling for honest, even pious, reasons, had good reason to travel with an attestation of their stable connections to family. Another 10 percent of attestations were for impoverished individuals or people with scandals in their past. These include people who had flirted with unorthodox beliefs, had some kind of family or sexual scandal behind them, or whose impoverished appearance or desperation might inspire suspicion. When such people came with an attestation, elders would put in some extra effort, as they did with Jan Kools in 1577.

Thus, it seems that attestations were not standard practice across the diaspora; instead, they were used by specific subgroups of people with a special reason for seeking an attestation. In Wesel, elders wrote an average of only

200 Hochstadt, "Migration in Preindustrial Germany," 203–4. Often that travel was regional, not long distance. Prak et al., "Access to the Trade," 11–13.

201 Kamp, "Female Crime"; Rublack, *Crimes of Women*, 92–162.

9.5 attestations per year, a small fraction of the people moving in and out of Wesel's Reformed community in the 1570s and 1580s. Attestations were usually unnecessary and not common. Those who did bring attestations included social elites looking to document their status and piety as a means of integrating into similar circles in their new homes. For others, having an attestation probably helped them avoid scrutiny and facilitated their acceptance because something about their situation risked provoking suspicion.

Compared to Petrus Dathenus and Gaspar van der Heyden's vision for a transnational system of exchanging attestations in 1570, the practice looks like an utter failure. In most cases, requiring attestations for every migrant indicating their hometown, occupation, reason for traveling, and the proposed length of stay proved either impractical or impossible. Few Reformed migrants seem to have traveled with them. As a result, consistories developed other means of judging newcomers' suitability to join Christ's church. It's not clear whether this discrepancy between ideal and reality was primarily a result of the fact that people were so mobile, political circumstances so precarious, church members so unreliable, consistories so overwhelmed with work, or a combination of these factors.

Looked at in another light, though, the system of attestations served the necessary purposes exactly. Consistories maintained pragmatic procedures for integrating new members arriving without attestations. Meanwhile, those people who wanted special assurances that their honor and piety would be recognized could secure it by requesting an attestation before they left. If they knew where they were heading, they could request the more detailed kind of attestation recommended by the synod of Emden. Given the uncertainties of the period—beset by sieges, large-scale military campaigns, religious persecutions, economic uncertainties, and outbreaks of plague—consistories also proved willing to write more open-ended letters of recommendation. In that sense, the system of attestations adapted to serve the needs of the individuals of the Dutch Reformed diaspora. That said, transnational networks of coordination were not nearly as vigorous as delegates at Emden had once hoped or as historians have sometimes portrayed them.

Support for Military Operations and Printing Campaigns

There are two other ways that historians have sometimes identified transnational bonds between Dutch Reformed Protestants across the diaspora: supporting the military and political resistance against Catholic rule—especially in the Dutch Revolt—and publishing proevangelical or anti-Habsburg books to be smuggled into the Netherlands. Both types of transregional activities have been important means by which scholars have measured the strength and impact of "international Calvinism."[202] In both of these arenas, however, we found that the congregations in our study only ever played a minor role.

The Dutch Reformed migrant congregations provided little support for the military campaigns or political stratagems in support of William of Orange, or his allies, against Habsburg rule. This fact disappointed Orange, as he admitted.[203] Orange's agents, including Diederik Sonoy and Dirck Volckersz Coornhert, did make a collection in Wesel for the prince's military campaign in the fall of 1568.[204] However, we do not know how much they collected. The elder Jan Bayen later explained in a letter to Amsterdam that he had loaned one hundred *dalar* to Sonoy in 1568 but that he had intended that "not for the common good [*gemeynen nuts*], but for Sonoy's own personal use."[205] Sonoy had also been expelled from Wesel in May 1568 for helping to organize Orange's rebellion, and it seems that Orange canceled an intended visit to the city himself.[206] Otherwise, the Dutch Reformed migrants devoted little activity to supporting the revolt. Refugees and other migrants surely watched closely for news of the war, especially when it threatened them directly or affected their business dealings. But we find little evidence of active support for military action against the Habsburg government in Brussels. We have not found even one prayer-and-fast day in support of Orangist armies in any of the surviving records of the congregations in our study.[207] Indeed, when elders at Wesel proposed a fast day in February 1575, it was not to pray for victory for Orange but for a peace treaty between him and the "court of Burgundy."[208] When Orange's general Philip of Hohenlohe-Neuenstein wrote to Wesel's Dutch Reformed consistory in November 1579 to collect funds to support "the general fatherland and the building up of the church of God," elders explained that they could not give because they had too many impoverished refugees coming from Guelders, Jülich, and Limburg. Even if they had the resources to spare, they

202 Holt, "International Calvinism," in Holder, *John Calvin in Context*, 375–82.

203 Roosbroeck, *Emigranten*, 68; Nijenhuis, *Adrianus Saravia*, 38, 270; Spicer, *French-speaking Reformed Community*, 129–31. In England, there seems to have been more support for Orange's cause among some wealthy English Protestants. David Trim, "Immigrants, the Indigenous Community, and International Calvinism," in Goose and Luu, *Immigrants*, 211–22.

204 For Sonoy, see Kipp, *Landstädtische Reformation*, 412, 415. For Coornhert's role on Orange's behalf, see chapter 1.

205 EKAW Gefach 72,2 fol. 108r.

206 Spohnholz, *Convent of Wesel*, 39, n. 71.

207 See also Jelsma, "'Weakness of Conscience'"; Muylaert, *Shaping the Stranger Churches*.

208 EKAW Gefach 72,2 fol. 58r.

added, they would not send them to support the Orangist cause because doing so would anger Wesel's magistrates, risking their welcome there.[209] The former pastor in Frankenthal, Petrus Dathenus, even sought to reconcile with King Philip II in 1583 if he could just convince him to grant permission for Reformed Protestants to worship in the Netherlands.[210]

We see a similarly limited role for the Dutch Reformed communities in our study when it comes to printing in support of the evangelical cause in the Low Countries. As Andrew Pettegree has shown, Emden played a major role in printing Reformed literature to be smuggled into the Netherlands.[211] Between 1555 and 1565 several presses operated in Wesel, publishing at least eighty-six books.[212] While this output was substantial, there are a few characteristics that differentiate Wesel as a printing center from Emden. First, over half of the publications were in English, not Dutch, German, or Latin. They were thus printed to serve English Protestant refugees who had fled the Catholic rule of Mary Tudor, or for smuggling back into England. Second, they included far more Lutheran and spiritualist works than Reformed titles. The most books published in Wesel in a single year—eighteen—was in 1567, led by the printing activities of Augustijn van Hasselt (Christoph Plantin's agent in the city) and Hans de Braeker—both Lutherans.[213] After that year, though, Wesel's confessionally charged printing waned. In 1572 and 1573, we find a surge in German-language news publications about recent political events, but these did not focus on theology, liturgy, or confessional polemic, like so much of what was coming out of Emden's presses.[214] Thereafter, Wesel's presses essentially shut down. Wesel's printing industry was thus more confessionally diverse and less oriented toward the Dutch market than Emden's and thus did not play a central role in supporting the Dutch Reformed movement or "international Calvinism."

There were a few other places with presses that published Reformed literature. In Emmerich there seems to have been a short-lived press run by a

209 EKAW Gefach 72,2 fol. 159r. The surviving copy of this letter is incomplete, so it is unclear whether they sent it as written. However, the missive provides an explanation of their attitude.

210 Alastair Duke, "Calvinist Loyalism: Jean Haren, Cimay and the Dimise of the Calvinist Republic of Bruges," in his *Dissident Identities*, 271.

211 Pettegree, *Emden*, 87–108; Pettegree, "Emden as a Center." Geneva played a similar role for France. Gilmont, *Le livre réformé*.

212 See the records in the University Short Title Catalogue (www.ustc.ac.uk). Spohnholz, *Tactics of Toleration*, 57–58, 75–76; Valkema Blouw, "Augustijn van Hasselt"; Rotscheidt, "Eine Weseler Ausgabe."

213 See the essays on printing in Wesel during these years, in Valkema Blouw, *Dutch Typography*.

214 Stempel, "Zeitungen aus Wesel."

Reformed migrant from Ghent, Jan Canin, after he was expelled from Wesel for publishing illegal literature in 1570. Canin soon shifted his operations to Dordrecht.[215] In Frankfurt, the Wechel press produced a large number of Reformed books, but those were almost all in Latin, and none in Dutch.[216] None of the other communities in our study emerged as printing centers for Dutch-language books and pamphlets supporting Reformed Protestantism. That's not surprising, given the legally precarious situation for Reformed Protestants in most of these communities. Despite its support for the Reformed faith, Frankenthal also never emerged as a printing center in the sixteenth century either. While Jean Barsanges was printing there from 1578, he printed just five books, only one of which was in Dutch. Similarly, in nearby Heidelberg, a leading center of Reformed printing, only two editions of Dathenus's psalm translations were ever published in Dutch, in 1566 and 1567–68.[217]

Conclusion

There is some truth to earlier claims that the experience of exile helped support the construction of the Dutch Reformed Church. Certainly, the pastors and elders who oversaw these migrant congregations understood themselves to be part of a broad transnational community of faith whose members supported one another through advice, charity, gentle reprimands, and shared information. However, we should not thereby conclude that transnationalism was unique to the Reformed tradition, nor should we see it as the natural outcome of the widespread experience of persecution and exile faced by Reformed Protestants. Rather, this orientation was probably just as much the same inheritance of medieval Christianity's universalism that many other Christians inherited. This reorientation in examining this diasporic community encouraged us to begin tracing social networks between congregations—through ecclesiastical institutions, pastoral staffing, gifts of charity, correspondence, and letters of attestation—to understand the regional, transregional, and transnational relationships that migrants chose to maintain. What we found is that leaders of these churches did understand themselves to be part of a diasporic community of fellow believers from the Low Countries with bonds of mutual association and support. However, that did

215 Valkema Blouw, "Jan Canin in Wesel."

216 Evans, *Wechel Presses*. Maclean, "André Wechel in Frankfurt," in his *Learning and the Market Place*, 163–225.

217 See records at https://www.ustc.ac.uk/editions/411331 and https://www.ustc.ac.uk/editions/415380.

not mean that they necessarily saw themselves as tied to the new rebel state that began forming in the summer of 1572. That also did not mean that they prioritized a shared native language over affiliations of belief. Local, regional, and transregional bonds within the Empire—which transcended linguistic and political boundaries—also proved critical to their social networks. Earlier historians were not wrong when they described a kind of transnational Reformed identity that developed among Dutch migrant communities whose members were eager to liberate the fatherland for Christ's church. However, they have stressed that identity at the expense of other forms of identity that crossed language and polity. Thus, by looking at the social networks migrants built, we are able to see the regional and transregional affiliations that were developing among the Dutch Reformed in the diaspora.

Chapter Six

Returning and Remembering

After the military successes of William of Orange in the summer of 1572, migrants from parts of the northern Low Countries, at least, were able to return home. Those who came from the lands still controlled by the Habsburgs, of course, could also move to the northern provinces as well, but for them this was not a return home. In either case, the successes of Orange in Holland and Zeeland brought with it an influx of former exiles to the rebel-held territories. Political and religious leaders of the revolt tried to convince Netherlanders living abroad to resettle in Holland to help rebuild. Orange urged merchants living in England and the Empire to immigrate, to support Holland's economy.[1] In October 1571, delegates at the synod in Emden had already encouraged ministers to prioritize serving congregations in the Netherlands instead of the refugee communities.[2] After Orange gained a foothold in Holland, starting the following summer, Emden's statement became relevant. Sometimes, congregations in the Orangist territories reminded ministers in Dutch Reformed churches abroad that they should prioritize supporting churches in the newly independent parts of the Netherlands.[3] Requests for ministers from foreign churches were sometimes successful, but on other occasions ministers stayed in the Empire. A minister named Lambertus Pithopeus, for example, declined a call from Harderwijk, preferring to stay in the Palatine town of Neustadt where the salary was far higher.[4] Johannes Seu, writing from Frankenthal where he worked as a schoolmaster, also recommended that Arent Cornelisz call those ministers living in the Palatinate back to help the "fatherland."[5] He likely had

1 Janssen, "Exiles," especially 42.
2 Rutgers, *Acta*, 74.
3 Gorter, *Gereformeerde migranten*, 174–75.
4 Hendrik van den Corput to Arent Cornelisz, September 14, 1590, in WMV 3/2, ep 14, 137.
5 Johannes Seu to Arent Cornelisz, Frankenthal, May 18, 1575, in WMV 3/5, ep 1, 266. See also Taffin to Arent Cornelisz, Middelburg, January 4, 1575, in WMV 3/5, ep 6, 148. Taffin to Thomas Van Thielt, Middelburg, March 1, 1577, in WMV 3/5, ep 3/5, 181.

in mind the students studying at the University of Heidelberg. Seu moved to Frankfurt to become a minister, but soon after beginning his new office, Middelburg's church offered him a post, and he felt obliged to serve "the fatherland." Apparently, members of the Dutch Reformed consistory in Frankfurt were not too enthusiastic about the prospect of Seu's departure, though they did ultimately allow him to move to Zeeland.[6] Arent Cornelisz himself wrote in 1576 that Delft (his native town) claimed him ("*pretendant droict sur moy*"), although he had planned to return to Frankenthal, the town where he ministered at the time. Frankenthal was (reluctantly) ready to let him go and Cornelisz was happy to stay in Delft: he felt that his ministry bore fruit for his fellow citizens.[7]

The signing of the Union of Utrecht in 1579 probably also encouraged a number of migrants to move to rebel-held parts of the southern Netherlands. As we mentioned in chapter 1, Elisabeth Zeghers returned home as soon as the situation in Antwerp became more stable, and, from a Reformed perspective, more promising. Some ministers did the same. Gaspar van der Heyden, who came from Mechelen, apparently did everything he could to return to his region of origin. He fled several times to different places, but as soon as circumstances allowed, he returned to Brabant. But his return to Antwerp in 1579 was only temporary. After the Spanish military victories in 1585, Van der Heyden was one among many who migrated again. He died en route to Frankenthal in 1586.

This chapter is dedicated to the return of migrants and the subsequent memory culture that later developed about their time abroad. Many historians have made extensive claims about the profound influence of former migrants on the religious landscape of the Dutch Republic. As we explained in the introduction, they suggested that the experience of exile resulted in refugees embracing a more theologically rigid Calvinism independent of interference from government officials. According to this narrative, returning exiles spread this worldview in the newly independent United Provinces. Former exiles, in this view, became the backbone of orthodox Calvinism in the first years of the Dutch Republic, including at the Synod of Dordt in 1618–19.[8] According to Alastair Duke, their stay abroad also incited the exiles to foster the idea of a Dutch "fatherland."[9] As we emphasize through-

6 Frankfurt, consistory records, July 17, 1576, August 5, 1576, and September 11, 1576, in Meinert and Dahmer, *Das Protokollbuch*, 139–40, 141, 143.

7 Arent Cornelisz to Estienne Gyonin, July 3, 1576, in WMV 3/5, ep 2, 327.

8 Asaert, *1585*; Oberman, *John Calvin*; De Jong, *Nederlandse Kerkgeschiedenis*, 189.

9 Alastair Duke, "In Defence of the Common Fatherland: Patriotism and Liberty in the Low Countries, 1555–1576," in *Dissident Identities*, 50, 69–70.

out this book, such causal connections between exiles' experiences and these later outcomes are implausible. Exiles' experiences were shaped by diverse local circumstances, variable church structures, different demographics within the communities, and, of course, individual personalities. A second problem with this common picture of the influence of former exiles on the Dutch religious landscape is that it also presupposes that most migrants returned home. In fact, however, most migrants never returned home. Many died before they even had the option of moving back to the Low Countries; many others made new homes abroad.

It is therefore necessary to reevaluate the significance of this migration on the migrants as well as on later generations. How did their experiences influence their later lives? How did they write about those experiences? How did others and later generations write about their migration? Did these stories share common patterns? And, finally, if there was something like a common exile narrative, how did this narrative influence the religious landscape of the Dutch Republic? Several scholars have pointed to the importance of exile narratives, whether told by migrants or later generations. After all, it was only due to these narratives that the diverse forms migrations we have examined became understood primarily as "confessional migration." In their stories, former exiles or later generations explained the decision to move as a religious act to which they ascribed a spiritual meaning.[10] Understanding the actual influence of sixteenth-century mass migration is hard to measure for at least two reasons. First, the existing evidence simply does not prove that migration encouraged the development of a specific belief system. There are simply too many examples of believers who accommodated to their environment and developed compromising strategies while living in exile to make such a link between exile and strictly confessionalized forms of belief plausible.[11] Similarly, there is no reliable evidence that those refugees who did later move to the Dutch Republic were especially influential there. However, we can describe the way people remembered these migrations and utilized the discourse of exile within subsequent memory culture. In the case of the Dutch Republic, Johannes Müller insightfully highlights how later generations created a specific memory culture about sixteenth-century Dutch Reformed refugees. To do so, they draw on older stories and images, including medieval Christian ideas about pilgrimage and suffering as a way to follow Christ's footsteps.[12] Rather than tracing the direct influence of the refugees themselves, we can better understand the influence of the

10 Niggemann, "Confessional Migration."

11 Van Veen and Spohnholz, "Calvinists vs. Libertines."

12 Breedvelt-Van Veen, *Louis de Geer*, 1–2; Müller, *Exile Memories*, 124–46.

sixteenth-century mass migration on the Dutch religious landscape by analyzing this memory culture.

But first, we need to understand the diverse ways that the migrants themselves described their experiences at the time, as well as how they remembered those experiences. To do so, we use the correspondence of the Van der Meulen and the Van den Corput families—which included individuals living in one or more of the eleven refugee centers covered in our study. While previous chapters focused on the eleven migrant communities in the Empire, in this chapter we are more expansive because (1) we are examining communication networks across the diaspora, and (2) we are examining correspondence networks that are personal or familial, rather than ecclesiastical, in function. We have also compared these letters to the correspondence of Dirck Volckertsz Coornhert, who lived as a refugee in the duchy of Cleves but was never a member of a Reformed congregation, to avoid making unwarranted conclusions about the confessional distinctiveness of particular responses to life abroad. Similarly, we also compare these letters to the correspondence of a group of migrants from Ypres who settled in England as well as to several other writings on the suffering of believers during the years of the revolt in order to compare the Van der Meulen and the Van den Corput correspondence to that of people who share the same faith but lived in more supportive political and religious environments. This correspondence allows us to describe the diversity of exile experiences as well as to trace the later consolidation of memories of those experiences.

During the last few decades, historians have started to recognize that religious migrants were more than mere victims. Using strategies to build themselves a better future, these people made their own decisions as agents to shape their lives. As we described in the previous chapters, migrants had their own agency about when they decided where to go, how they interacted with their neighbors, and how they organized their congregations and worship.[13] At the same time, however, migrants still sometimes described themselves as passive victims. In several letters written to her siblings, Sara van der Meulen, for example, downplayed her own agency: she blamed the "circumstances" for the dispersal of the family, ignoring the decision of the Van der Meulens to settle in a variety of places.[14] In a song, Coornhert described his stay in the Empire as an exile, caused by the rulers in his home country.[15] In 1581, Johanna van den Corput saw the movements of the family members within an almost providential framework. She described her move with her husband Hendrik de Smet as part of the larger plan of

13 Cf. Janssen, "Legacy of Exile." See also Lougee, *Facing the Revocation*.

14 See also Sadler, "Family in Revolt, 563–66.

15 Coornhert, *Lied-boeck*, b7r.

Count Palatine Johann Casimir to create a refuge for believers in Neustadt, and she assured her addressee that the "pure doctrine" was preached in her new home.[16]

According to Jesse Sadler, the Van der Meulen family developed a discourse of exile in their letters. [17] Actually, the word "exile" rarely occurs in these texts. The same goes for Hendrik van den Corput's letters, although he mentioned his return "*ab exilio*" in one letter from 1597, nineteen years after moving from the Palatinate to Dordrecht. [18] Instead, it might be more appropriate to speak of a discourse of suffering in refugees' letters.[19] Migrants spoke extensively about the suffering of the true believers, but this suffering was not confined to refugees. Apparently, Johanna van den Corput, Hendrik's sister, regarded exile as a better option than staying at home.[20] She foresaw that circumstances in the Netherlands would deteriorate and, in an apocalyptic letter, bemoaned the fate of those who hadn't left the country.[21] Likewise, Johan Badius explained to Coornhert that those staying at home were probably worse off. While Coornhert lived in freedom in his place of exile, Badius explained that people back home had to endure imprisonment and even severe torture.[22] Other correspondents staying in the Low Countries reminded the migrants that living in the "fatherland" was probably worse. Katharina Court, for example, wrote from Breda that Anna van den Corput could probably hardly imagine how

16 Johanna van den Corput to a cousin, [1581], in CPG 841, 1r.

17 Sadler, "Family in Revolt," 527.

18 Sadler, "Family in Revolt," 527, 541. Hendrik van den Corput to Hendrik de Smet, May 3, 1597, in CPG 838i, 3–13v.

19 On this point as it relates to John Calvin, see Pitkin, *Calvin, the Bible and History*, 122–140. On sixteenth-century ways of coping with suffering, see Kuijpers, "Emotional Narratives."

20 Johanna van den Corput to Anna van den Corput, undated, in CPG 841, 11v. Johanna wrote that "moeike Bruyninx" (a woman unknown to us) would regret it if she remained in the "fatherland."

21 Johanna van den Corput to Anna van den Corput, July 18, [1568], in CPG 841, 9r. "*Ick hadde beter geraden te vlieden die plaetsen daer die plagen vallen als ons Esaias en Apocalypse voorseyt:* "*Gaet wt mijn volck*", *want ic beduchte dat over onse landen noch harde straffe sal comen.*" She was referring to Isaiah 48:20 and Revelations 18:4, which called on believers to distance themselves from sin. Johanna also applied the message to her "fatherland" where unjust judges shed "innocent blood."

22 Coornhert, *Een Lieffelijcke tsamenspreeckinge, van de droefheydt*, WW 3, 381v.

it was for a Christian to live in the Netherlands and that she would have preferred to live in Duisburg with Anna.[23]

The awareness that people back home were probably worse off made it impossible for the Van den Corputs and Coornhert to ascribe a heroic role to migrants or regard them as exemplary believers. Some migrants from Ypres fleeing to England, however, seemed to understand fleeing as a way to follow in Christ's footsteps. Some of their letters describe migration as a mark of religious virtue.[24] In this line of reasoning, they even went beyond John Calvin. As we saw in chapter 1, early modern Europeans were inclined to regard staying at home as a duty. Calvin's polemic against the Nicodemites painted the decision to flee as the safer option. In his view, it was simply unrealistic to expect ordinary believers to keep themselves uncontaminated from "idolatry" as long as they lived at home in what he called "Babylon."[25] The believers from Ypres described flight as the more pious option and as a religious virtue. But although members of the Van den Corput family, the Van der Meulens, and Coornhert were aware of the miseries back home, they occasionally struggled with the consequences of having left their homeland.

A dialogue between Coornhert and Basius, published in Coornhert's collected works, reveals the troubles Coornhert experienced during his stay in exile. He missed his homeland, its benefits, and his friends, and he was concerned about the loss of social status. He also feared adversities like illness, poverty or even death that he might encounter while living among foreigners. But the awareness that "evildoers" rejoiced in the miseries of true believers and the "tyranny against the pitiful and innocent Christians" made things truly hard to bear.[26] The absence of friends, the dispersal of families, the uncertainty of each other's well-being, and the impossibility of attending one another's weddings, births, and deaths, could be a heavy burden for migrants. This burden differed from person to person. Whereas Coornhert mentioned the absence of his friends repeatedly, the Van der Meulens were, as it seems, primarily concerned about the dispersal of their family. As we will see below, Sara van der Meulen worried that the next generation might grow up without getting to know each other and, hence, without establishing a

23 Katharina Court to Anna van den Corput, Breda, December 11, 1567, in CPG 841, 36v. See also her letter written on December 9, 1567, to Anna van den Corput, in CPG 841, 33v.

24 An unknown person to Jacob Balde, June 24, 1568, Janssen, "De Hervormde vlugtelingen," 262. For other examples, see Janssen, "De Hervormde vlugtelingen," 216, 224, 228.

25 Van Veen, *'Verschooninghe van de roomsche afgoderye'*, 35–96.

26 Coornhert, *Een lieffelijcke tsamenspreeckinge, van de droefheydt*, WW 3, 380r/v.

mutual bond of friendship.[27] As we mentioned in chapter 1, the Van den Corputs struggled to keep track of each other and grew concerned when they did not know one another's whereabouts.[28] Anthonina's sickness was a second source of suffering. Anthonina herself longed for news from her parents while she was ill.[29] But their arrival in Lemgo in later 1567 came too late. By then, their daughter had already passed away.[30]

Migrants used various coping strategies to soften their feelings of loss and loneliness. Writing letters helped them to keep in touch and compensated for the absence of family and friends; a discourse of suffering helped them to understand their sorrow and to put it into perspective. Letters offered an important means of maintaining contact with family members and friends elsewhere. Writing letters helped those facing uncertainty assure one another of their well-being. Writers often asked about the health of their correspondent or other loved ones and shared information about their own health or that of loved ones who were with them. Another important goal of letter writing was to preserve the bonds between family members and friends.[31] At the same time, these letters served a more practical goal: correspondents shared information about the well-being of other relatives, about the successes and failures of the rebels in the Netherlands, and on other political and economic developments. Additionally, writers used their letters to exhort one another to behave in a certain way or to comfort each other.[32] The letters we analyzed reveal a remarkable variety in tone. The Van den Corput sisters wrote letters reminiscent of the Pauline epistles. They were careful to start with an apostolic greeting and to apply scripture to their daily lives. By contrast, the Van der Meulen letters were more down to earth. God is not absent from their letters, but their main goal was to share information and preserve their mutual bonds.

The letters written by women were also often far more pious in tone than those written by men. Many women even wrote letters in a Pauline style, recalling the apostolic letters of the early church.[33] The women exhorted each other to take biblical examples to heart and were quite explicit about the meaning they ascribed to their experiences. Some of these women felt

27 See below, n. 84.

28 See chapter 1, n. 148.

29 Johanna van den Corput to an unknown person, [November/December 1567], in CPG 841, 8r.

30 See chapter 1, n. 118.

31 See Sadler, "Family in Revolt."

32 Schipper, "Across the Borders of Belief," 188–224.

33 See for example: Anthonina van den Corput to Anna van den Corput, Lemgo, November 12, 1567, in CPG 841, 64r.

called to admonish (*vermanen*) their correspondent. They regarded their ability to apply Scripture to their lives and to admonish each other as a gift that they were eager to use to benefit others. To be sure: they didn't confine their admonishments to female readers but extended them to male readers as well. For example, in 1567 Anthonina van den Corput wrote a letter on the necessity of suffering to Peeter Meere and his wife. Peeter thanked Anthonina for the comfort she offered and embraced her interpretation of the religious meaning of their persecutions.[34] On one occasion in early 1568, Johanna van den Corput entered into a written debate with a Catholic woman she referred to only as "Miss Vervloet," still living in Breda. She tried to convince Vervloet of the truth of the Reformed faith. Although Johanna asked her minister for theological advice, she definitely took the lead in writing the letters and deciding which arguments to use in them.[35] She also exhorted her brother Nicolaas to stay true to the Reformed faith, too.[36] During his imprisonment in 1582, Johanna wrote him a letter offering comfort and urging him to confess the truth. In her view, those who denied the faith were not better off because their own consciences troubled them as well as God's wrath. She urged Nicolaas to rejoice in his suffering, which was for the sake of Christ.[37]

While sources produced by and for the migrant churches mostly only discuss women as the subjects of church discipline or the recipients of charity, these women's letters show a remarkable self-confidence and demonstrate their extensive familiarity with biblical texts and theological arguments.[38] Johanna van den Corput was confident about her gift for "warning" her brethren and she felt that others recognized her gift as well. In a letter from July 1568, one replete with warnings and exhortations, she wrote that she wouldn't mind if the addressee shared the content of the letter with others.[39] Johanna was probably just one example of many women who seized the opportunities that renewal movements offered. The temporary absence of formal ecclesiastical structures reduced the centrality of formally ordained pastors and increased the importance of charisma. This offered new

34 Peeter Meere and his wife to Anthonina van den Corput, Breda, August 24, 1567, in CPG 841, 38v.

35 Schipper, "Across the Borders of Belief," 184–87.

36 Nicolaas may well have been born as an extra-marital son of Johan de Oude. See Postema, *Johan van den Corput*, 18.

37 Johanna van den Corput to Nicolaas van den Corput, April 11, 1582, in CPG 841, 13r.

38 Dorothea Mercator to Anna van den Corput, Duisburg, November 5, [1568], in CPG 841, 41r.

39 Johanna van den Corput to Anna van den Corput, July 18, [1568], in CPG 841, 9r, 10v.

opportunities to women. The Van den Corput sisters may have been familiar with the important role Reformed women played in their hometown of Breda, where Philipotte van Belle (Philip van Marnix's wife) and Henrica des Barres were at the forefront of the Reformed movement. Henrica des Barres had probably helped to spread the Reformed message, including having someone only known to us as Master Adriaen teach Calvin's Genevan Catechism at her house.[40]

In their pious letters, correspondents used a discourse of suffering. Their letters resembled other letters of comfort that early modern people wrote to loved ones suffering from illness or from the loss of a close family member or friend. For example, in November 1568 Dorothea Mercator wrote of the suffering of those in exile, those persecuted, and those suffering from illness all at the same time. Suffering belonged to life on earth, she explained, since it pleased God to send his afflictions upon his children.[41] Believers were proud of their suffering and took it as a sign that God would, in the end, give them martyrs' crowns. They attributed no special role to their exile experience—they understood all true believers who faced persecution within this framework. True believers, in this mindset, had always been persecuted by infidels. The might of these infidels was, however, limited. They were unable to kill the soul of believers and, ultimately, God would punish the infidels for their deeds, as Peeter Meere wrote to Anthonina van den Corput in August 1567.[42] The early modern perception of the suffering of true believers was thus highly ambiguous. On the one hand, many Reformed Protestants were sure that their suffering was caused by non-believers and they comforted each other with an apocalyptic vision according to which God would eventually take revenge.[43] They occasionally presented suffering as a test offering believers the opportunity to demonstrate the strength of their faith. In September 1585, Anna van der Meulen tried to comfort her mother, who had been traveling from Antwerp to Geertruidenberg, even though she was old and fragile. It was clear to her that God wanted to test believers to see whether they were steadfast. "It is heavy to bear in our eyes, but God sends us only [afflictions] that serve our best."[44] On the other

40 Beenakker, *Breda*, 46–47.

41 Dorothea Mercator to Anna van den Corput, [Duisburg], November 5, [1568], in CPG 841, 41v.

42 Cf. Matthew 10:28. Peeter Meere to Anthonina van den Corput, August 24, 1567, in CPG 841, 38v.

43 Katharina Court to Anthonina van den Corput, Outside Zevenbergen, July 19, 1567, in CPG 841, 29v. Coornhert, *Een lieffelijcke tsamenspreeckinge, van de droefheydt*, WW 3, 383r.

44 Anna van der Meulen to Sara van der Meulen, Cologne, September 18, 1585, in RGP 196, bijlage LXVII, 507.

hand, Reformed writers sometimes blamed themselves for all the evils happening. They confessed their sins, saw suffering as divine punishment for those sins, and exhorted one another to repent and convert. Migrants sometimes also applied this framework to their life abroad.[45]

Awareness of the suffering of believers in the "fatherland" and their own remorse about their sins as the cause of misery were reason enough to take their forced migration as it was. Although Dirck Volckertsz Coornhert and Johanna van den Corput differed in many ways, they agreed that their exile was in accordance with divine will, which prevented them from labeling exile as evil. In their view, a believer should not resist God's providence but rather remain steadfast and bear adversities with patience. According to the writings of migrants, believers embraced patience as an essential virtue. According to early modern thought, perfect exiles were neither fanatics nor immoderate zealots. Instead, they were moderate and patient. Believers urged each other to rest in God's will and forsake their own wills, which only led to evil.[46] The fact that Coornhert and the Van den Corput family did quite well in exile certainly helped them to embrace these virtues. Anthonina van den Corput wrote extensively about her house in Lemgo and recommended living there: she was happy with the local bread and judged the women she met as friendly and beautiful.[47] Coornhert cooperated during his stay in the duchy of Cleves with notable artists.[48] Hendrik van den Corput reminded Gillis van Musenhole of the prosperity he acquired during his exile. Since God had blessed him with a thriving business, Van Musenhole was now obliged to allow his son to study theology instead of becoming a merchant, and to pay for his studies.[49] But besides the more practical advantages that sometimes befell migrants during their time abroad, they were also confident about the spiritual benefits of suffering. According to Johanna, this suffering ensured the growth of the church, since as the Church Father Tertullian understood, the blood of martyrs was the seed of the church.[50] Early modern Reformed Protestants equated suffering with the passing of a test: the ability to bear suffering marked someone as a follower of Christ. But this

45 Johanna van den Corput to Anna van den Corput, Lemgo [November 14, 1567], in CPG 841, 11r. Anna van den Corput to (unknown), January 20, 1568, in CPG 841, 58r–v. See also Coornhert, *Een lieffelijcke tsamenspreeckinge, van de droefheydt*, WW 3, 381v.

46 Maria Adriaensdr to Anna van den Corput, January 15, 1568, in CPG 841, 45r.

47 Anthonina van den Corput to Anna van den Corput, Lemgo, November 12, 1567, in CPG 841, 65r.

48 Veldman, "Coornhert en de prentkunst."

49 Hendrik van den Corput to Gillis van Musenhole, undated, CPG 841, 20r.

50 Johanna to a cousin, [1581], in CPG 841, 1r.

interpretation of exile as a trial from God and an opportunity for spiritual growth was not limited to Reformed authors. Coornhert too was convinced that God used his exile to teach him to improve. His own feelings of loss were due to his attachment to things he did not own. They really belonged to God, he explained, though had had wrongly treated them as his possessions. Exile taught him that he had made idols out of his wealth, friends, and the love of his "fatherland." The cross of exile forced him to quit his sins. For that reason, Coornhert agreed that exile was not a punishment but a blessing. Hence exile should be endured with patience and gaiety.[51]

According to migrants, exile and the suffering that went along with it were quite normal. They quoted biblical stories on fleeing patriarchs and Jesus's flight to Egypt to show that exile was an ordinary part of the Christian life. The references to these stories also offered comfort because they testified to God's care for his people when they lived among foreigners.[52] The use of these Old Testament narratives was also not confined to Reformed authors, as Coornhert's example shows. He referenced the story of Joseph and Jacob in a spiritualist-mystical framework: this story showed that God used exile to force believers to distance themselves from their carnal belongings and concentrate on divine goodness.[53] Even more important was the influence of Augustine's idea that believers were ultimately strangers in this world on their way to the heavenly home. For example, Maria Adriaens, who had been a member of Breda's Reformed community too, applied this insight to the decision of Johan van den Corput and Antonina Montens to leave their homeland. She lamented over their hardships but also reminded them that they were pilgrims on their way to the heavenly fatherland.[54] Johannes Basius urged Coornhert to see earthly distance from an eternal perspective: he was still living on the same earth and enjoying the warmth of the same sun.[55] In 1569, one unknown correspondent of Johanna van den Corput called all life on earth "a Babylonian exile" from which believers

51 Coornhert, *Een lieffelijcke tsamenspreeckinge, van de droefheydt*, WW 3, 384v.

52 Maria Adriaensdr to Anna van den Corput, January 15, 1568, in CPG 841, 45v. Anna van den Corput to Johanna van den Corput and her husband Hendrik de Smet, January 20, 1568, CPG 841, 58v.

53 Coornhert, *Een lieffelijcke tsamenspreeckinge, van de droefheydt*, WW 3, 384r.

54 Maria Adriaensdr to Anna van den Corput, January 15, 1568, in CPG 841, 45r. Maria Adriaensdr probably remained in Breda, since she did not send her greeting to Hendrik who was still in Breda at the time. Ibidem, 45v. In March 1568, she wrote a letter describing the dire circumstances in Breda. See below, n. 93.

55 Coornhert, *Een lieffelijcke tsamenspreeckinge, van de droefheydt*, WW 3, 381r.

were only delivered by death.[56] No doubt migrants also had more down-to-earth ideas of what it meant to be at home. Coornhert, for example, longed for the Netherlands, his "earthly paradise" *("aardsch prieel")*.[57] But his poem about his "aardsch prieel" shows that his understanding was embedded in a religious framework. Coornhert understood the miseries of exile as a divine punishment for human sins. One of these sins was, precisely, longing for one's earthly home while forgetting the heavenly home.[58] This religious framework induced John Calvin to define "home" in purely religious terms: believers were at home where they could listen to the pure preaching of God's Word.[59] Many Reformed believers, at least in theory, agreed with him. Anna van den Corput only wanted to return home when the preaching of the true Word of God could be reintroduced.[60] Katharina Court, a correspondent of Anthonina van den Corput, defined the quality of life of a particular place by the preaching of the word in different languages.[61] Longing for the preaching of the "pure Word" allowed for some flexibility. Reformed were willing to balance the pursuit of Reformed purity with other interests and were willing to live and work in Lutheran or even Catholic lands.[62]

When early modern people spoke of their home in a more literal, earthly sense, their understanding of being at home was not limited to a specific spot. The presence of family and friends enabled early modern people to feel at home. As we saw, the Van der Meulens regarded their dispersal as an exilic drama. Especially the female correspondents of this family longed to be together again. Likewise, the Van den Corput family connected their return home with being reunited.[63] Dorothea Mercator longed to live in the same place as her friend Anna van den Corput and to have the opportunity to admonish and comfort others. This place could be Brabant, but it

56 An unknown person to Johanna van den Corput, after February 26, 1569, in CPG 841, 54r.

57 Coornhert, *Liedboeck* Amsterdam: Herman Janszoon, [1575]), b7r.

58 Coornhert, *Liedboeck*, b7r.

59 Calvin to Agneti Angliae, 1553, CO 14, ep. 1890, 739–42.

60 Katharina Court to Anna van den Corput, December 9, 1567, in CPG 841, 33r.

61 Katharina Court to Anthonina van den Corput, July 19, 1567, in CPG 841, 30r.

62 Hans van Dursten to Hendrik de Smet, Franckfurt, November 9, [1589], in CPG 804, 191r. Van Dursten was a cousin of De Smet and was well known to Hans van den Corput.

63 Cornelis Ymans (a cousin of Johan) to Johan van den Corput, Speyer, November 30, 1568, in CPG 841, 68v. See also Postema, *Johan van den Corput*, 43. For another example, see Van Roijen, "Een familiecorrespondentie," especially 141.

could just as well be Duisburg.[64] Coornhert was happy to return home after his second exile because this implied the renewed proximity of family and friends.[65] But, as the presence of family and friends as well as the preaching of the Word were so important to early modern believers, many people were able to develop a sense of belonging even while living abroad. The Dutch Reformed pastor Lubbertus Fraxinus, for example, a native of Brabant, was at first glance destined to remain homeless. After serving as pastor to the Dutch Reformed congregation in Cologne, his attempt to return home ultimately failed; in 1581, he moved to Oudenaarde and later to Antwerp, but Farnese's military conquest of that city in 1585 prompted him to flee again. This time, Fraxinus went to Holland where he became a valued minister in the early Dutch Republic.[66] It is uncertain whether a man like Fraxinus ever considered himself an exile and whether he felt he had suffered while living in Cologne.

The interpretation of exile as a disruptive experience that fundamentally altered the lives of migrants and induced them to embrace a specific belief system, fails to take into account the early modern understanding of what it meant to be *at home* and overlooks the frequency of suffering in a sixteenth-century context. Much like other sorts of suffering, exile could breed Christian virtues like patience, resignation, and steadfastness. Coornhert's play, *Abraham's Uytgangh* (*Abraham's Exodus*), offers a striking example of the interplay between migration and this type of spiritual growth. Coornhert wrote this play during his own exile and dedicated it to Arend van Wachtendonk, a nobleman in the service of the duke of Cleves. The play was first published in 1575 in Rees.[67] A character named "Cruysvlucht" (fleeing the cross), who wants to avoid the plagues savaging his own country, is told to take Abraham's example to heart.[68] But Abraham's migration is, according to this play, a spiritual one for Abraham, who decides to leave his evil life.[69] Nevertheless, literal migration is not absent in this play: the concerns "Cognatio" raises against migration are very much the concerns of early modern migrants and of Coornhert himself: the loss of friends, the uncertainties and loneliness that went with living among foreigners, the duty

64 Dorothea Mercator to Anna van den Corput, [Duisburg], November 5, [1568], CPG 841, 41r.

65 Coornhert to Frans Coornhert, undated, Coornhert, *Hondert Brieven*, ep. 6, 8.

66 BLGNP, sv.

67 Fleurkens, *Stichtelijke lust*, 221–22.

68 Coornhert, *Abrahams Uytgangh*, in Van der Meulen, *Het roerspel*, line 1–62.

69 See, Coornhert, *Abrahams Uytgangh*, line 1038–1041 in Van der Meulen, *Het roerspel*.

to stay in one's "fatherland," and the dangers of traveling.[70] It is tempting to see autobiographical elements interwoven with the biblical story of Abraham. In Coornhert's play, Abraham is worried about Sara's readiness to follow him, even as Sara is, indeed, severely tempted by "Communis opinion," "Cognatio" and "Affectus."[71] As the biblical story doesn't even mention the option of any doubts on Sara's side, this part of the play seems to mirror Coornhert's doubts about Neeltje's willingness to follow him and the attempts of others to convince her to stay in Holland.[72] Coornhert's lesson is, in fact, a pretty general one: believers should leave their worldly concerns behind them and submit themselves to God's eternal will.

As we outlined above, migrants' longing for home took diverse forms in practice. Some migrants seemed to have hoped for a return within a short time, but as their stay in the Empire was prolonged, the metaphorical distance between them and their homeland grew. People became part of their host society and sometimes even grew alienated from their homeland. Hence, the decision to return (if possible) was not always easy to make. In the following, we will describe some of the push and pull factors.

Werner Helmichius (1551–1608) returned home.[73] He was born and raised in Utrecht, but in 1566 he left to enroll in the Genevan Academy. In 1570, he continued his studies abroad, in Heidelberg. William of Orange's military successes starting in 1572 didn't inspire him to move to Holland. Instead, in 1576 he became minister in the Dutch Reformed congregation in Lutheran Frankfurt. A year later, fellow believers seized the opportunity to organize a Reformed church in Utrecht. Helmichius soon returned home to become a minister in his hometown. Wherever Orangist troops gained ground, Reformed leaders intensified their efforts to provide the nascent church in the new state with a minister. Sometimes, the migrant congregations helped them.[74] The farewell speech of refugees in Wesel to the city

70 Coornhert, *Abrahams Uytgangh*, line 337–66; 535–47; 795–806, in Van der Meulen, *Het roerspel.*

71 Coornhert, *Abrahams Uytgangh*, line 471–622, in Van der Meulen, *Het roerspel.*

72 See chapter 1, n. 103.

73 BLGNP, sv.

74 Philip van Marnix to [the consistory of the Dutch stranger community in London], Middelburg, January 27, 1577, in Hessels, *Epistulae et Tractatus*, vol. 2, ep. 154, 572. Gaspar Heydanus to [the consistory of the Dutch Stranger community in London], Middelburg, March 8, 1577, in Hessels, *Epistulae et Tractatus*, vol. 2, ep. 158, 584. The Dutch church in London felt obliged to send ministers to the rebel-held lands of the Netherlands because ministers could make a greater contribution there than they could in small congregations in England. See: the consistory of the Dutch community in

council in 1578 and the presentation of chalices as signs of gratitude for the hospitality the city had shown, are probably the most notable example of believers making plans to travel home.[75] Sometimes, members of the refugee communities mentioned changes they had undergone as a result of the rebels' successes. The Dutch Reformed community at Yarmouth, England, for example, witnessed the departure of the wealthier members "as God had opened part of our fatherland"[76] Other Reformed refugees also returned after Orange's initial victories.[77]

In the case of the migrants in our study, however, many people stayed in the refugee communities, moved to elsewhere in the Empire, or died before they had the option of returning home. Elizabeth Zeghers, the founding mother of the Van der Meulen firm, died in Bremen, just as so many other migrants died while living in exile.[78] Her children were unable to return home after 1585 when Antwerp came under Spanish rule. Some of them visited Antwerp occasionally, but this was not without risks. In 1588, Daniel van der Meulen planned to go to Antwerp, but his sister Sara expressed concern, warning him of the dangerous journey and of friends in Antwerp behaving like "foxes."[79] In 1598, Jan della Faille urged Daniel to come to Antwerp: his coming would be useful in resolving a family conflict, but Jan also encouraged Daniel to see his relatives again.[80] Sara van der Meulen continued longing for a return to Antwerp. Brabant and Flanders were their "fatherland" and Holland was only second best. Living in Holland was better than living in Bremen, but only because it was closer to Antwerp.[81]

London to the consistory of the Dutch community in Maidstone, London, August 8, 1577, in Hessels, *Epistulae et Tractatus*, vol. 3, ep 492, 464.

75 Janssen, "De Nederlandsche hervormden in Kleefsland," 307–318, 320–422. See also Spohnholz, "Calvinism and Religious Exile."

76 The consistory of the Dutch church in Yarmouth to the consistory of the Dutch church in London, Yarmouth, May 15, 1576, in Hessels, *Epistulae et Tractatus*, vol. 3, ep. 388, 369.

77 De Jong, *Nederlandse Kerkgeschiedenis*, 149; Selderhuis, *Handboek Nederlandse Kerkgeschiedenis*, 318. See also Fagel and Pollmann, *1572*, 88, 177, 196.

78 Sadler, "Family in Revolt," 541–54.

79 Sara van der Meulen to Daniel van der Meulen, Cologne, September 5, 1588, DvdM, 295 Brieven van Sara van der Meulen.

80 Jan della Faille to Daniel van der Meulen, Antwerp, January 3, 1598, DvdM, 270 Brieven van Jan della Faille, 33.

81 Sara van der Meulen to Daniel van der Meulen, Bremen, December 7, 1592, DvdM, 295 Brieven van Sara van der Meulen.

Gradually, migrants' hopes to return to their homeland evaporated.[82] The desire to live in Antwerp again was closely connected with Sara van der Meulen's ardent wish to live as a united family in one place, instead of being dispersed among different countries.[83] Once Sara had settled in Utrecht, she joyfully watched the sons of both Daniel and Andries playing with her own boys. She prayed that the Lord would bless their friendship.[84] The unity of the family—so tested by its dispersal—was a matter of high significance to Sara. Brothers and sisters were able to remain in touch via written correspondence, but a second generation grew up without having the opportunity to know each other. Sara was worried about how to keep the dispersed family together, especially when a new generation was growing up apart. Behind her description of the scene of her nephews playing together one can almost detect a sigh of relief.[85]

Whereas some members of the Van der Meulen family moved from the Holy Roman Empire to the Dutch Republic beginning in the early 1590s, other migrants decided to stay in the Empire: apparently, they had found a new home. Johanna van den Corput, for example, never returned to the Dutch Republic. In 1578, she and her husband made plans to settle in Dordrecht, together with her mother and sister Elisabeth. However, as Johanna explained in a letter, Count Johann Casimir was not willing to let her husband, Hendrik de Smet, go, and so they stayed in Neustadt. The two later moved to Heidelberg. Elisabeth married Franciscus Junius, the renowned professor of theology, and postponed moving to the Republic as well. Dorothea Mercator longed for her homeland, as she testified in a letter to Anna van den Corput, although she was aware that a return might take longer than they anticipated.[86] In fact, she seems to have felt perfectly at home in the Empire: she gave birth to several children and, as far as we know from their biographies, these children stayed in the Empire just like

---

82 Spohnholz, "Calvinism and Religious Exile." For another example, see Müller, *Exile Memories*, 64.

83 Sara van der Meulen to Daniel van der Meulen, Bremen, December 7, 1592: "*Je me suis resjoui de veoir vostre filz et le filz de notre frere Andries. Ils sont ici comme estants freres avecque les notres s'asbatant et s'entrejouissant en toute modestié. J'espere que le Seigneur nourira et liera leur amytié.*" DvdM, 295 Brieven van Sara van der Meulen.

84 Sara van der Meulen to Daniel van der Meulen, Utrecht, July 22, 1599, DvdM, 295 Brieven van Sara van der Meulen.

85 Likewise, Hendrik van den Corput rejoiced when he reunited with family members. Hendrik van den Corput aan Hendrik de Smet, September 16, 1592, in CPG 804, 76r.

86 Dorothea Mercator to Anna van den Corput, Duisburg, February 9, 1569, in CPG 841, 43r.

their mother. Hendrik van den Corput did not rush to move to the Republic either. In 1573 his main goal was not to help build the Dutch Reformed Church, but rather to obtain a pastorate in the Palatinate. Only in 1578 did he move to Dordrecht.[87] And indeed many migrants became members of their host societies: they acquired citizenship, married locals, and participated in local politics.[88]

At first glance, Holland offered favorable conditions for exiles to return. William of Orange granted former exiles privileges such as housing, occasionally confiscated property from Catholic exiles who had fled, and made it clear that returning exiles were to have an honorable position in the newly forming government. As Geert Janssen has shown, the world was turned upside down, as Orange replaced Catholic officeholders (who had fled) with arriving Protestant exiles and allowed them to take a visible role in the new state.[89] When Coornhert returned to Holland in 1572, he was given back his belongings, including his house, which was being repaired after apparently being damaged.[90] At the same time, despite these enticements, some migrants may well have found the circumstances in the Empire more promising. After years of war, the Dutch economy was evidently in a bad state. Wouter Jacobsz's dramatic account of the poverty, hostilities, and damage caused by the war is particularly moving.[91] To be sure: regions like the duchy of Cleves had suffered from war as well, and both rebel and royal troops looted the lands. But at least until the Thirty Years' War, circumstances in the Empire were often better. A second factor that an objective observer could not fail to see was the uncertainty about the near future in the Low Countries, where the situation was extremely unstable as Johannes Ceporinus (1541–1626), for example, experienced. After living as a refugee in Goch, his return to Nijmegen, where he had begun his ecclesiastical career, came too early. After Farnese's successes he had to flee again; this time he went to Medemblik. In 1617 we find him back in Goch. This was not the end of his journey, for in 1620, he had to flee yet again after which he returned to Nijmegen. He ended his life in Zaltbommel, about fifty kilometers to the west.[92] He was not the only person for whom the miseries of war and the violence of religious discord was practically omnipresent. When

87 Hendrik van den Corput to an unknown person, [March 2, 1573], in CPG 841, 19r. See also Hendrik van den Corput to [Hendrik de Smet?], March 1573, in CPG 841, 19v. See also BLGNP, sv.

88 Schilling, *Niederländische Exulanten*, 158–59. See also chapter 3.

89 Janssen, "Exiles."

90 Becker, *Bronnen*, no 97, 63–64.

91 Van Eeghen, *Dagboek van Broeder Wouter Jacobsz.*

92 Acquoy, *Jan van Venray.*

the return of the exiles began, in the summer of 1572, the revolt, with its mutual hatred, religious and political violence, and economic misery still had a tremendous impact. Even people who were able to keep themselves at a distance from the economic, political, and religious distress heard stories of people who had to flee, saw the damage caused by outbreaks of violence, or had witnessed the trials of heretics.[93] People in the new state watched the military maneuvers with a keen eye. Military successes and failures affected the lives of people they knew and endangered their own lives. In 1581, for example, Hendrik van den Corput apologized for writing a rather chaotic letter, one in which he expressed serious concern about his family and friends in Breda who were suffering through a brutal Spanish military occupation.[94] Ministers watching what happened in the southern Netherlands lumped this military threat together with the actions of the opponents of their Reformed endeavors. In their view, enemies were everywhere and were endangering everything.[95]

Migrants may well have had also more personal reasons to stay in their places of refuge. According to Henricus Caesarius, who described the history of Zaltbommel in a treatise, Johannes Ceporinus's heart tended toward the Palatinate.[96] As we outlined above, as people became involved in their host societies, they grew more distanced from their homeland. Members of the Van der Meulen family managed to stay in touch and keep each other posted on their well-being, but in other families the bond between brothers and sisters or parents and children weakened. Carolus Batten reported to Hendrik de Smet that he did not know how many children his brothers and sisters had. He reminded his addressee that he hadn't been in his hometown for twelve years.[97] To people who had fled during their childhood, their native town or village sometimes became just a hazy memory. Bonaventura Vulcanius asked De Smet for more information on his family: because of his flight he knew little of his family history.[98] As time passed, migrants integrated into their host societies, including, as we have seen, sometimes becoming citizens.[99] For the children of migrants, especially, their place of

93 Maria Adriaensdr to Anna van den Corput, March 1568, in CPG 841, 47r.

94 Hendrik van den Corput to Arent Cornelisz, August 4, 1581, in WMV 3/2, ep. 20, 156.

95 W. Helmichius to Arent Cornelisz, Utrecht, April 25, 1584, in WMV 3/4, ep xx, 45–46.

96 Caesarius, *Danck Sermoon*, 4r.

97 Carolus Batten to De Smet, Dordrecht, February 6, 1591, in CPG 804, 165v.

98 Bonaventura Vulcanius to De Smet, Leiden, March 18, 1592, in CPG 804, 109r.

99 See chapter 3.

refuge gradually became home. Some children of migrants ceased speaking Dutch altogether. In the case of Hendrik van den Corput, the question of where one belonged caused tension between the first and second generation of migrants. Hendrik felt that his sons should return to their "fatherland" and assist in building the Dutch Reformed Church.[100] But his sons were probably not entirely sure that the Republic was really their fatherland. Abraham planned to buy a house and marry in the Palatinate, but his father felt that he and his sons were obliged to serve their fatherland and the Dutch Reformed Church. Men like Hendrik van den Corput grew concerned that their children had become alienated from the Netherlands. Buying a house and marrying someone from one's place of refuge enlarged the distance to one's home country. In the case of Hendrik van den Corput and his sons, the first and second generation of migrant families had different perceptions of the meaning of their land of origin and their obligations to it.[101] The son of Hendrik de Smet returned to the Republic to help build the church, even though he didn't speak Dutch. Hendrik van den Corput offered help: he had learned German by reading it aloud every day and was now ready to teach Dutch by reading it to his son daily.[102] After decades away, the place where one belonged could become unclear. The Anabaptist writer Joost van den Vondel is probably the most famous example of how difficult it became to define "home" for early modern migrants. His parents had left Flanders and found a refuge in Cologne. They went to the Republic and Joost van den Vondel eventually went to Amsterdam, but he continued to identify himself as a native of Cologne.[103]

Ministers often had more reason than ordinary citizens to return to the Netherlands since they often received requests to come help them build and grow new congregations. Since the new Reformed congregations struggled with a shortage of ministers, the prospects for ministers willing to work were good. Although Reformed pastors always asked for stronger support from the authorities than they received, the circumstances under which they

---

100 Hendrik van den Corput felt that the Netherlanders should have their own ministers instead of relying on foreign ministers. Hendrik van den Corput to Gillis van Musenhole, undated, in CPG 841, 20r.

101 Hendrik van den Corput to Hendrik de Smet, October 2, 1590, in CPG 804, 171v. Hendrik van den Corput to Hendrik de Smet, December 1590, in CPG 804, 166r. Hendrik van den Corput to Hendrik de Smet, December 1590, in CPG 804, 168r. We see a similar thought process in the correspondence of the Thijs family. See Müller, *Exile memories*, 64. On this family correspondence, see Van Roijen, "Een familie-correspondentie," 126, 130.

102 Hendrik van den Corput to Hendrik de Smet, December 26, 1592, in CPG 804, 56r.

103 On Vondel, see Sneller, *De gouden eeuw in gedichten*.

worked were overall favorable. Reformed pastors were allowed to use the main church buildings in cities and towns, and they received stable salaries from secular authorities. But as far as we have been able to ascertain, fewer than 25 percent of ministers in exile returned.[104] Whereas new congregations in the independent Netherlands sometimes put pressure on ministers to assist in building the new church, the Dutch congregations in the Empire also had good reason to urge their ministers to stay. Often the congregations in our study only let their ministers go reluctantly.[105] After all, losing a pastor might mean that their church would have to function without a pastor.[106] Migrant communities sometimes refused to give their ministers permission to leave or otherwise tried to keep them. In 1586, Emmerich prevented Henricus Helmichius from accepting a call to a church in Utrecht. People from Emmerich had been ready to pay his ransom to have him relieved from prison. So long as he had not paid them back, he had to stay there.[107] Jacobus Rolandus was ready to accept a call to Amsterdam in 1602, but his flock in Frankenthal insisted that he stay.[108] Ultimately, however they were unsuccessful. In 1603 we find Rolandus back in Amsterdam.[109] The migrants' congregations, of course, aimed to protect their own survival and were probably as interested in the flourishing of Reformed Protestantism in their own region as in the thriving of the Dutch Reformed Church in the Republic.[110]

---

104 This is only a rough estimate. Our database lists 168 ministers; we know of 29 who later served in a congregation in the Republic. We compared a list of pastors in the eleven Reformed congregations that form the center of our study to Van Lieburg, *Repertorium*.

105 On this point, see also chapter 5.

106 When Helmichius left Frankfurt, consistory members opted to worship by reading pious writings. Frankfurt consistory records, May 3, 1579, Meinert, Dahmer, *Das Protokollbuch*, 186–87.

107 Werner Helmichius to Arent Cornelisz, Utrecht, September 6, 1586, in WMV 3/4, ep. xxv, 57. Likewise, Petrus Gellius Faber was obliged to stay in Lehr (near Emden). Since the church at Emden had paid for his ransom, Emden was unwilling to permit him to accept a calling to The Hague. Bernardus Faile (minister in The Hague) to the consistory of Emden, August 28, 1584, ub WMV 3/2, ep. 12, 28–30.

108 Werner Helmichius to Arent Cornelisz, Amsterdam, April 2, 1603, WMV 3/4, ep. 79, 180. On Rolandus's readiness to accept a call to Amsterdam see: Helmichius to Arent Cornelisz, Amsterdam, December 23, 1602, in WMV 3/4, ep. 74, 169. On Rolandus, see Harline, *Jacobs vlucht*, 17–142.

109 BLGNP, sv.

110 In 1573 the classis of Birkesdorf attempted to establish a church in Dusseldorf and Essen, WMV 3/5, ep. 35, 79. See also Gorter, *Gereformeerde migranten*,

They were not alone in their endeavors, as others also took an interest in their well-being. Certainly, the articles of the synod held in Emden in October 1571 urged ministers to prioritize serving churches in the Netherlands. Yet they also took measures to organize ecclesiastical life abroad and safeguard the bonds among the churches in the diaspora.[111] Some ministers in the Republic took an interest in the congregations in the diaspora, including discussing how to support them. In 1586, Johannes Kuchlinus, a Reformed minister in Amsterdam, was concerned about the Dutch Reformed community in Danzig (present-day Gdańsk) since so many merchants from Brabant had moved there. He felt called to help keep Danzig's flock of Christ awake and he assisted in the search for a new minister.[112] Apparently the duchy of Cleves continued to be a promising place to live and work. Rutger Topanus, for example, was a minister in Amersfoort, but at some point in the 1590s he left for the duchy of Cleves. Werner Helmichius held him in high esteem and attempted to draw his attention to the vacant churches in the Dutch Republic.[113] But in 1610, he probably still lived in Moers and attended the synod of Duisburg, representing *Herrschaft* Hardenburg, a Reformed noble enclave within the duchy of Berg.[114] No wonder many Dutch Reformed congregations in the Empire persisted long after the rebels had secured a foothold in the northern Netherlands. The Dutch community in Frankfurt am Main, for example, thrived into the eighteenth century.

It is not clear that those who had stayed at home were always happy to welcome former migrants back. As we outlined in chapter 1, early modern Europeans fostered mixed feelings about people who moved. On the one hand, cities needed newcomers to survive and developed mechanisms for integrating foreigners. On the other hand, early modern societies often perceived foreigners as infringing on the natural order. The difference between migrants and vagabonds was blurry, and the decision to leave one's homeland evoked mixed feelings. Indeed, many sixteenth-century people were inclined to consider the decision to move as a sign of a lack of loyalty rather than of steadfastness. It seems that some of those who returned struggled with the early sixteenth-century axiom that people ought to stay at home. Van den Corput, for example, wished that those living in Frankenthal would

---

173–79. See also chapter 5.

111 Rutgers, *Acta*, 59–61.

112 Kuchlinus to Arent Cornelisz, November 5, 1586, in WMV 3/5, ep. 20, 263–64. See also Kuchlinus to Arent Cornelisz, February 17, 1586, in WMV 3/5, ep. 18, 260.

113 Helmichius to Arent Cornelisz, Amsterdam, January 10, 1603, in WMV 3/4, ep. 76, 174. Helmichius to Arent Cornelisz, Amsterdam, March 22, 1603, in WMV 3/4, ep. 77, 176.

114 Rosenkranz, *Generalsynodalbuch*, 1:17.

come to Holland and Zeeland to contribute to the local economy. Yet he understood the decision to stay abroad since, as he wrote in 1585, nobody really cared about those "poor expelled people."[115] Doede van Amsweer, whose treatise was published in 1613, felt compelled to write on his return that he now really longed to help build the fatherland. His former life in exile mattered to him, but he was well aware that those who had stayed at home sometimes had mixed feelings about former exiles, and he wanted to assure his readers that he was not seditious or unfaithful to the country.[116] Bartholomeus van den Corput had to settle the estate of the deceased Hendrik van den Corput, but after years in exile he found that people on the streets in Breda no longer knew him.[117] The same went, of course, for the next generation: they did not know the people of Breda either.[118]

Neither migrants themselves nor those who had stayed at home regarded the former exiles as a spiritual elite. The fact that the Reformed movement didn't leave a wealth of exile literature—as the Lutheran movement did—is telling. Whereas Lutheran authors used exile as a pious example worth imitating, sixteenth-century Reformed authors rarely discussed this topic.[119] In 1568, Dorothea Mercator even complained about the lifestyles of her fellow exiles. The majority were more interested in idle things than in pious speech, she explained. She saw this as reason enough to keep herself at a distance from them.[120] Coornhert did the same: according to him, many exiles lacked the right mindset because they fled to distance themselves from the economic miseries that oppressed the country rather than to distance themselves from their evil thoughts, wills, and inclinations.[121] In his correspondence with Hendrik de Smet, Hendrik van den Corput described those who had adhered to the Reformed truth from the very beginning of the troubles as a spiritual elite—and not just those who had experienced exile. Apparently, this long-standing commitment to the truth created a bond among people, for, as Van den Corput stated, the commitment of his

115 Van den Corput to Arent Cornelisz, August 14, 1585, in WMV 3/2, ep 54, 253–54.

116 [Doede van Amsweer], *Een Christelijcke Tragedia*, b6v.

117 Jean and Jacob van den Corput to Hendrik de Smet, Dordrecht, May 22, 1602, in CPG 838, 2–31v.

118 Jean van den Corput to Hendrik de Smet, Dordrecht, November 13, 1603, in CPG 838i, 1–78r. Jean complained that he knew nobody in Breda that could be trusted with the administration of his inheritance. He expressed his relief that in Dordrecht he finally found someone who could serve this role.

119 Van Veen, "'Reformierte Flüchtlinge."

120 Dorothea Mercator to Anna van den Corput, Duisburg, November 5, 1568, in CPG 841, 41r.

121 Coornhert, *Abrahams Uytgangh*, line 25, Van der Meulen, *Roerspel.*

parents to the Reformed faith should induce De Smet to watch over Arent Cornelisz's son more carefully than other students.[122] Johannes Kuchlinus's request of Arent Cornelisz to help a young exiled man start his theological studies at Leiden University is another clear example of exilic status mattering little. In this case, it was the fact that he belonged to the poor and the hungry who deserved support that Kuchlinus thought would move Arent Cornelisz to offer the man aid.[123] The short biography of the Flemish pastor Pieter Hazaert published after his death is yet another example of exile failing to provide people with an aura of piety or steadfastness. In this short description of Hazaert's life, the pastor of Naaldwijk, Pieter Louwijc, did not praise him because of his exile experiences in Norwich, Wesel, Emmerich, and elsewhere but because of his willingness to help build the church in the Habsburg Netherlands, despite the dangers.[124]

In the sixteenth century, Reformed authors hardly ever ascribed an exemplary role to exiles. The diversity of migrants' experience that we have described in the proceeding chapters shows that forced migration did not inherently promote any specific belief system. The influence of the sixteenth-century mass migration was less concrete and more ambiguous than historians have sometimes claimed. It is unclear to what extent their former exile continued to influence these mobile people: it often seems as if the memory of their exile barely mattered to them. The correspondence between Arent Cornelisz and Hendrik van den Corput, two ministers firmly rooted in the diaspora Reformed communities, attests to the minor role exile played in the correspondence of former exiles. In their letters, the two ministers remembered the persecutions and the suffering under Spanish tyranny but not their exile experience. This memory of suffering, however, called for action: it obliged believers to do their utmost to preserve the pure religion and to prevent "papal idolatry" from taking possession of the land again.[125] This memory of suffering became a founding myth of both the Dutch Republic and its public church. The brave steadfastness of the ancestors in the midst of suffering continued to be a call for commitment to the Republic, to freedom,

122 Hendrik van den Corput to Hendrik de Smet, May 22, 1590, in CPG 804, 175r. See also Hendrik van den Corput to Hendrik de Smet, April 15, 1590, in CPG 804, 178r.

123 Johannes Kuchlinus to Arent Cornelisz, Amsterdam, January 9, 1579, in WMV 3/5, ep. 1, 234. Johannes Kuchlinus from Amsterdam also wrote to Arent Cornelisz, on April 24, 1579. "*Non enim mentitur os, quod dixit: Quicquid fecisti uni ex istis minimis, mihi fecistis.*" WMV 3/5, ep. 2, 235. Cf. Matthew 23:40.

124 Louwijc, *De wtkomste der wandelinge*, b6v.

125 See, for example, Hendrik van den Corput to Arent Cornelisz, Dordrecht, May 14, 1579, in WMV 3/ 2, ep. 4, 100.

and to the true faith. Later generations viewed the revolt as a golden age of true faith and contrasted it with the lukewarm faith of their own time.[126]

Ministers often interpreted the revolt against Spain and the suffering of the Dutch in biblical terms. They used Old Testament stories like the exodus from Egypt or the Babylonian exile to explain what happened to the faithful in earlier years. In their explanations, they identified themselves with Israel and their adversaries with Israel's enemies. This framework helped them call on true believers to stay firm against Spain, ascribe meaning to the suffering of the rebels, and assure their audience of God's providence for his people.[127] This narrative of the deliverance of the Republic from tyranny clearly impacted how Dutch Reformed authors described their new state and how they characterized their identity. Dutch Reformed authors were also inclined to take suffering as a hallmark of their church and in their histories created a lineage of martyrs to which the Christians of the first centuries and Reformed Protestants of their own days belonged. Whereas Catholic theologians developed the concept of apostolic succession, Protestant authors (Reformed Protestants, but also Lutherans and Anabaptists) invented a succession of persecuted believers to demonstrate continuity with the ancient church.[128] Reformed Protestants took the sufferings of members of their church as a clear sign of the verity of their faith. They often referred to earlier periods of suffering to promote the authority of, for example, the Belgic Confession and Heidelberg Catechism. The fact that their confession and the church order were rooted in a time of suffering bestowed them religious gravitas.[129] Abraham van den Corput, a grandson of Hendrik van den Corput, used the argument that the true church had always been persecuted to polemicize against the Catholic Church. In his view, the splendor and wealth of clerics had nothing to do with the example of Christ and his apostles who had been ready to suffer and to bear the cross.[130] His focus on history allowed him to juxtapose the Catholic cooperation with the mighty and the powerful with the cross-bearing of the true Christians.[131] The emphasis on suffering also influenced how Dutch Reformed authors understood the place of

---

126 Cleyn, *Dank-offer*, 56–57; Hoornbeeck, *Belydenis Predicaty*, *2r–**2v; Van der Sloot, *Twe honderdjarige gedagtenis*, 76–79. More generally, see Monge and Muchnik, *Early Modern Diasporas*, 25–54. See also Fagel and Pollmann, *1572*, 184–92.

127 Groenhuis, "Calvinism and National Consciousness."

128 Van Veen, "Protestantse martelaarsgeschiedenis"; Gordon, "Changing Face of Protestant History."

129 Van den Corput to Arent Cornelisz, August 15, 1587, in WMV 3/2, ep. 62, 281.

130 Van den Corput, *De Goddelicke Vierschare*, 6v–7r.

131 Van den Corput, *De Goddelicke Vierschare*, ******3v.

their church within the history of Christianity. The awareness that the true church was always a suffering church encouraged believers to sympathize with those who suffered, especially, of course, those who suffered from persecution.[132]

And yet, this memory of suffering could lead believers in different directions, as the polemic between Coornhert, on the one hand, and Arent Cornelisz and Hendrik van den Corput, on the other, so clearly shows. Their parallel exilic experiences and their parallel memory of suffering did not result in them having shared worldviews. On the contrary. Cornelisz and Van den Corput, ministers in Delft and Dordrecht, counted the freedom to worship according to a Reformed liturgy as the main heritage of the revolt. Consequently, they called on magistrates to defend this freedom for Reformed Protestants and to keep other religious groups in check. But they saw their efforts endangered from all sides: foreign enemies were but one threat to the heritage of the revolt, internal enemies were another. These Reformed pastors were not sure that magistrates or the states would continue to uphold the Reformed cause rather than begin supporting the enemies of the pious.[133] By contrast, Coornhert was wary of Reformed ministers seizing power and replacing the Spanish Inquisition with a Genevan variant. He urged people to be on their guard against Reformed ministers, who threatened to introduce what Coornhert described as a new inquisition. According to Coornhert, the revolt had not been about freedom for Reformed Protestantism, but about a more general freedom that allowed all believers to worship, each in their own way.[134] Similar experiences of suffering clearly inspired opposing visions and contributed to a ferocious debate.

In addition to the memory of suffering, the international outlook of former migrants influenced the Dutch religious landscape. An outspoken example of this international outlook was presented by Hendrik van den Corput. As we saw, Hendrik moved to the Republic and became a minister in Dordrecht. His two sisters, however, together with their husbands, stayed in the Palatinate. Van den Corput used his relationship with De Smet and

132 See also Pollmann, "Met grootvaders bloed bezegeld." For an example of Reformed Protestants cultivating a memory of suffering elsewhere, see Richter, *Koexistenzen und Konflikte,* 18–20.

133 For some examples: Jean Taffin to Arent Cornelisz, Dordrecht, May 11, 1575, in WMV 3/ 5, ep 11, 156. Arent Cornelisz to Estienne Guyonin, July 3, 1576, in WMV 3/5, ep. 2, 328. Hendrik van den Corput to Arent Cornelisz, Dordrecht, November 15, 1579, in WMV 3/2, ep. 10, 119. *Antwoort Lamberti Danei*, 12. (This part was written by Arent Cornelisz); Werner Helmichius to Arent Cornelisz, Utrecht, October 22, 1586, WMV 3/4, ep. xxvi, 60.

134 Van Veen, "'De aert van Spaensche Inquisitie'."

Junius to strengthen the influence of Heidelberg's theology at the cost of Leiden's influence. He esteemed Heidelberg, possibly in part because his brothers-in-law worked there, while he now regarded Leiden University as a hotbed of heresies.[135] Since in his view Leiden would only improve if the professors were replaced by more pious men, he urged his correspondents to send young students who wanted to study theology or law to Heidelberg. He was sure that Daniel Tossanus, Franciscus Junius, and Hendrik de Smet, then professors at the Collegium Sapientia in Heidelberg, would be happy to help students to obtain permission to attend the seminary there at a reasonable price.[136] One of the young men he sent to Heidelberg was his own son, Johannes Nicolaus: a clear sign that his esteem for the University of Heidelberg was heartfelt.[137] Educating future ministers to serve the Dutch Reformed Church was a concern of Van den Corput.[138] His efforts to support students must have been a considerable task, for in 1590 he complained that his involvement in the training of students came at the cost of his work as a minister.[139] His support included the writing of letters of recommendation, financial help, assistance in securing proper housing, and keeping the fathers updated on the well-being of their sons.[140] On some occasions, Van den Corput felt highly responsible for the spiritual well-being of his students. In the case of Andries Cornelisz and David Balthasar, whose parents had belonged to the "true church" from the very beginning, he asked De Smet to keep them under Christian discipline and to consider himself as their father.[141] The historian Anton Beenakker was able to trace fourteen

---

135 Hendrik van den Corput to Hendrik de Smet, August 13, 1589, in CPG 804, 202r–v.

136 Hendrik van den Corput to Arent Cornelisz, November 28, 1586, in WMV 3/2, ep. 57, 265–66. Hendrik van den Corput to Arent Cornelisz, January 10, 1587, in WMV 3/2, ep. 58, 270.

137 Hendrik van den Corput to Hendrik de Smet, August 13, 1589, in CPG 804, 202r–v. Hendrik van den Corput to Hendrik de Smet, July 25, 1589, in CPG 804, 192v.

138 See also 304–5.

139 Hendrik van den Corput to Hendrik de Smet, December 13, 1590, in CPG 804, 167r.

140 In a letter from April 14, 1590, Hendrik van den Corput recommended Theodoricus Adriaen to Hendrik de Smet. Since Adriaen wanted to study law, Van den Corput explained, he would be best off if he shared a house with jurists, which would help him to learn the language properly and further aid his studies. CPG 804, 181r.

141 Hendrik van den Corput to Hendrik de Smet, April 15, 1590, in CPG 804, 178r–179r. See also Hendrik van den Corput to Hendrik de Smet, May 22, 1590, in CPG 804, 174r.

students who were part of Van den Corput's endeavors: René van der Warck, the son of Hendrik de Vorst (whose first name we do not know), Johannes van Mijlen, Erasmus Putwaert, Andries Cornelisz de Witt, Dyrck Adriaensz, Michiel Hendrickxsz, David Balthasar, Balthasar Fransz, the brother of Andries Cornelisz, Michiel Wittensz, Adriaen Verstraten, Theodoricus Adriaen, and Michiel Dircksz. There were probably even more. According to Beenakker, Van den Corput started his student support system in 1589, but, as his correspondence with Arent Cornelisz shows, he had already started promoting Heidelberg in 1586.[142] In this correspondence, he recommended that students of Arent Cornelisz go to Heidelberg.

Van den Corput was not the only one who highly valued the University of Heidelberg. At the time it was a center of international Reformed learning, attracting students from all over Europe. Students attending Heidelberg mixed with other students from across Europe and brought a new international outlook back home.[143] This cosmopolitan Reformed perspective was probably the most important and most specific contribution former migrants made to the religious culture in the early Dutch Republic. They kept in contact with people in the Empire, and they used these networks to exchange news, offer support, and to exhort each other to stay true to the faith. These networks were a constant reminder that the members of the Dutch Reformed Church indeed saw themselves as members of a catholic (that is, universal) church. To members of the Van der Meulen and Van den Corput family, the familiarity with the diasporic Dutch Reformed and their interest in the well-being of the church in the Republic and the churches abroad bolstered their belief in that sense of a "reformed catholic church." They understood the Reformed Church, in this sense, not as bound to a single place but, as in a truly catholic sense, everywhere.[144] To be sure: an international outlook was not a specifically Reformed characteristic. Catholics shared such an identity as well.[145]

Besides promoting a memory of suffering and a more international worldview, in later generations the sixteenth-century mass migrations also encouraged a memory of some former refugee churches in the diaspora as "model churches" that might serve as guides from an idealized past. By the

142 Beenakker, "Brieven 1585–1612," 12. We haven't been able to trace these students back to the Netherlands. They are not listed in Van Lieburg's *Repertorium*. Only three of them appear in Heidelberg's list of students: René van der Warck, Andries Cornelisz and David Balthasar.

143 Selderhuis, "Eine attraktive Universität." See also chapter 5.

144 For example, Bernardus Faille to the Consistory in Emden, The Hague, August 28, 1584, in WMV 3/2, ep. 12, 29.

145 Janssen, *Dutch Revolt and Catholic Exile*, 104–28; Hsia, *World of Catholic Renewal*.

early seventeenth century, believers sometimes revered the Dutch-speaking congregations in Emden and London as "mother churches."[146] Many glorified Emden, especially for the asylum it had offered to so many pious believers.[147] Its hospitality was not the only reason that Emden obtained a special place in some Reformed narratives; the other reason was the foundational role later ascribed to the synod held at Emden in 1571. That synod had, according to many Reformed authors, laid the foundations for the Dutch Reformed Church. Reformed believers in the Dutch Republic continued to watch developments in Emden with a keen eye and to regard "Emden" as a part of the history of their church.[148]

The Palatinate, with the University of Heidelberg and the model church in Frankenthal, sparked the imagination of many Dutch Reformed authors as well.[149] This appreciation of the Palatinate was deeply rooted, as Leiden's actions in 1624 showed. That year, after the Spanish conquest of the Palatinate, Leiden's university felt called to help students from the Palatinate, precisely because the Palatinate had been a place of refuge for the Dutch brethren and because Heidelberg had sent so many excellent ministers to the Netherlands.[150]

The eleven Dutch Reformed communities in our study, however, played only a minor role in this sixteenth- and seventeenth-century memory culture. Only in the seventeenth century did Wesel's Dutch Reformed community acquire any status as the town where the so-called Convent of Wesel had purportedly convened in November 1568 and where the first foundations of Dutch Reformed ecclesiastical organization had thus supposedly been laid.[151] In the mid-seventeenth century, Jacobus Trigland marked a new development in describing Wesel and Emden as the churches that had laid the foundations of the church order. In his view, "*Ballinghen om des Evangeliums wille*" (exiles for the Gospel) had convened in Wesel in 1568 to summarize the basis of a future church order. Trigland was keen to list the names of those who had supposedly met in Wesel that autumn because he

146 Simon Ruytinck to ministers and elders of the Dutch Church in London, Middelburg, July 25, 1604, in Hessels, *Epistulae et Tractatus*, vol. 3, ep. 1620, 1145.

147 Kuchlinus to Arent Cornelisz, February 8, 1580, in WMV 3/5, ep. 6, 244.

148 Kuchlinus to Arent Cornelisz, Amsterdam, March 12, 1580, in WMV 3/5, ep. 8, 247.

149 Kuchlinus to Arent Cornelisz, Amsterdam, April 21, 1586, in WMV 3/5, ep. 19, 262.

150 The professors of the faculty of theology in Leiden to the ministers and elders of the Dutch stranger community in London, September 10, 1624, in Hessels, *Epistulae et Tractatus*, vol. 3, ep. 1833, 1310–11.

151 See Spohnholz, *Convent of Wesel.*

believed that readers might be happy to learn the names of their ancestors.[152] His church history was highly polemical, however. He wrote it as a reply to Johannes Uytenbogaert's vision, which linked orthodox Calvinism together with the bigotry of zealous Lutherans of the sixteenth century. According to Uytenbogaert, orthodox Calvinists resembled zealous Lutherans who had never been ready to grant more moderate Reformed a secure place in the Empire.[153] By contrast, Trigland insisted that it was the Reformed refugees in the Empire who had been the first staunch defenders of a Reformed confession.

Trigland's understandings were part of a general trend of Reformed authors from the mid-seventeenth century romantically remembering a heroic past. The children and grandchildren of former exiles also started to write family histories that remembered the exilic experiences of their ancestors. Abraham van den Corput (1599–1670), for instance, explained the decision of his ancestors to leave Breda as a refusal to yield to Spanish tyranny.[154] Andries van der Muelen interpreted Elisabeth Zeghers's decision to live in Cologne as a form of exile. He emphasized the commitment of his ancestors to the Reformed faith and described how his father Andries had left Antwerp immediately after Farnese's victory.[155] In other historical writings too, authors increasingly remembered going into exile as an act of piety. In his short description of the Reformation in Zaltbommel, for example, published in 1609, Henricus Caesarius (1550–1628) mentioned the exiles as among the first believers who dared to confess the Reformed faith.[156]

Gradually "exile" acquired a special place within the memory culture of the Dutch Reformed Church. The new waves of Reformed migrants in the late seventeenth and early eighteenth centuries, including the Bohemian Brethren, the French Huguenots, and the Salzburg Emigrants, were important factors in the growing relevance of "exile" for Dutch Reformed Protestants.[157] In particular, the Revocation of the Edict of Nantes in 1685 shocked the Dutch Republic and had a profound impact on Dutch Reformed identity. The support of persecuted brothers and sisters continued to be an important characteristic of Reformed communities. Later, stories

---

152 Trigland, *Kerckelycke Geschiedenissen*, 160–62.

153 Uytenbogaert, *Kerckelicke Historie*, part 2, 68.

154 Van den Corput, *De Goddelicke Vierschare, eerste deel*, *4v. Van den Corput first published his four volumes between 1659 and 1669.

155 Het Utrechts archief, 57 Familie Van der Muelen, inv. nr. 3. Müller, "Permeable Memories," 290.

156 Caesarius, *Danck Sermoon*, 3v.

157 Van der Linden, *Experiencing Exile*; Walker, *Salzburg Transaction*; Janssen, "Legacy of Exile."

of the persecution of Protestants and their mutual support for one another cemented the conviction of many Reformed authors that the Catholic Church was inherently tyrannical.[158] They apprehended stories on the sufferings of their coreligionists as a warning against the Catholic threat, and writers called on their audience to be on their guard against the "papists." Even as Reformed Protestants in the Dutch Republic maintained a privileged position from political authorities, allowing them to push expressions of Catholic piety into the hidden corners of Dutch society, these actions of solidarity and the stories of persecuted Protestants confirmed their self-perception as a minority under threat.

While many sixteenth-century Reformed authors had been in doubt about whether escape was even permitted, Huguenot leaders in the Republic after 1685 were especially inclined to portray exiles as martyrs of the true faith.[159] They were sure of their exemplary role and hallowed their fellow refugees as the purest part of Christ's flock.[160] Huguenot authors in the Republic often described exiles as having laudable virtues, such as a steadfast faith and an industrious work ethic. This changing image of exiles influenced the memory culture of sixteenth-century Dutch exiles as well. New migrants used older stories and older visions to interpret their experiences, but their stories also influenced how the older stories were retold. And although the Huguenots and the Salzburg Exiles praised migrants as models of steadfast faith, they did not explain exile itself as promoting any specific theological outlook. This link only later came into being.

Nineteenth-century Reformed church leader and Dutch political giant Abraham Kuyper (1837–1920) proved key in creating a rather specific image of both the refugee churches and the refugees. His use of the refugee churches is a clear example of an invented history. Starting in the later 1860s, Kuyper advocated for churches whose members were ready to commit themselves to the Reformed confession independent from state interference. He described those sixteenth-century refugee churches as the forerunners of the independent churches he envisioned and idealized the sixteenth-century exiles as paragons of Calvinist steadfastness.[161] Thus, references to sixteenth-century Reformed Protestants helped him claim authority for his late nineteenth-century vision. According to him, voluntary

---

158 Grell, *Brethren in Christ*, 229–48.

159 Benoit, *Historie der Gereformeerde Kerken van Vrankryk*, d2r–d3r; Gillis, *Kerckelijcke historie*, 6.

160 Van der Linden, *Experiencing Exile*, 96.

161 Kuyper, "De eerste Kerkvergaderingen of de vesting onzer Hervormde Kerk, en de strijd over haar zelfstandig bestwaan 1550–1618," and "De eeredienst," in Ter Haar and Moll, *Geschiedenis der christelijke kerk*, 71–86, 87–113; Kuyper, *De Hollandsche gemeente te Londen*.

church membership, confessional commitment, and ecclesiastical discipline had been the core of Calvinism from its beginning. Kuyper's involvement in the publication of sixteenth-century sources, the quality of his work, and his many students enabled him to have an impact on historical research on exiles up to the present day. A striking example of Kuyper's influence is the use of A. A. van Schelven's extensive history of the Dutch refuge churches by modern historians. Van Schelven's work, written as a PhD dissertation at the Vrije Universiteit Amsterdam that Kuyper founded, is in many ways an admirable piece of work. It is also permeated by Kuyper's ecclesiastical ideals. Historians continue to use Van Schelven's work, in large part because he provides us access to sources that do not survive. To a large extent, a century later the historian Heiko Oberman took over the general picture that Kuyper drafted. According to Oberman, sixteenth-century Reformed migrants formulated a "theology of exile," that is to say a theology that embraced predestination, promoted a strong ecclesiastical discipline, and drew clear confessional boundaries.[162]

The sixteenth-century picture of migrants, however, was more diverse than this picture suggests. Migrants did not invent a new theology but applied old theological ideas to ascribe meaning to their experiences and did so in various ways. Their interpretations were primarily embedded in a narrative of suffering. Sixteenth-century Dutch Reformed believers had interpreted their persecutions and troubles in terms of Christian suffering. Their readiness to endure tribulations marked them as true believers who were ready to follow Christ's footsteps and to bear his cross. In this larger story, suffering migrants did not play a major role. Some migrants saw flight as the better option, describing it as a form of obedience to Christ's commandments. Others became convinced that they fared better than those who stayed at home. How migrants classified themselves varied as well: some identified as exiles, others as pilgrims. On the chalices Dutch migrants offered to Wesel in 1578, they had themselves depicted as pious strangers receiving hospitality. This identification mattered: the term "exile" suggests a forced displacement and recalls Old Testament stories of the exile of ancient Israelites. The term "pilgrim" does not necessarily imply forced displacement and rather refers to medieval pilgrimage stories.[163]

The idea that exiles developed a specific theology stems from the idea that they did so as a way of competing with extraordinary suffering. In fact, many of them fared quite well abroad and even integrated into their host societies in a variety of ways (as we have seen throughout this book), even if doing so required a range of often frustrating compromises and sometimes even

162 Spohnholz and Van Veen, "Disputed Origins," 418–25.

163 Van Veen, "Reformierte Flüchtlinge."

Figure 6.1. The stranger from atop a chalice given by Wesel's Dutch Reformed congregation to Wesel's magistrates in 1578. Stadtarchiv Wesel 01a.

dangers. Only a small minority of those who had the opportunity returned home. It is difficult to pinpoint the extent to which their former migration continued to influence returnees. Their stay abroad probably stimulated an international outlook. After his decision to move to Dordrecht, for instance, Hendrik van den Corput continued to exchange letters with people who stayed in the Empire. His contacts in the Palatinate allowed him to establish an early modern student exchange program: for years he helped students attend the University of Heidelberg. This international outlook was probably the most important fruit of this sixteenth-century mass migration. This was, however, not a result of any specific Reformed way of thinking, since Europeans of all faiths—especially educated Europeans living in cities—were increasingly adopting international worldviews as well.

However, theologically, migrants mostly draw on intellectual traditions they already knew. Reformed migrants used old theological concepts about Christian suffering to make sense of their experiences. They draw on ideas about pilgrimage for the same reason. There has been little recognition of Protestant migrants' emphasis on pilgrimage and on being strangers in this world, but the topic is worth further research. Decades after the end of the Reformation, even after securing a privileged position in the Dutch Republic, Dutch Reformed Protestants continued to identify as a minority under threat. The sins of the world, in this view, never stopped troubling "true Christians." The decision of the so-called Pilgrim Fathers who migrated to North America is probably the most well-known example of this migration-related rhetoric in the seventeenth century. In other instances, authors used this rhetoric of pilgrimage in a more spiritual sense. John Bunyan's 1678 *Pilgrim's Progress* is a clear example of how important the idea of distancing oneself from a hostile world through an inner migration continued to be. Yet there is still much research to be done regarding the extent to which later puritan rhetoric drew on narratives of earlier Reformed migration experiences.

Afterword

As noted in the introduction of this book, historians of sixteenth-century Dutch Reformed migrants have often instrumentalized them to serve two kinds of arguments. The first, often favored by authors sympathetic to Reformed orthodoxy, explain how the experience of exile allowed "Calvinists" to form model churches, free from the constraints of governmental supervision that characterized other leading strands of early modern Christianity. Astonishingly, some authors even celebrated these refugee congregations for establishing the principle of the separation of church and state![1] In the second, often proffered by those who favored secularism and liberalism, exile transformed these migrants into militant and doctrinaire "Calvinist" culture warriors intent on imposing their vision on an otherwise tolerant and nondogmatic society. Astute commentators on the historiography of the Dutch Reformation and the early Dutch Republic have usefully contrasted these two traditions, showing the flaws of each.[2] However, when we began zeroing in on just the question of the refugees themselves, we were struck by a similarity of the two opposing arguments: both suggested that Calvinism had some kind of natural affinity to exile, or that the experience of exile itself was sufficient to explain the strength of Reformed orthodoxy in the Dutch Republic. As we continued to work, we saw example after example in which historians did not even require evidence to make such claims. The story told itself. Meanwhile, forceful challenges to these assertions have simply been overlooked.[3]

This book has been an effort to retell these migrants' stories, severed from the historiographical shadows that have long haunted them, whether they expressed some fundamentally "Calvinist" character or stood in stark contrast to some fundamentally "Dutch" character. Both claims about sixteenth-century Dutch-speaking refugees anachronistically essentialize confessional or nationalist characteristics in ways that obscure efforts to understand who they were. While historians in the nineteenth and early twentieth centuries

1 Lang, *Reformation und Gegenwart*, 202–3.

2 Nauta, "De Reformatie in Nederland"; Kaplan, "'Dutch' Religious Tolerance," in Hsia and Van Nierop, *Calvinism and Religious Toleration*, 8–26.

3 Rogier, "Over karakter en omvang."

sometimes did this in abashedly jingoistic or Romanticist prose, in recent years, these claims have remained remarkably resilient, if more matter of fact.

As we have seen time and time again in this book, the categories of analysis that historians use, often inherited from intervening centuries, can sometimes obscure elements of the experiences of these migrants that are critical to understanding the reasons why they left (chapter 1), the terms of their arrival (chapter 2), the relationships they developed with their hosts (chapter 3), the forms of their worship (chapter 4), the ties they developed across the diaspora (chapter 5), and their decision whether or not to return to the Low Countries (chapter 6). To be honest, with each chapter we struggled about how to sever our own history from the legacies of intervening centuries. Of course, modern historians (including ourselves) still *greatly* profit from the diligence of eighteenth-, nineteenth-, and twentieth-century record collectors and historians for compiling, preserving, and publishing sources. However, this dependence on earlier materials sometimes also makes it difficult to look across categories of difference, whether those were confessional, political, linguistic, national, or otherwise as well as to critically assess the extent to which printed primary source collections might have played a role in highlighting some voices and silencing others. We hope that this book offers one model for how others might be able to dispel some of the shadows that obscure elements of their historical quarry, too.

In the end, the research presented here offers little to contribute to the historiography of toleration in the Dutch Republic or to the development of Reformed orthodoxy in the Dutch-speaking world. It's clear enough that the experience of being a refugee, exile, or forced migrant played no essential role in shaping these migrants in the ways that scholars have sometimes suggested. As a group, they did not become more tolerant or less tolerant, more Calvinist or less Calvinist, more committed to state supervision of religious life or less. They did not possess a shared ethnic or political identity. Neither did they possess a shared commitment to the Dutch Revolt or a shared political ideology. While these conclusions are largely negative, their significance lies in that they challenge much of what has been previously written.

Indeed, what most characterized the Dutch Reformed refugees of the late sixteenth century is their diverse range of experiences. As we explained in chapter 1, people fled for a wide range of reasons, with multiple push and pull factors shaping their decision-making process. Their travels were not just one way; migrants sometime moved back and forth between the Low Countries and the Holy Roman Empire or between various cities within the diaspora. Once they arrived, a range of local forces shaped what terms host governments demanded for their stay, including the local balance of confessional groups, how people understood the boundaries between those groups, how magistrates understood and applied imperial law, as well as the interventions of nonlocal powers. In chapter 3, we learned that treating all these migrants using the same confessional and ethnic categories obscures much about migrants' relations with their hosts. Diversities in refugees' experiences mean that scholars need to be cautious about markers of foreigners' social integration into host populations. An action that might be taken as indicative of assimilation in one community might have meant something very different in another. The compromises required for preserving sacred devotions also depended greatly on location, as we saw in chapter 4. Dutch Reformed migrants chose from a range of options, including traveling to nearby territories, worshipping in private houses or barns, or worshipping in services alongside people of different confessions. This last category of compromises proved easier for rites of passage than for the celebration of the Lord's Supper, but there were even diverse ways to manage communion services. For all this variety, of course, the Dutch-speaking Reformed migrants in our study maintained important ties to one another, sharing ecclesiastical institutions, pastors, social welfare, and correspondence, as we showed in chapter 5. They were deeply committed to the welfare of fellow believers across the diaspora, imagining themselves to be part of a community of faith that was not only well-defined but also connected to a universal, divine, and eternal spiritual community. But not only were the networks they developed to support that community less oriented to Netherlands than historians have often assumed, but the political, social, cultural, and religious arrangements still had to be developed according to local demands, meaning that diversity of experiences still reigned.

Facing this range of experiences, migrants drew on preexisting personal, intellectual, and emotional resources to make sense of what they were going through, as explained in chapter 6. They did not understand those experiences through the same lens, and they certainly did not all understand them as traumatic or exilic. One of the most surprising conclusions of our study is that, when faced with the opportunity to abandon the compromises required in their new homes, return to the Netherlands, and join the new public Dutch Reformed Church, most did not do so. Even for those who did go to the Dutch Republic, few experienced this move as returning "home." Rather, their move was yet another remigration, impelled by a variety of political, economic, and familial factors. It was only after several generations that a shared memory culture of these forced migrations started to emerge. Over the centuries, that memory culture developed into a single historical narrative, first among coreligionists either celebrating their own ancestors or seeking to integrate themselves to the migrants' descendants. Later, that narrative got picked up by critics of Reformed orthodoxy, for whom the same story served opposite purposes—presenting them as introducing a foreign intolerance into an otherwise tolerant Dutch society.

When we pan out from national narratives and consider this book's contributions relative to the recent scholarship on early modern migration, our research takes on a different light. Rather than exile promoting more tightly defined, militant, and rigid thinkers, perhaps it just as often promoted habits of living and thinking that encouraged flexibility, creativity, and a willingness to compromise. The anthropologist Anton Blok has suggested that such life-changing challenges like fleeing one's home as an exile and or living in social exclusion as a stranger can lead to what he calls the "blessings of adversity" (*de zegeningen van tegenslag*) that allow for high degrees of creativity.[4] Peter Burke has similarly suggested that the experience of exile can promote a "deprovincialization" that can spur on innovation and creative hybridization in thinking for both migrants and their hosts.[5] Regarding sixteenth-century Reformed refugees, Nicole Grochowina and Michael Bruening have both recently suggested that sixteenth-century Reformed refugee communities were places where heterodox, nonconfessional, and even tolerant ideas could flourish.[6] This claim points to the exact opposite of Heiko Oberman's argument about an *Exulantentheologie*.

For the refugees in our study, there is something to commend such an interpretation. First, their experiences in the Empire required these migrants to flexibly adapt the ways they thought, behaved, worshipped, and communicated with remarkable creativity and resilience. One can see traces of this trend in every chapter of this book, from the decisions to flee or to creatively recast themselves as adherents to the Augsburg Confession in order to secure their stay. We see it too in the diverse liturgical compromises they developed depending on local needs, or the kind of alliances and collaborations they made with German- and French-speaking coreligionists abroad, but also at times with Lutherans, Anabaptists, and Catholics. We can also see it in the ways they adapted practices used by Reformed Protestants elsewhere—including disciplinarily procedures, letters of attestations, and purposes of classis institutions—to serve their distinct needs. Earlier historians have argued that a strict system of ecclesiastical discipline, a well-structured theology, and a strong pattern of coordination across vast distances proved critical to the Dutch Reformed diaspora. In fact, it might have been the ability of these migrants to adapt locally in ways that were often not well coordinated that proved critical.

4 Blok, *De vernieuwers.*

5 Burke, *Exiles and Expatriates.*

6 Grochowina, *Indifferenz und Dissens*, 402–3; Bruening, *Refusing*, 188–92.

Second, it was not just relations across the diaspora that held it together but the migrants' ability to build substantive relations with those outside the diaspora. In that sense, rather than seeing refugee communities as isolated in a foreign land, we need to understand the constructive associations that they built with others, which many carried with them through their entire lives. Here too, we see examples in every chapter. It certainly was true for those who studied at the University of Heidelberg. It was also true for those who developed international correspondence networks while living in the Empire. We can also see it in the cooperation that they built with refugees from France, as well as coreligionists from the Empire. It was also true in the patrons they developed among political and religious elites within their host communities. We see it in the friendships and mutual dependencies they developed that allowed some to look the other way at their unorthodoxy. We can see in in the critical alliances they built with influential German Reformed princes who proved crucial to providing protection, finances, and worship spaces for the migrants. The most important of these, until his death in October 1576, was Elector Friedrich III of Palatine. Other noble patrons included members of the Neuenahr, Myllendonk, and Goor families.

There is a critical limitation to this interpretation, though: those who fled were already likely to be both more adaptable and more connected to the wider world. After all, migrants rarely traveled to a new community unless they already knew that place existed, already had some knowledge about how to get there, and had the means to make such a trip happen. Dutch Reformed who fled, that is, were more likely than those who stayed to be educated, to know travel routes, to be in contact with family or friends who had already fled, and to have occupations that relied on specialized skills rather than (for instance) the possession or use of a specific tract of land. In that case, life as a refugee merely exacerbated preexisting attributes. Further, there is no real evidence of any particularly innovative intellectual productivity in any of these refugee communities. Their discourses for describing suffering were part of conventional Christian repertoires. Yes, they learned to compromise, but learning to grudgingly compromise with religious difference was part of a general experience in post-Reformation Europe, not something specific to refugees. While a few influential Dutch Reformed leaders came out of these communities—Arent Cornelisz and Werner Helmichius, instance—their impact did not stem from their intellectual creativity or originality but from their energy, focus, and organizational skills.

The experience of life in the Empire, though, did provide these migrants extensive practice with multilingualism and expanded opportunities to interact with people from different backgrounds. If these "blessings of adversity" did not have direct intellectual impacts on the refugees themselves, such assets may have had intergenerational impacts. As Johannes Müller has shown, second-generation descendants of the Dutch Reformed migrants who stayed in Frankfurt emerged as important translators and publishers of new nonconfessional forms of pious literature that began offering alternatives to the dogmatic confessionalism of earlier generations.[7] In that sense, if Nicholas's Terpstra was right that the sixteenth century saw the first emergence of religious refugees as a mass phenomenon, then perhaps the consequential creation of intellectual and cultural creativity promoted by exile was also only long term and intergenerational. After all, later commenters on these forced migrations assigned specific meanings to refugees' experiences. And in later centuries that subsequent meaning-making proved generative of new identities that shaped varieties of local, regional, and national politics. Of course, before such conclusions can be sustained, there remains much research to do. We need deeper understandings of the relationships between refugees across language and culture systematically. We need more studies by scholars capable of working in the full range of languages that the refugees they study used. And we need more collaborative projects, like this one, that can grapple with the enormous challenge of working against the archival grain.

If we have been cognizant that politics of the seventeenth, eighteenth, nineteenth, and twentieth centuries has deeply shaped the study of sixteenth-century refugees, we are also aware that our own scholarship is shaped by the politics of our moment in history. Today, exile and migration in early modern Europe have become an important focus of scholarly attention, largely inspired by increasing debates about refugees and immigrants in Europe and the United States. These migrations have challenged some self-understandings of people in the West and provoked deep debates that seem to be reshaping global politics. The stakes of that migration could be high, as movements of people from the Global South challenge Western political and economic dominance that began just about the time that our own study of migration begins: in the mid-sixteenth century. Like today, the forced migrations of the sixteenth century sparked debates about the nature of political and economic order. They also forced similar questions also about whether the cultural and religious changes that necessarily accompany migration should be welcomed or minimized, and about whether the ways we manage the misunderstandings and disagreements that result are sustainable and constructive or volatile and dangerous. Certainly, the study of early modern migration makes it clear that questions about the relationship between the culture of settlers and settled, and related questions about religious coexistence, are much older than we are often inclined to think. Of course, historians cannot solve contemporary challenges or resolve debates

7 Müller, "Transmigrant Literature."

about the causes and consequences of migration and refugee resettlement today. But historians can contribute to contemporary debates by providing critical context necessary for a more mature understanding of both ourselves and others. In that sense, we hope our book helps readers check themselves from the easy lure to categorize members of an ethnic, religious, or national group of migrants according to some preset assumption about who they are, why they are leaving, how they experience their migration, or possible future impacts of their travels. Thus, we see this book not only as part of a scholarly discussion about the sixteenth century but a way that we can offer historical perspective that might allow others—in Mirjam van Veen's home in Europe, Jesse Spohnholz's home in the United States, or otherwise—to consider their views on refugees and forced migrations in more thoughtful, more self-critical, and more generous ways.

Bibliography

Manuscript Sources

Die autobiographischen Aufzeichnungen Hermann Weinsbergs: Digitale Gesamtausgabe < https://www.weinsberg.uni-bonn.de/>.
De briefwisseling van Willem van Oranje. <http://resources.huygens.knaw.nl/wvo/>.

Codex Palatinus Germanicus. Universitätsbibliothek Heidelberg. https://digi.ub.uni-heidelberg.de/de/bpd/virtuelle_bibliothek/codpalgerm/index.html.

804 (Briefe an Henricus Smetius, verschiedene Orte, 1585–1593)
838 Band 1 and 2 (Briefe an Henricus Smetius, verschiedene Orte, 1586–1613)
841 Briefe der Familie Corput—Urkunden, verschiedene Orte, 16./17. Jh.

Erfgoed Leiden en Omstreken

0096 Daniël van der Meulen en Hester de la Faille, zijn vrouw, 1550–1648.

Evangelisches Kirchenarchiv Wesel

Gefach 6,1 Acta Generalia. Kirchen und Konsistorial Sachen, 1444–1600
Gefach 6,4 Akten die Geschichte der evangelischen Gemeinde zu Wesel 1492–1635
Gefach 12,5 12,5 Originalprotocolle der ref. Classis Vesaliensis, 1572–1595
Gefach 21,1 Liturgical book from sixteenth-century Wesel
Gefach 37,6–8 Kirchenrechnungen Willibrordi, 1536–1615
Gefach 60,7 Kirchen Ordnungen 1561–1781
Gefach 65,1 Denkwürdige Sachen: unsere Stadt- und Landsachen … 1352–1629
Gefach 65,2 Unterschiedliche notwendige religions-articelen.
Gefach 72,1–3 Acta consistorii der gereformierder nederduytschen gemeente binnen Wesel 1. Sept. 1573–3. Dec. 1601

Gefach 74,1 Traubuch Willibrordikirche 1574–22.12.1582, Taufbuch der Willirbrordikirche Febr. 1578–26.10.1640
Gefach 74,37 Traubuch Mathenakirche, 1564–21.07.1620

Stadtarchiv Frankenthal

1/1/1–3 Kapitulationen
1/2/4–6. 13 Privelegien
1/11/82–91 Rats- und Gerichtsprotokolle

Stadtarchiv Wesel

A1/152,1 Landes Militaria und Defension-Sachen
A1/155 Landtags-Sachen 1454–1850
A1/275 Wallonische-französiche Kolonie, 1562–1586
A3/44–65, Ratsprotokolle, 1549–1600

Printed Primary Sources

[Amsweer, Doede van.] *Een Christelijcke Tragedia Die Coopman ofte dat oordeel geheeten. Daerinne die Hoovet-stucken ofte Gront-leeringhen van twee Religien, die Romische Papistische ende die Gereformeerde Evangelische....* Groningen: Hans Sas, 1613.

Antwoort Lamberti Danei... op drie voorghestelde vragen, nopende het ampt der overheydt inde regeeringhe der kercken... door Arnoldum Cornelii. Delft: Jan Andriesz, 1613.

Arend, Sabine, ed. *Die Evangelische Kirchenordnungen des XVI. Jahrhundert.* Vol. 9: Hesse II. Tübingen: Mohr Siebeck, 2011.

Augustijn, Cornelis and Frans Pieter van Stam, ed. *Ioannis Calvini Epistolae.* Geneva: Librairie Droz, 2005.

Becker, Bruno, ed. *Bronnen tot de kennis van het leven en de werken van D. V. Coornhert.* The Hague: Martinus Nijhoff, 1928.

Beenakker, A. J. M., ed. "Brieven van de familie van de Corput." https://www.yumpu.com/nl/document/view/20133579/pdf-brieven-1562–1584-brieven-van-den-corputnl.

Benoit, Élie. *Historie der Gereformeerde Kerken van Vrankryk: vervattende het begin en den voortgang der Reformatie, begonnen met het jaar 1517. en byzonderlyk de historie sedert het verlenen van 't edict van Nantes.* Amsterdam: Jan ten Hoorn, 1696.

Bonali-Fiquet, F. ed. *Jean Calvin: Lettres à Monsieur et Madame de Falais.* Geneva: Librairie Droz, 1991.

Booma, Jan G. J. van, ed. *Communio Clandestina: Archivalien der Konsistorien der heimlichen Niederländischen Reformierten Flüchtlingsgemeinden in Goch und Gennep im Herzogtum Kleve 1570–circa 1610.* 2 vols. Bonn: Verlag Dr. Rudolf Habelt, 2010.

———. and J. L. van der Gouw, eds. *Communio et Mater Fidelium: Acta des Konsistoriums der Niederländischen Reformierten Flüchtlingsgemeinde in Wesel, 1573–1582.* Cologne: Rheinland-Verlag, 1991.

Caesarius, Henricus. *Danck Sermoon over het teghenwoordighe ghemaeckte bestant van twaelf jaeren, wt de handelinghen des Apostelen, cap 9. Vers 31. tot Godts lof ende eere.* Utrecht: Jan a Meliszoon, 1609.

Calvin, John. *Ioannis Calvinis Opera Quae Supersunt Omnia.* Edited by G. Baum, E. Cunitz, and E. Reuss. 59 vols. Brunswick: C. A. Schwetschke, 1863–1900.

———. *L'Excuse du Noble Seigneur Jacques de Bourgogne Seigneur de Falais et de Bredam.* Edited by A. Cartier. Geneva: A. Jullien, 1911.

Cleyn, Cornelis, *Dank-offer voor de eerstelingen van Neerlands vrijheid, by het vieren van het twede eeuwgety der inneminge van Den Briele door de watergeuzen.* Den Briel: Wed. Verhell en Zoon, 1772.

Cochrane, Arthur C., ed. *Reformed Confessions of the Sixteenth Century.* Louisville, KY: Westminster John Knox Press, 2003.

Coornhert, Dirck Volkerstz. *Brieven-boeck, inhoudende honderdt brieven.* Amsterdam: Jacob Aertsz Colom, 1630.

———. *Dieryck Volckertsz. Coornherts wercken, waer van eenige noyt voor desen gedruct zyn.* 3 vols. Amsterdam: Jacob Aertsz Colom, 1630.

———. *Hondert Brieven van verscheyden ghewightighe en stichtelijcke materien.* [Amsterdam: Jacob Aertsz Colom], 1626.

———. *Liedboeck.* Amsterdam: Herman Janszoon, [1575].

[———.], *Remonstrance of vertooch by die van Leyden* ([Leiden: A. Verschout], 1582

Corput, Abraham van den. *De Goddelicke Vierschare, dat is, ontdeckinge der Hemelsche Oordeelen, Het eerste deel.* Amsterdam: Joannes van Waesberge, 1681.

———. *De Goddelicke Vierschare. Dat is ontdeckinge der Hemelsche Oordeelen, Het III deel.* Amsterdam: Jan Jansz van Waesbergen, 1665.

Dathenus, Petrus. *Bestendige Antwort Etlicher Fragstück, so die Predicanten zu Franckfurt am Mayn zur Prob uber die Jüngst zu Dreßden der Churfürstlichen Sächsischen Theologen gestelte Bekandtnuß, in Truck zur Warnung haben Außgehen lassen.* Heidelberg: Johann Mayer aus Regensburg, 1572.

———. *Kurtze und Warhafftige Erzelung, welcher Massen, den Frantzösischen unnd Niderländischen verjagten Christen, in der Stadt Franckfurt am Meyn* ... Heidelberg: Schirat, 1563.

Dodt van Flensburg, J. J., ed. *Archief voor kerkelijke en wereldsche geschiedenissen inzonderheid van Utrecht*, vol 1. Utrecht: N. van der Monde, 1839.

Drecoll, Volker Henning, ed. *Der Passauer Vertrag (1553): Einleitung und Edition.* Berlin: Walter de Gruyter, 2000.

Eeghen, I. H. Van, ed. *Dagboek van Broeder Wouter Jacobsz (Gualtherus Jacobi Masius) prior van Stein. Amsterdam, 1572–1578 en Montfoort, 1578–1579.* Groningen: J. B. Wolters, 1959.

Franckfurtischer Religions-Handlungen. 2 vols. Frankfurt am Main: Franz Varrentrapp, 1735.

Gillis, Pierre. *Kerckelijcke historie, vande Gereformeerde Kercken, vergadert in eenighe valeyen van Piedmont, en haere nagebueren, eertijds genaamt Waldensen ... Uyt het Frans in het Nederduyts vertaalt door Gillis van Breen.* Amsterdam: Jaques Boursse, 1657.

Groen van Prinsterer, G. *Archives ou correspondence inédite de la maison d'Orange-Nassau*, première série, t. 3: 1567–1572. Leiden: S. et J. Luchtmans, 1836.

Hessels, J. H., ed. *Epistulae et tractatus cum Reformationis tum ecclesiae Londino-Batavae historiam illustrantes.* 3 vols. Cambridge: Ecclesiae Londino-Batavae, 1889–97.

Hooijer, Cornelis, ed. *Oude kerkordeningen der Nederlandsche hervormde gemeenten (1563–1638), en het Concept-Reglement, op de organisatie van het Hervormd Kerkgenootschap in het Koningrijk Holland (1809).* Zalt-Bommel: Johannes Noman, 1865.

Hoornbeeck, Johannes. *Belydenis Predicaty.* Utrecht: Jan van Waesberge, 1648.

Janssen, H. Q., ed. *Handelingen van den kerkeraad der Nederlandsche gemeente te Keulen, 1571–1591.* Werken der Marnix-Vereeniging, serie I, deel III. Utrecht: Kemink & zoon, 1881.

——— and J. J. van Toorenenbergen, eds. *Brieven uit onderscheidene kerkelijke archieven.* Werken der Marnix-Vereeniging, serie III, deel II. Utrecht: Kemink en zoon, 1878.

——— and J. J. van Toorenenbergen, eds. *Brieven uit onderscheidene kerkelijke archieven.* Werken der Marnix-Vereeniging, serie III, deel IV. Utrecht: Kemink en zoon, 1880.

——— and J. J. van Toorenenbergen, eds. *Acten van classicale en synodale vergaderingen der verstrooide gemeenten in het land van Cleef, Sticht van Keulen en Aken, 1571–1589.* Werken der Marnix-Vereeniging, serie II, deel V. Utrecht: Kemink & zoon, 1882.

Jensma, Th. W. *Uw rijk kome: Acta van de kerkeraad van de Nederduits gereformeerde gemeente te Dordrecht 1573–1579.* Dordrecht: J. P. van den Tol, 1981.

Jongbloet-Van Houtte, Gisela, ed. *Brieven en andere bescheiden betreffende Daniel van der Meulen, 1584–1600*, vol 1: augustus 1584–september 1585. Rijks Geschiedkundige Publicatiën, 196. The Hague: Martinus Nijhoff, 1986.

Keller, Ludwig, ed. *Die Gegenreformation in Westfalen und am Niederrhein: Aktenstücke und Erläuterungen.* 2 vols. Leipzig: S. Hirzel, 1881–87.

Kirchenordnung, Wie es mit der Christlichen Lehre, Heiligen Sacramenten, und Ceremonien, inn der Chur und fürtlichen Pfalz bey Rhein, Gehalten wirdt. Heidelberg: Jacob Müller, 1585.

Kuyper, Abraham, ed. *Johannes á Lasco Opera tam edita quam inedita.* 2 vols. Amsterdam: Frederic Muller, 1866.

Langhans, Adolf, ed. *Die Bürgerbücher der Stadt Wesel: Die Listen Der Neubürger von 1308–1677.* Duisburg: Druck von O. Hecker, 1950.

Lanzinner, Maximilian, ed. *Der Reichstag zu Speyer 1570.* 2 vols. Göttingen: Vandenhoeck & Ruprecht, 1988.

Livre synodal contenant les articles résolus dans les synodes des églises wallonnes des Pays-Bas. Vol. 1: 1563–1683. The Hague: Martinus Nijhoff, 1896.

Louwijc, P. *De wtkomste der wandelinge vanden eerweerdigen, ghetrouwen ende godsaligen Dienaer Jesu Christi ende zijns heyligen woorts Pieter Hasaert …* Delft: Bruyn Harmansz Schinckel, 1598.

Meinert, Hermann, ed. *Die Eingliederung der Niederländischen Glaubensflüchtlinge in die Frankfurter Bürgerschaft, 1554–1596: Auszüge aus den Frankfurter Ratsprotokollen.* Frankfurt am Main: Waldemar Kramer, 1981.

——— and Wolfram Dahmer, eds. *Das Protokollbuch der Niederländischen Reformierten Gemeinde zu Frankfurt am Main, 1570–1581.* Frankfurt am Main: Waldemar Kramer, 1977.

Meulen, P. van der, ed. *Het roerspel en de comedies van Coornhert. Uitgegeven en van commentaar voorzien.* [Leiden: Brill, 1955].

Noll, Mark A., ed. *Confessions and Catechisms of the Reformation.* Grand Rapids, MI: Baker Book House, 1991.

Nopp, Johann. *Aacher Chronik, Das ist eine Kurtz historische Beschreibung aller Gedenkwürdigen Antiquitäten und Geschichten … Dess Königlichen Stuls und H. Römischen Reichs Statt Aach.* Cologne: Jodicus Kalcoven, 1643.

Orange, William of. *De verantwoordinghe des princen van Oraengien tegen de valsche logenen, daer mede sijn Wedersprekers hem soecken t'onrecht te beschuldighen.* Wesel: Augustijn van Hasselt, 1568.

Pontanus, Johannes Isacius. *Historische beschrijvinghe der seer wijt beroemde coopstadt Amsterdam*, trans. Petrus Montanus. Amsterdam: J. Hondius, 1614.

Poullain, Valérand. *Liturgia Sacra (1551–1555)*. Edited by A. C. Honders. Leiden: Brill, 1970.

Protocoll, Das ist, alle handlung des gesprechs zu Frankenthal inn der Churfürstlichen Pfalz. Heidelberg: Johannes Mayer, 1571.

Quick, John, ed. *Synodicon in Gallia Reformata, or, the Acts, Decisions, Decrees, and Canons of Those Famous National Councils of the Reformed Churches in France*. London: T. Parkhurst and J. Robinson, 1692.

Rosenkranz, Albert, ed. *Generalsynodalbuch: Die Akten der Generalsynoden von Jülich, Kleve, Berg und Mark, 1610–1793*. Vol. 1. Düsseldorf: Presseverband der evangelischen Kirche im Rheinland, 1966.

Rotscheidt, Wilhelm, ed. "Confessio D. Johannis Badij." *Monatshefte für Rheinische Kirchengeschichte* 1 (1907): 555–58.

Rutgers, F. L., ed. *Acta van de Nederlandsche synoden der zestiende eeuw*. Dordrecht: J. P. van den Tol, 1980.

Ruytinck, Simeon. *Gheschiedenissen ende handelingen die voornemelick aengaen de Nederduytsche natie ende gemeynten: Wonende in Engelant ende int bysonder tot Londen*. Edited by J. J. van Toorenenbergen. Werken der Marnix-Vereeniging, serie III, deel I. Utrecht: Kemink en zoon, 1873.

Schilling, Heinz, ed. *Die Kirchenratsprotokolle der Reformierten Gemeinde Emden, 1557–1620*. 2 vols. Cologne: Böhlau, 1989.

Schmidt, Benno, ed. *Frankfurter Zunfturkunden bis zum Jahre 1612*. Vol. 1. Wiesbaden: Dr. Martin Sändig oHG, 1968.

Sehling, Emil, ed. *Die evangelischen Kirchenordnungen des XVI. Jahrhundert: Kurpfalz*. Tübingen: Mohr Siebeck, 1969.

Simons, Eduard, ed. *Kölnische Konsistorial-Beschlüsse: Presbyterial-Protokolle der heimlichen Kölnischen Gemeinde, 1572–1596*. Bonn: P. Hanstein's Verlag, 1905.

———, ed. *Synodalbuch: Die Akten der Synoden und Quartierkonsistorien in Jülich, Cleve und Berg, 1570–1610*. Neuwied: Louis Heuser, 1909.

Sloot, Augustys van der. *Twe honderdjarige gedagtenis der verlossinge van Middelburg uit de Spaansche en Antichristische dwingelandye, plegtig geviert op zondag namiddag den xx. February 1774*. Middelburg: Levinus Moens, [1774].

Someren, J. F. van. "Oranjes Briefwisseling met Jacob van Wesenbeke en andere geheime agenten in de Nederlanden 1570–1573, voor het eerst volledig uitgegeven." *Oud Holland* (1892): 81–96; 147–209; (1893): 7–29; 105–124; 179–92; 236–54.

Teschenmacher, Werner. *Annales Ecclesiastici*. Düsseldorf: Presseverband der Evangelischen Kirche im Rheinland, 1962.

Toorenenbergen J. J. van, ed. *Philips van Marnix van St. Aldegonde: Godsdienstige en kerkelijke geschriften.* The Hague: Martinus Nijhoff, 1878.

———, ed. *Brieven uit onderscheidene kerkelijke archieven.* Werken der Marnix-Vereeniging, serie III, deel V. 2 vols. Utrecht: Kemink en zoon, 1882–84.

Trigland, Jacobus. *Kerckelycke Geschiedenissen begrypende de swaere en bekommerlijcke geschillen, in de vereenigde Nederlanden voorgevallen, met derselver beslissinge ende aenmerckingen op de kerckelycke historie van Johannes Wtenbogaert.* Leiden: Adriaen Wyngaerd, 1650.

Ulenberg, Caspar. *Summarische Beschreibung eines ungefehrlichen Gesprächs.* Cologne: Gerwinus Calenius, 1590.

Utenhove, Jan. *Simplex et fidelis narratio de instituta ac demun dissipata Belgarum, aliorumque peregrinorum in Anglia, Ecclesia: & potissimum de suspectis postea illius nomine itineribus, quaeque eis in illis evenerunt.* [Basel]: n.p., 1560.

Uytenbogaert, Johannes. *Kerckelicke Historie vervatende verscheyden gedenckwaerdige saken, in de christenheyt voor-gevallen.* Rotterdam: Bastiaen Wagens, 1647.

Velden, Adolf von den, ed. *Registres de l'eglise réformée Néerlandaise de Frankenthal au Palatinat, 1565–1689.* 2 vols. Brussels: Librairie évangélique, 1911–13.

Vries van Heekelingen Herman de, ed. *Genève Pépinière du Calvinisme Hollandais,* vol II: *Correspondance des élèves de Théodore de Bèze après leur départ de Genève.* The Hague: Martinus Nijhoff, 1924.

Wied, Hermann von. *Einfältiges Bedenken: Reformationsentwurf für das Erzstift Köln von 1543.* Edited by Helmut Gerhard and Wilfried Borth. Düsseldorf: Presseverband der evangelischen Kirche im Rheinland, 1972.

Secondary Sources

Abt, Josef, and Wolfgang Vomm. *Der Kölner Friedhof Melaten: Begegnung mit Vergangenem und Vergessenem aus Rheinischer Geschichte und Kunst.* Cologne: Greven, 1980.

Acquoy, J. G. R. *Jan van Venray (Johannes Ceporinus) en de wording en vestiging der Hervormde Gemeente te Zalt-Bommel.* 's-Hertogenbosch: G. H. van der Schuyt, 1873.

Aldrin, Emilia. "Choosing a Name = Choosing Identity? Toward a Theoretical Framework." *Biblioteca tècnica de politíca lingüística onomàstica* 11 (2014): 392–401.

Arnade, Peter J. Beggars, *Iconoclasts, and Civic Patriots: The Political Culture of the Dutch Revolt.* Ithaca, NY: Cornell University Press, 2008.

Arndt, Johannes. *Das Heilige Römische Reich und die Niederlande 1566 bis 1648: Politisch-konfessionelle Verflechtung und Publizistik im achtzigjährigen Krieg*. Cologne: Böhlau, 1998.

Arnold, Matthieu. "Migration und Exil as Signum des Internationalen Calvinismus." *Verkündigung und Forschung* 57, no. 2 (2012): 73–80.

Asaert, Gustaaf. *1585: De val van Antwerpen en de uittocht van Vlamingen en Brabanders*. Tielt: Lannoo, 2004.

Asten, Herbert von. "Religiöse und wirtschaftliche Antriebe im niederrheinischen Montangewerbe des 16. und 17. Jahrhunderts." *Rheinische Vierteljahrsblätter* 28 (1963): 62–83.

Atherton, Ruth. "Power and Persuasion: Catechetical Treatments of the Sacraments in Reformation Germany, 1529–1597." PhD diss., University of Birmingham, 2017.

Augustijn, Cornelis. "Die Ketzerverfolgungen in den Niederlanden von 1520–1545." In *Ketzerverfolgung im 16. und 17. Jahrhundert*, edited by Silvana Seidel Menchi, 49–63. Wiesbaden: Otto Harrassowitz, 1992.

———. "Die Reformierte Kirche in den Niederlanden und der Libertinismus in der zweiten Hälfte des 16. Jahrhunderts." In *Querdenken: Dissens und Toleranz im Wandel der Geschichte. Festschrift zum 65. Geburtstag von H. R. Guggisberg*, edited by Michael Erbe, 107–121. Mannheim: Palatium Verlag, 1996.

Badea, Andrea. *Kurfürstliche Präeminenz, Landesherrschaft und Reform: Das Scheitern der Kölner Reformation unter Hermann von Wied*. Münster: Aschendorf, 2009.

Bakker, Frens and Roeland van Hout. "Twee vrienden: jij en ik? Twee pronomina en de scheiding tussen het Zuidnederfrankisch and Kleverlands." *Leuvense Bijdragen* 99–100 (2016): 337–52.

Barton, Peter Friedrich. *Um Luthers Erbe: Studien und Texte zur Spätreformation: Tilemann Heshusius (1527–1559)*. Witten: Luther-Verlag, 1972.

Bauer, Karl. *Valérand Poullain: Ein Kirchengeschichtliches Zeitbild aus der Mitte des Sechzehnten Jahrhunderts*. Elberfeld: Buchhandlung des Erziehungsvereins, 1927.

Baumann, Wolf-Rüdiger. *The Merchants Adventurers and the Continental Cloth Trade (1560s–1620s)*. Berlin: W. de Gruyter, 1990.

Becker, Judith. *Gemeindeordnung und Kirchenzucht: Johannes a Lascos Kirchenordnung für London (1555) und die Reformierte Konfessionsbildung*. Leiden: Brill, 2007.

———. "Kirchenordnung und Reformierte Identitätsbildung am Beispiel Frankenthals." In *Kommunikation und Transfer im Christentum der frühen Neuzeit*, edited by Irene Dingel and Wolf-Friedrich Schäufele, 275–95. Mainz: Verlag Philipp von Zabern, 2007.

Beenakker, A. J. M. *Breda in de eerste storm van de opstand: Van ketterij tot beeldenstorm, 1545–1569.* Tilburg: Stichting Zuidelijk Historisch Contact, 1971.

———. "Pendelen tussen Heidelberg en Breda in de zestiende eeuw," https://docplayer.nl/7757511-Pendelen-tussen-heidelberg-en-breda-in-de-zestiende-eeuw-dr-a-j-m-beenakker-samengebracht-zijn-hier.htm.

Benedict, Philip. *Christ's Churches Purely Reformed: A Social History of Calvinism.* New Haven: Yale University Press, 2002.

———. *The Huguenot Population of France, 1600–1685: The Demographic Fate and Customs of a Religious Minority.* Philadelphia: American Philosophical Society, 1991.

———. *Rouen During the Wars of Religion.* Cambridge: Cambridge University Press, 1981.

———, Guido Marnef, Henk van Nierop, and Marc Venard, eds. *Reformation, Revolt and Civil War in France and the Netherlands, 1555–1585.* Amsterdam: Royal Netherlands Academy of Arts and Sciences, 1999.

Berg, A. J. van den. "Herman Herberts (ca. 1540–1607) in conflict met de gereformeerde kerk." In *Kerkhistorische Opstellen*, edited by C. Augustijn, P. N. Holtrop, G. H. M. Posthumus Meyjes, and E. G. van der Wall, 20–29. Kampen: Uitgeversmaatschaapij J. H. Kok, 1987.

Bergerhausen, Hans-Wolfgang. *Die Stadt Köln und die Reichsversammlungen im Konfessionellen Zeitalter: Ein Beitrag zur Korporativen Reichsständischen Politik, 1555–1616.* Cologne: Kölnischer Geschichtsverein, 1990.

Besser, Gustav Adolf. *Geschichte der Frankfurter Flüchtlingsgemeinden, 1554–1558.* Halle: Druck von E. Karras, 1906.

Blok, Anton. *De Vernieuwers: De zegeningen van tegenslag in wetenschap en kunst, 1500–2000.* Amsterdam: Prometheus, 2013

Blom, N. van der. *Grepen uit de geschiedenis van het Erasmiaans gymnasium, 1328–1978.* Rotterdam: W. Backhuys, 1978.

Blum, Daniella. *Multikonfessionalität im Alltag: Speyer zwischen politischem Frieden und Bekenntniserust (1555–1618).* Münster: Aschendorff, 2015.

Boer, David de. "De verliezers van de opstand." In *De Vluchtelingenrepubliek: Een migratiegeschiedenis van Nederland*, edited by David de Boer and Geert Janssen, 15–30. Amsterdam: Prometheus, 2023.

Bonger, H. *Leven en werk van D. V. Coornhert.* Amsterdam: G. A. van Oorschot, 1978.

Bonterwek, K. W. "Die Reformation im Wupperthal und Peter Lo's Antheil an Derselben." *Zeitschrift des Bergischen Geschichtsvereins* 4 (1867): 273–336.

Boom, H. ten. *De reformatie in Rotterdam, 1530–1585.* [Amsterdam]: Bataafsche Leeuw, 1987.

Booma, Jan G. J. van. *Onderzoek in Protestantse kerkelijke archieven in Nederland. Handleiding, tevens beknopte gegevens over de geschiedenis van de kerkelijke instellingen, over het kerkelijk archiefrecht en het kerkelijk archiefbeheer.* The Hague: Centraal Bureau voor Genealogie, 1994.

Bosbach, Franz. *Die Katholische Reform in der Stadt Köln (1550–1662): Ein Beispiel für erfolgreiche kirchliche Erneuerung.* Cologne: Presseamt des Erzbistums Köln, 1988.

———. "Köln—Erzstift und Freie Reichsstadt." In *Die Territorien des Reichs im Zeitalter der Reformation und Konfessionalisierung: Land und Konfession 1500–1650, vol. 3: Der Nordwesten*, edited by Anthon Schindling and Walter Ziegler, 58–84. Münster: Aschendorff, 1991.

Bossy, John. "The Mass as a Social Institution, 1200–1700." *Past and Present* 100 (1983): 29–61.

Bothe, Friedrich. *Die Entwicklung der direkten Besteuerung in der Reichsstadt Frankfurt bis zur Revolution, 1612–1614.* Leipzig: Duncker & Humblot, 1906.

———. *Frankfurts Wirtschaftlich-Soziale Entwicklung vor dem dreissigjährigen Kriege und der Fettmilchaufstand (1612–1616).* Frankfurt am Main: Baer, 1920.

Bott, Heinrich. *Gründung und Anfänge der Neustadt Hanau, 1596–1620.* Marburg: Elwert, 1970.

Brady, Thomas A., Heiko Oberman, and James D. Tracy, eds. *The Handbook of European History.* 2 vols. Leiden: Brill, 1995.

Breedvelt-Van Veen, Foukje. *Louis de Geer 1587–1652.* Amsterdam: H. J. Paris, 1935.

Bremmer, Rolf H. *Reformatie en rebellie.* Franeker: Wever, 1984.

Breustedt, Sonja. "Bürger- und Beisassenrecht: Die Rechtspolitische Steuerung der Immigration im Frühneuzeitlichen Frankfurt am Main." *Zeitschrift für Historische Forschung* 44 (2017): 597–633.

Briels, J. G. C. A. *Zuidnederlanders in de Republiek, 1572–1630: Een demografische en cultuurhistorische studie.* Sint-Niklaus: Damthe, 1985.

———. "Zuidnederlandse goud- en zilversmeden in Noordnederland omstreeks, 1576–1625." *Bijdragen tot de Geschiedenis* 55 (1972): 89–112.

Broeke, C. [Leon] van den. "No Funeral Sermons: Dutch or Calvinistic Prohibition?" In *Preparation for Death, Remembering the Dead*, edited by Tarald Rasmussen and Jon Øygarden Flæten, 361–77. Göttingen: Vandenhoeck & Ruprecht, 2015.

———. *Een geschiedenis van de classis: Classicale typen tussen idee en werkelijkheid (1571–2004).* Kampen: Uitgeverij Kok, 2005.

Bruening, Michael W. *Refusing to Kiss the Slipper: Opposition to Calvinism in the Francophone Reformation.* Oxford: Oxford University Press, 2021.

Brulez, W. "De diaspora der Antwerpse kooplui op het einde van de 16e eeuw." *Bijdragen voor de geschiedenis der Nederlanden* 15 (1960): 279–306.

Burghartz, Susanna. *Zeiten der Reinheit, Orte der Unzucht: Ehe und Sexualität in Basel während der frühen Neuzeit.* Paderborn: Schöningh, 1999.

Burke, Peter. *Exiles and Expatriates in the History of Knowledge, 1500–2000.* Waltham, MA: Brandeis University Press, 2017.

Chaix, Gérald. "Die Schwierige Schule der Sitten—Christliche Gemeinden, Bürgerliche Obrigkeit und Sozialdiziplinierung im frühneuzeitlichen Köln, etwa, 1450–1600." In *Kirchenzucht und Sozialdisziplinierung im Frühneuzeitlichen Europa*, edited by Heinz Schilling, 199–217. Berlin: Duncker & Homblot, 1994.

Clossey, Luke. *Salvation and Globalization in the Early Jesuit Missions.* Cambridge: Cambridge University Press, 2010.

Coenen, Dorothea. *Die Katholische Kirche am Niederrhein von der Reformation bis zum Beginn des 18. Jahrhunderts.* Münster: Aschendorff, 1967.

Coleman, D. C. "An Innovation and Its Diffusion: The 'New Draperies.'" *The Economic History Review* 22, no. 3 (1969): 417–29.

Corens, Liesbeth. *Confessional Mobility and English Catholics in Counter-Reformation Europe.* Oxford: Oxford University Press, 2019.

———, Kate Peters, and Alexandra Walsham, eds. *The Social History of the Archive: Record-Keeping in Early Modern Europe,* Past & Present Supplement 11. Oxford: Oxford University Press, 2016.

Cornelissen, Georg. *Kleine Niederrheinische Sprachgeschichte (1300–1900): Eine regionale Sprachgeschichte für das deutsch-niederländische Grenzgebiet zwischen Arnheim und Krefeld.* Geldern: Stiftung Geschichte des Raumes Peel-Maas-Niels, 2003.

Corpis, Duane J. *Crossing the Boundaries of Belief: Geographies of Religious Conversion in Southern Germany, 1648–1800.* Charlottesville: University of Virginia Press, 2014.

Coy, Jason P. *Strangers and Misfits: Banishment, Social Control, and Authority in Early Modern Germany.* Leiden: Brill, 2008.

Cuno, Friedrich Wilhelm. *Geschichte der Wallonisch-Reformirten Gemeinde zu Frankenthal.* Magdeburg: Heinrichshofen, 1894.

———. *Geschichte der Wallonisch- und Französisch-Reformirten Gemeinde zu Wesel.* Magdeburg: Heinrichshofen, 1895.

———. *Die Pfälzischen reformierten Fremdengemeinden.* Westheim: Verlag des evangelischen Vereins für die Pfalz, 1886.

Daniell, Christopher. *Death and Burial in Medieval England, 1066–1550.* London: Routledge, 1997.

Dankbaar, Willem Friedrik. "Marnix van St. Aldegonde en zijn betekenis voor de vestiging van de Nederlandsche gereformeerde kerk." In *Hoogtepunten uit het Nederlandsche Calvinisme in de zestiende eeuw*, 41–85. Haarlem: H. D. Tjeenk Willink & zoon, 1946.

Davis, Natalie Zemon. "The Sacred and the Body Social in Sixteenth-Century Lyon." *Past & Present* 90 (1981): 40–70.

Decavele, Johan. *De dageraad van de reformatie in Vlaanderen (1520–1565)*. Brussel: Paleis der Academiën, 1975.

———. *Het eind van een rebelse droom: Opstellen over het Calvinistisch bewind te Gent (1577–1584) en de terugkeer van de stad onder de gehoorzaamheid van de koning van Spanje (17 September 1584)*. Ghent: Stadsbestuur, 1984.

———. "De Gentse poorterij en buitenpoorterij." In *Recht en instellingen in de oude Nederlanden tijdens de middeleeuwen en de nieuwe tijd: Liber Amicorum Jan Buntinx*, edited by Gustaaf Asaert, 63–79. Leuven: Universitaire Pers, 1981.

Dechent, Hermann. *Kirchengeschichte von Frankfurt am Main seit der Reformation*. Vol. 1. Leipzig: Kesselringsche Hofbuchhandlung Verlag, 1913.

Deen, Femke. *Publiek debat en propaganda in Amsterdam tijdens de Nederlandse Opstand. Amsterdam 'Moorddam' 1566–1578*. Amsterdam: Amsterdam University Press, 2015.

Denis, Philippe. *Les églises d'étrangers en Pays Rhénans (1538–1564)*. Paris: Sociéte d'Édition „Les Belles Lettres", 1984.

———. "Jacques de Bourgogne, Seigneur de Falais." In *Bibliotheca Dissidentium. Répertoire des non-conformistes religieux des seizième et dix-septième siècles*, edited by Andre Séguenny, 9–52. Vol. 4. Baden-Baden: Éditions Valentin Koerner, 1984.

Deursen, A. Th. van. *Bavianen en Slijkgeuzen: Kerk en kerkvolk ten tijde van Maurits en Oldenbarnevelt*. Franeker: Van Wijnen, 1998.

———. "Kerk of parochie? De kerkmeesters en de dood tijdens de Republiek." *Tijdschrift voor Geschiedenis* 89 (1976): 531–37.

Diefendorf, Barbara. "The Reformation and Wars of Religion in France." *Oxford Bibliographies*. (https://www.oxfordbibliographies.com). Oxford: Oxford University Press, 2019.

Dietz, Alexander. *Frankfurter Handelsgeschichte*. Vol. II. Frankfurt: Gebrüder Knauer, 1921.

Dietz, Burghard and Stefan Ehrenpreis, eds. *Drei Konfessionen in einer Region: Beiträge zur Geschichte der Konfessionalisierung im Herzogtum Berg van 16. bis zum 18. Jahrhundert*. Cologne: Rheinland-Verlag, 1999.

Dingel, Irene. "Religionssupplikationen der Französisch-Reformierten Gemeinde in Frankfurt am Main." In *Calvin und Calvinismus: Europäische Perspektiven*, edited by Irene Dingel and Herman J. Selderhuis, 281–96. Göttingen: Vandenhoeck & Ruprecht, 2011.

Doedens, Anne and Jan Houter. *De Watergeuzen: Een vergeten geschiedenis, 1568–1575*. Zutphen: Walburg Pers, 2020.

Dölemeyer, Barbara. "Kapitulations und Transfix: Die Gründung der Neustadt Hanau unter rechtshistorischen Aspkecten." In *Auswirkungen einer Stadtgrundung*, edited by Magistrat der Stadt Hanau, Wallonische-Niederländische Gemeinde Hanau, and Hanauer Geschichtsvereins, 44–51. Hanau: CoCon-Verlag, 1997.

Dooren, J. P. van, ed. *De Nationale Synode te Middelburg in 1581: Calvinisme in opbouw in de noordelijke en zuidelijke Nederlanden*. Middelburg: Koninklijk Zeeuws Genootschap der Wetenschappen, 1981.

Duke, Alastair C. *Dissident Identities in the Early Modern Low Countries*, edited by Judith Pollmann and Andrew Spicer. London: Routledge, 2009.

———. "The Elusive Netherlands: The Question of National Identity in the Early Modern Low Countries on the Eve of the Revolt." *Bijdragen en Mededelingen betreffende de Geschiedenis der Nederlanden* 119, no. 1 (2004): 10–38.

———. *Reformation and Revolt in the Low Countries*. London: The Hambledon Press, 1990.

Dünnwald, Achim. *Konfessionsstreit und Verfassungskonflikt: Die Aufnahme der Niederländischen Flüchtlinge im Herzogtum Kleve, 1566–1585*. Bielefeld: Verlag für Regionalgeschichte, 1998.

Dürr, Renate. "Die Migration von Mägden in der Frühen Neuzeit." In *Frauen und Migration*, edited by Martina Krauss and Holger Sonnabend, 117–32. Stuttgart: Franz Steiner Verlag, 2001.

Ebrard, Friedrich Clemens. *Die Französisch-Reformierte Gemeinde in Frankfurt am Main, 1554–1904*. Frankfurt am Main: R. Ecklin, 1906.

Eells, Hastings. *Martin Bucer*. New York: New York, Russell & Russell, 1971.

Ehrenpreis, Stefan. *'Wir sind mit blutigen Köpfen davongelaufen': Lokale Konfessionskonflikte im Herzogtum Berg 1550–1700*. Bochum: D. Winkler, 1993.

——— and Ute Lotz-Heumann. *Reformation und Konfessionelles Zeitalter*. Darmstadt: Wissenschaftliche Buchgesellschaft, 2002.

Elmentaler, Michael. "Die Schreibsprachengeschichte des Niederrheins: Ein Forschungsprojekt der Duisburger Universität." In *Sprache und Literatur am Niederrhein*, edited by Dieter Heimböckel, 15–34. Bottrop: P. Pomp, 1998.

Enderle, Wilfried. "Die Katholischen Reichstädte im Zeitalter der Reformation und Konfessionalisierung." *Zeitschrift der Savigny-Stiftung für Rechtsgeschichte/Kanonistische Abteilung* 106 (1989): 228–69.

Ennen, L. "Die Reformirte Gemeinde in der Stadt Köln am Ende des sechzehnten Jahrhunderts." *Monatsschrift für rheinisch-westfälische Geschichtsforschung und Alterthumskunde* 1 (1875): 397–438, 493–528.

Esser, Raingard. "Citizenship and Immigration in 16th- and Early 17th-Century England." In *Citizenship in Historical Perspective*, edited by Seven G. Ellis, Gudmundur Hálfdanarson, and Ann Katherine Isaacs, 237–52. Pisa: Pisa University Press, 2006.

———. *Niederländische Exulanten im England des 16. und frühen 17. Jahrhunderts.* Berlin: Duncker & Humblot, 1996.

Evans, Robert John Weston. *The Wechel Presses: Humanism and Calvinism in Central Europe, 1572–1627.* Oxford: Past and Present Society, 1975.

Evenhuis, R. B. *Ook dat was Amsterdam, vol. II: De kerk der hervorming in de gouden eeuw.* Amsterdam: Uitgeverij W. ten Have, 1967.

Fagel, Raymond and Judith Pollmann. *1572: Burgeroorlog in de Nederlanden.* Amsterdam: Prometheus, 2022.

Fehler, Timothy G. "Coping with Poverty: Dutch Reformed Exiles in Emden, Germany." In *Religious Diaspora in Early Modern Europe: Strategies of Exiles*, edited by Timothy G. Fehler, Greta Grace Kroeker, Charles H. Parker, and Jonathan Ray, 121–36. London: Pickering & Chatto, 2014.

———. *Poor Relief and Protestantism: The Evolution of Social Welfare in Sixteenth-Century Emden.* Aldershot, UK: Ashgate, 1999.

———. "Refugees Wives, Widows, and Mothers." In *Embodiment, Identity, and Gender in the Early Modern Age*, edited by Amy E. Leonard and David M. Whitford, 187–96. London: Routledge, 2021.

Fitzsimmons, Richard. "Building a Reformed Ministry in Holland, 1572–1585." In *The Reformation of the Parishes: The Ministry and the Reformation in Town and Country*, edited by Andrew Pettegree, 175–94. Manchester: Manchester University Press, 1993.

Fleurkens, Anneke C. G. *Stichtelijke lust: De toneelspelen van D. V. Coornhert (1522–1590) als middelen tot het geven van morele instructie.* Hilversum: Verloren, 1994.

Flüchter, Antje. *Der Zölibat zwischen Devianz und Norm: Kirchenpolitik und Gemeindealltag in den Herzogtumern Jülich und Berg im 16. und 17. Jahrhundert.* Cologne: Bölau, 2006.

François, Etienne. *Die unsichtbare Grenze: Protestanten und Katholiken in Augsburg 1648–1806.* Sigmaringen: Jan Thorbecke Verlag, 1991.

Franzen, August. *Bischof und Reformation: Erzbischof Hermann von Wied in Köln vor der Entscheidung zwischen Reform und Reformation.* Münster: Aschendorff, 1971.

———. *Die Kölner Archidiakonate in Vor- und Nachtridentinischer Zeit.* Münster: Aschendorff, 1953.

Freist, Dagmar. *Glaube - Liebe - Zwietracht: Religiös-Konfessionell Gemischte Ehen in der frühen Neuzeit.* Munich: De Gruyter Oldenbourg, 2017.

Frijhoff, Willem. *Embodied Belief: Ten Essays on Religious Culture in Dutch History.* Hilversum: Verloren, 2002.

———. "Marnix over de opvoeding." In *Een intellectuele activist: Studies over leven en werk van Philips van Marnix van Sint Aldegonde*, edited by H. Duits and T. van Strien, 59–76. Hilversum: Verloren, 2001.

Fuchs, Ralf-Peter, and Arnt Reitmeier. "Konfession und Raum: Die Klevisch-Geldrische Region im Rhein-Maas-Raum." In *Handbuch Landesgeschichte*, edited by Werner Freitag, Michael Kißener, Christine Reinle, and Sebine Ulmann, 579–93. Berlin: De Gruyter Oldebourg, 2018.

Funke, Nikolas Maximilian. "Religion and the Military in the Holy Roman Empire c.1500–1650." PhD diss., University of Sussex, 2012.

Fussel, G. E. "Low Countries' Influence on English Farming." *English Historical Review* 74 (1959): 611–22.

Gelder, H. A. Enno van. *Revolutionnaire Reformatie: De vestiging van de Gereformeerde Kerk in de Nederlandse gewesten, gedurende de eerste jaren van de opstand tegen Filips II, 1575–1585.* Amsterdam: P. N. van Kampen & zoon, 1943.

Gelder, Maartje van. *Trading Places: The Netherlandish Merchant Community in Venice, 1590–1650.* Leiden: Brill, 2009.

Gelderblom, Oscar. *Cities of Commerce: The Institutional Foundations of International Trade in the Low Countries, 1250–1650.* Princeton: Princeton University Press, 2013.

———. "The Governance of Early Modern Trade: The Case of Hans Thijs, 1556–1611." *Enterprise & Society* 4, no. 4 (2003): 606–39.

———. *Zuid-Nederlandse kooplieden en de opkomst van de Amsterdamse stapelmarkt (1578–1630).* Hilversum: Verloren, 2000.

Geurts, J. H. J. "'Onsser stadt in sulken gedranghe': Maastricht tussen Brabant en het Rijk, 1500–1550." PhD diss., Katholieke Universiteit Nijmegen, 1993.

Geyl, Peter. *The Revolt of the Netherlands, 1555–1609.* London: Ernest Benn Limited, 1958

Gielis, Gert and Violet Soen. "The Inquisitorial Office in the Sixteenth-Century Habsburg Low Countries: A Dynamic Perspective." *The Journal of Ecclesiastical History* 66, no. 1 (2015): 47–66.

Giesbers, Charlotte. "Dialecten op de grens van twee talen: Een dialectologische en sociolinguistisch onderzoek in het kleverlands dialectgebied." PhD diss., Radboud University, 2008.

Gillner, Bastian. *Freie Herren, Freie Religion: Der Adel des Oberstifts Münster zwischen konfessionellem Konflikt und staatlicher Verdichtung, 1500–1700.* Münster: Aschendorff, 2011.

Gilmont, Jean François. *Le livre réformé au XVIe siècle.* Paris: Bibliothèque nationale de France, 2005.

Goeters, J. F. G. "Der Katholische Hermann von Wied." *Monatshefte für evangelische Kirchengeschichte des Rheinlandes* 35 (1986): 1–17.

Goose, Nigel. "The 'Dutch' in Colchester: The Economic Influence of an Immigrant Community in the Sixteenth and Seventeenth Centuries." *Immigrants and Minorities* 1 (1982): 261–80.

——— and Lien Luu, eds. *Immigrants in Tudor and Early Stuart England.* Brighton: Sussex Academic Press, 2005.

Goosens, Aline. *Les inquisitions modernes dans les Pays-Bas meridionaux (1520–1633).* Brussels: Éditions de l'université de Bruxelles, 1998.

Gootjes, Nicolaas. H. *The Belgic Confession: Its History and Sources.* Grand Rapids, MI: Baker Academic, 2007.

Gordon, Bruce. "The Changing Face of Protestant History and Identity in the Sixteenth Century," In *Protestant History and Identity in Sixteenth-Century Europe*, vol. 1, edited by Bruce Gordon, 1–22. Aldershot, UK: Ashgate, 1996.

——— and Peter Marshall, eds. *The Place of the Dead: Death and Remembrance in Late Medieval and Early Modern Europe.* Cambridge: Cambridge University Press, 2000.

Gorter, Peter. *Gereformeerde migranten: De religieuze identiteit van Nederlandse gereformeerde migrantengemeenten in de rijkssteden Frankfurt am Main, Aken en Keulen (1555–1600).* Hilversum: Verloren, 2021.

Graaf, Ronald P. de. *Oorlog, mijn arme schapen: Een andere kijk op de Tachtigjarige Oorlog 1565–1648.* Franeker: Van Wijnen, 2004.

Gramulla, Gertrud Susanna. *Handelsbeziehungen Kölner Kaufleute zwischen 1500 und 1650.* Cologne: Böhlau, 1972.

Greengrass, Mark. "Protestant Exiles and Their Assimilation in Early Modern England." *Immigrants and Minorities* 4, no. 3 (1985): 68–81.

Grell, Ole Peter. *Brethren in Christ: A Calvinist Network in Reformation Europe.* Cambridge: Cambridge University Press, 2011.

———. "The Creation of a Transnational, Calvinist Network and Its Significance for Calvinist Identity and Interaction in Early Modern Europe." *European Review of History* 16, no. 5 (2009): 619–36.

Grochowina, Nicole. *Indifferenz und Dissens in der Grafschaft Ostfriesland im 16. und 17. Jahrhundert.* Frankfurt: Peter Lang, 2003.

Groenhuis, G. "Calvinism and National Consciousness: The Dutch Republic as the New Israel." In *Britain and the Netherlands, vol. 7: Church and State since the Reformation*, ed. A. C. Duke and C. A. Tamse, 118–33. The Hague: Martinus Nijhoff, 1981.

Groenveld, Simon. "'Natie' en 'patria' bij zestiende-eeuwse Nederlanders." *In Vaderland: Een geschiedenis vanaf de vijftiende eeuw tot 1940*, edited by N. C. F. van Sas, 55–81. Amsterdam: Amsterdam University Press, 1999.

Gunther, Karl. *Reformation Unbound: Protestant Visions of Reform in England, 1525–1590.* Cambridge: Cambridge University Press, 2014.

Haar, Alisa van de. *The Golden Mean of Languages: Forging Dutch and French in the Early Modern Low Countries (1540–1620)*. Leiden: Brill, 2019.

Haar, Bernard ter and Willem Moll, *Geschiedenis der christelijke kerk in Netherland, in tafereelen*. Vol. 2. Amsterdam: Portieltje en zoon, 1869.

Hantsche, Irmgard. *Atlas zur Geschichte des Niederrheins*. Bottrop: Peter Pomp, 1999.

———. "Niederländische Glaubensflüchtlinge am Niederrhein im 16. Jahrhundert und die reformierten Gemeinden in Wesel und Düren." *Annalen des Historischen Vereins für den Niederrhein, insbesondere das alte Erzbistum Köln* 213 (2010): 127–51.

Harding, Vanessa. *The Dead and the Living in Paris and London, 1500–1670*. Cambridge: Cambridge University Press, 2002.

Harline, Craig. *Jacobs vlucht: Een familiesaga uit de Gouden Eeuw*. Nijmegen: Vantilt, 2016.

Harreld, Donald. *High Germans in the Low Countries: German Merchants and Commerce in Golden Age Antwerp*. Leiden: Brill, 2004.

Harrington, Joel F. *Reordering Marriage and Society in Reformation Germany*. Cambridge: Cambridge University Press, 1995.

Hassall, Meredith. "Dialect Focusing and Language Transfer in Sixteenth Century Germany." PhD diss., University of Wisconsin-Madison, 2001.

Haude, Sigrun. *In the Shadow of "Savage Wolves": Anabaptist Münster and the German Reformation during the 1530s*. Boston: Humanities Press, 2000.

Hendriks, Jennifer Boyce. "Immigration and Linguistic Change: A Socio-Historical Linguistic Study of the Effect of German and Southern Dutch Immigration on the Development of the Northern Dutch Vernacular in 16th/17th Century Holland." PhD diss., University of Wisconsin-Madison, 1998.

Heppe, Heinrich. *Geschichte des Deutschen Protestantismus*. Vol. I. Marburg: Elwert'sche Universitäts-Buchhandlung, 1852.

Herborn, Wolfgang. "Die Protestanten in Schilderung und Urteil des Kölner Chronisten Hermann von Weinsberg (1518–1598)." In *Niederlande und Nordwestdeutschland: Studien zur Regional- und Stadtgeschichte Nordwestkontinentaleuropas in Mittelalter und in der Neuzeit*, edited by Wilfried Ehbrecht and Heinz Schilling, 136–53. Cologne: Böhlau, 1983.

———. "Die Reisen und Fahrten des Hermann von Weinsberg: Zur Mobilität eines Kölner Bürgers im 16. Jahrhundert." In *Köln als Kommunikationszentrum*, edited by Georg Mölich and Gerd Schwerhoff, 141–66. Cologne: DuMont, 2000.

Hibben, C. C. *Gouda in Revolt: Particularism and Pacifism in the Revolt of the Netherlands 1572–1588*. Utrecht: HES, 1983.

Hill, Kat. *Baptism, Brotherhood, and Belief in Reformation Germany: Anabaptism and Lutheranism, 1525–1585.* Oxford: Oxford University Press, 2015.

Hippel, Wolfgang. *Armut, Unterschichten, Randgruppen in der Frühen Neuzeit.* Munich: Oldenbourg, 2013.

Hochstadt, Steve. "Migration in Preindustrial Germany." *Central European History* 16, no. 3 (1983): 195–224.

Holder, R. Ward, ed. *John Calvin in Context.* Cambridge: Cambridge University Press, 2020.

Hollweg, Walter. "Calvins Beziehungen zu den Rheinlanden." In *Calvinstudien: Festschrift zum 400. Geburtstage Johann Calvins*, edited by J. Bohatec, 129–86. Leipzig: Rudolf Haupt, 1909.

Holt, Mack. *The Duke of Anjou and the Politique Struggle during the Wars of Religion.* Cambridge: Cambridge University Press, 1986.

Houtte, J. A. van. *Die Beziehungen zwischen Köln und den Niederlanden vom Hochmittelalter bis zum Beginn des Industriezietalters.* Cologne: Forschungsinstitut för Sozial- und Wirtschaftgeschichte an der Universität zu Köln, 1969.

Hsia, R. Po-Chia. "The Myth of the Commune: Recent Historiography on City and Reformation in Germany." *Central European History* 20, no. 3/4 (1987): 203–15.

———. *Social Discipline in the Reformation: Central Europe, 1550–1750.* London: Routledge, 1989.

———. *The World of Catholic Renewal, 1540–1770.* 2nd ed. Cambridge: Cambridge University Press, 2005.

———, and H. F. K. van Nierop, eds. *Calvinism and Religious Toleration in the Dutch Golden Age.* Cambridge: Cambridge University Press, 2002.

Hullu, J. de. "Bijdrage tot de geschiedenis der Hervorming te Deventer, 1567–1575." *Nederlands Archief voor Kerkgeschiedenis* 30, no. 1 (1937): 167–241.

Hund, Johannes and Henning P. Jürgens. "Pamphlets in the Theological Debates of the Later Sixteenth Century: The Mainz Editorial Project 'Controversia et Confessio." In *The Book Triumphant: Print in Transition in the Sixteenth and Seventeenth Centuries*, edited by Malcolm Walsby and Graeme Kemp, 158–77. Leiden: Brill, 2012.

Hürkey, Edgard J., ed. *Kunst, Kommerz, Glaubenskampf: Frankenthal um 1600.* Worms: Wernersche Verlagsgesellschaft, 1995.

Irrgang, Stephanie. *Peregrinatio Academica: Wanderungen und Karrieren von Gelehrten der Universitäten Rostock, Greifswald, Trier und Mainz im 15. Jahrhundert.* Stuttgart: Steiner, 2002.

Jaanus, Hendrik Johan. *Hervormd Delft ten tijde van Arent Cornelisz (1573–1605).* Amsterdam: Nordemann, 1950.

James, Mervyn. "Ritual, Drama, and Social Body in the Late Medieval English Town." *Past & Present*, no. 98 (1983): 3–29.

Janssen, Geert H. *The Dutch Revolt and Catholic Exile in Reformation Europe.* Cambridge: Cambridge University Press, 2014.

———. "Exiles and the Politics of Reintegration in the Dutch Revolt." *History* 94 (2009): 36–52

———. "The Legacy of Exile and the Rise of Humanitarianism." In *Remembering the Reformation*, edited by Brian Cummings, Ceri Law, Karis Riley, and Alexandra Walsham, 226–42. London: Routledge, 2020.

Janssen, Gustaaf. "Verjaagd uit Nederland: Zuidnederlandse emigratie in de zestiende eeuw: Een historiographisch overzicht (ca.1968–1994)." *Nederlands Archief voor Kerkgeschiedenis* 75 (1995): 102–19.

Janssen, H. Q. "De Hervormde vlugtelingen van Yperen in Engeland, geschetst naar hunne brieven." *Bijdragen tot de Oudheidkunde en geschiedenis inzonderheid van Zeeuwsch-Vlaanderen* 2 (1857): 211–304

———. "Petrus Dathenus aan den avond zijns levens: Een bezoek bij hem te Staden." *Bijdragen tot de oudheidkunde en geschiedenis, inzonderheid van Zeeuwsch-Vlaanderen* (1858): 1–27.

Janssen, L. J. F. "De Nederlandsche hervormden in Kleefsland, vooral te Wezel, in de XVI eeuw." *Archief voor kerkelijke geschiedenis, inzonderheid van Nederland* 5 (1834): 307–460.

Jelsma, Auke. *Frontiers of the Reformation: Dissidence and Orthodoxy in Sixteenth-Century Europe*. Aldershot, UK: Ashgate, 1998.

———. "The 'Weakness of Conscience' in the Reformed Movement in the Netherlands: The Attitude of the Dutch Reformation to the Use of Violence between 1562 and 1574." In *The Church and War*, edited by W. J. Sheils, 217–29. Oxford: Blackwell, 1983.

Johann, Anja. *Kontrolle mit Konsens: Sozialdisziplinierung in der Reichsstadt Frankfurt am Main im 16. Jahrhundert.* Frankfurt am Main: Verlag Waldemar Kramer, 2001.

Jong, O. J. de. *Nederlandse Kerkgeschiedenis.* Nijkerk: G. F. Callenbach, 1985.

Jürgens, Henning P. *Johannes a Lasco in Ostfriesland: Der Werdegang eines europäischen Reformators.* Tübingen: Mohr Siebeck, 2002.

Jütte, Robert. *Obrigkeitliche Armenfürsorge in deutschen Reichsstädten der frühen Neuzeit: Städtisches Armenwesen in Frankfurt am Main und Köln.* Cologne: Böhlau, 1984.

Kaller, Gerhard. "Wallonische und Niederländische Exulantensiedlungen in der Pfalz im 16. Jahrhundert: Entstehung und Stadterhebung." In *Oberrheinische Studien*, edited by Alfons Schäfer, 327–51. Vol. 3. Karlsruhe: Braun-Verlag, 1975.

Kamen, Henry. *The Iron Century: Social Change in Europe, 1550–1660.* London: Weidenfeld and Nicolson, 1971.

Kamp, Jeannette. *Crime, Gender, and Social Control in Early Modern Frankfurt am Main.* Leiden: Brill, 2020.

———. “Female Crime and Household Control in Early Modern Frankfurt am Main.” *The History of the Family* 21, no. 4 (2016): 531–50.

Kaplan, Benjamin J. *Calvinists and Libertines: Confession and Community in Utrecht, 1578–1620.* Oxford: Clarendon Press, 1995.

———. *Divided by Faith: Religious Conflict and the Practice of Toleration in Early Modern Europe.* Cambridge, MA: Belknap Press, 2007.

———. “Fictions of Privacy: House Chapels and the Spatial Accommodation of Religious Dissent in Early Modern Europe.” *The American Historical Review* 107, no. 4 (2002): 1031–64.

———. “Integration vs. Segregation: Religiously Mixed Marriage and the ‘Verzuiling’ Model of Dutch Society.” In *Catholic Communities in Protestant States: Britain and the Netherlands, c.1570–1720*, edited by Benjamin J. Kaplan, Bob Moore, Henk van Nierop, and Judith Pollmann, 1–17. Manchester: Manchester University Press, 2009.

———. “The Legal Rights of Religious Refugees in the ‘Refugee-Cities’ of Early Modern Germany.” *Journal of Refugee Studies* 32, no. 1 (2019): 86–105.

Karant-Nunn, Susan C. *The Reformation of Ritual: An Interpretation of Early Modern Germany.* London: Routledge, 1997.

Kasper-Holtkotte, Cilli. *Die Jüdische Gemeinde von Frankfurt/Main in der Frühen Neuzeit: Familien, Netzwerke und Konflikte eines Jüdischen Zentrums.* Berlin: De Gruyter, 2010.

Keller, Ludwig. “Herzog Alba und die Wiederherstellung der Katholischen Kirche am Rhein.” *Preußischen Jahrbücher* 48 (1881): 586–606.

Kernkamp, J. H. “Het Van der Meulen-archief ca.” *Bijdragen en Mededelingen betreffende de Geschiedenis der Nederlanden* 85 (1970): 49–62.

Kessel, H. “Reformation und Gegenreformation im Herzogtum Cleve (1517–1609).” *Düsseldorfer Jahrbuch* 30 (1920): 1–113.

Kingdon, Robert M. *Adultery and Divorce in Calvin’s Geneva.* Cambridge, MA: Harvard University Press, 1995.

Kipp, Herbert. *‘Trachtet zuerst nach dem Reich Gottes’: Landstädtische Reformation und Rats-Konfessionalisierung in Wesel (1520–1600).* Bielefeld: Verlag für Regionalgeschichte, 2004.

Kirchner, Thomas. *Katholiken, Lutheraner und Reformierte in Aachen, 1555–1618.* Tübingen: Mohr Siebeck, 2015.

Kist, N. C. “Petrus Bloccius: Eene bijdrage tot de inwendige geschiedenis der Nederlandsche kerkhervorming en eene proeve van haren onafhankelijken oorsprong en hare zelfstandigheid.” *Archief voor kerkelijke geschiedenis, inzonderheid van Nederland* 3 (1842): 1–113.

———. “De synoden der Nederlandsche Hervormde Kerken onder het Kruis, gedurende de jaren 1563–1577, gehouden in Braband, Vlaanderen enz.” *Nederlandsch archief voor kerkelijke geschiedenis* 9 (1849): 113–218.

Klein, Adolf. "Die Kölner Kirche im Zeitalter der Glaubensspaltung und der Katholischen Erneuerung." *Almanach für das Erzbistum Köln* 2 (1982): 334–402.

Klueting, Harm. "Obrigkeitsfreie Reformierte Flüchtlingsgemeinden und obrigkeitliche reformierte Landeskirchen – Zwei Gesichter des Reformiertentums im Deutschland des 16. Jahrhunderts." *Jahrbuch der Hessischen Kirchengeschichtlichen Vereinigung* 49 (1998): 13–49.

Knetsch, F. R. J. "The National Synod of Dordrecht, 1578 and the Position of the Walloon Churches." *The Low Countries History Yearbook/Acta Historiae Neerlandicae* 13 (1980): 52–67.

———. "Ortsgemeinden und Synoden in den frühen französischen und niederländischen reformierten Kirchenordnungen um 1564." *Zwingliana* 19, no. 2 (1991–92): 173–81.

Koch, Hans. *Geschichte des Seidengewerbes in Köln vom 13. bis zum 18. Jahrhundert.* Leipzig: Verlag von Duncker & Humblot, 1907.

Kooi, Christine. *Calvinists and Catholics during Holland's Golden Age: Heretics and Idolaters.* Cambridge: Cambridge University Press, 2012.

———. *Liberty and Religion: Church and State in Leiden's Reformation, 1572–1620.* Leiden: Brill, 2000.

———. *Reformation in the Low Countries, 1500–1620.* Cambridge: Cambridge University Press, 2022.

Kooijmans, Luuc. "Andries & Daniel: Vriendschap in de vroegmoderne Nederlanden." *Groniek: Historisch Tijdschrift* 130 (1995): 9–25.

Koslofsky, Craig. *The Reformation of the Dead: Death and Ritual in Early Modern Germany, 1450–1700.* New York: St. Martin's Press, 2000.

Kuijpers, Erika. "Fear, Indignation, Grief and Relief: Emotional Narratives in War Chronicles from the Netherlands (1568–1648)." in *Disaster, Death, and the Emotions in the Shadow of the Apocalypse, 1400–1700*, edited by Jennifer Spinks and Charles Zika, 93–111. London: Palgrave, 2016.

Kuyper, Abraham. *De Hollandsche gemeente te Londen in 1570/1.* Hardewijk: M. C. Bronsveld, 1870.

Lachenicht, Susanne. "Refugees and Refugee Protection in the Early Modern Period." *Journal of Refugee Studies* 30, no. 2 (2016): 261–81.

Lang, August. *Reformation und Gegenwart: Gesammelte Aufsätze, Vornehmlich zur Geschichte und zum Verständnis Calvins und Der Reformierten Kirche.* Detmold: Meyersch Hofbuchhandlung, 1918.

Langer, Ute. "Die konfessionelle Grenze im frühneuzeitlichen Köln: Das Zusammenleben von Reformierten und Katholiken zwischen Anpassung und Abgrenzung." *Geschichte in Köln: Zeitschrift für Stadt- und Regionalgeschichte* 53 (2015): 35–62.

Leibring, Katharina. "Given Names in European Naming Systems." In *The Oxford Handbook of Names and Naming*, edited by Carole Hough, 199–213. Oxford: Oxford University Press, 2016.

Lejeune, Jean. *Land zonder grens: Aken/Luik/Maastricht: Studie over de geschiedkundige ontwikkeling der drie steden*. Brussels: Charles Dessart, 1958.

Lem, Anton van der. *De Opstand in de Nederlanden, 1568–1648: De Tachtigjarige Oorlog in woord en beeld*. Nijmegen: Vantilt, 2018.

Lennep, M. F. van. *Gaspar van der Heyden, 1530–1586*. Amsterdam: Müller, 1884.

Lesger, Clé. "Informatiestromen en de herkomstgebieden van migranten in de Nederlanden in de vroegmoderne tijd." *Tijdschrift voor sociale en economische geschiedenis* 3, no. 1 (2006): 3–23.

———. *The Rise of the Amsterdam Market and Information Exchange: Merchants, Commercial Expansion and Change in the Spatial Economy of the Low Countries, c.1550–1630*. Aldershot, UK: Ashgate, 2006.

———. "Variaties in de herkomstpatronen van nieuwe burgers in Nederlandse steden omstreeks het midden van de zeventiende eeuw." *Tijdschrift voor sociale en economische geschiedenis* 3 (2006): 118–39.

Lieburg, Fred A. van. *Profeten en hun vaderland: De geografische herkomst van de gereformeerde predikanten in Nederland van 1572 tot 1816*. Zoetermeer: Boekencentrum, 1997.

———. *Repertorium van Nederlandse hervormde predikanten tot 1816*. 2 vols. Dordrecht: F. A. van Lieburg, 1996.

Lieuwes, Lieuwe. "Dorpsreglementen in de Meierij van 's-Hertogenbosch, 1648–1795: Van onstuurbaar naar stuurbaar bestuur." PhD diss., Tilburg University, 2020.

Linden, David van der. *Experiencing Exile: Huguenot Refugees in the Dutch Republic*. Farnham, UK: Ashgate, 2015.

Lougee, Carolyn Chappell. *Facing the Revocation. Huguenot Families, Faith, and the King's Will*. Oxford: Oxford University Press, 2017.

Lucassen, Jan, and Leo Lucassen. "The Mobility Transition Revisited, 1500–1900." *Journal of Global History* 4, no. 3 (2009): 347–77.

Luebke, David M. "Confessions of the Dead: Interpreting Burial Practice in the Late Reformation." *Archiv fur Reformationsgeschichte* 101 (2010): 55–79.

———. *Hometown Religion: Regimes of Coexistence in Early Modern Westphalia*. Charlottesville: University of Virginia Press, 2016.

———. "Ritual, Religion, and German Home Towns." *Central European History* 47 (2014): 496–504.

Lundin, Matthew. *Paper Memory: A Sixteenth-Century Townsman Writes His World*. Cambridge, MA: Harvard University Press, 2012.

Luria, Keith P. "Separated by Death? Burials, Cemeteries, and Confessional Boundaries in Seventeenth-Century France." *French Historical studies* 24, no. 2 (2001): 185–222.

Lurz, Friedrich. "Initiation im *Einfältigen Bedenken:* Die Formulare der Taufe, der Firming und der Abendmahlsfeier in der Kölner Reformationsdenkschrift von 1543." In *Kölnische Liturgie und ihre Geschichte: Studien zur interdisziplinären Erforschung des Gottesdienstes im Erzbistum Köln*, edited by Albert Gerhards and Andreas Ordenthal, 291–307. Münster: Aschendorff, 2000.

Maclean, Ian. *Learning and the Market Place: Essays in the History of the Early Modern Book.* Leiden: Brill, 2009.

Majérus, Pascal. "What Language Does God Speak?: Exiled English Nuns and the Question of Languages." *Trajecta* 21 (2012): 137–52.

Margolin, J. C. "Réflexions sur l'emploi du terme Libertin au XVI siècle." In *Aspects du Libertinisme au XVI siècle: Actes du colloque international de sommières,* edited by M. Bataillon, 1–33. Paris: J. Vrin, 1974.

Marnef, Guido. *Antwerp in the Age of Reformation: Underground Protestantism in a Commercial Metropolis, 1550–1577.* Baltimore: Johns Hopkins University Press, 1996.

———. "Een Gentse proost in Keulen: Bucho Aytta en zijn rol in de Opstand, 1579–1581." In *Liber Amicorum Dr. J. Scheerder: Tijdingen uit Leuven over de Spaanse Nederlanden, de Leuvense Universiteit en historiographie*, 75–86. Leuven: Vereniging Historici Lovanienses, 1987.

Meer, Bernardus van. *De Synode te Emden, 1571.* The Hague: Martinus Nijhoff, 1892.

Meester, Jan de. "To Kill Two Birds with One Stone: Keeping Immigrants in by Granting Free Burghership in Early Modern Antwerp." In *Innovation and Creativity in Late Medieval and Early Modern European Cities*, edited by Karel Davids and Bert de Munck, 95–113. Farnham, UK: Ashgate, 2014.

Mentzer, Raymond A. "'*Disciplina Nervus Ecclesiae*': The Calvinist Reform of Morals at Nîmes." *Sixteenth Century Journal* 18 (1987): 89–115.

———. "Reformed Liturgical Practices." In *A Companion to the Eucharist in the Reformation*, edited by Lee Palmer Wandel, 231–50. Leiden: Brill, 2014.

———, ed. *Sin and the Calvinists: Morals Control and the Consistory in the Reformed Tradition.* Kirksville, MO: Truman State University Press, 1994.

———, Françoise Moreil, and Philippe Chareyre, eds. *Dire l'interdit: The Vocabulary of Censure and Exclusion in the Early Modern Reformed Tradition.* Leiden: Brill, 2010.

Meyn, Matthias. *Die Reichsstadt Frankfurt vor dem Bürgeraufstand von 1612 bis 1614: Stuktur und Krise.* Frankfurt am Main: Verlag Waldemar Kramer, 1980.

Mihm, Arend. "Rheinmaasländische Sprachgeschichte von 1500 bis 1650." In *Rheinisch-Westfälische Sprachgeschichte*, edited by Jurgen Macha and Elber Neuss, 139–64. Cologne: Böhlau, 2000.

———. "Sprache und Geschichte am unteren Niederrhein." *Jahrbuch des Vereins für niederdeutsche Sprachforschung* (1992): 88–122.

———. "Sprachwandel in der frühen Neuzeit: Augsburg und Köln im Vergleich." In *Deutsch im 17. Jahrhundert: Studien zu Sprachkontakt, Sprachvariation und Sprachwandel: Gedenkschrift für Jürgen Macha*, edited by Markus Denkler, Stephan Elspaß, Dagmar Hüpper and Elvira Topalović, 265–319. Heidelberg: Universitätsverlag Winter, 2017.

Militzer, Klaus. "Gaffeln, Ämter, Zünfte': Handwerker und Handel vor 600 Jahren." *Jahrbuch des Kölnischen Geschichtsvereins* 67, no. 1 (1996): 41–59.

Miller, Jaroslaw. "Early Modern Urban Immigration in East Central Europe: A Macroanalysis." *Austrian History Yearbook* 36, no. 2 (2005): 2–39.

Molitor, Hansgeorg. "Reformation und Gegenreformation in der Reichsstadt Aachen." *Zeitschrift des Aachener Geschichtsvereins* 98/99, no. 1 (1992/1993): 185–203.

Monge, Mathilde. *Des communautés mouvantes: Les "sociétés des frères chrétiens" en Rhénanie du nord: Juliers, Berg, Cologne vers 1530–1694*. Geneva: Librairie Droz, 2015.

———. "Dans la couronne d'épines…: Communautés et indivus à Cologne (v.1550–v.1615)." In *L'expérience de la differénce religieuse dans l'Europe moderne (XVIe–XVIIIe siècles)*, edited by Bertrand Forclaz, 117–36. Neuchâtel: Éditions Alphil-Presses Universitaires Suisses, 2012.

———. "Überleben durch Vernetzung: Die Täuferischen Gruppen in Köln und am Niederhein im 16. Jahrhundert." In *Grenzen des Täuftertums/Boundaries of Anabaptism: Neue Forschungen*, edited by Anselm Schubert, Astrid von Schlachta, and Michael Driedger, 214–31. Gütersloh: Gütersloher Verlaghaus, 2009.

——— and Natalia Muchnik. *Early Modern Diasporas: A European History.* London: Routledge, 2022.

Mout, M. E. H. N. "Armed Resistance and Calvinism during the Revolt of the Netherlands." In *Church, Change and Revolution: Transactions of the Fourth Anglo-Dutch Church History Colloquium*, edited by Jan van den Berg and Paul G. Hoftijzer, 57–68. Leiden: Brill, 1991.

Muchnik, Natalia, and Mathilde Monge. "Fragments d'exils: Pour une histoire non linéaire des diasporas." *Diasporas: Circulations, migrations, histoire* 31 (2018): 7–20.

Mühling, Andreas. *Heinrich Bullingers europäische Kirchenpolitik.* Bern: Peter Lang, 2000.

Muir, Edward. *Ritual in Early Modern Europe.* Cambridge: Cambridge University Press, 1997.

Müller, Johannes. *Exile Memories and the Dutch Revolt: The Narrated Diaspora, 1550–1750*. Leiden: Brill, 2016.

———. "Permeable Memories: Family History and the Diaspora of Southern Netherlandish Exiles in the Seventeenth Century." In *Memory before Modernity: Practices of Memory in Early Modern Europe*, edited by Erika Kuijpers, Judith Pollmann, Johannes Müller, and Jasper van der Steen, 283–95. Leiden: Brill, 2013.

———. "Transmigrant Literature: Translating, Publishing, and Printing in Seventeenth-Century Frankfurt's Migrant Circles." *German Studies Review* 40, no. 1 (2017): 1–21.

Muller, Richard A. "Demoting Calvin: The Issue of Calvin and the Reformed Tradition." In *John Calvin, Myth and Reality: Images and Impact of Geneva's Reformer*, edited by Amy Nelson Burnett, 1–17. Eugene, OR: Cascade Books, 2011.

Munck, Bert De, and Anne Winter, eds. *Gated Communities?: Regulating Migration in Early Modern Cities*. Farnham, UK: Ashgate, 2012.

Münker, Herbert. *Die Weseler Schiffahrt vornehmlich zur Zeit des spanisch-niederländischen Krieges: Ein Beitrag zur Verkehrsgeschichte des Niederrheins*. Wesel: Carl Kühler, 1908.

Murdock, Graeme. *Beyond Calvin: The Intellectual, Political, and Cultural World of Europe's Reformed Churches, c.1540–1620*. Basingstoke, UK: Palgrave Macmillan, 2004.

Murphy, Emilie. "Exile and Linguistic Encounter: Early Modern English Convents in the Low Countries and France." *Renaissance Quarterly* 73, no. 1 (2020): 132–64.

Muylaert, Silke. "The Accessibility of the Late Medieval Goldsmith Guild of Bruges." *TSEG/ Low Countries Journal of Social and Economic History* 16, no. 2 (2019): 47–70.

———. *Shaping the Stranger Churches: Migrants in England and the Troubles in the Netherlands, 1547–1585*. Leiden: Brill, 2021.

Naphy, William. *Calvin and the Consolidation of the Genevan Reformation*. Louisville, KY: Westminster John Knox Press, 1994.

Nauta, Doede. "De Nationale Synode van Dordrecht (1578)." In *De Nationale Synode van Dordrecht, 1578: Gereformeerden uit de Noordelijke en Zuidelijke Nederlanden bijeen*, edited by Doede Nauta and J. P. van Dooren, 9–52. Amsterdam: Buijten & Schipperheijn, 1978.

———. "De Reformatie in Nederland in de historiographie." In *Geschiedschrijving in Nederland, Deel II: Geschiedbeoefening*, edited by P. A. M. Geurts and A. E. M. Janssen, 206–227. The Hague: Martinus Nijhoff, 1981.

———. "Wesel (1568) en Emden (1571)." *Nederlands Archief voor Kerkgeschiedenis* 36 (1949): 220–46.

———. J. P. van Dooren, and O. J. de Jong, eds. *De Synode van Emden, oktober 1571: Een bundel opstellen ter gelegenheid van de vierhonderdjarige herdenking*. Kampen: Kok, 1971.

Neuser, Wilhelm. "Die Aufnahme der Flüchtlinge aus England in Wesel (1553) und ihre Ausweisung trotz der Vermittlung Calvins und Melanchthons (1566/57)." In *Weseler Konvent, 1568–1968: Eine Jubiläumschrift*, 28–49. Düsseldorf: Pressverband der Evangelischen Kirche im Rheinland, 1968.

Nierop, Henk van. "A Beggar's Banquet: The Compromise of the Nobility and the Politics of Inversion." *European History Quarterly* 21 (1991): 419–44.

———. "Coornherts huwelijk: Een bijdrage tot zijn biografie." *Bijdragen en Mededelingen betreffende de Geschiedenis der Nederlanden* 106, no. 1 (1991): 33–44.

———. *Het foute Amsterdam*. Amsterdam: Vossiuspers, 2000.

Nierop, Leonie van. "De bruidegoms van Amsterdam van 1578 tot 1601." *Tijdschrift voor Geschiedenis* 49 (1934): 136–60, 329–44.

Niggemann, Ulrich. "Confessional Migration," in *European History Online* (EGO). Published by the Leibniz Institute of European History (IEG), Mainz 2020–02–06. URL: http://www.ieg-ego.eu/niggemannu-2019-en URN: urn:nbn:de:0159–2020020406 [2020-August-10].

Nijenhuis, Willem. *Adrianus Saravia (c.1532–1613): Dutch Calvinist, first Reformed Defender of the English Episcopal Chucrh Order on the Basis of the Ius Divinum* (Leiden: Brill, 1980).

———. *Ecclesia Reformata: Studies on the Reformation*. 2 vols. Leiden: Brill, 1972–1994.

Nischan, Bodo. "The Exorcism Controversy and Baptism in the Late Reformation." *Sixteenth Century Journal* 18 (1987): 31–51.

———. "The 'Fractio Panis': A Reformed Communion Practice in Late Reformation Germany." *Church History* 53 (1984): 17–29.

———. *Lutherans and Calvinists in the Age of Confessionalism*. Aldershot, UK: Ashgate 1999.

Norwood, Frederick. *The Reformation Refugees as an Economic Force*. Chicago: American Society of Church History, 1942.

Oakley, Anne M. "The Canterbury Walloon Congregation from Elizabeth I to Laud." In *The Huguenots in Britain and their French Background*, edited by Irene Scouloudi, 56–71. London: Macmillan Press, 1987.

Oberman, Heiko A. "'Europa Afflica:' The Reformation of the Refugees." *Archiv für Reformationsgeschichte* 83 (1992): 91–111.

———. *John Calvin and the Reformation of the Refugees*, Geneva: Librairie Droz, 2009.

Ogilvie, Sheilagh. *A Bitter Living: Women, Markets and Social Capital in Early Modern Germany*. Oxford: Oxford University Press, 2003.

———. *The European Guilds: An Economic Analysis.* Princeton: Princeton University Press, 2019.

Ó hAnnracháin, Tadhg, *Confessionalism and Mobility in Early Modern Ireland.* Oxford: Oxford University Press, 2021.

Olson, Jeanine E. *Calvin and Social Welfare: Deacons and the* Bourse française. Selinsgrove, PA: Susquehanna University Press, 1989.

Olson, Oliver K. "The 'Fractio Panis' in Heidelberg and Antwerp." In *Controversy and Conciliation: The Reformation and the Palatinate, 1559–1583*, edited by Derk Visser, 147–53. Allison Park, PA: Pickwick Publications, 1986.

Onnekink, David. "Models of an Imagined Community: Huguenot Discourse on Identity and Foreign Policy." In *The Huguenots: History and Memory in a Transnational Context: Essays in Honour and Memory of Walter C. Utt*, edited by D. J. B. Trim, 193–215. Leiden: Brill, 2011.

Parker, Charles H. "Moral Agency and Moral Autonomy of Church Folk in the Dutch Reformed Church of Delft, 1580–1620." *Journal of Ecclesiastical History* 48 (1997): 44–70.

Paul, Herman. "Johannes Calvijn." In *Het Gereformeerde Geheugen: Protestantse Herinneringsculturen in Nederland, 1850–2000*, edited by George Harinck, Herman Paul, and Bart Wallet, 41–50. Amsterdam: Bert Bakker, 2009.

Peters, Robert. "Mittelniederdeutsche Sprache." In *Niederdeutsch: Sprache und Literatur: Eine Einführung*, edited by Jan Goossens, 66–115. Neumünster: Wachholtz, 1973.

Pettegree, Andrew. *Emden and the Dutch Revolt: Exile and the Development of Reformed Protestantism.* Oxford: Clarendon Press, 1992.

———. "Emden as a Center of Sixteenth-Century Book Trade. A Catalogue of the Bookseller Gasper Staphorst." *Quaerendo* 24 (1994): 114–35.

———. *Foreign Protestant Communities in Sixteenth-Century London.* Oxford: Clarendon Press, 1986.

———. "The London Exile Community and the Second Sacramentarian Controversy, 1553–1560." *Archiv für Reformationsgeschichte* 78 (1987): 223–51.

———. "The Politics of Toleration in the Free Netherlands, 1572–1620." In *Tolerance and Intolerance in the European Reformation*, edited by Old Peter Grell and Bob Scribner, 182–98. Cambridge: Cambridge University Press, 1996.

———. "The Struggle for an Orthodox Church: Calvinists and Anabaptists in East Friesland, 1554–1578." *The Bulletin of the John Rylands Library* 70 (1988): 45–59.

———. "'Thirty Years On': Progress Towards Integration Amongst the Immigrant Population of Elizabethan England." In *English Rural Society*, edited by John Chartres and David Hey, 297–312. Cambridge: Cambridge University Press, 1990.

———, Alastair Duke, and Gillian Lewis, eds. *Calvinism in Europe, 1540–1620.* Cambridge: Cambridge University Press, 1994.

Pijper, Fredrik. *Jan Utenhove: Zijn leven en werken.* Leiden: A. H. Adriani, 1883.

Pitkin, Barbara. *Calvin, the Bible and History: Exegesis and Historical Reflection in the Era of Reform.* Oxford: Oxford University Press, 2020.

Plaizier, Kees. *Herman Herbers, Gouds predikant van 1582–1607: Een mystieke weg.* Gouda: Historische Vereniging Die Goude, 2011.

Plath, Uwe. "Zur Entstehungsgeschichte des Wortes 'Calvinist.'" *Archiv für Reformationsgeschichte* 66 (1975): 213–23.

Poelhekke, J. J. "Het naamloze vaderland van Erasmus." *BMGN: Low Countries History Review* 86, no. 1 (1971): 90–123.

Poettering, Jerun. *Migrating Merchants: Trade, Nation, and Religion in Seventeenth-Century Hamburg and Portugal.* Translated by Kenneth Kronenberg. Berlin: De Gruyter, 2019.

Pohl, Walter. "History in Fragments: Montecassino's Politics of Memory." *Early Medieval Europe* 10, no. 3 (2001): 343–74.

Pohlig, Matthias. "Wahrheit als Lüge - Oder: Schloss der Augsburger Religionsfrieden den Calvinismus aus?." In *Konfessionelle Ambiguität: Uneindeutigkeit und Verstellung als Religiöse Praxis in der Frühen Neuzeit*, edited by Andreas Pietsch and Barbara Stollberg-Rilinger, 142–69. Gütersloh: Gütersloher Verlaghaus, 2013.

Pollmann, Judith. "Internationalisierung en de Nederlandse Opstand." *BMGH—Low Countries History Review* 124, no. 4 (2009): 515–36.

———. "Met grootvaders bloed bezegeld: Over religie en herinneringscultuur in de zeventiende-eeuwse Nederlanden." *De zeventiende eeuw: Cultuur in de Nederlanden in interdisciplinair perspectief* 29, no. 2 (2013): 154–75.

———. "Off the Record: Problems in the Quantification of Calvinist Church Discipline." *Sixteenth Century Journal* 33 (2002): 423–38.

———. *Religious Choice in the Dutch Republic: The Reformation of Arnoldus Buchelius, 1565–1641.* Manchester: Manchester University Press, 1999.

Postema, Jan. *Johan van den Corput (1542–1611): Kaartmaker, vestingbouwer, krijgsman.* Kampen: Stichting Ijsselakademie, 1993.

Prak, Maarten, Clare Crowston, Bert De Munck, Christopher Kissane, Chris Minns, Ruben Schalk, and Patrick Wallis. "Access to the Trade: Citizens, Craft Guilds, and Social and Geographical Mobility in Early Modern Europe—a Survey of the Literature, with Additional New Data." *BEUCITIZEN Working Paper* 1 (2014): 1–32.

———. "Access to the Trade: Monopoly and Mobility in European Craft Guilds, 17th and 18th Centuries." *Economic History Working Papers*, no. 282 (2018): 1–46, https://www.lse.ac.uk/Economic-History/Assets/Documents/WorkingPapers/Economic-History/2018/WP282.pdf.

Prestwich, Menna. "The Changing Face of Calvinism." In *International Calvinism, 1541–1715*, edited by Menna Prestwich, 1–14. Oxford: Clarendon Press, 1985.

Prieur, Jütta, ed. *Wesel: Beiträge zur Stadtgeschichte*. Wesel: Stadtarchiv Wesel, 1985.

Prims, Floris. *Antwerpse stadsschulden in Duitsland in de XVIe eeuw*. Antwerp: Standaard-Boekhandel, 1948.

Puttevils, Jeroen. "The Ascent of Merchants from the Southern Low Countries: From Antwerp to Europe, 1480–1585." PhD diss., University of Antwerp, 2012.

Raitt, Jill. *The Colloquy of Montbélaird: Religion and Politics in the Sixteenth Century*. Oxford: Oxford University Press, 2014.

Redlich, Otto R. *Staat und Kirche am Niederrhein zur Reformationszeit*. Leipzig: M. Heinsius Nachfolger, 1938.

Reiss, Ansgar and Sabine Witt, eds. *Calvinismus: Die Reformierten in Deutschland und Europa*. Dresden: Sanstein Verlag, 2009.

Reitsma, Johannes. *Geschiedenis der Hervorming en de Hervormde Kerk in der Nederlanden*. Groningen: J. B. Wolters, 1893.

Reitsma, Rients. *Centrifugal and Centripetal Forces in the Early Dutch Republic: The States of Overijssel, 1556–1600*. Amsterdam: Rodopi, 1982.

Richter, Thomas. *Koexistenzen und Konflikte: Die Entwicklung der protestantischen Gemeinden in der katholischen Reichsstadt Aachen an den Grenzen des Alten Reiches (1645–1794)*. Bonn: Dr. Rudolf Habelt, 2021.

Ridder, Bram de, Violet Soen, Werner Thomas, and Sophie Verreyken, eds. *Transregional Territories: Crossing Borders in the Early Modern Low Countries and Beyond*. Turnhout: Brepols, 2020.

Rogghé, P. "Pieter Anastasius de Zuttere: Zuidnederlandse apostel van de verdraagzaamheid in de 16e eeuw." *Appeltjes van het Meetjesland: Jaarboek van het Heemkundig Genootschap van het Meetjesland* 17 (1966): 138–89.

Rogier, L. J. "Over karakter en omvang van de Nederlandse emigratie in de zestiende eeuw." *Historisch Tijdschrift* 16, no. 4 (1937): 325–67; 17 no. 1 (1938): 5–27.

Rohls, Jan. "A Lasco und die Reformierte Bekenntnisbildung." In *Johannes a Lasco (1499–1560): Polnische Baron, Humanist und europäischer Reformator*, edited by Christoph Strohm, 101–33. Tübingen: Mohr Siebeck, 2000.

Roijen, R. van. "Een familiecorrespondentie van omstreeks 1600." *Leidsch Jaarboekje* 34 (1943): 124–50.

Roitman, Jessica Vance. *The Same but Different?: Inter-Cultural Trade and the Sephardim, 1595–1640*. Leiden: Brill, 2011.

Roodenburg, Herman. *Onder censuur: De kerkelijke tucht in de gereformeerde gemeente van Amsterdam, 1578–1700*. Hilversum: Verloren, 1990.

Roosbroeck, Robert. *Emigranten: Nederlandse vluchtelingen in Duitsland, 1550–1600*. Leuven: Davidsfonds, 1968.

———. "Die Niederländischen Glaubensflüchtlinge in Deutschland und die Anfänge der Stadt Frankenthal." *Blätter für pfälzische Kirchengeschichte und Volkskunde* 30 (1963): 2–28.

Roper, Lyndal. "'The Common Man,' 'The Common Good,' 'Common Women': Gender and Meaning in the German Reformation Commune." *Social history/Histoire Sociale* 12, no. 1 (1987): 1–22.

Rotscheidt, Wilhelm. "Übergang der Gemeinde Wesel von dem lutherischen zum reformierten Bekenntnis im 16. Jahrhundert." *Monatshefte für evangelische Kirchengeschichte des Rheinlandes* 13 (1919): 225–56.

———. "Eine Weseler Ausgabe des Augburger Konfession und der Apologie vom Jahre 1558." *Monatshefte für Rheinische Kirchengeschichte* 5 (1911): 129–36.

Rubin, Miri. *Cities of Strangers: Making Lives in Medieval Europe*. Cambridge: Cambridge University Press, 2020.

———. *Corpus Christi: The Eucharist in Late Medieval Culture*. Cambridge: Cambridge University Press, 1992.

Rublack, Ulinka. *The Crimes of Women in Early Modern Germany*. Oxford: Clarendon, 2007.

———. *Reformation Europe*. Cambridge: Cambridge University Press, 2005.

Ruys, Theodorus. *Petrus Dathenus*. Utrecht: G. J. A. Ruys, 1919.

Sadler, James Robert J. "Family in Revolt: The Van der Meulen and Della Faille Families in the Dutch Revolt." PhD diss., UCLA, 2015.

Sarmenhaus, Wilhelm. *Die Festsetzung der Niederländischen Religionsflüchtlinge im 16. Jahrhundert in Wesel und ihre Bedeutung für die wirtschaftliche Entwicklung dieser Stadt*. Wesel: Historische Vereinigung Wesel, 1986.

Sas, N. C. F. van. *Vaderland: Een geschiedenis vanaf de vijftiende eeuw tot 1940*. Amsterdam: Amsterdam University Press, 1999.

Scharff, Friedrich. "Die niederländische und die französische Gemeinde in Frankfurt a.M." *Archiv für Frankfurts Geschichte und Kunst*, Neue Folge 2 (1862): 245–317.

Schatorjé, Jos M. W. C. "Kirchengeschichtliche Hintergründe des ersten Buches des Reformators Engelbert Faber aus Gustorf (1563)." In *Adel, Reformation und Stadt am Niederrhein*, edited by Gerhard Rehm, 133–68. Bielefeld: Verlag für Regionalgeschichte, 2009.

Scheffler, Wolfgang. *Goldschmiede Rheinland-Westfalens.* Vol. 2. Berlin: Walter de Gruyter, 1973.

Schelven, A. A. van. De *Nederduitsche Vluchtelingenkerken der XVIe eeuw in Engeland en Duitschland.* The Hague: Martinus Nijhoff, 1909.

———. "Petrus Dathenus." *Nederlands Archief voor Kerkgeschiedenis* 10, no. 1 (1917): 328–43.

Schilling, Heinz. "Christliche und jüdische Munderheitengemeinden in Vergleich: Calvinistische Exulanten und westliche Diaspora der Sephardim im 16. und 17. Jahrhundert." *Zeitschrift für historische Forschung.*" 36, no. 3 (2009): 407–44.

———. *Niederländische Exulanten im 16. Jahrhundert.* Gütersloh: Gütersloher Verlagshaus G. Mohn, 1972.

———. "Reformation und Bürgerfreiheit: Emdens Weg zur Calvinistischen Stadtrepublik." In *Stadt und Kirche im 16. Jahrhundert*, edited by Bernd Moeller, 128–62. Gütersloh: Mohn, 1978.

——— and Heribert Smolinsky, eds. *Der Augsburger Religionsfrieden, 1555.* Münster: Aschendorff, 2007.

Schindling, Anton. "Wachstum und Wandel von konfessionellen Zeitalter bis zum Zeitalter Ludwigs XIV: Frankfurt am Main 1555–1685." In *Frankfurt am Main: Die Geschichte der Stadt in Neuen Beiträge*, 205–60. Frankfurt am Main: Thorbecke, 1994.

Schipper, Ingeborg. "Across the Borders of Belief: Netherlandish Reformed Migrants and Confessional Boundaries in the Duchy of Cleves, c. 1550–1600." PhD diss., Vrije Universiteit Amsterdam, 2021.

Schmale, Wolfgang. "Grenze in der deutschen und französischen Fruhneuzeit." In *Menschen und Grenzen in der frühen Neuzeit*, edited by Wolfgang Schmale and Reinhard Stauber, 50–75. Berlin: Berlin Verlag Arno Spitz GmbH, 1998.

Schmitz, Walter. *Verfassung und Bekenntnis: Die Aachener Wirren im Spiegel der kaiserlichen Politik (1550–1616).* Frankfurt am Main: Lang, 1983.

Schnetttger, Matthias. "Die Reformation in Frankfurt am Main—Voraussetzungen, Verlauf und Ergebnisse." In *Migration und Modernisierung: 450-jähriges Bestehen der Evangelischen Französisch-reformierten Gemeinde Frankfurt am Main*, edited by Georg Altrock, Hermann Düringer, Matthias von Kriegstein, and Karin Weintz, 25–51. Frankfurt am Main: Haag + Herchen, 2006.

Schnurr, Eva-Maria. *Religionskonflikt und Öffentlichkeit: Eine Mediengeschichte des Kölner Kriegs (1582 bis 1590).* Cologne: Böhlau, 2009.

Scholz, Luca. *Borders and Freedom of Movement in the Holy Roman Empire.* Oxford: Oxford University Press, 2020.

Scholz, Maximillian Miguel. "Religious Refugees and the Search for Public Worship in Frankfurt am Main, 1554–1608." *Sixteenth Century Journal* 50, no. 3 (2019): 765–82.

———. *Strange Brethren: Refugees, Religious Bonds, and Reformation in Frankfurt, 1554–1608.* Charlottesville: University of Virginia Press, 2021.

Schreiber, Tobias. *Petrus Dathenus und der Heidelberger Katechismus: Eine traditionsgeschichtliche Untersuchung zum konfessionellen Wandel in der Kurpfalz um 1563.* Göttingen: Vandenhoeck & Ruprecht, 2017.

Schunka, Alexander. "Konfession und Migrationsregime in der frühen Neuzeit." *Geschichte und Gesellschaft* 35, no. 1 (2009): 28–63.

———. "Migrations in the German Lands: An Introduction." In *Migrations in the German Lands, 1500–2000*, edited by Jason Coy, Jared Poley, and Alexander Schunka, 1–34. New York: Berghahn Books, 2016.

———. *Migrationserfahrungen - Migrationsstrukturen.* Stuttgart: Steiner, 2010.

Schutte, G. J. *Het Calvinistisch Nederland: Mythe en Werkelijkheid.* Hilversum: Verloren, 2001.

Schützeichel, Rudolf. "Rheinische und Westfälische 'Staffel'/'Stapel'-Namen und die Bedeutung der Benrather Linie." *Rheinische Vierteljahrblätter* 30 (1976): 30–57.

Schwerhoff, Gerd. *Köln im Kreuzverhör: Kriminalität, Herrschaft, und Gesellschaft in einer frühneuzeitlichen Stadt.* Bonn: Bouvier, 1991.

Scribner, R. W. "Why Was There No Reformation in Cologne?" *Bulletin of the Institute of Historical Research* 49 (1976): 217–41.

Seibt, Ferdinand. *Karl V, der Kaiser und die Reformation.* Berlin: Wolf Jobst Siedler, 1990.

Selderhuis, H. J. "Eine attraktive Universität: Die Heidelberger Theologische Fakultät 1583–1622. In *Bildung und Konfession*, edited by H. J. Selderhuis and M. Wriedt, 1–30. Tübingen: Mohr Siebeck, 2006.

———. ed. *Handboek Nederlandse Kerkgeschiedenis.* 2nd rev. ed. Kampen: Kok, 2010.

Selwood, Jacob. *Diversity and Difference in Early Modern London.* Farnham, UK: Ashgate, 2010.

Sepp, Christiaan. *Drie evangeliedienaren uit den tijd der Hervorming.* Leiden: Brill, 1879.

Sijs, Nicoline van der. *15 eeuwen Nederlandse taal.* Gorredijk: Sterck & De Vreese, 2019.

Simons, Eduard. "Ein Rheinisches Synodalschreiben aus dem Jahr 1576." *Zeitschrift des Bergischen Geschichtsvereins* 36 (1903): 145–51.

———. *Niederrheinisches Synodal- und Gemeideleben 'Unter dem Kreutz.'* Freiburg: J. C. B. Mohr, 1897.

Slenczka, Björn. *Das Wormser Schisma der Augsburger Konfessionsverwandten von 1557.* Tübingen: Mohr Siebeck, 2010.

Soen, Violet, Bram De Ridder, Alexander Soetaert, Werner Thomas, Johan Verberckmoes, and Sophie Verreyken. "How to Do Transregional History: A Concept, Method, and Tool for Early Modern Border Research." *Journal of Early Modern History* 21 (2017): 343–64.

———, Alexander Soetaert, Johan Verberckmoes, and Wim François, eds. *Transregional Reformations: Crossing Borders in Early Modern Europe.* Göttingen: Vandenhoeck & Ruprecht, 2019.

Solzbacher, Joseph. *Kaspar Ulenberg: Eine Priestergestalt aus der Zeit der Gegenreformation in Köln.* Münster: Aschendorff, 1948.

Sommerville, Johann P. "The 'New Art of Lying': Equivocation, Mental Reservation, and Casuistry." In *Conscience and Casuistry in Early Modern Europe*, edited by Edmund Leites, 159–84. Cambridge: Cambridge University Press, 1988.

Sneller, A. Agnes. *De Gouden Eeuw in gedichten van Joost van den Vondel (1587–1679).* Hilversum: Verloren, 2014.

Spicer, Andrew. *The French-Speaking Reformed Community and Their Church in Southampton, 1567–c.1620.* London: Huguenot Society of Great Britain and Ireland, 1997.

———. "A Process of Gradual Assimilation: The Exile Community in Southampton, 1567–1635." *Proceedings of the Huguenot Society of London* 26 (1995): 186–98.

———. "'Rest of Their Bones': Fear of Death and Reformed Burial Practices." In *Fear in Early Modern Society*, edited by William G. Naphy and Penny Roberts, 167–83. Manchester: Manchester University Press, 1997.

Spierling, Karen E. *Infant Baptism in Reformation Geneva: The Shaping of a Community, 1536–1564.* Louisville, KY: Westminster John Knox Press, 2017.

Spohnholz, Jesse. "Calvinism and Religious Exile during the Revolt of the Netherlands (1568–1609)." *Immigrants & Minorities* 32, no. 3 (2014): 235–61.

———. "Confessional Coexistence in the Early Modern Low Countries." In *Multiconfessionalism in the Early Modern World*, edited by Thomas Max Safley, 47–73. Leiden: Brill 2011.

———. *The Convent of Wesel: The Event That Never Was and the Invention of Tradition.* Cambridge: Cambridge University Press, 2017.

———. "Exile Experiences and the Transformations of Religious Cultures in the Sixteenth Century: Kleve, England, East Friesland, and the Palatinate." *Journal of Early Modern Christianity* 6, no. 1 (2019): 43–67.

———. "Instability and Insecurity: Dutch Women Refugees in Germany in England." In *Exile and Religious Identity, 1500–1800*, edited by Jesse Spohnholz and Gary K. Waite, 111–25. London: Pickering & Chatto, 2014.

———. “Multiconfessional Celebration of the Eucharist in Sixteenth-Century Wesel.” *Sixteenth Century Journal* 39, no. 3 (2008): 705–29.

———. “Olympias and Chrysostom: The Debate over Wesel’s Reformed Deaconesses, 1568–1609.” *Archiv für Reformationsgeschichte* 98 (2007): 84–106.

———. “Overlevend non-conformisme: Anabaptistische tradities en hun regulering in laat zestiende-eeuws Wezel.” *Doopsgezinde Bijdragen* 29 (2003): 89–109.

———. *Ruptured Lives: Refugee Crises in Historical Perspective.* Oxford: Oxford University Press, 2020.

———. *The Tactics of Toleration: A Refugee Community in the Age of Religious Wars.* Newark: University of Delaware Press, 2011.

———. “Turning Dutch? Conversion in Early Modern Wesel.” In *Conversion and the Politics of Religion in Early Modern Germany*, edited by David M. Luebke, Jared Poley, Daniel C. Ryan, and David Warren Sabean, 49–68. New York: Berghahn Books, 2012.

——— and Mirjam G. K. van Veen. “The Disputed Origins of Dutch Calvinism: Religious Refugees in the Historiography of the Dutch Reformation.” *Church History* 86, no. 2 (2017): 398–426.

Springer, Michael. *Restoring Christ’s Church: John a Lasco and the Forma ac Ratio.* Aldershot, UK: Ashgate, 2007.

Stein, Robert and Judith Pollmann, eds. *Networks, Regions, and Nations: Shaping Identities in the Low Countries, 1300–1650.* Leiden: Brill, 2010.

Stempel, Walter. “Zeitungen aus Wesel unterstüzten den Aufstand der Niederlande: Ein Beitrag zur Geschichte des Weseler Buchdrucks im 16. Jahrhundert.” *Monatschefte für Evangelische Kirchengeschichte des Rheinlands* 37/38 (1988/89): 363–71.

Stipriaan, René van. *De Zwijger: Het leven van Willem van Oranje.* Amsterdam: Querido Facto, 2022.

Strohm, Christoph. “Die Universität Heidelberg als Zentrum der späten Reformation.” In *Kirche und Politik am Oberrhein im 16. Jahrhundert*, edited by Ulrich Wien and Volker Leppin, 197–214. Tübingen: Mohr Siebeck, 2015.

Subacci, Paola. “Italians in Antwerp in the Second Half of the Sixteenth Century.” In *Minderheden in Westeuropese steden (16de–20st eeuw)*, edited by Hugo Soly and K. L. Thijs, 73–90. Brussels: Belgisch Historisch Instituut te Rome, 1995.

Sunshine, Glenn S. *Reforming French Protestantism: The Development of Huguenot Ecclesiastical Institutions, 1557–1572.* Kirksville, MO: Truman State University Press, 2003.

Terpstra, Nicholas. *Religious Refugees in the Early Modern World: An Alternative History of the Reformation.* Cambridge: Cambridge University Press, 2015.

Tervooren, Helmut. "Sprache und Sprachen am Niederhrein (1550–1900)." In *Sprache an Rhein und Ruhr: Dialektologische und soziolinguistische Studien zur sprachlichen Situation im Rhein-Ruhr-Gebiet und ihrer Geschichte*, edited by Arend Mihm, 30–47. Stuttgart: Franz Steiner Verlag, 1985.

———. *Van der Masen tot op den Rijn: Ein Handbuch zur Geschichte der mittelalterlichen volkssprachlichen Literatur im Raum von Rhein und Maas.* Berlin: Erich Schmidt Verlag, 2006.

Thimme, Hermann. "Der Handel Kölns am Ende des 16. Jahrhunderts und die internationale Zusammensetzung der Kölner Kaufmannschaft." *Westdeutsche Zeitschrift für Geschichte und Kunst* 31 (1913): 389–473.

Tilmans, C. P. H. M. "De ontwikkeling van een vaderland-begrip in de laatmiddeleeuwse en vroeg-moderne geschiedschrijving van de Nederlanden." *Theoretische Geschiedenis* 23, no. 1 (1996): 77–110.

Tol, Jonas van. *Germany and the French Wars of Religion, 1560–1572.* Leiden: Brill, 2019.

Valkema Blouw, Paul. "Augustijn van Hasselt as a Printer in Vianen and Wesel: Part Two." *Quaerendo* 16 (1986): 83–109.

———. *Dutch Typography in the Sixteenth Century: The Collected Works of Paul Valkema Blouw*, edited by T. Croiset van Uchelen and P. Dijstelberge. Leiden: Brill, 2013.

———. "Jan Canin in Wesel, and in Emmerich?." *Quaerendo* 28, no. 3 (1998): 225–29.

Vanwelden, Martine. *Productie van wandtapijten in de regio Oudenaarde: Een symbiose tussen stad en platteland (15de tot 17de eeuw).* Leuven: Universitaire Pers Leuven, 2006.

Veen, Mirjam G. K. van. "'De aert van Spaensche Inquisitie': Coornherts opvattingen over de verhouding tussen kerk en staat." *Nederlands Theologisch Tijdschrift* 58 (2004): 61–76.

———. *Dirck Volckertsz Coornhert.* Kampen: Kok, 2009.

———. "'... in excelso honoris gradu...': Johannes Calvin und Jacques de Falais." *Zwingliana* 32 (2005): 5–22.

———. "'... polué et souillee...': The Reformed Polemic against Anabaptist Marriage, 1560–1650." In *Sisters: Myth and Reality of Anabaptist/Mennonite Women, c.1525–1900*, edited by Mirjam van Veen, Piet Visser, Gary K. Waite, Els Kloek, Marion Kobelt-Groch, and Anna Voolstra, 88–104. Leiden: Brill, 2014.

———. "'Verjaeght, vervolght, vermoordt te zijn, en is niet quaet': Protestantse martelaarsgeschiedenis." *Tijdschrift voor Nederlandse Kerkgeschiedenis* 20, no. 3 (2017): 85–91.

———. "*Verschooninghe van de Roomsche afgoderye": De polemiek van Calvijn met Nicodemieten in het bijzonder met Coornhert.* 't Goy-Houten (Utrecht): HES & De Graaf, 2001.

———. "'...Wir sind ständig unterwegs...': Reformierte Flüchtlinge des 16. Jahrhunderts als Exulanten." *Archiv für Reformationsgeschichte* 109, no. 1 (2018): 442–58.

——— and Jesse Spohnholz. "Calvinists vs. Libertines: A New Look at Religious Exile and the Origins of 'Dutch' Tolerance." In *Calvinism and the Making of the European Mind*, edited by Gijsbert van den Brink and Harro M. Höpfl, 76–99. Leiden: Brill, 2014.

Veldman, I. M. "Coornhert en de prentkunst." in *Dirck Volckertszoon Coornhert: Dwars maar recht*, edited by H. Bonger, 134–43. Zutphen: Walburg Pers, 1989.

400 Jahre Bedburger Synode: Eine Festschrift. Niederaußem: Evangelische Kirchengemeinde Bedburg, 1971.

Vloten, J. van. *Onderzoek van 's Koningswege ingesteld omtrent de Middelburgsche Beroerten van 1566 en 1567.* Utrecht Kemink en zoon, 1873.

Waite, Gary K. "From Apocalyptic Crusaders to Anabaptist Terrorists: Anabaptist Radicals after Münster, 1535–1544." *Archiv für Reformationsgeschichte* 80, no. 1 (1989): 173–93.

Wal, J. de. *Nederlanders, studenten te Heidelberg.* Leiden: Brill, 1886.

Walker, Mack. *German Hometowns: Community, State, and General Estate, 1648–1871.* Ithaca, NY: Cornell University Press, 1998.

———. *The Salzburg Transaction: Expulsion and Redemption in Eighteenth-Century Germany.* Ithaca, NY: Cornell University Press, 1992.

Wandel, Lee Palmer. *The Eucharist in the Reformation: Incarnation and Liturgy.* Cambridge: Cambridge University Press, 2006.

Watt, Jeffrey R. "Divorce in Early Modern Neuchâtel." *Journal of Family History* 14, no. 2 (1989): 137–55.

Weis, Monique. "Philip of Marnix and 'International Protestantism': The Fears and Hopes of a Dutch Refugee in the 1570s." *Reformation and Renaissance Review* 11, no. 2 (2009): 203–20.

———. *Philipp de Marnix et le Saint Empire (1566–1578): Les connexions allemandes d'un porte-parole de la révolte des Pays-Bas.* Brussels: Société royale d'histoire du protestantisme Belge, 2004.

Whaley, Joachim. *Germany and the Holy Roman Empire. Volume 1, Maximilian I to the Peace of Westphalia, 1490–1648.* Oxford: Oxford University Press, 2012.

Wilcox, Peter. "'Églises plantées' and 'églises dressées' in the Historiography of Early French Protestantism." *The Journal of Ecclesiastical History* 44, no. 4 (1993): 689–95.

Wilke, Jürgen. "Der Einfluss der Hugenotten auf die gewerbliche Entwlick-lung." In *Hugenotten in Berlin*, edited by Gottfried Bregulla, 227–80. Berlin: Union, 1988.

Wilson, Stephen. *The Means of Naming: A Social and Cultural History of Personal Naming in Western Europe*. London: UCL Press, 1998.

Witzel, Georg. "Gewerbgeschichtliche Studien zur niederländischen Einwanderung in Deutschland im 16. Jahrhundert." *Westdeutsche Zeitschrift für Geschichte und Kunst* 29 (1910): 117–82.

Wolgast, Eike. *Reformierte Konfession und Politik im 16. Jahrhundert: Studien zur Geschichte der Kurpfalz im Reformationszeitalter*. Heidelberg: Universitätsverlag C. Winter, 1998.

Wolters, Albrecht. *Reformationsgeschichte der Stadt Wesel*. Bonn: Adolph Marcus, 1868.

Woltjer J. J. *Friesland in hervormingstijd*. Leiden: Universitaire Pers, 1962.

———. *Tussen vrijheidsstrijd en burgeroorlog: Over de Nederlandse Opstand, 1555–1580*. Amsterdam: Uitgeverij Balans, 1994.

Zagorin, Perez. *Ways of Lying: Dissimulation, Persecution, & Conformity in Early Modern Europe*. Cambridge, MA: Harvard University Press, 1990.

Zalinge-Spooren, Lia van. *Gemeint en gemeenschap: Jaargeboden in Peelland circa 1300–1795*. Hilversum: Verloren, 2018.

Index